NUCLEAR AMERICA

NUCLEAR AMERICA

Military and Civilian
Nuclear Power
in the United States
1940–1980

Gerard H. Clarfield
and
William M. Wiecek

1817

HARPER & ROW, PUBLISHERS, New York

Cambridge, Philadelphia, San Francisco, London
Mexico City, São Paulo, Singapore, Sydney

FOR LESLIE, AND FOR JUDY

l'chaim

NUCLEAR AMERICA. Copyright © 1984 by Gerard Clarfield and William M. Wiecek. All rights reserved. Printed in the United States of America. No part of this book may be used or reproduced in any manner whatsoever without written permission except in the case of brief quotations embodied in critical articles and reviews. For information address Harper & Row, Publishers, Inc., 10 East 53rd Street, New York, N.Y. 10022. Published simultaneously in Canada by Fitzhenry & Whiteside Limited, Toronto.

FIRST EDITION

Designed by Ruth Bornschlegel

Library of Congress Cataloging in Publication Data

Clarfield, Gerard H.
　　Nuclear America.

　　Bibliography: p.
　　Includes index.
　　1. United States—Military policy. 2. Atomic weapons.
3. Atomic energy—United States. I. Wiecek, William M.,
1938-　　. II. Title.
UA23.C558 1984　　355'.0335'73　　84-47565
ISBN 0-06-015336-9

84 85 86 87 88 10 9 8 7 6 5 4 3 2 1

Contents

Acknowledgments

We have incurred debts to individuals and institutions for assistance in the preparation of this book. Nuclear and chemical engineers, and several scientists as well, have answered our questions, criticized our ideas, helped us locate materials, and educated us in the history and the technology of nuclear power. We will forbear mentioning them by name, however, since some of their colleagues might associate them with the views expressed in this book, or with inferences and implications the reader might see between the lines. Our historian colleagues at the University of Missouri—John Lankford, Claudia Kren, and Robert Collins—will suffer no such embarrassment, and we record our gratitude for their assistance while absolving them from any errors that might have survived their criticism.

Chronology

1895	Wilhelm Roentgen discovers X-ray radiation.
1932	James Chadwick discovers the neutron.
1938	Otto Hahn and others achieve atomic fission.
October 1939	Albert Einstein and others persuade FDR to support research on an atomic bomb.
December 1941	FDR approves the Manhattan Project.
December 1942	Enrico Fermi and others achieve controlled and sustained chain reaction.
July 1945	First atomic bomb detonated at Alamogordo, New Mexico.
August 1945	Hiroshima and Nagasaki are destroyed by atomic bombs.
June 1946	U.S.A. proposes Baruch Plan for international control of nuclear weapons; U.S.S.R. rejects it.
July 1946	First Atomic Energy Act enacted.
August 1949	U.S.S.R. detonates its first fission bomb.
January 1950	President Truman approves development of the hydrogen bomb.
May 1950	NSC-68 outlines plan for massive U.S. rearmament and military spending.
January 1951	AEC begins weapons testing at Nevada test site.
December 1951	First experimental production of electricity from a nuclear reactor.
November 1952	U.S.A. detonates its first hydrogen bomb, followed by U.S.S.R. in 1953.
December 1953	President Eisenhower's Atoms for Peace address.
January 1954	John Foster Dulles announces a new strategic policy, massive retaliation.
June 1954	AEC affirms denial of security clearance to J. Robert Oppenheimer.
August 1954	Second Atomic Energy Act enacted.
September 1957	Congress enacts the Price–Anderson Act, indemnifying the nuclear power industry in the event of nuclear accidents.

October 1957	U.S.S.R. launches Sputnik. The missile gap is born.
December 1957	Shippingport, the world's first exclusively non-military power reactor, comes on stream.
? 1957	U.S.S.R. nuclear disaster near Sverdlovsk.
Spring 1958	Worldwide protests begin against atmospheric nuclear testing.
January 1961	President Kennedy advances a new strategy, flexible response.
June 1962	Robert McNamara announces No Cities doctrine.
July 1963	U.S.A., U.S.S.R., U.K. sign Partial Test Ban Treaty, ending atmospheric testing.
February 1964	Mutually assured destruction becomes the nuclear strategy of U.S.A.
October 1966	Nuclear accident at Fermi-1, a commercial breeder reactor near Detroit.
September 1967	U.S.A. announces it will deploy a "thin" antiballistic missile system.
January 1972	AEC generic rule-making hearings begin on ECCS.
May 1972	SALT I is signed in Moscow. ABM deployment is sharply limited.
August 1974	Rasumussen report released, downplaying likelihood of reactor accidents.
October 1974	Congress abolishes AEC, substituting NRC and ERDA (which is later replaced by Department of Energy).
November 1974	Karen Silkwood killed in accident.
November 1974	U.S.A., U.S.S.R. agree to Vladivostok accords.
January 1975	Browns Ferry reactor accident.
March 1979	Three Mile Island; concurrent but coincidental release of film *The China Syndrome*.
June 1979	SALT II signed in Moscow.
December 1979	SALT II withdrawn from Senate by President Carter.

I have set before you life and death,
blessing and curse; therefore choose life,
that both thou and thy seed may live.

Deuteronomy 30:19

Prologue: "The Italian Navigator"

IT WAS BITTERLY COLD OUTSIDE, as Chicago's notorious lake wind drove the windchill below zero, making it colder than normal even for the second day of December. Arthur Compton, Nobel laureate and director of the obscurely named "Metallurgical Laboratory" at the University of Chicago, phoned his colleague James B. Conant, president of Harvard University. "The Italian navigator has just landed in the new world," he said. It was a cryptic statement, but then so many messages in 1942 were communicated in odd codes. An eavesdropper would have been puzzled—as he was meant to be. Conant did not seem to be surprised by the peculiar message; he simply asked, "Were the natives friendly?" Compton replied, "Everyone landed safe and happy," hung up, and went to join the impromptu celebration already under way on the floor below.[1]

The message conveyed in amateurish code by the Chicago physicist to the Cambridge chemist was as momentous as Columbus's landfall 450 years earlier. For Conant had just announced that humanity had achieved a controlled and sustained chain reaction in the fission of atomic nuclei. American scientists had cleared a path for the development of the world's first atomic bomb. Prometheus-like, humankind had seized nuclear fire, and now found itself capable either of destroying itself or of transforming the material world with a virtually limitless source of energy. Before Enrico Fermi, the "Italian navigator," demon-

1

strated the possibility of controlled fission, physicists were unsure whether the energy locked in the atom could be deliberately released. Doubters had on their side the authority of Sir Ernest Rutherford, Nobel laureate in chemistry and doyen of the international nuclear science community, who dismissed hopes of controlling nuclear energy as "moonshine."[2] But other scientists believed that a chain reaction was possible. Spurred on by the fear that German scientists might produce an atomic weapon for the Third Reich, American scientists organized the most massive research effort the world has ever seen, code-named the "Manhattan Project." As part of this effort, Compton organized a centralized research effort at Chicago, one of the centers of U.S. nuclear research, and code-named it with the uninformative but altogether accurate title of Metallurgical Laboratory, or Met Lab for short. The Met Lab's foremost task was to determine whether a chain reaction was feasible.

Compton invited Fermi, who was a fellow Nobel laureate in physics and an anti-Fascist refugee then teaching at Columbia University, to lead the project. He found space for Fermi's group in unused football facilities at Stagg Field. By November 1942, working in an empty squash court under the stands, Fermi and his assistants began the laborious construction of a "pile" of graphite blocks with slugs of uranium embedded throughout; hence the name of the world's first nuclear reactor: CP-1 (Chicago Pile Number One). In this unlikely place, physicists, chemists, graduate students, and craftsmen labored in secrecy to achieve a self-sustaining chain reaction. The scientists worked under eleventh-hour deadlines and a disheartening suggestion from England that boron impurities might prematurely detonate any uranium chain reaction, producing a fizzle. They nevertheless processed four hundred tons of graphite, six tons of uranium metal, and fifty tons of uranium oxide to build the pile. Fermi and other professionals even pitched in with the tedious, dirty construction work. After helping laborers haul, saw, drill, and emplace the forty thousand graphite blocks, physicists would sometimes end their day's work looking like dust-blackened, sweat-streaked coal miners.

Heavy, dirty work was not the only problem at CP-1. When

Compton informed Conant that the pile was to be in the heart of Chicago, rather than in the Argonne Forest Preserve some twenty-five miles southwest of the Loop, Conant was so appalled that the blood drained from his face.[3] Despite Fermi's confidence in his own calculations, the official historians of the Atomic Energy Commission have concluded that Compton's decision constituted a "gamble with a possibly catastrophic experiment in one of the most densely populated areas in the nation."[4] Fortunately for the people of Chicago, however, Fermi's calculations proved correct, and on December 2, 1942, CP-1 went critical: it achieved a chain reaction—without blowing up Chicago.

As luck would have it, on December 2, the squash court's heaters were not working, and the inside temperature remained just above freezing. Fermi's assistants, still piling graphite bricks, had to catch and handle the slippery blocks—graphite is an excellent dry lubricant—with hands nearly frostbitten. Fermi had designed three sets of cadmium-coated control rods for the pile, the earliest example of redundancy in reactor design for safety purposes. The first was mechanically operated from the control console on a balcony overlooking the court. The second, called "Zip," was a special emergency rod that moved vertically through the pile so that gravity would pull it down into the pile if anything went wrong—assuming that the force of gravity would still be adequate to bring the rod down into a supercritical pile. When Fermi decided to go for criticality, he ordered Zip withdrawn and held above the pile by a rope tied via a pulley to the balcony railing. One of his assistants stood by with an ordinary ax to chop the rope and drop Zip back into the pile if the reaction got out of hand. As a sort of fail-safe precaution, a group of three other scientists, known as the suicide squad, stood on staging above the pile with a bucket of liquid cadmium solution, to dump on the pile in an emergency, flooding it with the neutron absorber.

The third control rod was the one used to begin the chain reaction. Another of Fermi's assistants, the physicist George Weil, moved it by hand. Fermi orchestrated the whole operation behind a bank of dials on the balcony, making calculations with a six-inch pocket slide rule and then checking his predictions against the gauges that were recording neutron activity in the pile. Near the threshold of criticality, Fermi ordered Weil to begin withdrawing the calibrated manual control rod, then watched the neutron activity first soar and then level off. He waited, calculated, and repeated. For the observers the drama was as intense as the neutron activity.

Finally, after lunch, Fermi's slide-rule calculations indicated that criticality was at hand. He ordered the final withdrawal; the clicking of the neutron counters became a steady buzz; an automatic recording pen on a galvanometer drew an exponential curve. Fermi, calm and smiling, announced simply, "The reaction is self-sustaining." He let it run twenty-eight minutes, then shut it down. The Hungarian physicist Eugen Wigner proffered a bottle of Chianti, Fermi poured it into paper cups for a toast, and all present autographed the straw basket of the empty bottle.

Because of the drive of a few score scientists working to build a bomb, humankind now found itself in what would soon be called the "atomic age."

1

"$E = mc^2$"

THE PHYSICAL REVOLUTIONS OF THE TWENTIETH CENTURY

Shortly before World War I, some members of the international scientific community were dazzled by a vision: the release of unimaginable amounts of energy from small quantities of ordinary matter. The English science-fiction writer H. G. Wells spoke for them in his prophetic novel *The World Set Free* (1914) through the fictional Professor Rufus, lecturing on radioactivity at the University of Edinburgh. Holding up a beaker of uranium oxide, Rufus declared:

> In the atoms in this bottle there slumbers at least as much energy as we could get by burning a hundred and sixty tons of coal. If at a word, in one instant I could suddenly release that energy here and now it would blow us and everything about us to fragments; if I could turn it into the machinery that lights this city, it could keep Edinburgh brightly lit for a week.

Professor Rufus and his audience became carried away at the thought of the ways in which atomic energy might change their society.

> Not only should we have a source of power so potent that a man might carry in his hand the energy to light a city for a year, fight a fleet of battleships or drive one of our giant liners across the Atlantic; but we should also have a clew that would enable us at last to quicken the process of disintegration in all the other elements, where decay is still so slow as to escape our finest measurements. Every scrap of solid matter in the world would become an

5

available reservoir of concentrated force. . . . It would mean a change in human conditions that I can only compare to the discovery of fire, that first discovery that lifted man above the brute. We stand to-day towards radioactivity exactly as our ancestor stood towards fire before he had learned to make it . . . just when it is becoming apparent that our ever-increasing needs cannot be borne indefinitely by our present sources of energy, we discover suddenly the possibility of an entirely new civilisation. The energy we need for our very existence, and with which Nature supplies us still so grudgingly, is in reality locked up in inconceivable quantities all about us.[1]

This breathless hope had come into being because physicists began to sense that they were living in a revolutionary era, a time when the received wisdom of Newtonian physics ceded place to unnerving, previously unthinkable modes of imagining physical reality.

As far as nuclear science was concerned, the nineteenth century had belonged to the chemists. They established bold, imaginative paradigms for thinking about the structure of matter and predicting its behavior. The chemists drew the outlines of modern atomic theory; they constructed the periodic table of the elements; and they discovered radiation. From their work, the twentieth century inherited a new image of the physical world.

The day of the chemists began with the work of John Dalton, the Manchester scientist who worked in meteorology, mathematics, optics, and physics, as well as chemistry. Dalton's work capped the efforts of a line of distinguished European scientists —Pierre Gassendi, Robert Boyle, John Locke, Isaac Newton— who since the fifteenth century had revived the concept of "atomism": the idea that, as Newton put in the *Opticks,* "God in the Beginning, form'd Matter in solid, massy, hard, impenetrable, moveable Particles. . . . these primitive Particles being Solids, are incomparably harder than any pourous Bodies compounded of them; even so very hard, as never to wear or break in pieces; no ordinary Power being able to divide what God himself made one in the first Creation."[2] As part of efforts to explain the behavior of gases, Dalton in 1803 formulated a table of atomic weights, reasoning that elements differed from each other because they were composed of different atoms, and that these atoms had different properties, including weights. He visualized atoms as little billiard-ball-like bits of matter differing from atoms of another element chiefly by their weights. He also suggested that atoms of different elements combine to form what are now called molecules. His hypotheses about atomic weights were soon confirmed by experiments in electrolysis carried out by the English chemists Humphry Davy and Michael Faraday, who broke molecules of compounds into elements, for example water into hydrogen and oxygen.

Classification and taxonomy mark the beginnings of all scientific fields; witness Linnaeus at the dawn of modern biology. So it was with chemistry. Refinements in measuring atomic weights led to the next momentous advance: the periodic table. This classification was first proposed by the French geologist Alexandre de Chancourtois (1862) and the English chemist John A. R. Newlands (1865). De Chancourtois' "table" was a vertical helix, like a spiral staircase. Newlands observed that his arrangement produced a suggestive periodicity, which he called the "law of octaves": a recurrence to similar chemical properties with every eighth element after helium (atomic number 2). For example, the gas chlorine (atomic number 17) exhibits behavior similar to another gas, fluorine (atomic number 9), eight places above it in the modern periodic table. This periodicity led the Russian chemist Dmitri Mendeléev to postulate a periodic table in 1869, based on an arrangement of known elements organized according to recurring similarity in their chemical properties. Mendeléev even predicted that gaps in his table would be filled by the discovery of thitherto-unknown elements, whose properties he predicted on the basis of his table. When these were in fact discovered—gallium in 1875, scandium in 1879, germanium in 1886—Mendeléev was vindicated.

This dramatic proof demonstrated some of the most valuable features of Mendeléev's system of classification. His periodic table gave clues about elements not yet discovered; it suggested hypotheses about the inner structure and behavior of atoms; and it provided an exploratory and explanatory tool that carried scientists far beyond the speculative ruminations of Dalton. This was essential, because no apparatus on earth before World War II could see, weigh, or dissect an atom as a neurologist might dissect a frog. A refined conceptual tool like the periodic table had to substitute for the electron microscopes of today.

Later achievements in nuclear science were recognized by the award of a Nobel prize in chemistry or physics, beginning with the first physics Nobel given to Wilhelm Roentgen in 1901 for his discovery of the X ray. So Mendeléev's contribution of a generation earlier had to be recognized in another way. When Glenn Seaborg and others produced the artificially created transuranic element 101 in 1955, it was named mendelevium. Other elements similarly honoring the early nuclear scientists are: curium (96), einsteinium (99), fermium (100), lawrencium (103), rutherfordium (104), and hahnium (105). Nobelium (102) honors Nobel himself. The Soviets, who claim priority in the creation of element 104, call it kurchatovium, honoring the father of the Soviet atomic bomb, Igor Kurchatov.

After these advances in chemistry, it was the physicists' turn. Often by accident, experimentalists would stumble on the presence of mysterious phenomena that seemed to have the ability to penetrate matter, as when the German physicist, Wilhelm Roentgen, discovered X rays in 1895. While working with an evacuated, pear-shaped glass apparatus called a Crookes tube, Roentgen was astonished to see that the tube, though covered, could nevertheless project a "shadow" of a solid object on a fluorescent screen or a photographic plate. Not knowing the nature of this radiation, he called it, simply, X rays. Medical and physical scientists eagerly began experimenting with this new form of radiation. In the year after Roentgen's discovery of X rays, the French physicist Antoine Henri Becquerel accidentally discovered the X ray's near relative, gamma radiation, while experimenting with a compound containing uranium. (Gamma rays are very short wavelength forms of electromagnetic radiation.)

Gamma and X rays assisted scientists in chemical analysis, among other things. A husband-and-wife team of chemists, the Pole Marie Sklodowska Curie and the Frenchman Pierre Curie, worked with uranium in an ore called pitchblende. They discovered that even after all the uranium was extracted, the ore displayed a high radioactivity, suggesting the presence of some unknown element more potently radioactive than uranium. After more than a year of laboriously processing the dark, lustrous ore, in 1902 the Curies extracted a tiny amount of the new element, which they called radium. At the same time, they discovered and isolated another radioactive element—polonium (named in honor of Marie's native land). For their work with radioactivity, the Curies shared a Nobel in physics with Becquerel in 1903, and Marie became the first double laureate when she was awarded the Nobel in chemistry in 1911 for the discovery of radium and polonium. Her work, however, proved fatal; she died in 1934 of leukemia probably induced by exposure to radioactivity. Her daughter Irène Joliot-Curie, also a Nobel laureate in chemistry, suffered the same fate.

British scientists at the same time discovered two other forms of radiation. Unlike X ray and gamma radiation, which are electromagnetic, the new radiation consisted of particles. In 1897, J. J. Thomson, the English physicist who was director of the Cavendish Laboratory, demonstrated that cathode rays from a Crookes tube could be deflected by an electric charge. He concluded that they consisted of minute, light, electrically charged particles, to which he gave the name "electrons." Physicists quickly accepted the idea that these were subatomic particles. The atom was no longer indivisible. Shortly thereafter Ernest Rutherford, a New Zealander then working at McGill University in Montreal, distinguished alpha particles, which were later identified as helium nuclei, consisting of two protons and two neutrons.

The ancient conception of atoms as ultimately indivisible units of matter now had to be scrapped. Nuclear scientists replaced it with theories of subatomic structure and behavior. Rutherford moved on to Manchester and then to Cambridge, where he worked with the German physicist Johannes Geiger, who later invented the radiation counter that bears his name. When they fired streams of alpha particles at a gold foil target, they noticed that a few of the projectiles were sharply deflected or even bounced back from the foil. In a benchmark 1911 paper, Rutherford sketched a model of the atom as a planetary structure. He suggested that the mass of the atom was concentrated in a central region and consisted of relatively massive, positively charged protons. The bounce-back effect he noticed in the gold foil experiments occurred because of the repulsion of two positively charged nuclei. Surrounding it in orbital paths like satellites were the electrons, whose negative charges equaled the positive charges of the protons.

The first of the great revolutions that characterize twentieth-century physics had begun, as scientists probed the structure of the atom, seeking to explain the behavior of subatomic particles. Later, Rutherford's simple and neat planetary model had to be scrapped, replaced by a model of a nucleus surrounded not by little "planets" in orbit, but rather by charged "clouds" or "smears" of electrons, complex in shape, representing regions where the electron is likely to be found. But for following a narrative of the early history of nuclear physics, the planetary simile still remains useful, especially since nuclear physicists of the World War I era like Rutherford and the Danish physicist Niels Bohr not only thought in planetary terms but actually sketched models of different orbital patterns for the elements.

The planetary model posed a troublesome problem though: it could not behave according to classical Newtonian theory. If it did, the orbiting electrons would lose energy, their orbits would contract, and they would collapse into the nucleus. Bohr resolved this difficulty in 1913 by applying the quantum theory suggested in 1900 by the German physicist Max Planck: at the atomic level, energy is not emitted in a steady and continuous stream, but rather in packets or "quanta" of energy. Bohr suggested that the orbits of electrons were organized in specific patterns. They did not transmit a quantum of energy until they moved from one orbit to another. In 1916, two Americans working independently, Gilbert Lewis and Irving Langmuir, elaborated on Bohr's theory by introducing the concept of "valence shells" to explain the chemical behavior of elements in terms of the arrangement of electrons around the nucleus. The hydrogen atom has just one electron and combines readily; the helium atom has two and is inert, that is, disinclined to form chemical combinations with other elements. Lithium, with three electrons, combines; and so on up to the next inert element, neon with ten. The pattern that emerged indicated that the innermost shell was composed of no more than two electrons, while the outer shells were each composed of no more than eight. A "full" outer shell of eight electrons, with no more electrons and shells beyond it, characterized the "noble" gases (so-called because they did not combine with other elements): helium, neon, argon, krypton, xenon, and radon. The pattern of eight-electron shells explained the law of octaves that Newlands had intuited a half-century earlier in listing atomic numbers. The concept of "completing" shells through elements sharing electrons explained chemical combinative behavior: for example, lithium, with one electron in its second shell, readily combines with fluorine, which has seven electrons in its outer shell, to form a molecule of lithium fluoride, in which each component "fills" the outer shell of the other. With the valence-shell model of the atom, scientists had a readily comprehensible sketch of the structure and workings of the atom.

In the same year, 1913, that Bohr applied quantum theory to explain atomic structure, one of Rutherford's young associates, the English chemist Frederick Soddy, was developing a theory to explain several oddities in atomic behavior. Earlier, Becquerel, Rutherford, and others had noticed that a few radioactive elements—uranium, thorium, actinium—increased in radioactivity over time. Further, more accurate calculations of atomic weights indicated that the weights were not precisely whole numbers. Nitrogen, for example, is not 14, but 14.0067; oxygen is not 16, but 15.9994. Why this minute but real deviation? J. J. Thomson, who had just constructed a device for measuring radiation by means of bending it through electrical and magnetic fields, was turning up evidence of different masses for the same element. Soddy resolved all these problems with the theory of "isotopes" (from Greek roots meaning "same place," that is, same place in the periodic table). Elements were not simply unitary, but consisted of siblings, as it were, having different atomic weights (determined by the total of their protons and neutrons) but the same atomic number (determined by the number of protons alone). Uranium (atomic number 92), for example, has three naturally occurring isotopes: U-234, U-235, U-238.

With the refinements made possible by the concept of isotopes, and the application of quantum theory, an adequate working model of the atom was available for further experimentation, and the stage was set for the next great advance: nuclear transmutation.

Centuries earlier, alchemists had dreamed of transmuting one element into another, but the idea was abandoned as alchemy evolved into scientific chemistry. Around 1902, the Curies and Rutherford speculated on the possibility of a spontaneous, naturally occurring transmutation, by which an element such as radium "decays" into an element lower in the periodic table by giving off protons, which are the basis of its atomic number and therefore its place in the table. It occurred to Rutherford that transmutation might be induced artificially by "firing" alpha particles as projectiles at nuclei to knock off or add a proton or two and thus transmute the element. He accordingly experimented with alpha bombardment before the war, reasoning that if an element absorbed an alpha particle, it would move two places down the periodic table, and if it emitted a beta particle (an electron), it would move up one place since it now had a surplus of positive charge, which had the same effect as adding a proton to it.

In 1919, Rutherford hit pay dirt and produced the most significant leap forward in nuclear physics since 1911 when he postulated the planetary structure. While bombarding nitrogen (atomic number 7) with alpha particles, Rutherford discovered that he was getting an end product with the atomic number of eight: oxygen. He thereby achieved the first laboratory transmutation of elements, proving that transmutation could occur and could be induced artificially. But inherent limitations in the process restricted what physicists could achieve with alpha particles: they could move elements up or down the periodic table only one or two places (the leapfrog effect); and they could work only with lighter elements. The positively charged alpha particle would be repelled by the nuclei of the heavier elements, which, having more protons, had a much greater electrical charge. Transmutation, for the time being, was limited to the lightest elements of the periodic table: lithium, beryllium, boron, carbon, nitrogen, oxygen, fluorine. Rutherford's process, as Ronald Clark has observed, was a matter of "chipping, rather than splitting" atoms.[3] Rutherford thus remained convinced that the more radical form of transmutation, fission, was impossible; hence his "moonshine" address of 1933.

Despite Rutherford's skepticism, his work with alpha particle bombardment opened the doors to the discovery of nuclear fission. The relatively modest and simple transmutation he achieved led others to recall the special theory of relativity, propounded by the German-Swiss physicist Albert Einstein in 1905. Einstein suggested the equivalence of mass and energy, a concept later embodied in the famous equation $E = mc^2$. This formula indicated that the conversion of even a tiny amount of matter (m = mass) would release unbelievably great energy (E = energy, measured in ergs) because the constant that served as the multiplier was so huge (the speed of light squared = 3.45×10^{10}). The English physicist Francis Aston's precise measurements with the mass spectrograph demonstrated a slight loss of mass as an atomic nucleus is built up, indicating that some mass had been converted to energy to hold the components of the nucleus together. This "binding energy," as physicists call it, is measured in millions of electron volts, and hence is a potential source of immense energy. If the nucleus could somehow be disrupted, its binding energy might be released.

A few scientists sensed this potential, though before 1932 they lacked a specific theory, technique, and material to accomplish it. Moreover, some doubted that fission would be desirable. Rutherford and Aston both worried that the release of atomic energy, once begun, might prove uncontrollable. Aston mordantly suggested in a 1922 address to the Franklin Institute in Philadelphia that it might be possible

> that the energy once liberated will be completely uncontrollable and by its intense violence detonate all neighboring substances. In this event, the whole of the hydrogen on the earth might be transformed at once, and the success of the experiment published at large to the universe as a new star.

Rutherford uneasily speculated that if "a proper detonator could be found, it was just conceivable that a wave of atomic disintegration might be started through matter, which would indeed make this old world vanish in smoke."[4]

Winston Churchill's imagination ran free among the military possibilities opened up by fission:

> Might not a bomb no bigger than an orange be found to possess a secret power to destroy a whole block of buildings or blast a township at a stroke? Could not explosives even of the existing type be guided automatically in flying machines by wireless or other rays, without a human pilot, in ceaseless procession upon a hostile city, arsenal, camp, or dockyard?

Others were more sanguine. Shortly after the armistice, the British physicist Oliver Lodge mused that nonmilitary applications of atomic power would "greatly ameliorate the conditions of factory life. There would be no smoke due to imperfect combustion and no dirt due to the transit of coal or ashes, while the power would be very compact and clean."[5] (Nuclear utilities in the 1980s would make precisely the same claims for nuclear power.) A decade later, the English astronomer Sir Arthur Eddington disclosed his

> vision of vast supplies of energy far surpassing the wildest desires of the engineer. . . . Instead of pampering the appetite of our engine with delicacies of coal or oil, we shall induce it to work on a plain diet of sub-atomic energy. If that day ever arrives the barges, the trucks, the cranes will disappear, and the year's supply of fuel for the station will be carried in a tea cup, namely thirty grams of water, or of anything else that is handy.[6]

The practical applications of nuclear power were pushed out of the realm of speculation and much closer toward realization by three events occurring in 1932. Thanks to advances in the theory of wave mechanics, the British team of John Cockcroft and Ernest T. S. Walton, working under Rutherford at the Cavendish, produced the first transmutation of an atomic nucleus by bombarding it, not with naturally occurring radiation as Rutherford had done, but with artificially accelerated protons. They bombarded lithium, atomic mass 7. Occasionally, a lithium nucleus would capture one of the accelerated protons, acquiring a mass of 8, and then immediately split into two helium nuclei, each with a mass of 4. (For this, they were awarded the Nobel in physics in 1951.) In distant California, Ernest O. Lawrence announced that his particle accelerator, the cyclotron, had speeded up protons to an energy of more than a million electronvolts, an energy level previously considered unattainable. For this he got the 1939 Nobel in physics. Most important of all, though, the English physicist James Chadwick, also working at the Cavendish, discovered the neutron, a subatomic particle having roughly the mass of a proton and bound with it in the nucleus, but having no electric charge. Seen in retrospect, Chadwick's discovery proved to be the most significant event in the prehistory of military and civilian nuclear power between the discovery of radioactivity (1896) and the achievement of fission (1938). The new particle had no electric charge—hence its name. It thereby overcame the limitations of alpha particles and protons as bombardment projectiles, and gave scientists a powerful new weapon for subatomic research. Chadwick received the Nobel in physics for his discovery in 1935; seldom has a Nobel prize recognized a more significant scientific achievement.

At the same time that Chadwick achieved this vital breakthrough, politics began the fateful collision with science that has characterized the later twentieth century. The Weimar Republic, rotting from within, nonetheless presented to the rest of the world a façade of scientific leadership. Einstein, director of theoretical physics at the Kaiser Wilhelm Institute in Berlin, was at work on his field theory, his special and general theories of relativity having already made him one of the world's most eminent physicists. He had received the Nobel in physics in 1921 for work on photoelectricity. Berlin and the medieval university of Göttingen shared, with the Cavendish Laboratory, the distinction of being world centers of physical, chemical, and mathematical research. But the Nazis came to power in 1933 and began implementing their race theories immediately. They fired Jewish faculty at Göttingen and elsewhere, and stripped Einstein of his German citizenship. Under the reign of *dozentenführers* ("the leaders of professors") who imposed Nazi ideological purity, the German universities shriveled as centers of learning as many of their illustrious scientists emigrated to Great Britain, the United States, Switzerland, and elsewhere. Later, the Nazis tried to implement their lunatic program of "Aryan physics," deliberately hobbling their scientific research by purging physics of the influence of Jewish scientists, Einstein above all.

Political upheaval notwithstanding, the newly discovered neutron's usefulness as a bombardment particle touched off a burst of laboratory research throughout Europe and the United States. Scientists bombarded the elements at the heavy end of the periodic table, probing the tantalizing possibility that they might be able to discover or create something beyond the heaviest naturally occurring element, uranium (atomic number 92). The possibility of creating these new man-made elements—transuranics—beckoned alluringly to Enrico Fermi in Italy, Otto Hahn in Berlin, and others. But most physicists still assumed that any transmutations they achieved with neutrons would be accomplished along lines similar to Rutherford's leapfrog alpha particle transmutations, by a step or two along the periodic table.

Fermi worked energetically and systematically from 1932 to 1938 in Rome, bombarding every element from hydrogen (atomic number 1) to uranium (atomic number 92) with neutrons. Bombarding uranium, he produced a highly radioactive product and, in 1934, announced that he had produced the first transuranic element. In fact, he had not; instead he had unknowingly achieved something more momentous, nuclear fission. (The first authentic creation of element 93, neptunium, did not take place until 1940, when it was achieved by Edwin McMillan and Philip Abelson at the University of California.) Only one scientist demurred to Fermi's announcement, the German chemist Ida Noddack, who suggested that Fermi had really split the uranium atom. But orthodox scientists of the day considered that impossible. Rutherford and Hahn both rejected the possibility. Noddack's suggestion was to lie on the shelf for five years.

In the course of his bombardment work, Fermi made an important practical contribution to nuclear technology when he discovered that ordinary household compounds like water or paraffin, both rich in hydrogen, could moderate the speed of neutrons. Slower or "thermal" neutrons had a better chance of hitting their target, thus improving the technique of bombardment. Though Fermi did not foresee it at the time, neutron moderators also make controlled nuclear reactions possible, and hence are an essential basis for fission reactors. For his achievements, multiple honors were heaped on Fermi: the Nobel in physics, 1938; the element fermium named after him in 1955; the first American breeder reactor named after him (Fermi-1, Detroit, 1956).

At the same time, in Europe's other fascist nation, the research team of Otto Hahn, Lise Meitner, and Fritz Strassmann were also bombarding uranium and getting results that perplexed them. Their product seemed to display the chemical properties of actinium (atomic number 89), a radioactive element close enough in the periodic table to uranium to be within the range of transmutations then thought possible. In Paris, another research team composed of Irène Joliot-Curie (daughter of Pierre and Marie Curie, who succeeded her mother as director of the Radium Institute) and the Yugoslav Pierre Savitch carried on the same experiment and got the same results. They, however, concluded that they were producing lanthanum (atomic number 57), which lies above actinium in the periodic table and hence displays similar chemical behavior. Shaken, Hahn and Strassmann returned to their lab to redo their experiments, convinced the Paris team was in error. But late in 1938 they concluded that Joliot-Curie and Savitch were right, and that they were getting lanthanum and its periodic table neighbor, barium (atomic number 56). Beset with doubt and second thoughts, they reported their findings.

Hahn and Strassmann now had to do their work without their female colleague, because politics had again cut across scientific research. Meitner was an Austrian Jew. Her nationality previously exempted her from harassment under the Nazi "race laws," so she was able to carry on her long association with Hahn in Berlin after the Nazis came to power. But after the Anschluss (1938) which incorporated Austria into the Third Reich, Meitner was obliged to flee Berlin. She carried on her work alone in Stockholm. This proved to be an opportunity. Removed from the Berlin lab, Meitner had a chance to reflect on the significance of

Hahn's work, and, in early 1939, she and her nephew, the German physicist Otto Frisch, published a letter in the British scientific periodical *Nature*, an extraordinarily modest and understated announcement of one of the most momentous laboratory experiments of all time. They argued that the Paris and Berlin experiments were in fact producing not element 93, but rather barium, by a process of fission that they analogized to the splitting of a drop of water.[7] Frisch conveyed this theory personally to Bohr in Copenhagen, who immediately perceived its validity and propagated it at a congress of physicists then meeting in Washington, D.C. Scientists in the United States and Europe quickly replicated the experiment.

The sinister significance of the Hahn–Strassmann–Meitner work was immediately apparent to Fermi. After journeying to Stockholm to accept his physics Nobel in 1938, he declined to return to Fascist Italy because his wife was Jewish, choosing instead to immigrate to the United States. Sitting in his office in Columbia University's physics lab, he gazed thoughtfully out his window toward most of downtown Manhattan, and formed a large ball with his hands. "A little bomb like that, and it would all disappear," he mused.[8]

With the reality of fission established, the next major experimental goal became the chain reaction. Physicists reasoned that when an atom split, one or more of its neutrons would be released, and these might serve as further bombardment projectiles, going off to strike other nuclei, which in turn would release more neutrons, and so on. Among the most eager investigators of this idea were Frédéric and Irène Joliot-Curie. With Europe arming and on the verge of war, 1939 was scarcely a propitious time for experimentation, but the Joliot-Curies pushed ahead anyway, unwilling to let the unstable world around them deflect their research.

The Joliot-Curies were not the only ones interested in the potential of the chain reaction. Fermi was also working on it at Columbia. Another anti-Fascist émigré there, the Hungarian Leo Szilard, had recognized the weapons possibilities presented by the chain reaction as early as 1934, and worried that the Nazis might develop it for a superbomb. Fragmentary bits of intelligence coming out of Germany five years later suggested (incorrectly as it turned out) that German scientists were doing just that: Germany placed a large order for heavy water, an excellent neutron moderator, from a Norwegian supplier. It also cut off uranium exports from the Joachimsthal mines in Bohemia, which came under German control after Munich and the subsequent dismemberment of Czechoslovakia.

Szilard was an extraordinary figure in the development of nuclear weapons. An exuberant impresario of ideas, he enjoyed a self-confidence that some of his associates thought bordered on the intemperate. He once explained to a colleague after World War II that he was writing a history of the Manhattan Project not for publication but for the information of God. His colleague suggested that God might know the facts already, but Szilard replied, "Not *this* version of the facts."[9] Viewing the course of Nazi foreign and military policy, Szilard feared the worst, and recommended to the British and American network of émigré scientists, including his Hungarian colleagues Eugen Wigner and Edward Teller, that they impose a voluntary moratorium on their nuclear research, or at least on the publication of it. (Szilard in 1936 had arranged to have British patents he had taken out on the chain reaction be kept secret by having them assigned to the Admiralty.) But Fermi was cool to the idea, to say the least, and Frédéric Joliot-Curie was flatly opposed. Szilard then turned to the idea of urging the United States to take diplomatic initiatives to keep the output of Belgian Congolese uranium mines from falling into German hands. Because he and his émigré colleagues were unknown outside scientific circles, Szilard decided to secure the cooperation of Einstein, then at Princeton's Institute for Advanced Studies. Szilard drafted a letter for Einstein's signature to President Franklin D. Roosevelt, in which the physicist informed the politician that "it may become possible to set up a nuclear chain reaction in a large mass of uranium, by which vast amounts of power and large quantities of new radium-like elements would be generated. . . . This would also lead to the construction of bombs, and it is conceivable—though much less certain—that extremely powerful bombs of a new type may thus be constructed."[10] Szilard then secured the services of one of FDR's informal advisers, the banker Alexander Sachs, to present the letter. When Sachs read the letter to the president on October 11, 1939, FDR at first seemed uninterested, perhaps uncomprehending. But Sachs proved persuasive, getting FDR to grasp at least the idea that the Nazis might beat the Allies to some sort of superweapon. The president called in his military attaché, General Edwin M. "Pa" Watson, and said, "Pa, this requires action."[11]

The "action" that FDR mandated in his dramatic gesture produced few significant results in the next two years, however. The American government approached the goal of a nuclear weapon sluggishly before Pearl Harbor. Szilard and other scientists could promise only a remote theoretical possibility of a nuclear weapon. No one had yet validated the chain reaction experimentally, nor even shown that nuclear fission could be achieved on anything more than a laboratory scale. French scientists at the time thought that the critical mass necessary to sustain a chain reaction might require a mound of uranium weighing forty tons, clearly beyond the range of anything that might be delivered as a bomb. Moreover, in 1939 the federal government had only rudimentary organizations that could support research and production on something as technically daunting as the fission project. The federal civilian and military bureaucracies were staffed by men who were conservative both in their approach to scientific research and in their social attitudes. They harbored a xenophobic distrust of European émigrés like Einstein, Szilard, Wigner, and Fermi—precisely the group most knowledgeable in the possibilities of nuclear research.

For their part, the émigrés had little patience with the conservatism of the military bureaucracies. Ten days after FDR's demand for action, Szilard, Wigner, Teller, and Lyman Briggs, head of the National Bureau of Standards, met with army and navy officers to discuss the military potential of nuclear power. One of the army representatives expressed skepticism, insisting that it would be naïve to think that the outcome of a war could be affected by a new explosive. In addition, he insisted, new weapons ordinarily required two wars for field testing, and besides, what counted in warfare was not weapons but the morale of the troops. To this, Wigner impatiently responded that if that were the case, then the army's budget should be cut.[12] With such attitudes prevalent, a year passed with only faint stirrings about nuclear power in the federal establishment. Briggs, chairman of the Advisory Committee on Uranium and the top scientist on the federal payroll, was temperamentally cautious and had other priorities. Funding was minimal: in 1940, six *thousand* dollars to buy graphite and uranium ore, out of a total federal defense budget of one *billion* dollars. Nuclear research was scattered among a half dozen universities, and was hampered by a self-imposed censorship on publication of articles dealing with fission research.

During this languid period in the United States, British and émigré scientists working in Great Britain established a short-lived British lead in the theoretical aspects of fission. Otto Frisch and Rudolph Peierls, an Austrian refugee physicist, both working at Birmingham, wrote a remarkably far-sighted estimate of the possibility of producing what they called a "Super-Bomb." They got around the technical problem of amassing forty tons of uranium by proposing instead a concentration of the fissile isotope U-235 in two hemispheres that would be brought together suddenly to form the critical mass necessary for a nuclear explosion. As much to the point from a present perspective, the authors also considered the impact of radiological warfare—fallout—and its moral implications. The Frisch–Peierls assumptions were shortly to be blasted aside by the bombings of London, Rotterdam, Coventry, and Dresden. They read today like a naïve voice from an age of lost innocence. After noting that radioactive fallout "will kill everybody within a strip estimated to be several miles long" and that rainfall would complicate the problem by making fallout cling to the ground, prolonging its lethal effect, the authors speculated that

> owing to the spreading of radioactive substances with the wind, the bomb could probably not be used without killing large numbers of civilians, and this may make it unsuitable as a weapon for use by this country [Great Britain]. Use as a depth charge near a naval base suggests itself, but even there it is likely that it would

cause great loss of civilian life by flooding and by the radioactive radiations.[13]

The Frisch–Peierls memorandum piqued enough interest in the British scientific community to lead to the formation of the MAUD committee,[14] a group composed of leading British scientists including Chadwick, J. J. Thomson, and John D. Cockcroft, who were charged with evaluating the feasibility of producing a uranium bomb for use against Germany.

The MAUD report, issued in April 1940, was a detailed survey of nuclear fission, not only as a bomb source, but also for postwar civilian power production by a "uranium boiler."[15] Interest in the "boiler" led someone at Imperial Chemical Industries, the British chemical giant that is the equivalent of the American DuPont, to an insight that has characterized the relationship between military and civilian nuclear power ever since:

> There must always be a very close relation between the exploitation of nuclear energy for military explosive purposes and for power production in peace and war. The development of one will have a considerable effect on the development of the other.[16]

The MAUD report also reflected advanced theoretical work being done by British scientists on such technical topics as the detonation of a fission weapon and the techniques for separating U-235. But the MAUD committee adopted only the technological, not the moral, insights of Frisch and Peierls. The official historian of the British wartime nuclear effort quotes an unnamed scientist working with the committee who reflected that "perhaps we should have studied the moral and political implications of the bomb and thought about its use. Perhaps, too, we should have considered whether radioactivity was a poison outlawed in spirit by the Geneva Convention. But we didn't."[17] Unencumbered by such doubts, British scientists for a brief period in 1940 to 1941 leaped to the forefront of nuclear research, a lead soon lost as Britain struggled to survive the Battle of Britain and the projected German invasion.

The Americans, by contrast, seemed to be awash in indecision, much to the distress of Szilard. None of the scientists involved in nuclear research agreed on ultimate goals or on the technological means necessary to reach them. Einstein's letter spoke of a bomb delivered by a naval vessel that could blow up a port; others were thinking of bombs dropped from the air; some contemplated radiological warfare by scattering radioactive fission products; the few naval personnel who knew something of the chain reaction's potential sought a new propulsive force, especially for submarines; and some hoped for nonmilitary applications for nuclear fission.[18]

Nor was there any unanimity in 1939–1941 about basic engineering problems. After Glenn Seaborg and others at Berkeley produced plutonium in 1941, there were two candidates, plutonium and uranium, for the source of explosive. If uranium was to be the choice, only the relatively scarce isotope U-235 would prove fissionable. It occurs naturally in uranium ores in a ratio of one part to 140 parts of U-238. Some means had to be found to separate the two to get a serviceable amount of U-235. Three approaches seemed possible: centrifugation, gaseous diffusion, and an electromagnetic process. All three promised to be slow, costly, and uncertain. If plutonium was to be the fuel, manufacturing it from U-238 by neutron bombardment looked just as unpromising.

But momentum picked up slightly in mid-1940, when a new organization, the National Defense Research Committee, was created to organize scientific and technological research for military purposes. Its head was Vannevar Bush, an electrical engineer who had been dean of engineering and vice-president of MIT, and was at the time president of the Carnegie Institute in Washington. Joining Bush on the NDRC were James B. Conant, a chemist and president of Harvard from 1933 to 1953, and Bush's former superior, Karl Compton, president of MIT.

Bush, Conant, and Compton themselves did not participate in any fission research, but they played crucial roles in bringing the scientific community into the bomb project, in subordinating science to the military and political objectives of the American government, and in making or approving fundamental policy decisions on wartime nuclear policy, such as the decision to drop the bombs on Hiroshima and Nagasaki. To political leaders like

President Roosevelt and Secretary of War Henry Stimson, Bush and Conant were the voice of the scientific community, even when many members of that community disagreed with policies that Bush and Conant accepted.

The Americans' seeming drift came to an end on December 6, 1941, the day before Pearl Harbor, when Bush informed his colleagues that FDR had ordered the reorganized Uranium Advisory Committee, now known as the S-1 Committee, to determine whether a bomb could be built at all, and if so, at what cost. The President wanted them to report back in six months. Despite the uncertainties, Fermi, Bush, Compton, and the others remained optimistic. Fermi succinctly summed up the problem facing them:

> The fundamental point in fabricating a chain reaction machine is of course to see to it that each fission produces a certain number of neutrons and some of these neutrons will again produce fission. If an original fission causes more than one subsequent fission then of course the reaction goes. If an original fission causes less than one subsequent fission than the reaction does not go.[19]

Physicists at the time referred to this "reproduction rate" of neutrons as k. Fermi and others had proved that they could achieve a k of $+1$ in the lab—Fermi had already got 1.73. The fundamental problems remained matters of engineering, not basic science: how to build a reactor to optimize k, given such essential constraints as building in adequate instrumentation, effective control rods, and shut-down mechanisms to prevent the chain reaction from getting out of hand. Karl Compton's brother, Arthur, proposed a timetable that proved to be remarkably close to the actual unfolding of events:

1. determine theoretically whether a chain reaction was possible by July 1942
2. actually achieve a chain reaction by January 1943
3. begin producing plutonium by January 1944
4. build the bomb (uranium or plutonium) by January 1945[20]

In January 1942, Arthur Compton organized a centralized research project at his own institution, known by the code name

Metallurgical Laboratory, to determine the feasibility of the chain reaction. He brought in Fermi to head up research and construction of a nuclear reactor that would accomplish the chain reaction. This the "Italian navigator" achieved on December 2, 1942, and from then on, the United States was plunged headlong into a feverish secret race to produce nuclear weapons.

2

"The Radiance of a Thousand Suns"
DEVELOPMENT OF THE ATOMIC BOMB
DURING WORLD WAR II

BETWEEN DECEMBER 1942 AND JULY 1945, American scientists and engineers built two uranium type and one plutonium type atomic bombs. By spending the then astronomical sum of two billion dollars, the nuclear community, working in total secrecy, constructed an enormous isotope-separation plant at Oak Ridge, Tennessee; a plutonium-production plant at Hanford, Washington; and a bomb laboratory at Los Alamos, New Mexico. At these sites, scientists, engineers, technicians, and working people labored under a blanket of tight security to launch the nuclear age.

During these years, the basic characteristics of Nuclear America emerged: nuclear power's intimate ties to the national security state, and the subordination of nonmilitary applications of nuclear power to military demands. The arms race mentality was spawned in this period too, out of the pressure scientists and policymakers alike felt about beating the Germans to the bomb. At the same time that nuclear weapons were becoming a reality in the laboratory, what George Kennan has described as "the nuclear delusion" was forming in the minds of America's political leadership. Increasingly, Presidents Roosevelt and Truman as well as those around them came to view nuclear weapons as some sort of panacea that would provide a cheap solution to the challenges and frustrations they encountered in conducting foreign relations. Finally, the nuclear-industrial complex was born, tying universities, the institutions that were to become the National

Laboratories, defense contractors, and the Defense Department into a tight web of mutual dependence.

During the summer and autumn of 1942, Bush and Conant decided to reorganize the entire atomic project to centralize its direction under the Army Corps of Engineers. The Corps appointed Brigadier General Leslie Groves to take charge of what was now code-named the Manhattan Engineering District—for short, MED or the Manhattan Project. At first, Groves, a career West Pointer who had up till then held only desk commands, approached his new assignment with little relish. He was hoping for a combat field command. Instead, his commanding officer asked him to stay on in Washington. Groves objected. "If you do the job right," the general responded, "it will win the war." Groves then realized what they were talking about. "Oh, that thing," he said unenthusiastically.[1]

Groves brought an abrasive mixture of attitudes to his new assignment. He shared his fellow army officers' contempt for the scientists, whom he and other soldiers called "doubledomes," "eggheads," "longbeards," and "oddballs." To the soldiers assigned to Los Alamos, Groves once stated, "At great expense we have gathered on this mesa the largest collection of crackpots ever seen."[2] But he had an insider's understanding of the army's internal politics. He was experienced in procurement and bureaucratic maneuver. As an engineer and supervisor of large-scale construction projects, including the Pentagon, he dealt with other engineers and the managers of large government contractors as an equal. His dynamism, his demand for results, even his crudeness, helped translate what might have been an academic and theoretical exercise in nuclear physics into an actual bomb.

Partly due to Groves's forceful personality, and partly because the project was finally being supported by adequate funding, during 1942 the Manhattan Project leaped forward. Scientists, confident that they could achieve a chain reaction, were turning from pure science and the experimental, laboratory stages of research to a phase dominated by engineering considerations aimed at building a bomb. The attitude of Ernest O. Lawrence was typical. He had "swept his laboratory clean of the customary patient research into Nature's laws; now he demanded results above all else. . . . Experiments, not theory, [became] the keynote. . . ."[3]

Groves's drive for results had a long-term consequence that has shaped nuclear policymaking to the present time. His contracting policies favored a few large corporations: DuPont, General Electric, Union Carbide, International Nickel, and Stone and Webster (a large Boston construction and engineering firm). In this, Groves was not unique. World War II procurement generally favored large, established corporations because only such enterprises had the production experience, facilities, trained workers, and laboratory staff necessary to produce something workable in a minimum amount of time. The federal government was infiltrated with "dollar-a-year men": executives of large corporations who served in civilian positions in various federal agencies, many involved with procurement. These executives injected a corporate mentality directly into the veins of the federal bureaucracy. Hence it was not surprising that 40 percent of federal wartime research and development contract dollars went to only ten corporations, while eight universities received 90 percent of the research expenditures of the Office of Scientific Research and Development.[4]

Groves was part of a trend when he favored DuPont, General Electric, and other industrial giants for building and running MED facilities.[5] But the trend continued unabated after the war, with the result that by the mid-1960s, more than half the Atomic Energy Commission's expenditures went to only seven contractors: Union Carbide, General Electric, Bendix, the Sandia consortium, DuPont, the University of California, and the University of Chicago.[6] Once started, the system tended to perpetuate itself: some managerial personnel of postwar nuclear contractors served "apprenticeships," as it were, in the AEC, thus providing their employers with invaluable contacts. AEC spending on research and development, as Admiral Hyman Rickover complained in 1960, "subsidizes and augments [large corporations'] own research and development efforts, and so enhances their competitive position."[7] This wartime association of big corporations and universities considerably strengthened the postwar military-industrial complex that President Dwight D. Eisenhower warned of in his 1961 Farewell Address. That alliance of universities and corporations was formalized in 1953 with the establishment of the Atomic Industrial Forum, which has become the nuclear power industries' principal voice and lobbyist.

But all this was a long way off in 1942. Then, the fundamental problem confronting scientists of the Manhattan Project was the separation of the fissile isotope U-235 from other uranium isotopes. The choice of separation techniques was narrowing to two: gaseous diffusion and electromagnetic separation. The Met Lab in Chicago could not be expanded to provide production facilities of the size required by either of those processes, so Groves sought a spacious site for a massive U-235 "factory." He soon located one in a chronically depressed area of eastern Tennessee on the Clinch River twenty miles west of Knoxville, near a hamlet called Oak Ridge. One of the advantages of the Oak Ridge site was that it nestled down between parallel ridges, which might provide some containment for Knoxville in case of a catastrophic accident at the plant. Groves hired the architectural firm of Skidmore, Owings, and Merrill to design an entirely new city there, and the Boston construction and engineering giant of Stone and Webster to build it. (Stone and Webster remains today one of the largest firms involved in building power plants, both conventional and nuclear.) Oak Ridge, destined to become the first of the National Laboratories, mushroomed in less than a year to an instant city with its own independent coal-fired power plant, sewage system, and housing for a wartime population of 13,000. Like so many later boomtowns spawned by nuclear power, Oak Ridge was a sprawl of bleak, barren trailer yards scattered around more conventional housing. Prefab plywood hutments and jerry-built cemesto houses went up atop the naked, scraped red earth.[8]

Oak Ridge was also the first of the "secret cities": three wartime installations—the others being Hanford, Washington, and Los Alamos, New Mexico—where research and production of the atomic bomb was carried out. A puzzled Tennessee native said of Oak Ridge in 1944: "It's a funny place. Everything goes in, but nothing comes out." The city was a cross between a federal military enclave and a company town, the company being Tennessee Eastman, a subsidiary of Eastman Kodak, a firm that had earlier impressed Groves by its performance in building an ordnance plant.

Gaseous diffusion, though it eventually emerged as the sole U-235 production process, seemed a long gamble in 1942. Its technical difficulties daunted nearly all the Columbia University scientists who had been working at it, because they had to create a system of thousands of metal filters with holes so tiny that, by comparison, a pinprick would be an enormous gap. As Oak Ridge rose on the red Tennessee earth, no one had yet constructed a pilot plant to prove that gaseous diffusion could be achieved on an industrial scale. Because of these uncertainties, Oak Ridge also pursued an electromagnetic separation process, accomplished by enormous electromagnetic runways called "racetracks." Deriving from Ernest O. Lawrence's work with the large cyclotron at Berkeley, a racetrack would in effect be a colossal mass spectrograph, which, instead of separating out minute amounts of an isotope like U-235 for laboratory work, would produce it in industrial quantities. Eventually the electromagnetic technique was abandoned after the war in favor of gaseous diffusion. But while it was in operation, it required the most valuable production machinery in existence at the time. In 1943, when the first racetracks were being built, copper was in short supply because of war production. Engineers at Oak Ridge heard that the United States Treasury might be able to release, for temporary use, about 80,000 tons of another metal that was an excellent electrical conductor: silver. So the Oak Ridge racetracks had magnetic windings of solid silver, and solid silver busbars an entire square foot in cross section.

DuPont and the Met Lab built a small-scale production reactor, CP-2, in the Argonne Forest Preserve near Chicago, a site that eventually became the Argonne National laboratory, a major postwar nuclear research facility. Oak Ridge also spawned Clinton Laboratory, organized to do research on specific production problems. But the Manhattan Project's need for production and laboratory facilities was still not satisfied. Oak Ridge was not a suitable place for producing plutonium, the alternative bomb material. The drain on its supply of electricity would be too great, and Groves considered it too accessible for comfort to would-be saboteurs. Army and DuPont engineers scouted several western sites, and finally came up with one in the deserts of southwest Washington near the town of Hanford. Hanford offered an ideal combination of criteria: it was near a large river, the Columbia; it was remote from the coast, so that the army could protect it against both sabotage and air attack; the surrounding country-side was arid and unpopulated; the Grand Coulee and Bonneville dams were nearby power sources. A railroad ran through the area, so labor and materials could be hauled in. Thus Hanford Reservation was born.

But the problems of building a second instant industrial city were more severe in the deserts of Washington State than they had been in the Tennessee hills. Dust storms in the summer discouraged imported workers. Remoteness and security restrictions imposed a spartan regime on the work force, especially in the first year before suitable housing had been completed. Nevertheless, DuPont managed to construct a self-contained industrial city that would begin producing plutonium by 1944.

The Hanford Reservation was not as immune to Japanese attack as the army thought, however. As the result of a bizarre Japanese military expedient, it almost blasted the United States with a nuclear disaster of some kind just months before the bomb manufactured there destroyed Nagasaki. Toward the end of the war, someone in the Japanese military came up with the imaginative scheme of lofting incendiary paper balloons across the Pacific, hoping they would fire the forests of the American Pacific Northwest. None of these balloons accomplished their mission, but one of them managed to complete its trans-Pacific journey and become entangled in power lines at Hanford. This shorted out the electrical supply, which in turn shut down pumps sending cooling water to the production reactor there. Emergency systems switched the pumps back on again in less than a second, but the reactor was down for three days.[9] The electrical transient produced the start of what later was called a loss-of-coolant accident (LOCA), and only the prompt resumption of power averted some kind of a massive accident.

Even the Met Lab, Argonne, and Clinton did not meet the Manhattan Project's requirements for research labs. At the beginning of the program, in 1941, research was scattered among some nine universities: Columbia, Princeton, Berkeley, Cornell, Johns Hopkins, Virginia, Chicago, Minnesota, and Iowa State College. Because scientists were concentrating on production problems for U-235 and plutonium, they had done little on the physics of explosion under the unearthly conditions of heat and pressure in a fission reaction. Nor had anyone yet begun working on the engineering problems of building and delivering a bomb. Recognizing the need to centralize and direct this research effort, J. Robert Oppenheimer, a prominent theoretical physicist from Berkeley, recommended to Groves that bomb research be concentrated in one location, preferably an isolated proving ground since the work would be in the area of ordnance, with tight security controls to prevent sabotage and the leakage of secret data. The site would have to be remote so that, as Groves put it in the euphemisms that come so readily to the tongue when speaking of nuclear disasters, "nearby communities would not be adversely affected by any unforeseen results from our activities."[10] In November 1942, the two men selected an isolated mesa near a town called Los Alamos, northwest of Santa Fe, New Mexico, where Oppenheimer had spent his boyhood summers. Shortly thereafter, Groves chose Oppenheimer to be the scientific head of the Los Alamos project.

The Los Alamos site, despite its beauty, was a challenge to those who came to live there during the war, especially the wives of the scientists, who found little there in the way of civilian amenities. The roads were almost impassable; a transplanted New Yorker remarked that New Mexico's roads made the back-country dirt roads of Alabama seem like the Merritt Parkway by comparison. Santa Fe was forty bone-crunching miles away on a rugged mountain road. The unpaved streets of Los Alamos were dusty in dry weather and muddy when wet. The dust, combined with soot from the coal stoves that served as kitchen ranges, made housekeeping miserable. The stoves, which were almost impossible to fire up, overheated kitchens in warm weather. One evening, on the pretext of having Groves instruct the women on the most efficient way to light the coal-burning stoves, one of the scientist's wives had him give a demonstration. One hour later, his uniform covered with soot, he at last coaxed a tiny flame from the stove. The next day, Groves supplied electric-resistance burners to all housing.

Groves, for his part, regarded the families of the scientists as a nuisance. He grudgingly consented to erection of a nursery school, but principally so that the mothers of some small children might be made useful as secretaries or statisticians. At one point, indignant about the birthrate among the wives of scientists, Groves is supposed to have said, "It has to stop."[11] Groves, the army, and its civilian contractors were indifferent to the natural beauty of the site. Only Oppenheimer's direct intervention prevented them from mindlessly stacking row after row of prefab housing in geometric rigidity. Instead he had them respect some site contours, to relieve the barracks-like layout. The housing itself ranged from unpleasant to unspeakable: Quonset huts, hutments, plywood fourplexes, square and rectangular prefabs that were the forerunners of today's modular housing.

Despite the difficulties of the site and the barracks-like atmosphere imposed by the army, Oppenheimer was able to recruit a brilliant array of individuals to work at Los Alamos, including a dozen present or future Nobel laureates. They later recalled the war years at Los Alamos with an extravagant nostalgia. Isidor Rabi spoke of "a certain magic, romance, devotion [that] causes people who were there to remember it as the most significant period in their lives." The Englishman James Tuck remembered "so many people doing a damned difficult job wresting the secrets of nature. Oppenheimer had to concert the fullest effort of the best minds of the Western world. Los Alamos is a phenomenon unique in history."[12] Alice K. Smith, an historian who was married to a metallurgist assigned to Los Alamos, caught the peculiar ambience of the wartime Mesa, what she calls "the general wackiness of the whole operation":

> Everyone had his own Los Alamos. It was one thing to those
> . . . who lived in the relative seclusion of Snob Hollow [an area of
> desirable apartment housing] and in ugly trailer camps along the
> road. It was different for a European getting his first taste of
> egalitarian America, and for a young wife from an industrial com-

munity casually playing "Twenty Questions" with Nobel Prize
winners. . . . The tension of those who worked in secrecy inside
[was] matched for those outside by maid shortages, milk shortages, electricity cutoffs, and water rationing.[13]

Security was another formidable drawback to life in Los
Alamos. The army's obsessive fear of leaks ceaselessly irritated
scientists on the Mesa. From Groves on down, secrecy, counterintelligence, and a "national security" mentality pervaded the
military administrators there. These attitudes were compounded
by a fear of foreigners and of Communism that sometimes threatened to paralyze research. Military counterintelligence personnel
were distressed to find that, of some twenty of the Allied nations'
scientific leaders who worked at Los Alamos, only four were
native-born Americans: Oppenheimer, Edwin McMillan, Richard
Feynman, and Luis Alvarez. Among the distinguished aliens were
Fermi, Rabi, Emilio Segrè, Niels Bohr, James Chadwick (head of
the British mission there), Victor Weisskopf, Hans Bethe, George
Kistiakowsky, Edward Teller, James Franck, Bruno Rossi, John
von Neumann, Stanislaw Ulam, and Rudolph Peierls. For some
reason he never disclosed, Groves was particularly suspicious of
Fermi, and insisted that he be excluded from Los Alamos. Oppenheimer considered that attitude preposterous and for once
rejected Groves's demand.

Because of security restrictions, the residents of Los Alamos
became, in some sense, nonpersons. Children born there could
not have the location entered on their birth certificates. No one
was allowed to tell the families and friends they left behind where
they lived; only in case of emergency, such as terminal illness in
the family, could the Mesa people refer to where they were, and
then only by stating that they lived in New Mexico. All incoming
mail was addressed simply to Box 1663, Santa Fe. Army counterintelligence corps personnel read all outgoing as well as incoming mail. All buildings except housing and community facilities (schools, PX, assembly hall) were restricted-access, enforced
by security badges and the ever-present military police. One MP
detachment, a cavalry unit sent to guard the bomb test site, added
a bizarre note to the operation. Its men, under the command of

a New York horse enthusiast and National Guard captain, patrolled the rugged terrain on horseback like the Indian-fighting cavalry of seventy years earlier. In their pith helmets and jodhpurs, they added an incongruous touch to the site of the most advanced scientific research in the world.

Though Bush, Oppenheimer, and the other high-level bureaucrats who ran the Manhattan Project supported these security precautions, some among those who lived and worked at Los Alamos kicked at the traces. Richard Feynman, who later proposed the existence of the quark and who in 1965 received the Nobel prize in physics for work in quantum electrodynamics, amused himself in his years at Los Alamos by sending coded messages in the mail to outwit the army censors, and by picking locks on safes that contained classified information. But despite such rare personal acts of rebellion, Groves's policy of secrecy prevailed, with one major exception.

Oppenheimer insisted on a free exchange of information among the scientists at Los Alamos, especially on the broad theoretical problems they faced, and he instituted a series of weekly seminars for this purpose. This became the renowned "Colloquium." Groves was horrified: the Colloquium flew in the face of a policy he called "compartmentalization" that he sought to impose on the entire Manhattan Project. According to this security concept, information could not flow freely among the components of the Manhattan Project, or even within the units themselves. All research data was handled on a need-to-know basis. Groves therefore resolutely fought the very idea of the Colloquium and bucked the dispute all the way up to FDR, who had letters sent to the leading scientific and administrative people reminding them of the need for secrecy. But the Colloquium survived, and, for its participants, became a highlight of the intellectual life on the Mesa.

Groves permitted only one known exception to his general policy of excluding scientists with leftist connections from work on the Manhattan Project: Oppenheimer himself. Oppenheimer freely disclosed his former radical connections to security investigators: His former fiancée had been a member of the Communist party, as had his brother Frank; his wife had friends in the party and had been married to a young Communist killed in Spain fighting with the Abraham Lincoln Brigade; he had attended party-sponsored events around Berkeley in the late 1930s. But this did not sate the craving of counterintelligence personnel for data that would link Oppenheimer more convincingly to the party and the Soviet Union. Working with rumor and innuendo, army counterintelligence (whom the scientists on the Mesa called "creeps") doggedly accumulated information on Oppenheimer and made bold inferential leaps in an attempt to label him a dangerous subversive. Colonel Boris Pash wrote Groves and other officers up the chain of command:

> All indications on the part of the Communist Party members who have expressed themselves with regard to the subject lead this office [Pash was referring to himself as "this office"] to believe that the Communist Party is making definite effort to officially divorce subject's ["subject" was Oppenheimer] affiliation with the Party, and subject himself is not indicating in any way interest in the Party. However, if subject's affiliation with the Party is definite and he is a member of the Party [Pash had no evidence to support this "if," much less the inferential daisy chain built around it] there is a possibility of his developing a scientific work to a certain extent, then turning it over to the Party without submitting any phase of it to the U.S. Government.

But Pash's logical pirouettes read like hard-edged analysis compared to the attitudes of other counterintelligence officers. Army Captain Peer DeSilva wrote in 1943 that

> J. R. Oppenheimer is playing a key part in the attempt of the Soviet Union to secure, by espionage, highly secret information which is vital to the Soviet Union.[14]

Groves, who usually devoured such security reports with fear and fascination, was in this case unmoved. He considered Oppenheimer essential to the success of the project and ordered him retained.

Groves's willingness to overlook Oppenheimer's former leftist associations constituted his only knowing lapse of anticommunist vigilance. Otherwise, he and army counterintelligence avidly searched for potential leaks to the Soviet Union. Reminiscing about his role as administrative head of the project years later, Groves stated that there was no "illusion on my part, Russia was our enemy and the project was conducted on that basis." Colonel John Lansdale, Jr., confirmed Groves's attitude. When counterintelligence personnel learned that one physicist working on the project had a Communist background they had him summarily drafted into military service over the objections of a number of project leaders. Another scientist lost his job simply because he made the mistake of attending a party at a restaurant in San Francisco given by the Russian vice-consul in honor of the violinist Isaac Stern.[15] All told, some 400,000 security checks were run on Manhattan Project employees. Those believed to be most likely to transmit classified project information to unauthorized persons were placed under surveillance.

Military counterintelligence was also worried, of course, about the possibility that America's Axis enemies might learn about the bomb project. Manhattan Project scientists shared their anxiety. The Germans had begun the war with a lead in nuclear research, and had both the scientific expertise and the raw materials necessary to produce a nuclear weapon. The haunting fear of a Nazi bomb troubled scientists until early 1945. At first, the Americans' fears were well founded. The German team of Hahn and Strassmann first knowingly achieved laboratory fission and thereby established what the Americans considered a head start in the nuclear race. After Munich, the Third Reich controlled one of the richest sources of uranium in the world, the Joachimsthal mines of Bohemia, and their occupation of Belgium in May 1940 gave them potential access to the output of the uranium mines of the Belgian Congo (modern Zaire). Despite the intellectual destruction of its universities, Germany retained a cadre of preeminent physicists, including men of the stature of Hahn, Werner Heisenberg, Walther Böthe, and Hans Geiger. Nazi Germany enthusiastically supported both basic and applied scientific research. The on-going work of the Kaiser Wilhelm Institute remained a constant reminder of the central role of science in the German war effort. Radioactivity was so widely understood throughout German society even before the war that a German firm marketed what it called the "Radioactive Toothpaste"—its hot ingredient was thorium—and advertised it by a little figure who said, "I am the radioactive substance. My rays massage the gums."

During the war, the German nuclear establishment was actively pursuing research in fission, U-235 separation, and the chain reaction. At a conference attended by high-ranking scientists and military officials in 1942, Field Marshal Erhard Milch, enraged by the British saturation-bombing of Rostock and Cologne, asked Heisenberg how large a nuclear weapon would have to be to inflict retaliatory devastation on an enemy city. Heisenberg formed an oval in the air with his hands and replied, "As large as a pineapple."[16] Throughout the war, in nuclear laboratories at Gottow, Dahlem, and Hechingen, combined civilian-military teams constructed imaginative piles using uranium in cubes, paraffin lattices, and frozen heavy water. By 1945, despite the turmoil of impending defeat, German physicists were racing toward criticality at a uranium pile in a cave at Haigerloch.

Yet despite these scientific efforts, Hitler's Germany did not even achieve a chain reaction, much less a nuclear weapon, because German nuclear technology remained underdeveloped. The Germans were long on theory, short on technology. They built no cyclotrons comparable in size to the American units that enabled the Allies to outstrip them in plutonium research and production. Though ingenious, the German piles were primitive. German scientists, unlike the Americans, never developed a satisfactory rapport with high civilian officials. Hitler, as well as lesser figures like Albert Speer, were of two minds about the possibilities of nuclear research. On the one hand, the Führer was excited by the prospect of a weapon powerful enough to destroy a city and kill hundreds of thousands; but on the other, anticipating quick victory, he directed the bulk of the German research effort to weapons promising short-term payoffs, like the V-1 flying bomb and the V-2 rocket. In striking contrast with the Manhattan Project, the German research effort never got central direction, adequate funding, full support at the highest levels, or intimate army sponsorship. Nor were the German scientists ever certain just what they hoped to produce: bomb, production reactor, or propulsion reactor for the submarine fleet.

Above all, German nuclear research was hampered by a simple, utterly human error of calculation. In early 1941, Walther Böthe, who was charged with computing the diffusion length of slow neutrons in carbon, greatly underestimated the length, with the result that the Germans from the outset abandoned graphite as a moderator, unlike the Americans, who built CP-1 out of graphite blocks. Instead, the Germans turned almost single-mindedly to heavy water as a moderator, and that, in turn, made them dangerously dependent on the world's only source of heavy water, a hydroelectric complex at Vermorsk in southern Norway.

British and Norwegian intelligence monitored the relationship of the Vermorsk plant to the Reich, both before and after Nazi occupation of Norway. When it became obvious that the Germans were taking large shipments of heavy water, the British decided to destroy the plant. Their first try, a glider-borne commando raid, was a tragic failure, with most of the aircraft crashing and the surviving commandos being shot on the spot by the occupying forces. But the second succeeded. It was a classic small-scale demolition raid every bit as thrilling as fictional commando attacks as portrayed in *The Guns of Navarone.* The commandos destroyed the facilities and dumped all the Norwegian heavy water into the fjord. The RAF subsequently bombed the plant, and a third commando raid sunk a lake steamer carrying heavy water to Germany. These strikes were a disastrous setback for the Nazi nuclear effort. Because I. G. Farben, the chemical giant, proved reluctant to build a heavy water plant, the German effort was always starved for the heavy water essential to research and production.

But American scientists and military leaders were not to learn just how retarded the German nuclear effort was until the war in Europe had almost ended. Desperate for information, Manhattan Project leaders organized a special team composed of civilian scientists and military men taken from the project's counterintelligence force. It was charged not only with responsibility for intelligence gathering, but also with seizing the Reich's nuclear materials and scientists. In a peculiar and unexplained breach of security, it was code-named *Alsos,* the Greek work for "grove" and hence a hint of the connection between its mission and the ultrasecret project headed by General Groves. Its military chief was the same Colonel Pash who played a prominent role in the security investigation of Oppenheimer. His civilian counterpart was the Dutch–American physicist, Samuel Goudsmit.[17] Following closely the advancing front lines, *Alsos* first interrogated Italian scientists in 1943, then established itself in its Paris headquarters after the Liberation. From there it sent its men into Germany, where it earned a reputation for being an insatiable consumer of captured documents and German scientists. *Alsos* men were called "bodysnatchers" because of their eager pursuit of scientists like Heisenberg and Hahn.

Indifferent to wartime agreements among the allies, *Alsos* did not hesitate to dash into designated zones of British, French, and Russian occupation as Germany was conquered, spiriting away documents and researchers just before allied troops arrived to take control. *Alsos* leaders were particularly eager to deny the Russians access to German data and personnel. Thus, on their recommendation, the Army Air Corps bombed the nuclear production works at Oranienburg near Berlin before the Soviets could occupy those facilities. *Alsos* snatched all uranium stocks from Strassfurt just ahead of the Russians, and rounded up scientists at Hechingen, deep in the projected Soviet zone of occupation. As Groves, the ultimate commanding officer of *Alsos,* admitted, at the time American units seized the scientists and uranium around Hechingen in April 1945, "our principal concern . . . was to keep information and atomic scientists from falling into the hands of Russians."[18]

President Roosevelt supported the determination of Manhattan Project leaders to keep the Soviets ignorant of American nuclear research while denying them access to German material and scientists.[19] FDR, who spoke frequently of the catastrophic potential of Manhattan Project research, cherished the American nuclear monopoly as an important element in his strategy to secure an acceptable and lasting peace. Roosevelt did not intend to rely on some crude form of nuclear blackmail to force the Soviets to acquiesce in a peace settlement dictated by Washington. On the contrary, he hoped to be able to work out differences with them through negotiations and without reference to the atomic bomb. But if diplomacy failed and confrontation erupted between the United States and the U.S.S.R., Roosevelt wanted the West to enjoy a nuclear advantage.

In 1943, Roosevelt's hopes for accommodation with the Soviets were clouded by Winston Churchill's fear that Stalin would prove more difficult to deal with once victory over the Axis powers had been achieved. Nor could the president have been exactly cheered by the views of his ambassador in Moscow. W. Averell Harriman doubted Stalin's revolutionary fervor but judged him to be an aggressive expansionist determined to take full advantage of the power vacuum that would be created in eastern and central Europe as German power waned. Then again, a number of the president's intimates, among them Harry Hopkins, Joseph P. Davies (a former ambassador to Moscow), and Vice-President Henry Wallace, believed that negotiations accompanied by a conciliatory demeanor would produce positive results.[20] Roosevelt would have preferred to believe the Hopkins–Davies view, but lacking any personal knowledge of Stalin, he remained undecided.

In late November 1943, Roosevelt set out to remedy this defect, journeying to Teheran for a conference with Churchill and Stalin. But it was the Soviet dictator he really wanted to meet. There is no way of knowing just what went through the president's mind as he waited to form his first impressions of the legendary Stalin. But he was probably unprepared for the smallish mustachioed man, neatly dressed in the uniform of a marshal of the Red Army, who came to greet him on the morning of the first day of the conference. Stalin exuded a relaxed self-confidence that set Roosevelt at ease almost immediately. In no time the two leaders were chatting like old compatriots. Stalin's blunt, at times even brusque conversation, so different from Roosevelt's own stylish evasiveness, charmed the president. FDR discovered that they shared a mutual distaste for the haughty leader of the Free French, Charles de Gaulle. More significantly, he discerned nothing doctrinaire about Stalin, nothing that indicated the Soviet leader was anything but a pragmatic and wholly nationalistic statesman. Encouraged by this first encounter, FDR told his son Elliott that Stalin was "altogether quite impressive." He left Teheran on excellent personal terms with Stalin, and satisfied that the Soviet leader was less a dedicated revolutionary than he was a traditional European statesman whose foreign policy aims, though undoubtedly imperialistic, were nevertheless limited. In short, Stalin seemed reasonable. FDR thought they might get along.[21] A second meeting between the two men at the Yalta conference, held in February 1945, only served to confirm Roosevelt's earlier impression. There, Stalin made more concessions than he won, while comporting himself like any other power politician.[22]

Roosevelt, convinced that a viable peace depended upon accommodation on the part of all the Allies, had feared that Stalin would prove to be the intractable zealot of the Churchill thesis. He found instead a traditional Russian expansionist, more an heir to the czars than to Marx. Encouraged by his view of Stalin as a tough, suspicious, but essentially reasonable man, Roosevelt persisted in his attempts to negotiate a postwar settlement to the end of his life. This is not to suggest, however, that had he lived, the president would have necessarily remained committed to peaceful diplomacy in his search for a resolution to differences between the Soviet Union and the West. In fact, during the weeks that followed Yalta, tensions mounted within the alliance as Stalin began to suspect that Roosevelt and Churchill might be negotiating a separate peace on the western front. Blunt, even angry cables were exchanged between the president and the Soviet dictator. More significantly, the sensitive German and Polish questions as well as a number of lesser problems remained unresolved. Roosevelt knew that the alliance might founder on these issues. For this reason he sought to strengthen the West by preparing a nuclear option in case his Soviet diplomacy failed.

Roosevelt's evolving views on the problem of sharing nuclear data with Great Britain provide further insight into his ambivalent, flexible attitudes. Despite Britain's early theoretical lead in nuclear research, evidenced by the MAUD report, after the summer of 1940 its effort stalled. The nation's industrial capacity was strained to the utmost simply to survive the Nazi air onslaught. Hence Great Britain could not undertake the massive economic commitment that would translate its head start into an actual weapon. The MAUD committee recommendations, supported by Prime Minister Winston Churchill, induced British policymakers to seek a "partnership between equals" with the United States in development of the bomb. The minister of aircraft production, Colonel John T. C. Moore-Brabazon, a man whose mind should have been preoccupied with other matters in the summer of 1940, promoted Anglo-American cooperation as the basis for a postwar dominance of the world by the two English-speaking nuclear policemen.[23]

But not many Americans were dazzled by this vision. By 1942, the United States had established insuperable advantages over the British in the number of its scientists and engineers, laboratory resources (even before Oak Ridge and Los Alamos were completed), and in access to raw materials. Some in Washington, especially James Conant and Secretary of War Henry Stimson, developed sour suspicions of British motives in seeking nuclear cooperation. The prominent role of Imperial Chemical Industries, Ltd., in the MAUD committee report led to speculation that the wily British were seeking a free ride on wartime American technology in order to develop a postwar civilian nuclear industry. Nor was General Groves enthusiastic about an Anglo-American partnership. Full cooperation would have violated his insistence on compartmentalization, and would have inducted scores of non-British aliens into the heart of the Manhattan Project, a prospect that appalled the xenophobic general and the counterintelligence personnel working under him.

In June 1942, despite all these American suspicions, President Roosevelt and Prime Minister Churchill arrived at an informal understanding that Churchill interpreted to mean that England and America were to be full partners in all future research. Six months later, however, acting on the advice of Conant and Stimson, FDR suddenly altered his course, adopting a policy of "restricted interchange" that cut the British off from much of the data being produced by the Manhattan Project. Not surprisingly, FDR's abrupt turnabout drew a sharp protest from Churchill, who insisted that the President was violating their June agreement. Churchill demanded restoration of full partnership.

James Conant was the most forthcoming of those who opposed

an Anglo-American nuclear partnership. He believed that while the United States was bearing virtually all of the financial burden of the Manhattan Project, the British were availing themselves of an immense amount of invaluable information relating to the peaceful uses of atomic energy. Distrustful of British purposes, Conant feared that at war's end they would use this information to become the United States' principal competitor in the promising field of nonmilitary nuclear energy. But Conant did not focus entirely on commercial issues in making his case. The atomic bomb, Conant argued, would so profoundly revolutionize international affairs that the mere fact that England and America alone among the powers controlled it would of necessity bind them together after the war. Conant believed that if the United States decided on a permanent alliance with Britain, that ought to be the result of a deliberate policy and not simply the accidental consequence of scientific cooperation.[24]

Churchill, desperate to sell Roosevelt on the advantages of Anglo-American cooperation, focused exclusively on political and diplomatic issues in rebutting the detractors of bilateralism. Europe, the prime minister warned, would become a vast power vacuum at the end of the war. With England weakened by her exertions, if America returned to her prewar isolationism, he feared that the Soviets would move in to fill the vacuum. In these perilous circumstances, British possession of nuclear weapons might prove to be the great equalizer, giving Britain the strength to stand up to the Soviets in a postwar confrontation. But the new American policy of restricted interchange would deny Britain the opportunity to develop a nuclear capability in time. Without that, Churchill feared, unless the United States was prepared to make guarantees, there was little hope for the future of Europe.

Though Roosevelt shared Conant's concern for the postwar commercial implications of continued Anglo-American cooperation, he was persuaded by the urgency of Churchill's arguments. In a secret agreement that he and the prime minister signed at Quebec on August 19, 1943, Roosevelt restored England to something akin to full partnership with the United States in the area of nuclear research. In exchange, Churchill disclaimed "any interest in . . . industrial and commercial aspects beyond what may be considered by the President of the United States to be fair and just and in harmony with the economic welfare of the world."[25] The rest of the agreement fit neatly into FDR's developing diplomatic plans. He intended to pursue a policy of cooperation with the USSR as long as that offered some hope of success. But what if accommodation proved impossible? FDR was not fighting to liberate Europe from the Fascists only to see it fall to the Soviets. Nor could he be certain that at war's end the American people would not revert to their traditional isolationism. Roosevelt wanted Britain to share the atomic bomb so that if his Soviet diplomacy failed and isolationism reemerged in the United States, Britain would be in a position to thwart Soviet ambitions in Europe.

In his pursuit of an accommodation with the Soviet Union, Roosevelt frequently emphasized the importance of assuring Stalin that the United States and Britain would not "gang up" on him after the war. Of course, the Quebec Agreement ran contrary to that notion. Yet, so long as it remained secret, the Anglo-American partners had little to fear. FDR was confident that the British were as anxious as he was to keep their nuclear research secret. Both parties pledged not to "communicate any information" about the weapons being developed to any third party. Too, the agreement stipulated that neither would use the weapon against any third party without the agreement of the other. Britain was to have the bomb: Roosevelt wanted that. But the British were also on leading strings held by Roosevelt. They could not use the weapon or even inform the world that they possessed it unless authorized to do so by Washington.

The eventual British participation in the Manhattan Project was more extensive and open than the terms of the Quebec Agreement might suggest. British scientists, including the refugee group, working in the United States and at an Anglo-Canadian laboratory at Montreal, made a significant contribution to the nuclear effort. Chadwick became the head of the British scientific delegation, and established a surprisingly warm working relationship with Groves. The two together scoured British industrial and academic laboratories for scientists, especially ordnance and metallurgical experts. The contributions made by this group only served to heighten British shock at the policy adopted by the United States in the McMahon Act of 1946, which brusquely excluded the British from further participation in American nuclear research.

The Quebec Agreement demonstrated that the president was prepared if necessary to use an Anglo-American nuclear monopoly to restrain the Soviets and preserve a balance of power in Europe. If it came to a confrontation, FDR wanted, like Theodore Roosevelt, to be prepared with his own version of the Big Stick. The question then became, *could* nuclear weapons be used for such a purpose? Would they provide security? Or had the logic of traditional statecraft been undermined by the very nature of the new weapon?

A few scientists, keenly aware of the revolutionary significance of the atomic bomb, tried to awaken American and British political leaders to the changed circumstances of the new nuclear world, especially to the long-range political implications of their work. Niels Bohr, the Danish physicist and Nobel laureate, was the earliest and most prominent among those to warn of the dangers that lay ahead. A leader of the international scientific community for decades, Bohr believed that scientists had a responsibility to encourage appropriate social and political responses to changes science brought about. "Every valuable human being must be a radical and a rebel," Bohr once wrote, "for what he must aim at is to make things better than they are."[26] Bohr was convinced that the development of nuclear weapons would have a profound, perhaps revolutionary impact on the old international order.

Late in 1943, after having been smuggled out of Nazi-occupied Denmark by the Danish underground, Bohr made his way to the United States, ostensibly to work on the Manhattan Project. But Bohr's services were not required by those working on the bomb. Nor had he really come for that purpose anyway. Instead, he hoped to make American leaders aware that they stood at a major crossroads in human history and that cooperation among the United States, Britain, and the Soviet Union to establish a system of international control of atomic energy was essential if the world was to be spared a potentially catastrophic nuclear arms race. Before Bohr left England, Sir John Anderson, the prime minister's principal science adviser and a man conversant with the situation in the United States, warned him that the bureaucrats who ran the Manhattan Project would be hostile. Bohr therefore bypassed Groves, Bush, and Conant, and instead sought direct access to the president. Felix Frankfurter, associate justice of the United States Supreme Court, a longtime presidential adviser and an old acquaintance, agreed to serve as his go-between.

Bohr's message, relayed to the president by Frankfurter probably in late February 1944, was clear and urgent. If nuclear energy was not brought under international control before the Western allies developed the weapon, the Soviets would undoubtedly build their own bomb. A nuclear arms race would ensue among the great powers, and sooner or later the weapons would be used. To head off this impending catastrophe, Bohr proposed that the United States and Britain inform the Soviets of the Manhattan Project and initiate negotiations leading to the creation of an international authority for the control of atomic energy. It was particularly important to inform the Soviets of nuclear research in the West before a bomb was developed, Bohr maintained. If the United States and Britain approached Stalin, after they perfected a bomb, the Soviet leader would undoubtedly feel that the Western initiative carried with it an implied threat and he would probably refuse to cooperate.

Bohr's plan called for a revolution in international politics comparable to the revolutionary changes taking place in nuclear physics. He was proposing a major modification in the idea of sovereignty. National states would have to surrender their power in the area of nuclear research and weapons development to an international authority if humanity was to survive in the nuclear age.

To Winston Churchill and to others who shared both his fear of the Soviets and his traditionalist approach to the conduct of foreign relations, Bohr seemed a muddleheaded idealist with utopian political views. And in some ways Bohr *was* being unrealistic. His own passionate commitment to reason led him to underestimate the power of tradition and established institutions in governing human behavior. He believed that rational statesmen, confronted by the possibility of a dreadful arms race and the final annihilation of the human species, would respond creatively regardless of the constraints placed upon them by a familiar order that was no longer suited to changed circumstances. But Bohr was not proposing that any scientific data be turned over to the Soviets. On the contrary, he suggested that Western statesmen make it clear to Moscow that the issue was so sensitive that they could not provide any data whatsoever until they were certain of Soviet cooperation. Nor was he confident that his approach would produce positive results. He believed, however, that the stakes were so high that the Western allies should do everything in their power to convince Stalin that they were not organizing a nuclear alliance against him. Soviet confidence on this score, Bohr believed, was an essential precondition to the establishment of a workable system of international controls.[27]

Justice Frankfurter left the White House thinking that Roosevelt had been impressed by Bohr's arguments. FDR told the jurist that he had for some time been "worried to death" about the implications of the bomb, and that he was "eager for all the help he could have in dealing with this problem."[28] But Roosevelt was not being candid. In reality, he was not willing to surrender the bomb, his ace in the hole if Soviet–American relations turned sour, to an international authority. Rather than explain his policy clearly, however, he sent Frankfurter back to Bohr with some encouraging but noncommittal words, and the suggestion that he explore his ideas with "our friends in London." He knew of course, how Prime Minister Churchill would react to the physicist's challenging recommendation.

Unaware of the president's real views and anxious to follow up on what seemed to him a promising beginning, Bohr hurried back across the Atlantic. But in London the prime minister kept him at arm's length. It was several weeks before Churchill granted him even a few minutes of his time. When at last the men met, Churchill was at his worst—gruff, inattentive, even impolite. Not long after the conference began he turned away from Bohr to discuss with Lord Cherwell the exact meaning of the terms of the Quebec Agreement. The Danish physicist was unable to turn the discussion back to the issue that concerned him, international control. At length, his allotted thirty minutes exhausted, he was ushered out. The meeting was a disaster. After the conference, a depressed Bohr remarked, "We did not even speak the same language."[29] Bohr would have been even more distressed had he known the real depth of Churchill's fierce, irrational suspicion of him. Writing to Lord Cherwell, his scientific adviser, Churchill noted "I did not like the man when you showed him to me, with his hair all over his head, at Downing Street." After noting that Bohr had corresponded with the Russian physicist Pyotr Kapitsa and advocated disclosure of the atomic project to the Soviets, Churchill suggested that "Bohr ought to be confined or at any rate made to see that he is very near the edge of mortal crimes."[30]

Dejected but still undeterred, Bohr returned to the United States determined to approach the seemingly sympathetic Roosevelt personally. A meeting was arranged and the two men talked together for more than an hour. There was a striking difference between Roosevelt's warmth and the frigid reception Bohr had received in London. They talked of Denmark, of international politics, and the importance of establishing an agency to control atomic energy. When he left the White House, like Frankfurter before him, Bohr felt certain that Roosevelt was in complete accord with his views and would soon approach the Soviets in a first step toward implementing plans for international control. But Bohr was misled by FDR's affability. Roosevelt had not changed his mind about maintaining a Western monopoly over nuclear weapons.

Less than a month later, meeting with Churchill to discuss the nuclear question at Hyde Park, Roosevelt officially endorsed not Bohr's but the prime minister's position. An aide-mémoire initialed by the two leaders specifically rejected Bohr's ideas about international control and reiterated the Anglo-American commitment to continued secrecy. Nor were Roosevelt and Churchill pleased about the openness with which Bohr seemed willing to discuss nuclear issues. Because of this and also because Bohr was known to have acquaintances among the scientific community in the Soviet Union, the two leaders agreed that Bohr ought to be watched carefully and "steps taken to ensure that he is responsible for no leakage of information, particularly to the Russians."[31]

In his impressive study, *A World Destroyed*, Martin Sherwin describes President Roosevelt's refusal to act on Bohr's advice as one of the great tragedies of modern times.[32] If ever there was a moment when the establishment of a system of international control of atomic energy had a chance, it was then, when no nation enjoyed a nuclear capability. But Bohr was asking too much, even of an enlightened traditionalist like Roosevelt. The president felt that Bohr was exaggerating the dangers posed by the development of nuclear weapons and, moreover, confusing means with ends. For centuries, statesmen had converted military advantage into diplomatic leverage. FDR pursued a similar course. He would try diplomacy first in an attempt to secure a peace settlement acceptable both to the Soviets and to the United States. But if diplomacy failed and tensions developed, he wanted to be prepared to deal with the Soviets from a position of strength. Roosevelt persistently sought a diplomatic solution to difficulties with the Soviets, but just as insistently determined to retain the American nuclear advantage over the Soviets. These two approaches to Soviet–American relations were not incompatible. They complemented one another, being components of a unitary and coherent diplomatic strategy.

But the Soviets could be impressed only by an actual bomb, not mere progress toward making one. Before FDR would be able to translate America's nuclear monopoly into political advantage, the Los Alamos scientists had to demonstrate that they could produce a workable bomb, not a dud. Even after it began to be apparent that their fears of a German nuclear weapon were unfounded, the bombmakers piled redundant experiment atop experiment in the race for the weapon. But they would not know that they had a workable device until they detonated an actual bomb. As Hans Bethe told the theoretical physicists, perhaps impiously, "Human calculation indicates that the experiment must succeed. But will nature act in conformity with our calculations?"[33]

Oppenheimer and Kenneth Bainbridge, technical orchestrator of the test explosion, began searching for test sites in late 1944. They finally settled on a remote desert area some seventy miles west of Alamogordo in southern New Mexico, a valley known as the Jornada de Muerto, "journey of death," so named for the many Spanish explorers and travelers who had died there of thirst or Indian attack. Like everything else connected with the Manhattan Project, the test explosion needed a code name, and Oppenheimer supplied a poetic one. At the time Bainbridge queried him for a suggestion, Oppenheimer happened to be reading a poem of John Donne's, with the line, "Batter my heart, three-person'd God." "Trinity," he decided.

Throughout early 1945, construction crews, military engineers, and scientists worked in the desert among fire ants, scorpions, and Gila monsters to erect the test-shot tower and lay cable for the instrumentation of Trinity. Bomb assembly teams took shipments of plutonium from Hanford and readied it for the final arming. Tension and drama mounted as Trinity approached. Oppenheimer chain-smoked and his weight dropped off to a sepulchral 115 pounds; Groves ordered in psychiatrists to assist scientists in keeping a mental equilibrium.

On July 15, the day before Trinity, a group of leading Manhattan Project scientists began gathering at the site to witness the test shot next morning. Enrico Fermi brought up once again a point that had been troubling Los Alamos scientists for nearly two years: would the detonation of a fission bomb initiate a chain reaction in the earth's atmosphere itself, possibly igniting it and incinerating life on the planet? Earlier, Arthur Compton had been so concerned about the possibility that he ordered a computation of the possibility of atmospheric ignition. Met Lab physicists decided the chance was three in a million, which they considered adequately improbable.[34] Fermi remained coolly detached about the possibility of doomsday catastrophe. At Trinity, he took bets on whether atmospheric ignition, if it took place the next day, would destroy only New Mexico, or all the earth. Gazing reflectively at the mountains to the west, he mused aloud, "Ah, the earth on the eve of its disintegration."[35]

The test shot occurred at dawn. Within the first second after detonation, it produced a light so intense it could have been seen by an observer on Venus. At the core of the explosion, temperatures reached a point never before attained on earth, ten thousand times the temperature at the surface of the sun. One hundred billion atmospheres of pressure hit the ground a hundred feet below the bomb. As the hell of radioactive debris roared and rolled, it fused the material at ground zero into ceramiclike green beads thereafter named "trinitite."[36]

The reaction of the human observers varied. Oppenheimer recalled lines from the *Bhagavad Gita*:

If the radiance of a thousand suns
were to burst at once into the sky,
That would be like the splendor of the Mighty One [Krishna]
I am become Death, the destroyer of worlds.

Equally in character, Fermi (presumably after concluding that the atmosphere had not ignited after all) exercised his uncanny skill at on-the-spot calculations by dropping bits of torn paper and estimating the blast by observing the effect of shockwaves on them. He arrived at the astonishingly correct approximation of the equivalent of 20,000 tons of TNT, a shock effect far higher than all but one or two of the Los Alamos scientists thought possible. Bainbridge at the site's control center responded to Oppenheimer's congratulatory handshake by stating calmly, "Now we're all sons of bitches." Later, George Kistiakowsky announced sententiously: "I am sure that at the end of the world, in the last millisecond of the earth's existence, man will see what we have just seen."[37]

I am become Death, the destroyer of worlds.

3

"The Destroyer of Worlds"
WHY HIROSHIMA AND NAGASAKI?

IN THE EARLY HOURS of August 6, 1945, a lone B-29 Superfortress, stripped of all nonessential gear and carrying a 9,000-pound uranium-type atomic bomb, waited at the end of the air strip on the captured island of Tinian. Colonel Paul Tibbets, USAAC, commander of the *Enola Gay,* understood that this was no ordinary mission. The bomb his plane was carrying would explode with a force of perhaps 20,000 tons of TNT, enough to destroy an entire city.

Tibbets had been warned by General Leslie Groves to expect "a little publicity" prior to takeoff. But what he found at the landing field took him completely by surprise. His plane was surrounded by floodlights that made a circle of harsh white light against the darkness beyond. Inside this circle were perhaps a hundred men—his own crew, scientists, military police, security personnel, and filmmakers sent by Groves to record the historic undertaking. William Laurence, the science reporter for *The New York Times* who had been flown in for a special briefing, was also on hand.

Tibbets later recalled his amazement at what he described as this "full-scale Hollywood premiere treatment. I expected to see MGM's lion walk onto the field or Warner's logo to light up the sky. It was crazy."[1] In a way it was crazy. That the atomic age should be ushered in with spotlights and public relations hoopla seems in retrospect to go beyond mere insanity to the genuinely macabre. But to General Groves it made perfect sense. The war was drawing to a close. When it was over, the man who headed the Manhattan Project wanted Congress and the public to remember that his organization had made an important contribution to victory. Not only would that be important in justifying expenditures that had already mounted to over $2 billion, it would mean a great deal to the future of nuclear power in the United States.

At 2:45 A.M., after a long picture-taking session, the *Enola Gay,* thousands of pounds overweight, began to rumble slowly down the runway. Fearing that the plane might not make it into the air, Tibbets decided to use every last foot of concrete before attempting to leave the ground. It was a risky gamble because the runway at Tinian ended at a cliff overlooking the ocean. Here, on this lonely island in the middle of the Pacific, Tibbets played what amounted to the most dangerous game of chicken ever conceived, and won. Just before running out of concrete, the *Enola Gay,* its engines screaming, lurched heavily into the air and began a slow ascent. Over the next several minutes she rose steadily until leveling off at an altitude of about 30,000 feet. After a rendezvous with two other B-29s, *The Great Artiste* and *No. 91,* the *Enola Gay* headed for her primary target, the city of Hiroshima, Japan.

It was a little past eight in the morning when the plane approached its target. All crew members save Tibbets, his copilot Robert Lewis, and bombardier Tom Ferebee, donned Polaroid goggles to protect their eyes. At 8:14 A.M. the bomb bay doors opened and a minute later Ferebee shouted, "Bomb away." He watched through the *Enola Gay*'s Plexiglas nose as the bomb seemed to stand for a moment suspended, and then began its descent. The tail gunner, "Bob" Caron, produced a striking account of what happened forty-three seconds later:

> A column of smoke rising fast. It has a fiery red core. A bubbling mass, purple-gray in color, with that red core. It's all turbulent. Fires are springing up everywhere, like flames shooting out of a huge bed of coals. I am starting to count the fires. One, two, three, four, five, six . . . fourteen, fifteen . . . it's impossible. There are

too many to count. Here it comes, the mushroom shape that Captain Parsons spoke about. . . . It's like a mass of bubbling molasses. The mushroom is spreading out. It's maybe a mile or two wide and half a mile high. It's nearly level with us and climbing. It's very black, but there is a purplish tint to the cloud. The base of the mushroom looks like a heavy undercast that is shot through with flames. The city must be below that. The flames and smoke are billowing out, whirling out into the foothills. All I can see now of the city is the main dock and what looks like an airfield.[2]

Tibbets was "surprised, even shocked. I had been expecting to see something big, but what is big? What I saw was of a magnitude and carried with it a connotation of destruction bigger than I had really imagined." Copilot Lewis wrote in his logbook, "My God, what have we done?"

In seconds, the center of Hiroshima was transformed into a hideous charred waste, four miles square. More than 130,000 persons, including a dozen American Navy fliers imprisoned in the city jail, were killed promptly; another 70,000 were to die by 1950, making the total fatalities for that city 200,000. Three days later, the U.S. Army Air Corps dropped a plutonium bomb on Nagasaki. Seventy thousand persons were killed, including some Dutch POWs; by 1950, a total of 140,000 had died of the second bombing.[3] On August 14, Japan surrendered, bringing World War II to an end.

Controversy has swirled around the decision to use the atomic bombs against Japan. Almost annually, usually in August, the anniversary of the bombings, the press runs articles reviving the debates of the 1940s. Historians and other scholars have returned repeatedly to the topic, producing whole schools of interpretation. Elsewhere throughout this book we avoid an explicit discussion of the literature of controversy, in the interests of presenting a narrative and analytical history of nuclear power's impact on our society. But here we must pause to review the contrasting opinions because attitudes about the world's only nuclear war to date pervade debates about the arms race and other applications of nuclear power today. By explicitly raising these attitudes at a conscious level, we hope to outline underlying questions and assumptions that give form to more recent debates about nuclear arms and reactors. Were the bombings of Hiroshima and/or Nagasaki necessary at all? Would Japan have surrendered shortly even if the United States had not used nuclear weapons? Or were the weapons our only alternative to the hideous slaughter of Japanese and Americans that would have accompanied the projected invasion of the home islands in late 1945? What precedents were set by the American decision to resort to nuclear war? How did this decision relate to the developing tensions in Soviet–American relations?

During the last stages of the war in Europe, the Allies succeeded in rounding up most of Germany's nuclear scientists, interning them at a country estate in England. There, on the evening of August 6, they learned of Hiroshima. Amidst excited debates on whether the reports were true—the Germans had doubted that the United States could produce a bomb before the war's end—they noted that some of their colleagues, most notably their leader Otto Hahn, were deeply distressed by the news. In fact the Nobel laureate Max von Laue insisted that some of them sit up with Hahn that evening to be sure he did not kill himself because of the news. The older internees concluded that it was just as well that they had not succeeded in building a bomb, for then they would have had to bear the guilt that now lay wholly on American shoulders.[4]

But Americans did not feel much guilt. The bombing of Hiroshima and Nagasaki was widely approved by the American people at the time. Ninety percent of the respondents to a *Fortune* magazine poll conducted in December 1945 supported the president's decision to use the bomb. One reason for this widespread endorsement was the assumption that by using nuclear weapons Truman had shortened the war, forcing Japan to surrender. A less obvious reason, a result of the secrecy that enshrouded the Manhattan Project, was that the public was unaware of the possible ramifications of the president's actions. Nor was there the slightest public hint that there had been any disagreement among those involved in the Manhattan Project over whether or not to use the bomb. Aware only that there was a war going on and convinced that the nuclear strikes had shortened it, most Americans quite naturally gave the president high marks.

This is not to suggest that President Truman escaped all contemporary criticism. The religious press in the United States was deeply troubled by the moral implications of his actions. On August 29, 1945, the *Christian Century Magazine* labeled the use of nuclear weapons "America's Atomic Atrocity." *Commonweal* charged that the names Hiroshima and Nagasaki would be forever identified "with American guilt and shame."[5] "Persons high in Vatican circles" reacted negatively to the news of the world's first nuclear attacks as well, denouncing them as "a useless massacre." And John Foster Dulles, who would one day promote the doctrine of massive retaliation, charged that in using nuclear weapons President Truman had not lived up to the standards of Christian statesmanship the world expected of an American leader.[6]

Outside the pages of the religious press, Dwight MacDonald, critic and political commentator, wrote two extraordinarily prescient pieces for his radical journal, *Politics,* in August and September 1945. Equating America's leadership with the Nazis who built the death camp at Maidanek, Poland, he declared that "those who wield such destructive power are outcasts from humanity. . . . We must 'get' the modern national state before it 'gets' us." MacDonald denounced as naïve or even worse those who claimed that atomic energy could be used for good as well as evil. It would not, in the cliché of the time, be "harnessed to constructive ends." Rather, "the new energy will be at the service of the rulers: it will change their strength but not their aims."[7]

In the immediate aftermath of the war, criticism of President Truman's decision to use the bomb was confined to scattered voices in the religious and scientific communities. But by summer 1946, critics outside these circles began to attack Truman for having failed to take advantage of the possibilities for international control of atomic weapons at a time when Soviet–American relations were relatively harmonious. In an article published in *The Saturday Review of Literature* in June 1946, Norman Cousins and Thomas Finletter, who would later become President Truman's secretary of the air force, condemned the administration for this "momentous blunder." Cousins and Finletter wondered whether in fact the president had been telling the entire truth about his decision. Was it possible that Washington wanted to end the war quickly in order to deprive the Soviet Union of a role in the occupation of Japan, at the cost of risking a nuclear arms race?[8]

In time, writers took up this theme, charging that the decision to use the atomic bomb had more to do with deteriorating Soviet–American relations than it did with ending the war in the Pacific. In *Fear, War, and the Bomb,* published in 1949, P. M. S. Blackett, a British physicist and Nobel laureate who played a role in the development of the atomic bomb, argued categorically that the Truman administration had used the weapon to check Soviet expansion in Asia. Blackett was struck by the speed with which the two remaining bombs were rushed across the Pacific and put into service after the Alamogordo test. Of the several possible reasons for this, he believed that Washington's concern over the future of Asia was foremost. The Soviets were scheduled to enter the war against Japanese forces in Manchuria and northern China on or about August 8. Nor could there be any doubt that the campaign would end with the Soviet Union "overrunning Manchuria and taking half a million prisoners." Under such circumstances it would be impossible to deny the Soviets a role in the occupation of Japan. By hurrying the use of the bomb, Blackett contended, the Truman administration insured "that the Japanese Government surrendered to American forces alone." To the British physicist, "the dropping of the atomic bombs was not so much the last military act of the Second World War as the first major operation of the cold diplomatic war with Russia now in progress."[9]

Well before 1950, then, a revisionist interpretation of the decision to use the atomic bomb had begun to take shape. Not surprisingly, an official explanation did, too. Some of those who had been decisionmakers in 1945 were provoked into print by the allegations made first by Finletter and Cousins. Others were simply indulging in the natural inclination of those who had been at the center of affairs to tell their story. Whatever their motives, these former policymakers offered an alternative to the revisionist view that, bolstered by the work of numerous respected historians, became the accepted explanation of the decision to drop the atomic bomb.

The administration's defenders were quick to point out that although the use of such genocidal weapons against civilian populations might in the abstract seem immoral, in the context of World War II the use of nuclear weapons appeared completely legitimate. Strategic bombing began as an attempt to destroy selected military and industrial targets in daylight attacks. But losses were so staggering that both sides soon resorted to indiscriminate nighttime terror bombings designed to kill as many civilians as possible. Royal Air Force as well as U.S. Army Air Corps tacticians deliberately devised "carpet bombing" patterns to achieve a fire-storm effect in order to maximize civilian casualties. Any reticence about using aerial bombing as a weapon of terror had been dispelled first by the Nazi air onslaught against London and then Conventry in 1940. Civilian casualties, measured first by the thousands, then by the tens of thousands, then by scores of thousands, and finally by hundreds of thousands, were mileposts in the brutalizing of the consciences of policymakers in all of the warring nations. In 1945, there seemed no difference between a single B-29 dropping one bomb that could destroy a city, and accomplishing the same end by employing a thousand planes dropping conventional explosives. At Dresden, 135,000 Germans had been incinerated in a fire storm created by a "conventional" raid.[10] And on the evening of March 9–10, 1945, B-29 bombers leveled fully one quarter of Tokyo, killing over 100,000 persons in a similar attack. Such massacres no longer evoked horror. For this reason, former Secretary of War Stimson later wrote, no one associated with the Manhattan Project ever questioned the legitimacy of using nuclear weapons.[11] President Truman put it even more matter-of-factly. Using the atomic bomb, he explained, was "not any decision you had to worry about."

But the bomb had not been used simply because it was thought to be legitimate. The centerpiece of the administration's position was that, terrible as the weapon was, its use forestalled an even more terrible bloodletting. In the summer of 1945, with the island of Okinawa in American hands, preparations were under way for the invasion of Japan. It was an undertaking that few wanted. During the Philippine and Okinawa campaigns, the United States Navy had taken a heavy battering from kamikaze attacks. All told, these pilots of the "divine wind" had sunk 34 ships and damaged another 285. Navy planners estimated that in an assault on Japan's home islands, as many as 5,000 such suicide planes might be hurled against the invasion fleet. Once ashore, American forces would fare little better. American planners had been awed by the suicidal determination of the defenders of Japan's Pacific island strongholds. The mass suicide of hundreds of Japanese women and children, who threw themselves from the cliffs of Okinawa rather than fall into the hands of American forces, was further convincing evidence that the invasion of Japan might be bloody beyond imagining. They estimated that the two million men that Japan still possessed to defend the home islands would be able to continue the war for twelve to eighteen months. They informed the president that he could expect another one million casualties, three times what the Pacific war had already cost in American casualties.[12]

Using the atomic bomb, then, seemed an attractive alternative to policymakers who were contemplating the costs of an invasion. Japan was already defeated; the problem was to convince her leaders to surrender. A nuclear attack might have the proper psychological effect. Such views were shared by many of America's scientific leaders. Throughout the winter of 1944–45 Vannevar Bush, prompted by a memorandum that Niels Bohr had prepared after his fruitless conversation with FDR, repeatedly recommended to Stimson the appointment of a special advisory committee to consider problems of postwar planning for nuclear weapons. At length, Stimson concurred and persuaded Truman to create what came to be known as the "Interim Committee," which consisted of Stimson as its chair, James F. Byrnes as the president's personal representative, Bush himself, James B. Conant, Karl Compton, and representatives of the Navy and State Departments. Conant and Bush in turn urged appointment of a body of experts, known as the "Scientific Panel," to express the views of scientists involved with the Manhattan Project. This body consisted of Arthur H. Compton, Fermi, Oppenheimer, and

Ernest O. Lawrence. Political leaders assumed that these men and the scientists on the Interim Committee spoke for the entire scientific community.

The Interim Committee and the Scientific Panel met jointly on May 31, 1945, and day-long debates carried on through lunch ranged over all policy issues concerning the use of the bomb against Japan. It reported to Stimson that scientific opinion was divided into two groups, one pressing for demonstration of the bomb in an uninhabited area, the other recommending that the bomb be dropped on some military target in order to save American lives. Members of the Scientific Panel, self-conscious about their lack of expertise in the area of public policy, were especially influenced by Oppenheimer, who insisted that the most effective method of impressing the Japanese would be to use it against a bona fide target. He pointed out that the bomb would explode in an awesome display of heat and light. Detonation would be followed by "a brilliant luminescence which would rise 10,000 or 20,000 feet" into the air. James Conant, who agreed with Oppenheimer, argued that in order to maximize the impact of a nuclear strike on Japan's leaders, the target selected should be a large war plant with workers' homes clustered nearby. It was important too that the target be intact prior to the attack so that the Japanese might properly gauge the power of the new weapon.

Members of the Committee and the Panel informally considered and rejected a number of alternatives to this plan, such as a demonstration of the weapon in some isolated spot with official Japanese observers present. Committee members feared that the militarists in control of the Japanese government would be unswayed. Moreover, there was always the chance that the bomb might be a dud, which would only reinforce Japanese determination to carry on. Or the Japanese might fill the test site with American and Allied POWs. For these varied reasons, the Scientific Panel concluded that "we can propose no technical demonstration likely to bring an end to the war; we can see no acceptable alternative to direct military use." Martin Sherwin, a preeminent scholarly authority on the subject, concluded that "no one could think of any way to employ the new weapon that offered the same attractive combination of low risk and high gain as a surprise attack; and no one was willing to argue that a higher risk should be accepted."[13]

Meanwhile, the administration had to consider the possibility that Japanese resolve to continue the war might be waning. An early indication that something was in the wind came from Switzerland, where Commander Yoshiro Fujimura, the Japanese naval attaché, and General Seigo Okamoto, the military attaché, each independently of the other made contact with Allen Dulles's OSS organization. Both men seemed eager to work for Japan's surrender. Washington authorized the OSS to maintain contact with the two Japanese and listen to anything they had to say. Ultimately, however, the State Department gave up on Fujimura and Okamoto when it became evident that neither was having any success convincing his superiors in Tokyo to accept the inevitability of defeat.

In June 1945, the Japanese government itself began a more serious attempt to end the war. The foreign ministry tried to open talks with the Soviet Union in the hope that Stalin, who was still at peace with Japan, might agree to tender his good offices. But at the Yalta conference held in the preceding February, the Russian dictator had already secretly agreed to enter the war against Japan within three months of Germany's defeat. In return, the Western allies had promised the Soviets significant territorial and economic concessions in Asia and the Pacific. Stalin had only to secure President Chiang Kai-shek's approval of these arrangements and then enter the war to secure the empire lost by the czars in 1905. It is not surprising, then, that Stalin, who had more to gain by entering the war than mediating the peace, showed little interest in playing Japan's game.

Stalin's attitude notwithstanding, the Truman administration was in an excellent position to form its own judgment of Japanese intentions. Even before the attack on Pearl Harbor, American cryptographers had cracked Japan's naval and diplomatic codes. The decrypting device, code-named *Magic,* allowed Washington to know in advance much of what the Japanese were thinking and doing throughout the war. The messages that were being sent back and forth between Tokyo and Moscow in June and July 1945 were being read in Washington, and by President Truman and

Secretary of State James Byrnes while they attended the Potsdam conference. But in official circles, these Japanese peace feelers counted for little. While it was clear that at least some of Japan's leaders sought an end to the war, the intercepted messages demonstrated that they were thinking in terms of a negotiated settlement based on specific conditions. In 1943, President Roosevelt had announced that the United States would accept nothing short of unconditional surrender. President Truman, who was intent upon carrying out Roosevelt's policies, was not prepared to deviate from that simple formula. Therefore, since there seemed no "weakening in the Japanese determination to fight rather than accept unconditional surrender," Washington decided to ignore Japan's July initiatives. "The nature of the purported 'peace feelers,'" Acting Secretary of State Joseph Grew wrote in a July issue of the *State Department Bulletin*, "must be clear to everyone. They are the usual moves in the conduct of psychological warfare by a defeated enemy. No thinking American, recalling Pearl Harbor, Wake, Manila, and Japanese ruthless aggression elsewhere, will give them credence." The policy of the American government, Grew reminded his readers, remained "unconditional surrender."[14]

On July 26, 1945, President Truman, Britain's Prime Minister Clement Attlee, and Generalissimo Chiang Kai-shek of China issued the Potsdam Declaration.[15] Here the Allies reiterated their demand for Japan's unconditional surrender and warned that if the war continued, the "Japanese homeland" would face "utter devastation." When Japan's prime minister, Admiral Suzuki Kantar, rejected the declaration as "unworthy of public notice" the stage was set for the flight of the *Enola Gay*.

Later, Secretary of War Stimson claimed that the bomb "served exactly the purpose we intended." Though a peace faction obviously did exist in Japanese government circles, he contended that until after Hiroshima, policy was still being determined by fanatical militarists determined to commit national suicide in one last great battle. The atomic attack, Stimson insisted, strengthened the peace faction, weakened the militarists, and convinced the emperor to become fully involved in the internal struggle for peace. Without the bomb, Stimson continued, the military would in all likelihood have maintained the upper hand in Tokyo. The war then would have been fought to its bitter hand-to-hand conclusion at terrible cost. In explaining why the atomic bomb was used, Stimson argued:

> My chief purpose was to end the war in victory with the least possible cost in the lives of the men in the armies which I had helped to raise. In the light of the alternatives which, on a fair estimate, were open to us I believe that no man, in our position and subject to our responsibilities, holding in his hands a weapon of such possibilities for accomplishing this purpose and saving those lives, could have failed to use it and afterwards looked his countrymen in the face.[16]

This orthodox explanation of the administration's decision to use nuclear weapons against Japan has for many years enjoyed wide currency. Yet it is vulnerable at a number of key points. For example, the contention that by using the bomb the United States avoided the enormous casualties American forces would otherwise have suffered in an invasion presupposes the need for an invasion. Yet from a military point of view, it is by no means certain that an invasion of the home islands was necessary. On the contrary: the reports of the Strategic Bombing Survey, made public in July 1946, suggest that Japan would in all likelihood have surrendered prior to an invasion whether or not the atomic bomb had been used. Colonel R. C. Kramer, the chief of the economic and scientific section at General MacArthur's head-quarters in Tokyo, made the same point to President Truman's personal emissary, Edwin Locke, a few weeks after the surrender. According to Kramer, American officers then in Japan were "amazed by the fact that resistance continued as long as it did." Bomb or no bomb, Kramer asserted, Japan could not have held out for long.[17]

Such post-surrender judgments, while they indicate how weak Japan actually was toward the end of the war, in themselves prove little. A more relevant question is whether or not American military leaders in July 1945 believed that an invasion would be required if the United States did not use the atomic bomb. The answer is quite startling. Three of the chiefs of staff as well as numerous other high-ranking officers believed that an invasion was unnecessary. General Dwight Eisenhower, informed of the bomb by Stimson while the two were at Potsdam in July 1945, argued fervently against using the weapon. Japan, he thought, was on the verge of surrender in any event. The administration should avoid "shocking world opinion by the use of a weapon whose employment was . . . no longer mandatory to save American lives."[18] Air force leaders were equally certain that victory could be attained without an invasion. General Curtis LeMay, who was never known to be modest about the potential of strategic bombing, recalled in his memoirs: "Most of us in the Army Air Forces had been convinced for a long time that it would be possible to defeat the Japanese without invading their home islands."[19] High-ranking naval officers felt similarly. Fleet Admiral Ernest King was convinced that a naval blockade would have starved Japan into submission without an invasion and without the use of the bomb. Admiral William D. Leahy, in total agreement with King, added

> My own feeling was that in being the first to use it we had adopted an ethical standard common to the barbarians of the Dark Ages. I was not taught to make war in that fashion, and wars cannot be won by destroying women and children.[20]

The fact that so many high-ranking officers believed that an invasion would be unnecessary raises a second question. To what extent were military leaders consulted with regard to the decision? The answer is again startling. Though each of the chiefs of staff knew of the weapons, as a group they neither discussed it nor were they asked to make recommendations to the president. In fact, although Truman described the use of the bomb as a military action, no high-ranking military officer participated in the decision to use it.

Did the atomic bomb persuade the Japanese to surrender, as administration defenders insist? Although this remains a debatable point, there is a good deal of evidence to suggest that it did not. In 1944, after the fall of Saipan and long before the attacks on Hiroshima and Nagasaki, a peace faction had emerged within the Japanese government. But the efforts of this group had been

hamstrung by America's failure to clarify the unconditional surrender doctrine on one specific point, the fate of the imperial
institution. Had the United States been willing to agree that the
dynasty would be preserved, peace might well have been attained
weeks or even months sooner. Without that guarantee, the progress of those in Japan working for a surrender was slow. Nevertheless, progress was being made. In fact by June, the emperor,
who usually remained above politics, had joined the peace movement and was using his immense influence to bring about a
surrender.

It would be difficult to find a person better placed during those
last critical weeks of the war than Kazuo Kawai, the editor of the
Nippon Times. Kawai, who had many intimate friends at the foreign office, insists that the two atomic bombs changed absolutely
nothing in Tokyo. Those militarists who had opposed surrender
prior to Hiroshima continued their opposition afterward, while
key members of the government who were working for a surrender continued to do so. At the most, Kawai has written, Hiroshima and Nagasaki only speeded the peace process by a few
days.

The official explanation for the decision to use the bomb, weak
in so many particulars, has been just as intensely questioned for
what it omits. By focusing upon the importance of the bomb as
a factor in ending the Pacific war, defenders of administration
policy either implicitly or in some cases explicitly deny that President Truman and his advisers saw the weapon as providing them
with any postwar diplomatic advantages vis-à-vis the Soviet
Union. Yet the allegations of Cousins, Finletter, and Blackett
remain unrefuted. Indeed, a number of scholars have found considerable merit in allegations made by critics. In 1959, William
Appleman Williams wrote in his influential book, *The Tragedy of
American Diplomacy,* that the Truman administration had used the
bomb against Japan in order to end the war in the Pacific quickly
"and thereby stop the Russians in Asia, and give them sober
pause in eastern Europe." Six years later, a young political economist, Gar Alperovitz, articulated a more advanced thesis in his
study, *Atomic Diplomacy: Hiroshima and Potsdam.* Whereas Williams
had contended that the principal reason for using the bomb was

to end the war quickly, Alperovitz thought that strictly military considerations had little to do with it. According to Alperovitz, President Truman actually had three options. Aware that the Japanese were seeking Soviet mediation, he might have pursued negotiations. Or he might have waited to see what the effect of the soon-to-be-announced Soviet declaration of war against Japan would be. He did neither, instead going ahead with plans to use the atomic bomb against Japan as soon as it became available. He did this for political reasons, Alperovitz insisted, to strengthen his hand in the difficult negotiations with the Soviets that lay ahead.

Already embroiled in difficulties with the Soviet Union over the future of eastern Europe, and concerned lest the Soviets expand too far in Asia, the administration saw the bomb as its diplomatic "mastercard." The use of the bomb as a demonstration of American power was essential to warn the Soviets that the United States not only had great power, but also the will to use it. Alperovitz viewed the Truman administration as practicing a particularly cynical brand of power politics in which the people of Hiroshima and Nagasaki were incinerated so that America's bargaining position vis-à-vis the Soviet Union might be substantially enhanced to arrange a postwar political settlement satisfactory to the United States.

Obviously, the introduction of nuclear weapons into modern warfare has had the most profound significance for all mankind. Facing thermonuclear catastrophe, modern critics point to the missed opportunity for establishing a system of international controls early and ask why the president decided to use the bomb against Japan. But is that the proper question? It may be more useful to ask whether President Truman had any reason *not* to use the bomb. By approaching the problem in this way, certain things immediately become clear. First, the decision to build the bomb was, for all intents and purposes, the decision to use it. No government would invest billions in such a project, produce a new and terrifying weapon during time of war, and then decide not to use it unless for some compelling reason. Although in retrospect it seems clear that the danger to humanity posed by nuclear weapons should have provided policymakers with sufficient incentives, that perspective simply was not apparent in the summer of 1945.

President Truman was particularly ill-equipped to decide against using the atomic bomb on Japan. Ignorant, and adrift on a sea of troubles, he wanted to adhere to the policies of his predecessor. But what was FDR's policy with regard to the bomb? Truman had no way of knowing, for Roosevelt had left nothing to guide him. Was it not then reasonable for the neophyte president to assume that if the bomb became available during the war it should be used? He had no reason to believe otherwise.

Lacking guidance from his predecessor, President Truman did not have access to sources of information that might have educated him to the broader issues raised by the development of nuclear weapons. He could not profit from a popular debate on the issues because an impenetrable cloak of secrecy kept the entire question out of the public arena. Nor did the president's political advisers provide him with a balanced analysis of the positive and negative aspects of the problem. Secretary of State James F. Byrnes favored use of the weapon against Japan because he believed it would end the war quickly while simultaneously providing the United States with added leverage in forthcoming talks with the Soviet Union over the postwar settlement. Secretary of War Stimson, though he clearly perceived that the existence of nuclear weapons was to have a profound effect on international affairs, nevertheless also supported using the bomb. The Interim Committee was similarly inclined. Created by Stimson to advise Truman on issues relating to nuclear weapons, the committee was dominated by men who assumed that the bomb would be used if it became available during the war.

To be sure, scientists working on the project did discuss the question; and some, including Leo Szilard, James Franck, and a number of others at Chicago's Metallurgical Laboratory did raise what turned out to be the most relevant long-range issues. American scientists knew by early 1945 that there was no German bomb, and that the Third Reich was on the verge of collapse and surrender. Sometime during the winter of 1944–45, Samuel Goudsmit, the civilian head of the *Alsos* team, remarked to an army major: "Isn't it wonderful that the Germans have no atom bomb? Now we won't have to use ours." But the soldier knew better. "Of course you understand, Sam," he replied, "that if we have such a weapon we are going to use it."[21] Goudsmit's shock was shared by other American scientists, especially when the focus of the question constricted from the broad issue raised by Bohr in 1944—should the bomb ever be used in any military way? —to the narrower but more imminent question of early 1945: Should the bomb be dropped on Japan? General Groves, reflecting the views of nearly all army officers, assumed that it should be, and he was seconded by the civilian political leadership, most notably Stimson, who insisted that the question was not *whether*, but *how* it should be used.

Certain Chicago scientists did not share that assumption. Szilard later recalled that "in 1945, when we ceased worrying about what the Germans might do to us, we began to worry about what the government of the United States might do to other countries."[22] In March 1945, Szilard collected his thoughts in a memorandum, "Atomic Bombs and the Postwar Position of the United States in the World," an extraordinarily prescient survey of nuclear policy.[23] Warning that the U.S.S.R. would soon develop its own nuclear capacity as well as more sophisticated delivery systems, including "rockets," Szilard warned that any American city would soon be vulnerable to nuclear attack. Thus international controls were essential, and the Soviet Union had to be persuaded to accept them by tactful approaches, not crude threats. He later cautioned that "a nation which sets the precedent of using these newly liberated forces of nature for purposes of destruction may have to bear the responsibility of opening the door to an era of devastation on an unimaginable scale."[24]

Meanwhile, others in the Met Lab group, including Glenn Seaborg, Eugene Rabinowitch, and James Franck, a Nobel laureate in physics who was one of the Göttingen exiles, as well as Szilard himself, collated the views of many of their colleagues in a document that has come to be known as the "Franck report." They viewed the problem of nuclear weapons as a matter "of long-range national policy rather than of military expediency." Like Bohr and Stimson, but unlike Truman, the Chicago scientists recognized that warfare in the atomic age would be qualitatively as well as quantitatively different from conventional war. One of the insidious peculiarities of nuclear warfare would be that no nation, no matter how well armed, could hope to defend itself against a nuclear attack. Moreover, the nature of nuclear weapons was such that they would necessarily be used against cities. The only realistic protection against nuclear war lay in the "political organization of the world," not in obsolete efforts to retain an evaporating monopoly of nuclear arms or a meaningless quantitative superiority.

The alternative to international control, Franck warned, was a "race for nuclear armaments" spurred by the threat of "total mutual destruction." Without an agreement on international control, the arms race would begin "in earnest not later than the morning after our first demonstration of the existence of nuclear weapons." Other nations, including the Soviet Union, would catch up to American capability in less than a decade. The U.S.S.R., Franck pointedly added, had access to uranium sources in the old Joachimsthal mines, by then effectively under Red Army control, and probably in the vast land expanse of the U.S.S.R. itself. The very nature of nuclear weapons would induce a first-strike mentality in a nation that felt itself threatened by the American nuclear lead, strongly tempting it to launch "a sudden unprovoked blow, particularly if he should suspect us of harboring aggressive intentions against his security or his sphere of influence."

Consequently, the report urged, the United States should be prepared to sacrifice some element of its sovereignty, relinquishing control over its ability to produce nuclear weapons and subordinate its head start in nuclear technology to effective international control. And this must be done *before* the United States revealed its bomb potential by using the weapon against Japan. Otherwise, America "would sacrifice public support throughout the world, precipitate the race for armaments, and prejudice the possibility of reaching an international agreement on the future control of such weapons."[25]

Such reasoning proved no more persuasive in the higher levels of the Truman administration than the report's condemnation of unannounced use of nuclear weapons against Japan. Oppen-

heimer cavalierly dismissed its suggestion of a demonstration
shot: "We did not think that exploding one of these things as a
firecracker over a desert was likely to be very impressive."[26]

Szilard correctly suspected that mere documents sent up
through channels might not reach those having ultimate decisionmaking authority. Recalling the impact he had made five
years earlier with the Einstein letter, he therefore decided to try
a direct personal approach. But FDR died before Szilard could
once again get his ear and the new president was too pressed by
other matters to see him. And so Szilard was shunted off to
Spartanburg, South Carolina, to present his views to James F.
Byrnes, former Justice of the United States Supreme Court, a
Truman intimate soon to be named secretary of state. The Spartanburg visit was as much a disaster as the earlier Bohr–Churchill
interview. Szilard's Hungarian accent and his effervescent personality were no more welcome to Byrnes than the substance of
his ideas. Instantly forming a dislike for this upstart alien, Byrnes
dismissed the Szilard overture with disdain. Long after the Spartanburg interview, Szilard wryly reflected to himself "how much
better off the world might be had I been born in America and
become influential in politics, and had Byrnes been born in Hun-
gary and studied physics. In all probability, there would have
been no atomic bomb, and no danger of an arms race between
America and Russia."[27]

If those men with access to the president who knew of the
atomic bomb all favored its use, a number of domestic and foreign political considerations also suggested that it was important
to go ahead. At the most primitive level were the twin factors of
racism and revenge. Prior to the beginning of the Pacific war
neither American policymakers nor the American people had
taken the Japanese entirely seriously. The "sneak attack" on the
Pacific Fleet at Pearl Harbor confirmed long-standing American
opinions about "double-dealing, slant-eyed Japs." The attack
and subsequent developments in the Pacific were especially in-
furiating because in the early months of the war, Allied forces
suffered a series of humiliating defeats in the Pacific.

The American reaction was extraordinary. James Montgomery
Flagg's famous poster picturing an angry Uncle Sam holding a

huge monkey wrench, rolling up his sleeves and saying "JAP
... YOU'RE NEXT!" only begins to tell the story. In San Francisco,
the Japanese Tea Garden was renamed the Oriental Tea Garden.
Kimonos were banned for the duration. On the popular radio
program, *The Green Hornet,* Bret Reed's faithful Japanese valet
Kato suddenly became a Filippino. A spate of Hollywood motion
pictures, including *The Flying Tigers, Bataan, The Sands of Iwo Jima,*
and dozens more, portrayed the Japanese as inhuman, cowardly
villains. This virulent wartime propaganda had the predictable
effect. In December 1944, a Gallup poll showed that Americans
hated the Japanese far more than the Germans. Thirteen percent
of those questioned recommended the extermination of the entire people, while some suggested mass sterilization, presumably
because it was more humane. "We are drowning and burning the
bestial apes all over the Pacific," Admiral "Bull" Halsey proclaimed in one newsreel. He thought it "just as much pleasure to
burn them as to drown them."

The political leadership in the United States was not immune
from such feelings. President Truman would in fact later justify
the use of nuclear weapons against Japan by comparing Hiroshima and Nagasaki with Pearl Harbor. "When you have to deal
with a beast you have to treat him as a beast," he said.[28] And
Truman was by no means among the most extreme. Consider, for
example, the ravings of Georgia's Senator Richard Russell who,
on learning of the Hiroshima raid, urged a policy of near genocide upon the president.

> Let us carry the war to them until they beg us to accept uncondi-
> tional surrender. . . . If we do not have available a sufficient num-
> ber of Atomic Bombs with which to finish the job immediately, let
> us carry on with TNT and fire bombs until we can produce them.
> . . . This was a total war as long as our enemies held all the cards.
> Why should we change the rules now, after the blood, treasure and
> enterprise of the American people have given us the upper hand?
> Our people have not forgotten that the Japanese struck us the first
> blow in this war without the slightest warning. They believe that
> we should continue to strike the Japanese until they are brought
> groveling to their knees.[29]

Truman did not use the bomb because he sought revenge. But he certainly understood that the American public would support horrible forms of retaliation against the Japanese.

By using the bomb, Truman not only satisfied the widespread desire for revenge, but he also avoided a potentially serious political threat to his administration. Congress had blindly appropriated $2 billion to fund the Manhattan Project on assurances from administration officials that the project was essential to the war effort. But it was clear that sooner or later the executive branch would have to answer for this expenditure. Project leaders realized this and took pains to prepare for the congressional investigation they were certain would come after the war. Truman understood this better than most. While a senator, he himself had threatened an investigation into this large and mysterious expenditure, only to be deterred by the personal assurances of Secretary Stimson. The president did not have to be particularly astute to conclude that if the bomb became available in time, it was important from a domestic political standpoint to use it. How, he might have asked himself, would Congress, the public, and the Republicans have responded to the knowledge that the administration had spent billions on the Manhattan Project, built a potentially decisive superbomb, and then decided against employing it?

A variety of foreign policy considerations also reinforced the assumption that if the bomb became available before Japan surrendered, it should be used. The Allies were already badly divided over the future of eastern Europe and Germany. The president realized that if the postwar settlement in Europe was to conform to American ambitions he would have to overcome strong Soviet objections. Truman and Secretary of State Byrnes both believed that an American nuclear monopoly, by virtue of its very existence, would force the Soviets into a more flexible position on issues of mutual interest. Somehow, both men believed, this enormous new force could be made to serve America's diplomatic advantage.

This is not to endorse the extreme revisionist view that holds that President Truman used the bomb against Japan solely in order to frighten the Soviets. As historian Barton Bernstein has shrewdly pointed out, Truman did not decide to use the bomb just to improve his chances of imposing a European settlement on the Soviets. Truman simply assumed that the bomb would be used. The diplomatic advantages that he believed would accrue to the administration as a result of having a nuclear monopoly were byproducts of the fact the United States controlled such power, and not the reason for using it.[30]

On a related point, there can be no question that the revisionist view is correct. After the bomb had been successfully tested in mid-July 1945, President Truman and Secretary of State Byrnes concluded that Soviet participation in the war against Japan was no longer either necessary or desirable. In his *Memoirs,* the president recalled that he went to the Potsdam conference for one reason only: to secure a Soviet agreement to enter the Pacific war. This is at best a half-truth. To be sure, early in the conference the president did inquire as to when Soviet forces might be ready to intervene in Asia. But after this initial inquiry he rapidly lost interest in pursuing the point. The reason for this is clear. Truman had deliberately delayed the opening of the conference to coincide with the first test of an atomic weapon at Alamogordo. News that the test had been successful arrived at Potsdam shortly after the conference began. Truman, who now believed that he had a weapon capable of forcing the Japanese into a swift surrender, no longer required a Soviet partner in the Pacific. In fact, the problem now seemed to be to find a method of keeping the Russians out. "It is quite clear," Prime Minister Churchill cabled London after learning of the first atomic test, "that the United States do not at the present time desire Russian participation in the war against Japan."[31]

But though the United States now controlled a weapon that could shock Japan into a surrender, the Soviets might nevertheless intervene in the war at any moment. Truman and Byrnes quickly contrived a strategy designed to delay a Soviet declaration of war against Japan. The Far Eastern aspect of the Yalta accords stipulated that prior to the Soviet Union's entry into the war, Stalin and Generalissimo Chiang Kai-shek were to agree on the precise terms of the territorial and economic concessions Russia was to receive in Asia at war's end. These negotiations had not produced an agreement prior to Stalin's trip to Potsdam. Fearing that if these talks aborted, the Soviets might enter the war sooner rather than later, Secretary Byrnes cabled Chiang urging him to carry on the negotiations no matter what. Simultaneously, however, he cautioned the Chinese leader against going beyond a narrow interpretation of exactly what the Yalta accords required in the way of concessions to the Soviets. Byrnes hoped that prolonged bargaining would ensue and that the atomic bomb would bring the war to a speedy conclusion before these talks had ended.

Because the Truman administration was anxious to end the war in Asia before the Soviets could intervene and saw the atomic bomb as one method of shocking Japan's leaders into a surrender, it is still necessary to inquire why the administration clung so long to the unconditional surrender formula while rejecting opportunities for an earlier settlement with Japan. The "peace feelers" of July 1945 constituted a serious attempt by important elements in Japan's government, supported by the emperor, to find a way out of the war. And at least one high-ranking Washington official, believing that a surrender was attainable, had for some time been urging the president to be flexible in his definition of what the unconditional surrender doctrine actually meant.

In May 1945, Acting Secretary of State Joseph C. Grew had developed a plan to secure Japan's surrender before the Soviets could intervene in Asia. Grew believed that the single greatest obstacle to peace was the fact that the United States had not as yet made its position clear concerning the future of Japan's emperor and the dynasty. Aware that the imperial institution was a vital feature of Japanese life and culture, and that Japan's leaders would never surrender unless the United States guaranteed its preservation, Grew urged the president to issue a declaration to the Japanese demanding that they lay down their arms while assuring them that unconditional surrender did not mean the end of the dynasty. If such assurances were offered just after a massive bombing attack such as the one that leveled more than eight square miles of central Tokyo, Grew felt certain that the carrot and the stick together would produce a surrender.

Initially, the president showed considerable interest in Grew's proposal, telling the acting secretary that his own thinking ran along similar lines. At a Pentagon meeting, Stimson and navy secretary James Forrestal as well as General George C. Marshall, all endorsed Grew's scheme. Nevertheless, "for certain military reasons, not then divulged" to the acting secretary, "it was considered inadvisable for the President to make such a statement at that juncture." Grew persisted, presenting newly appointed Secretary of State James F. Byrnes with a memorandum on the subject. But according to Grew, Byrnes, who was preoccupied with preparations for the upcoming Potsdam conference, showed little interest in the plan. The tragic results of this missed opportunity, Grew contended, included Hiroshima, Nagasaki, and a needlessly enlarged Soviet presence in Asia. Later he wrote, "If surrender could have been brought about in May, 1945, or even in June or July, before the entrance of Soviet Russia into the war and the use of the Atomic Bomb, the world would have been the gainer."[32]

Grew's charges, unfair to Byrnes, are based on a simplistic analysis of the problems confronting the new secretary. Byrnes was undoubtedly preoccupied with plans for the coming meeting at Potsdam, but he did not ignore the diplomat's proposals. There were good reasons for not rising to this bait. In the first place, Charles Bohlen and other Soviet experts in the State Department strongly opposed the idea, pointing out that Stalin would view the proposed modification in the unconditional surrender doctrine as an obvious attempt to cut the war short and thus deny him the Far Eastern concessions promised at Yalta. For Russophobes like Grew and James Forrestal, this was no problem. They wanted to repudiate the Yalta agreements and were even then thinking in terms of a confrontation with the Soviets. But Byrnes, still finding his way, had not yet given up on the idea of postwar collaboration among the Allies.

Former Secretary of State Cordell Hull gave Byrnes further cause to consider carefully before modifying the unconditional surrender formula. Grew's proposed statement, he warned, seemed "too much like appeasement of Japan, especially after the resolute stand we had maintained on unconditional surrender." Grew claimed that his plan provided a sure method of securing an early Japanese surrender. Hull, not so certain of this, warned that it was a gamble, one that might well backfire. If the administration made its "clarification" and the Japanese did not surrender, what then? He warned of "terrible political repercussions" at home if the unconditional surrender doctrine was modified. Hull evidently did not discuss the Soviet aspect of the problem with Byrnes. But it must have occurred to the secretary of state that if he took Grew's advice and Japan did not surrender he would also incur Soviet enmity and get nothing in return. That was not a very appealing prospect either.

At Potsdam, President Truman and his secretary of state faced an unhappy dilemma. They realized that Hull and Bohlen were right about the risks implicit in Grew's plan. On the other hand, as Byrnes explained to Army Air Force General "Hap" Arnold, "what we must do now is not to make the world safe for democracy, but make the world safe for the United States."[33] Asia would certainly be more safe for American interests if Japan surrendered before Russia intervened. Neither Truman nor Byrnes was as yet willing to provoke difficulties with the Soviets by overtly modifying the unconditional surrender formula. They were, however, willing to hint at the possibility that if Japan surrendered, the imperial institution might be preserved. Thus the Potsdam Declaration, which carried a warning of impending devastation if Japan did not promptly surrender, also promised that one of the final acts of the Allied occupation forces would be to see to it that there was "established in accordance with the freely expressed will of the Japanese people a peacefully inclined and responsible government."[34] Presumably then, if the people of Japan wanted to maintain the dynasty, they would be allowed to do so.

This was not as clear a hint to the Japanese as it might have been. Yet certain Japanese leaders, Foreign Minister Tōgō among them, did sense a certain flexibility in the terms of the Potsdam Declaration. At a meeting of the Japanese cabinet held on Friday, July 27, Tōgō recommended that the Japanese government make no reply to the Declaration until its terms were further clarified. The army chief of staff and the war minister opposed this delaying tactic, arguing that peremptory rejection of the Allied demand for surrender ought to be issued immediately. Because the cabinet could not agree on just how to respond, they decided at least for the time being to remain silent. In the interim the foreign office, which was still seeking Soviet good offices, would attempt to find out whether or not Stalin was prepared to play the role of peacemaker.

Since there had already been some mention of the Potsdam Declaration in the press, the cabinet also felt obliged to make some comment for domestic consumption. Again the military leaders urged that the Allied demands be rejected categorically. But the foreign minister as well as others of a more pacific disposition opposed this. They realized that stories in Japan's controlled press would be carefully monitored in Allied capitals and taken as statements of policy. Moreover, an outright rejection of the Potsdam demands would undoubtedly doom whatever chance remained that the Soviets would agree to play the role of mediator. While defending the views expressed by the foreign office, Prime Minister Suzuki insisted that the proper course would be to *mokusatsu* the declaration—in effect, to say nothing for the time being. The cabinet then agreed that the press would publish an abridged version of the Potsdam Declaration as straight news without commentary. Thus, as of Friday, July 27, the official policy of the Japanese government was neither to reject nor accept the Potsdam Declaration. At least for the time being, Japan would remain silent while attempting to involve the Soviets as mediators. The peace movement was once again gathering momentum.

All might have gone according to plan had not someone who attended that cabinet meeting leaked Suzuki's *mokusatsu* remark to the press, where it took on an altogether different meaning. The next morning Japanese newspapers published an expurgated version of the Potsdam Declaration as they had been instructed to do by the government. But they added plenty of commentary. The government's attitude, the public was informed, was *mokusatsu*. "Since the joint declaration of America, Britain, and Chungking is a thing of no great value," one paper editorialized, "it will only serve to re-enhance the government's resolve to carry the war forward unfalteringly to a successful conclusion!" Following the appearance of these stories, the army and navy chiefs of staff and the war minister met with Prime Minister Suzuki, this time demanding "an explicit and prompt rejection" of Allied demands. Incredibly, Suzuki agreed. At a press conference held late on the afternoon of July 28 he denounced the Potsdam Declaration as "a rehash of the Cairo Declaration. The Government does not regard it as a thing of any great value; the government will just ignore [mokusatsu] it. We will press forward resolutely to carry the war to a successful conclusion."

Suzuki's statement did not make any sense. The Japanese press was under strict government control and would not have published those editorial statements unless authorized to do so. Moreover, the prime minister's subsequent statement to the press was also in conflict with his own government's established policy. Perhaps Suzuki, under pressure from the military, hoped that the Allies would understand that the Japanese government was edging toward a surrender even though it was saying something else publicly. If so, he was sadly mistaken, for Japan's enemies took mokusatsu to mean point-blank rejection.

In the end, while the Japanese government vacillated, momentum triumphed. The Manhattan Project, begun one day before Pearl Harbor, reached its logical culmination a few thousand feet over Hiroshima on the morning of August 6, 1945. The peace process, under way in Japan for more than a year, came to final fruition four days later. But after two atomic bombings, little had actually changed in Japan. The government of Prime Minister Suzuki offered to accept the terms of the Potsdam Declaration "with the understanding that the said declaration does not comprise any demand which prejudices the prerogatives of His Majesty as Sovereign Ruler."[35] President Truman might have rejected Suzuki's qualified offer of surrender. But Stalin had declared war on the Japanese on August 8. With Soviet armies racing across Manchuria and into Korea while American forces were no closer to Japan and the Asian mainland than Okinawa, it would have been insane to prolong the war. In his carefully drafted reply to Japan's offer of surrender, Secretary of State Byrnes affirmed the "authority of the Emperor and Japanese

Government to rule the state" subject only to "the Supreme commander of the Allied Powers."[36] Here at last was the all important "clarification" of the unconditional surrender doctrine that brought World War II to its conclusion. Although President Truman claimed that Japan had surrendered unconditionally, that was not the case.

Whenever he was queried in the years that followed, President Truman remained remarkably consistent in explaining that during those last frantic weeks of World War II he gave little thought to the use of the atomic bomb against Japan. It was a military matter determined by the weapon's availability and the continuation of the conflict. There was no decision to use the atomic bomb, if by that one means the careful development of a plan or policy. The decision to use the bomb was implicit in the decision to create it. The president in effect stood aside, refusing to interfere with a process set in motion long before he came to the executive mansion.

But to leave the matter at that is to leave much unsaid. To decide not to act is, after all, a decision. And in this case the decision carried with it important implications for the future. In the first place, by using nuclear weapons in combat, the Truman administration established the principle that though genocidal they were legitimate. That precedent, though often contested, has never been upset. Second, and certainly as important, by using the weapon rather than seeking the establishment of a workable system of international control as proposed by Niels Bohr and Leo Szilard, the Truman administration made the proliferation of nuclear weapons inevitable. The Soviet Union could not be secure knowing that a potential adversary had such a weapon. Nor were the British and French willing to forego a nuclear capability. The nuclear arms race followed inevitably.

4

"Just Another Piece of Artillery"
NUCLEAR POWER IN THE EARLY TRUMAN YEARS

IN THE SHORT TERM, the atomic bombing of Hiroshima and Nagasaki had the heaviest impact not on the American public at large, but on two elites: political leaders in the executive branch entrusted with foreign and military policy, and the scientific community associated with the Manhattan Project. The reactions of these two groups have shaped American military and domestic nuclear policies ever since. Political leaders reaffirmed the 1945 decision to use nuclear weapons as a major instrument of our foreign policy; they determined to cling to the American nuclear monopoly; they adopted Churchill's world view that saw the Soviet Union as America's antagonist in an emerging bipolar division of the world; they both linked and subordinated nonmilitary applications of nuclear power to military demands, giving nuclear research an almost exclusively military orientation that lasted the better part of a decade.

The atomic age, born on August 6, 1945, created revolutions in war, politics, and science. But the new president of the United States, beset by enervating self-doubts, was poorly equipped to comprehend, let alone master, these revolutionary changes. He shrugged off the atomic bomb as "just another piece of artillery," as if it were nothing more than a larger version of the shells he had handled as a captain in the field artillery during World War I. Yet, though he underestimated the revolutionary effects of nuclear weapons, he and his successors had to develop a strategy for survival in a world in which humanity had achieved the ability to destroy itself. Truman's awesome task was complicated by the emergence of the Soviet Union as a potential adversary, and the growth of a conception of American national security that was global in nature and that defined any move by the Soviets outside their existing east European sphere as a threat to America's vital interests.

Franklin Roosevelt hoped that a conciliatory approach toward the Soviets would produce an acceptable postwar settlement. But this notion died with him. Truman, who had few informed opinions of his own in the area of international affairs, relied heavily upon advisers who did not share Roosevelt's optimism. Averell Harriman, wartime ambassador to Moscow and a man who wielded great influence in the new administration, told Secretary of the Navy James Forrestal that in dealing with the Russians "we might well have to face an ideological crusade just as vigorous and dangerous as Fascism or Nazism." He likened the advance of the Red Army westward to "a barbarian invasion of Europe" and insisted to Truman that it would require tough talk coupled with bold, decisive action to secure Russian cooperation in structuring a peace settlement satisfactory to the United States.[1] Harriman at least believed that by dealing with the Soviets from strength something positive could be accomplished. State Department experts, including Harriman's chargés d'affaires in Moscow, George Kennan, Loy Henderson, Elbridge Durbrow, and Charles Bohlen, believed that the Soviets, driven by ideological fervor, would prove totally uncooperative. To these men, confrontation seemed inevitable. They advised a strong stand in dealing with the Soviets and were prepared for conflict.

Although the advice coming from Harriman and the State Department's eastern European experts differed, they agreed on one thing—toughness was indispensable. This advice meshed with Truman's bantam-cock personality. He and his advisers assumed that the United States had to present a posture of unyielding strength because no compromise was possible with the Soviets. Unhappily, this proved to be a self-fulfilling prophecy. Differences over eastern Europe, Germany, Iran, the eastern Mediterranean, and Korea plagued Soviet–American relations in the early postwar years. American toughness was matched by Soviet intransigence, and tensions mounted. For the United States, each new unresolved issue served to reinforce the earlier assumptions that the Soviets were bent upon world domination, and that attempts at negotiation were pointless. By the end of 1946, relations between East and West were in disarray. The Truman administration, convinced that the Soviets would prove an intractable adversary for many years to come, set itself the goal of containing Soviet expansionism. Diplomacy was at an end. The Cold War had begun.

With relations between the two superpowers tense, military men and some in the academic community turned their attention to the role nuclear weapons might play in future wars. The first and the most forward-looking of this new group of strategic thinkers was Bernard Brodie, who published a pathbreaking essay on the issue in 1946. In *The Absolute Weapon: Atomic Power and World Order,* Brodie predicted the rapid proliferation of nuclear weapons and saw little hope that a reliable defense against them could ever be developed. Defense against them being impossible, he argued that it would be suicidal to use nuclear weapons in warfare, for this would invite retaliation. Brodie concluded that once the United States lost its monopoly, atomic weapons could not be used in an offensive mode but could function solely as a deterrent to attack. The only sensible strategy for a nuclear power to follow, he therefore maintained, was to concentrate on developing the capacity to retaliate with devastating effect against any nation foolish enough to strike first. Technology, it seemed, had made nuclear war obsolete. "Thus far the chief purpose of our military establishment has been to win wars. From now on its chief purpose must be to avert them. It can have almost no other useful purpose."[2]

Brodie's reasoning presupposed the existence of two or more nuclear powers, each with many atomic weapons. Although that was not the case in the early postwar years when the United States enjoyed a nuclear monopoly, the Truman administration never-theless rejected any thought of a first strike against the U.S.S.R. before the Soviets could develop a nuclear capability of their own. But why was the administration unwilling to seize the initiative? Given the several crises of 1947 and 1948, especially the Berlin blockade, Truman might have been able to maneuver the Soviets into "firing the first shot," thus justifying a war. He was probably even aware of the fact that other presidents had resorted to just this tactic. Yet he never gave the idea any serious thought. The president's conservative critics have ascribed his refusal to take action either to naïve optimism about Soviet intentions, or bumbling ineptitude, or a combination of the two. With the advantage of hindsight, it becomes obvious that neither explanation is sufficient. The Truman administration never contemplated preventive war because it was restrained by a sober and realistic assessment both of the international political scene in the late 1940s and the real state of America's military capability.

Many commentators have assumed that the world of the late 1940s was effectively bipolar, meaning that except for a number of nonaligned nations the United States and the Soviet Union had divided the world into spheres of influence. Such a description, however, belies the actual geopolitical situation, at least to the extent that it suggests relative equality between the U.S.A. and the U.S.S.R. The Soviets had lost between twenty and thirty million people, killed as a direct result of the war. Their economy was a shambles. Nevertheless, they did manage to establish a sphere of influence in eastern Europe, tightening their grip there between 1945 and 1949. The United States, in contrast, emerged from the war physically untouched and at the height of its powers. The war had in fact been an economic boon to the country, the gross national product actually doubling between 1941 and 1945. America's sphere of influence encompassed two thirds of prewar Germany (including the industrial heartland of the country), the United Kingdom and most of the British Commonwealth, southern and western Europe, the Middle East, Latin America, the Philippines, Japan, and until 1949, China. Many of the countries in this vast area had been devastated as a result of the war. But the United States had the capital and, after 1948, the will to aid in their reconstruction. In fact, in most of these (excluding China) the demographic, political, and industrial base essential for revival and steady economic growth was already in place. Two spheres there certainly were, but America's was of far greater importance than that relatively unimportant portion of the globe dominated by the Soviets. The Truman administration therefore did not entertain serious thoughts of a preventive war in part at least because the risk did not seem worth the gamble.

To be sure, America's policymakers recognized that the Soviets would sooner or later recover from the damage of the war. They believed that the Soviet leaders, driven by ideological fervor, might never be convinced to behave like traditional statesmen. "We have here," wrote George Kennan, who was soon to become the head of the State Department's policy planning staff, "a political force committed fanatically to the belief that with the United States there can be no permanent modus vivendi, that it is desirable and necessary that the internal harmony of our society be disrupted, our traditional way of life destroyed, the international authority of our state be broken, if Soviet power is to be secure."[3] The pessimism of Kennan as well as others not withstanding, this did not necessarily mean that war was inevitable. America's leaders hoped to be able to establish such a degree of stability, prosperity, and strength in the "free world" that the Soviets would be left permanently in a position of inferiority, unable to subvert the West politically or challenge it militarily.

If deterrence made more sense than confrontation from a foreign policy standpoint, that judgment was confirmed by the inadequacy of the American military establishment in the immediate postwar period. At the end of World War II the American military was speedily demobilized. Pressed by public and congressional demands to "bring the boys home," and embarrassed by widespread demonstrations on the part of the troops themselves, the administration moved swiftly. By the end of 1946 the armed services had been drastically reduced in size. Where once there had been more than 11 million men and women under arms, by 1946 no more than 1.6 million remained to guard the outposts of what had become a global empire. Moreover, the effectiveness of most of these units, which were made up of recent draftees, was questionable. Military budgets shrank faster than the services themselves. With the war at an end, the American people demanded relief from the high levels of taxation imposed during the fighting, and Congress was anxious to comply. Beginning in 1947, President Truman fought a running battle with Congress opposing what he believed were excessive tax cuts. But his efforts were fruitless. In the immediate postwar years, federal revenues dropped precipitately and the defense budget did too, averaging little more than $13 billion for each of the fiscal years 1947 through 1950. Making matters worse, at least from the viewpoint of the armed services, President Truman was a determined budget balancer who insisted that the government spend no more than it earned in any given year. The military budget prior to 1950 was determined by first subtracting the interest on the national debt, foreign aid, and all domestic costs from expected revenues. The remainder might be used for national security, although the president was reluctant to spend more than $14 billion on defense in any event. Truman was "a hard money man if ever I saw one" complained the then Secretary of Defense James Forrestal. He was "determined not to spend more than we take in taxes."[4]

Incapable of conducting a conventional war against the Soviet Union, the Truman administration relied upon its nuclear striking power in case of a conflict. But the Joint Chiefs of Staff did not really believe that the next war would be won in a few hours with atomic bombs. In the first place, the number of bombs available before 1950 was quite small. Although actual numbers are still classified, a reasonable estimate would be that at the time of the Korean War the American nuclear arsenal amounted to somewhere between 100 and 150 bombs. At the same time, conventional wisdom in the late 1940s had it that there was no difference between the effects of one nuclear strike and a mass raid similar to those that had leveled Dresden, Tokyo, and several other cities during the war. As the Strategic Bombing Survey pointed out, mass terror bombing had not brought Germany, Britain, or Japan to their knees. There was no reason to believe that it would have that effect on the Soviets. On the contrary, the Soviets suffered more than twenty million killed in the war, thousands of towns and cities destroyed, almost the entire industrial and agricultural base leveled or captured, and still they survived and in the end triumphed. When the Joint Chiefs considered what the Soviets had already endured, they were unable to believe that a war might be won with a few bombing raids. Even the air force, engaged in a struggle for scarce dollars with the other services, was careful not to claim too much for strategic airpower. In 1949, while in the midst of a bitter fight with the navy over the merits of the six-engined intercontinental B-36 bomber, air force spokesmen rejected the "illusory hope" that the next war would be won with atomic bombs alone. In urging Congress to authorize funds for the new bomber, the air force went no further than the modest claim "that the engagement of surface forces will take place with much greater assurance of success, and much fewer casualties . . . if an immediate, full-scale atomic offensive is launched against the heart of the enemy's war-making power."[5]

If American strategists did not view their nuclear monopoly as decisive, Soviet military policy made war even less inviting. Russia too had demobilized the greater part of its armed forces after the war. But Stalin kept large elements of what remained of the Red Army at forward bases in eastern Europe. Western analysts seem to have believed that 175 Soviet divisions were poised to move at the instant a new war broke out. Whether this many troops actually were deployed is debatable. But with even one half of this force, the Soviets could have swept almost unopposed to the English Channel in a matter of days. If Soviet cities were hostage to American bombers, western Europe, vital to the United States, was hostage to the Red Army. The result was an uneasy stalemate. Though frequently threatened by serious political crises in the last years of the decade, this de facto truce remained intact in part at least because neither side believed that it could win a military victory at an acceptable cost.

The question of just how long America's nuclear monopoly would last was a matter of considerable debate within the administration. General Leslie Groves insisted that it could be maintained perhaps for the indefinite future but certainly for the next twenty years. To support his argument he produced a study purporting to demonstrate that between them, Britain and the United States could monopolize the world's supply of uranium and thorium, thus making it impossible for the Soviets to develop a bomb, at least in the near term. The United States therefore need fear nothing: it would remain secure behind its nuclear shield for at least the next two decades, perhaps longer. This fatuous analysis not only underrated the importance of proven uranium deposits in the Joachimsthal region of Czechoslovakia, but also assumed that in all the vast land mass of the U.S.S.R. itself the raw materials for a bomb were not to be found. President Truman was even more ill-informed, largely because of his own low opinion of the Russian people, whom he referred to as "those Asiatics." Robert Oppenheimer later recalled this depressing conversation with the president:

> *Truman:* "When will the Russians be able to build the bomb?"
>
> *Oppenheimer:* "I don't know."
>
> *Truman:* "I know."
>
> *Oppenheimer:* "When?"
>
> *Truman:* "Never."[6]

American scientists, foremost among them Fermi, knew better. They tried to explain to political leaders who would listen that their colleagues throughout the world possessed an understanding of basic nuclear theory. The American nuclear lead lay in industrial technology, and that was not likely to assure an American monopoly of the bomb for longer than five years or so. Irving Langmuir, an American Nobel laureate in chemistry (1932), confirmed this belief when he returned from a trip to the Soviet Union in the autumn of 1945. Impressed by the advanced state of Soviet nuclear knowledge, Langmuir estimated they could develop their own bomb in five years.

Henry Stimson concurred with the scientists. He scorned the belief that the United States could establish a monopoly on raw materials dispersed widely around the globe. Americans were well aware of Canadian, African, and central European deposits, and had no reason to believe that these were unique. Aware that Groves's folly was widely shared, he began a major policy debate in the highest levels of the Truman administration over potential Soviet nuclear capability. On September 12, 1945, with Hiroshima still smoking, Stimson made a direct appeal to Truman, vainly trying to make the president see that there were no "atomic secrets," and that the theoretical knowledge necessary to construct a nuclear weapon was well understood throughout the world. During the war, the United States had developed certain processes for producing the bomb that would take other nations some time to duplicate. Just how much time was a matter of debate. Optimists like Groves believed that it might take the Soviets as long as twenty years; pessimists, including some of the Manhattan Project's most knowledgeable scientists, thought they could do it in four. But whether the nuclear monopoly lasted four or twenty years the results would be the same. Unless something was done, the world would face a nuclear arms race that might well destroy civilization.

Stimson also tried to make the president aware of how the current situation must appear to Soviet eyes. Great Britain and the United States were cooperating in the development of nuclear weapons while excluding the Russians. The Soviets, who could only view this as an alliance forming against them, were undoubtedly working to develop their own bomb. Stimson urged the president to head off a nuclear arms race by inviting the Soviets to participate with England and the United States in devising a plan for the international control of atomic energy. It is unclear just what Truman thought of Stimson's presentation. He was, however, sufficiently impressed to call a cabinet meeting to discuss the issue formally.

If all cabinet meetings are as badly organized or as confused as this one, we have good reason to fear for the future of the republic. Secretary of the Navy James Forrestal, whose pathological fear of the Soviets would lead first to a nervous breakdown and finally to suicide, was adamantly opposed to the Stimson proposal, without really understanding it. He seems to have believed that in some inexplicable way the nefarious Soviets would find a method of stealing the "secret" of the bomb from an international atomic authority. Nothing could convince him that there was no "secret," that the monopoly was a wasting asset. The bomb was "the property of the American people," he stormed, and the administration could not give it away without their permission.[7] A number of other cabinet members strongly disagreed. Robert Patterson, who had just replaced Stimson in the War Department, Secretary of Commerce Henry Wallace, and Acting Secretary of State Dean G. Acheson all supported the Stimson position. On studying the question, Acheson concluded that "a policy of secrecy is both futile and dangerous" for "if the invention is developed and used destructively there will be no victor and there may be no civilization remaining. The advantage of being ahead in the nuclear arms race," he concluded, "is nothing compared with not having the race."[8]

Surprising to note, the Joint Chiefs of Staff agreed at least initially with Acheson's analysis. They were convinced that if a nuclear arms race did develop, the United States would be at a serious disadvantage vis-à-vis the Soviet Union. On the one hand, the chiefs believed that nuclear weapons could most effectively be used in war as a first-strike weapon. In those innocent times they thought it inconceivable that the United States would ever adopt such a strategy. On the other hand, they were certain that the Soviets would have no such compunctions. Pearl Harbor had been bad enough, but a sneak attack on the American industrial base and large population centers with atomic weapons might well destroy American society before retaliation became possible. To make matters worse, all else being equal, the JCS believed that the United States would be at a considerable disadvantage in such a war with the Soviets because industrial and population centers in this country were more concentrated than in the Soviet Union, making them more vulnerable. These considerations convinced the chiefs that a workable system of international control would be more advantageous than relying on a short-lived nuclear monopoly and running the risk of a nuclear arms race.

Although Stimson's proposal had the endorsement of a number of cabinet officers as well as the JCS, President Truman would ultimately be guided by his old friend Secretary of State James Byrnes, and Byrnes was of two minds on this issue. Prior to leaving for the London foreign minister's conference in September 1945, he had in fact "begged" Stimson not to bring up the question of international control. Convinced that the nuclear monopoly could be translated into diplomatic leverage, he believed that "we must first see whether we can work out a decent peace" before surrendering so potent a weapon as the atomic bomb. Byrnes also had serious doubts about the feasibility of any system of international controls. It seemed to him that it would depend upon the development of a foolproof system of international inspections. It was doubtful that Congress would give foreign inspection teams carte blanche to poke around at will in the United States. Nor could he see how the Russians could be convinced to cooperate. "We can't get into Rumania and Bulgaria much less Russia," he exclaimed. He thought it "childish to think that the Russians would let us see what they are doing."[9]

Yet like Stimson, Byrnes realized that the nuclear monopoly was a wasting asset and that the alternative to the international control of nuclear weapons was a runaway arms race. Moreover, Byrnes's London experience raised serious questions about the effect the nuclear monopoly was having upon the Soviets. He had gone to London with, as Stimson put it, the bomb placed rather too ostentatiously "in his hip pocket." But the result had been exactly the reverse of his expectations. He found the Soviets more rigid and less inclined to deal because they found themselves in a position of inferiority. The bomb, it appeared, was not so potent a force as the secretary had at first imagined. On the contrary, its very existence now appeared an obstacle to an acceptable peace settlement. Probably for these reasons, and because the weight of cabinet opinion favored an attempt to find an acceptable formula for international control, Byrnes came around. Just prior to leaving for London and the opening session of the United Nations General Assembly, he telephoned Dean Acheson, who was at home in Georgetown ill with the flu. The assistant secretary of state was to head a committee to devise a plan for the international control of atomic energy.

The Acheson committee, composed of Acheson himself, former Assistant Secretary of War John J. McCloy, Vannevar Bush, James Conant, and General Leslie Groves, had a difficult assignment. As Byrnes and Acheson both knew, powerful congressmen and newspaper commentators opposed any program that endangered America's nuclear monopoly. When opponents charged that the Truman administration was preparing to give away the secret of the atomic bomb, the fear generated would be an extremely powerful force, one difficult to counteract. Therefore, the plan that the committee devised would have to be carefully drawn not only because national security was involved but also because it was essential to anticipate the opposition with a scheme that met the objections of those who had not yet realized that the development of nuclear weapons had changed international relations in fundamental ways.

Acheson, who knew nothing about atomic energy but a great deal about diplomacy, organized a working group of five experts from science, government, and industry who immediately set to work devising a program for international control. Before the middle of March 1946, this group, which included J. Robert Oppenheimer, David Lilienthal (head of the Tennessee Valley Authority), Harry A. Winne (vice-president in charge of engineering for General Electric), Charles A. Thomas (a vice-president of the Monsanto Company), and Chester I. Barnard (of the New Jersey Bell Telephone Company), issued a report that showed a great deal of promise. At Oppenheimer's urging, the working group proposed the creation of an international Atomic Development Authority. This agency was to be a well-funded organization at the forefront of nuclear research and capable of attracting the best minds in the field. The Authority would own and operate the mines from which the essential raw materials— uranium and thorium—were extracted. It would run the processing plants where fissionable materials were produced. The Authority would then denature these materials, making them unusable for bomb production, before distributing them to national governments and private organizations for nondangerous uses. The Authority alone would have the power to conduct experiments with nuclear explosives.

Acheson was immediately impressed by the subtleties of the plan. From the beginning he had assumed that any workable scheme would depend upon an absolutely foolproof system of international inspections. Yet no one had been able to come up with such a system. Even if they had, it probably would not have won the approval of the Soviets, who were intransigent on the subject of international inspections within the U.S.S.R. for any purpose. The beauty of the working group's proposal was that

while the ADA would have investigative powers it would not need
to exercise these except in extraordinary circumstances, for it
alone would control the world's supply of raw materials and the
processing plants essential for bomb production.

Oppenheimer's working group had performed a valuable service in defusing the issue of inspections, but Vannevar Bush felt
that it had not considered the issue of national security carefully
enough. Soviet–American relations were bad and growing worse
by the day. Bush noted that under such circumstances the United
States could not afford to renounce its nuclear monopoly immediately, for the Soviets enjoyed a great advantage in the area
of conventional weaponry. Acheson agreed. The creation of a
strong international Atomic Development Authority would be
the work of a decade. In the interim there would be crises in
Soviet–American relations that might wreck the entire undertaking. He therefore insisted that the move from national to international control be undertaken in stages. In the earliest phases the
United States would make promises but no actual concessions.
The other nations, including the Soviet Union, would have to
begin "playing pool" before the United States would dismantle
its nuclear arsenal, stop building bombs, discontinue research, or
turn over vital technical information to the international Authority. Playing pool obviously implied more than ratifying an agreement. Other countries would have to halt their nuclear research.
Moreover, the Authority would actually have to be in control of
all sources of raw material before the United States began making
concessions.

Oppenheimer, Lilienthal, and the rest of the working group
were just as concerned about "the Russian problem" as Acheson
and Bush. They too agreed that the ADA should be built in stages
and for precisely the reasons outlined by Bush and Acheson. But
they also believed that such delicate issues should be resolved in
private negotiations, which could be carried on at the United
Nations. They believed that by detailing in advance a plan such
as the one advocated by Bush and Acheson, the United States
would be needlessly complicating matters by publicly advertising
its distrust of the Soviets.

Acheson, a persuasive and skillful diplomat, knew that Oppen-

heimer's view was correct, that the chances for a successful negotiation with the Soviets would be enhanced if the talks were
private and the American position was developed gradually instead of being opened to public scrutiny at the very beginning of
the negotiating process. He opposed the Oppenheimer view on
political, not diplomatic, grounds. The Joint Chiefs would not go
along unless there was an ironclad guarantee that the United
States would surrender nothing until the Soviets had firmly committed themselves. The same was true of Senator Brien McMahon's Joint Committee on Atomic Energy, which was threatening
to seize the initiative in the matter if the State Department did not
produce a plan Congress could endorse. Congressmen and senators on both sides of the aisle, including Tom Connally of Texas
and Michigan's Arthur Vandenberg, instinctively opposed any
plan that even suggested the sharing of nuclear "secrets." The
administration had to convince skeptics that it was not going to
give the atomic bomb to our potential adversary for a mess of
pottage. This would constitute an open invitation for Congress
to take a hand in policy formulation. And Acheson was convinced
that nothing good could result from that.

The Acheson–Lilienthal Plan, as the Acheson committee report came to be known, was the Oppenheimer working group's
proposal, revised to make it clear that all other nations, including
the Soviet Union, would be required to abandon their nuclear
research and turn over their raw materials and processing plants
to the ADA before the United States would be required to make
any significant concessions. Acheson's committee had undoubtedly strengthened the plan in the eyes of its domestic critics by
insisting on these revisions. But then, as the committee's members must have realized, these same changes diminished the possibility that the Soviets would be willing to cooperate.

While the Acheson committee and its advisory group struggled
to find a formula for international control that might withstand
congressional and media scrutiny, Secretary of State Byrnes was
also working on the same problem. Byrnes believed that if the
administration could find someone who commanded widespread
respect to represent its policy when the United Nations Atomic
Energy Commission convened in June, chances of domestic ap-

proval would be enhanced. Byrnes thought the man for the job was his friend and benefactor, the South Carolina financier Bernard Baruch, self-styled adviser to presidents. On March 16, while the Acheson committee was winding up its work, Truman and Byrnes agreed that Baruch was the man for the job. In one sense at least there can be no doubt that Byrnes had made the appropriate move. Baruch's appointment was widely acclaimed. In the Senate, where the administration's approach to international control was under careful scrutiny, there was a collective sigh of relief: Baruch could be trusted. The Senate Foreign Relations Committee had such confidence in him that it did not even require Baruch to testify at appointment hearings. Baruch was confirmed, no questions asked.

If the Baruch appointment seemed to Truman and Byrnes to be the right move at the right time, Acheson was not so sure. "My own experience," he later wrote, "led me to believe that his reputation was without foundation in fact and entirely self-propagated." It wasn't long before Acheson's fears about Baruch were borne out. Byrnes had intended to use Baruch to front for administration policy. But shortly after his appointment, Baruch made it clear to the secretary of state as well as the president that he expected to be involved in policy formulation, and that he did not consider the Acheson–Lilienthal report entirely sound. He threatened to resign if the administration refused to allow him to redraft portions of the report. After three weeks of indecision, Truman gave in. He couldn't afford the political explosion that would accompany Baruch's departure. Baruch then used his own staff to redraw the outlines of nuclear policy. This staff included Ferdinand Eberstadt, a lawyer and investment banker who had worked with Baruch on the War Production Board; Fred Serles, a mining engineer who had worked in the Office of War Mobilization; John M. Hancock, who had been with Baruch during World War I on the old War Industries Board; and another old WIB colleague, the journalist Herbert Bayard Swope.

The Baruch group accepted the Atomic Development Authority, but for reasons wholly different from those that had motivated Oppenheimer, the author of the idea. They viewed the ADA as a splendid apparatus for monitoring the activities of the

Soviet Union. While content to allow the ADA the authority to conduct dangerous research, Baruch and his banker friends found the idea that the Authority should own and operate mines and processing plants dangerously socialistic. Instead, they proposed that these facilities remain either in state or private hands. The ADA would be granted extensive powers to inspect operations at these mines and processing plants, as well as other facilities that might be used by a nation to develop a nuclear military capability. The State Department objected that the Soviets were certain to reject any plan that relied upon a system of inspections. But Baruch ignored these objections, claiming that the Soviets would be no more averse to international inspections than to the ownership of facilities by the ADA.

Baruch made another change in the Acheson–Lilienthal report that was even more fundamental. The original plan had been conceived as essentially an elaborate warning device: if a nation decided to construct nuclear weapons, it would have to seize the processing plants and fuel stockpiles of the international Authority. At that, it would take even a technologically advanced nation nearly a year to fabricate its first bomb. The rest of the world would be furnished with a "clear, simple, and unequivocal danger signal." After that, everything would depend upon the "intelligence, power, and preparations" of other nations to meet the threat. Acheson and his colleagues had quite deliberately stopped short of recommending that the international Authority be granted police powers. In the first place, the Soviets would have rejected such a plan. In the second place, it was pointless. "If a major power disregarded a treaty and wanted a test of strength," Acheson explained to one of Baruch's aides, "no treaty clauses would have any value. Complete security was an illusion." If a transgression occurred under the Acheson–Lilienthal Plan, "the signatory countries would have a reasonable warning." "Provisions for paper police sanctions to be imposed by signatories to the treaty," Acheson intoned, "were only an illusion."[10]

Baruch, who vehemently disagreed with Acheson, again threatened to resign unless he was allowed to modify the Acheson–Lilienthal Plan on this fundamental point. Again the president

gave in. Under what came to be known as the Baruch Plan the
ADA would be entrusted with control over all phases of the
development and use of atomic energy. The Authority was to act
as a sort of international police agency with the power to inflict
"condign punishment" on any nation caught attempting to construct nuclear weapons. To be certain that the projected Authority would be free to act against any malefactor, the plan further
stipulated that no nation should be able to block the imposition
of sanctions by the use of its veto in the United Nations Security
Council. And of course, all of this was added to a scheme wherein
all other nations would have to cease nuclear research and agree
to terms laid down by the United States as preconditions to
significant American concessions.

Acheson was furious: he believed that Baruch's heavy-handed
approach had ended any chance of Soviet cooperation. "The
Soviet Union was undoubtedly doing all in its power to develop
nuclear weapons at the moment," he later wrote. If so, the "swift
and sure punishment" provision could be interpreted in Moscow
only as an attempt to turn the United Nations into an alliance to
support a U.S. threat of war against the U.S.S.R. unless it ceased
its efforts, for only the United States could conceivably adminis-
ter "swift and sure" punishment to the Soviet Union.[11] The
beauty of the Acheson–Lilienthal Plan was that it did not include
an unworkable system of international inspections or "paper
sanctions."

Acheson, then, was not at all surprised when Stalin's young
delegate to the United Nations Atomic Energy Commission, Andrei Gromyko, rejected the Baruch Plan. But Acheson was a
member of a tiny minority in 1946. By and large, the Baruch Plan
received plaudits in the press and elsewhere as a reasonable and
constructive proposal. Correspondingly, many took the Soviet
Union's refusal to go along as evidence of Stalin's aggressive
intentions.

Hysteria broke out in some quarters. Senator Brien McMahon,
chairman of the powerful Joint Committee on Atomic Energy,
openly discussed the possibility of preventive war against the
Soviet Union, remarking "that for the first time in human history,
the failure to agree to a sane, effective and righteous control of

weapons of war constitutes in and of itself an act of aggression." And Lord Bertrand Russell, who was soon to emerge as one of the founders of Britain's antinuclear movement, agreed with McMahon. In October 1946, Russell called for nuclear threats against the Soviets for the purpose of forcing them to accept "a world government under hegemony of the United States." "The only possible way" of accomplishing this, Russell seems to have believed, was through "a mixture of cajolery and threat, making it plain to the Soviet authorities that refusal will entail disaster, while acceptance will not."[12] Contemporary criticism of the Soviet position notwithstanding, it is clear in retrospect—as it was to Acheson, Lilienthal, and some few others at the time—that Stalin had a point. The Baruch Plan would have left the Russians at a severe disadvantage.

How are we to account for the fact that policymakers began with a reasonable, potentially workable proposal and moved progressively away from it? It was not for lack of real interest. A number of well-informed policymakers believed that the national interest would best be served by working with the Soviets to establish an acceptable system of international controls. But at home there was a great fear, played upon by those who insisted that national security depended on continued nuclear superiority, that the administration might sacrifice our "atomic secrets" and win in return a mere piece of paper, an ineffective system of international controls. And so, in order to co-opt the potential opposition and win wider domestic support for the idea of international control, Acheson felt called upon to "strengthen" the original Oppenheimer–Lilienthal proposal. In the process, he made it somewhat less likely that the Soviets would be willing to cooperate. The same process was repeated when Truman and Byrnes, fearing that Baruch's resignation would set off a political tempest, allowed him to make further revisions.

Conflict resolution in a democratic society calls for compromise among differing factions. But in this case each step down the road to a domestic consensus was a step back from the international objective. This progression validates Niels Bohr's 1944 warning to Franklin Roosevelt that the development of nuclear fission was a scientific revolution that would have to be matched by a revolution in international politics if civilization was to be preserved. The nation-state, Bohr insisted, had become a dangerous anachronism. In the long run, human survival would depend upon achieving important modifications in nationhood itself.

Skeptics may suggest that Bohr's prognosis was needlessly grim. Yet in the years since he first issued his warning, the United States (and the Soviets too) have unwaveringly sought security through more advanced weapons systems that only left each nation perched precariously on the verge of catastrophe. And in spite of the fact that both sides agree that the arms race is wasteful, dangerous, and should be brought to an end, nothing positive has been accomplished. Indeed, the last three and a half decades have been unremittingly regressive. Few propose disarmament any longer. The seemingly unattainable object of the 1980s is described as "arms control."

The same arguments that pertain now were valid when Acheson, Baruch, and Oppenheimer debated the issue in 1946. Advocates of disarmament believed that the nuclear revolution required an innovative response, that national security could not be maintained by attempting to keep ahead of the Soviets, and that an arms race should be avoided. Others, including Baruch, were prepared to accept nuclear disarmament only if as a result the Soviet Union was frozen into a permanently inferior military status. Short of that, they thought it best to be "cautious," to stick with tradition and maintain "strength." That point of view, so obviously flawed, nevertheless prevailed in 1946 as it does today.

What has provided it with such vitality? First, it is based on the very existence of the Soviet Union, a powerful adversary believed by most Americans to be bent upon our destruction. Second, there is the instinct, rooted in the consciousness of people throughout history, that in war victory will go to the strong. No matter that nuclear weapons have changed all that: ultimately instinct prevails. And because it does, the spiraling arms race continues as nations seek security and in the process produce only greater insecurity. They add to their strength only to find themselves increasingly vulnerable.

While members of the Truman administration were debating the question of international control of nuclear weapons, Congress and the American scientific elite were grappling with related questions. As early as 1943, scientists in the Manhattan Project had begun to give serious thought to the question of who should control the future development of nuclear power, both within the United States and in the world at large. Finding themselves less pressed than their colleagues elsewhere with the demands of the Manhattan Project, Met Lab scientists in Chicago began to consider the ethical and social questions that the existence of nuclear power had raised. Army officers at the Met Lab tried to squelch any outbreak of scientific conscience by threatening to ship the younger men to Guadalcanal,[13] but the Chicago scientists continued to debate the larger policy questions posed by their work. By the summer of 1944, some of the Met Lab scientists insisted on addressing the domestic and international implications of their project. Arthur Compton accordingly authorized two committees to gather the scientists' opinions and distill policy recommendations from them. The Committee on Postwar Policy, chaired by Richard C. Tolman, proposed the creation of a national authority after the war to promote nuclear research in order to maintain the U.S.A.'s military nuclear lead, and to adapt nuclear power to naval propulsion. The other group, headed by the industrial metallurgist Zay Jeffries, which included Fermi and Franck among its members, produced a report, the *Prospectus on Nucleonics,* that reflected the social concerns of the Chicago scientists.

Jeffries had recently coined the term "nucleonics" to replace the inaccurate and cumbersome "atomistics" that some still used to describe the entire field of nuclear science. The new word was appropriate to the broad-gauged approach of the Jeffries group. Its *Prospectus* articulated several ideas that paralleled the questions Niels Bohr was then raising with FDR, and that would be reflected in all scientists' contributions to nuclear policy debate in the next two years.

It tied postwar nuclear development to anticipated nonmilitary research that could benefit humanity, such as the medical uses of radioactivity and industrial applications of analytical irradiating techniques. The committee was pessimistic about the economic feasibility of using fission as a source of electric power, though it did speculate that waste heat from piles constructed for other purposes might be used locally for space heating. But central to the Jeffries group's report was the emphasis it placed on the international control of nuclear power. Postulating that "technological advances without moral development are catastrophic," the committee called for public education in the broader aspects of nuclear power to permit informed democratic support for policymaking, and insisted that "all nations [must] make every effort to cooperate now in setting up an international administration with police powers which can effectively control at least the means of nucleonic warfare." The issues of nonmilitary nuclear development, international control over nuclear arms, and public participation in nuclear policymaking were now explicit. Army censors did not permit circulation of the *Prospectus on Nucleonics;* it was not even declassified until 1957.[14]

The activism of Met Lab dissident scientists, which produced the *Prospectus on Nucleonics* and the Franck report, had little short-term impact on policymakers, but it did have unanticipated long-term effects. Social conscience plunged scientists into an unaccustomed role, requiring them to consider questions of conscience on social issues relating to their work, and to promote their view in the public arena. "We felt someone should attempt to represent the public conscience," a participant, Aaron Novick, recalled two years later, "and that at least we scientists should discuss among ourselves the tremendous social and political implications of atomic warfare."[15] Novick's observation may seem truistic today, but it betokened a radical new posture for American scientists. Before World War II, they had seldom felt compelled to take public stands, as scientists, on political issues. Even when science itself was directly threatened, as in the Scopes trial of 1925 contesting Tennessee's effort to prohibit the teaching of evolution in the public schools, the national community of scientists did not respond effectively as a body. Until the 1930s, most scientists adhered to the ideal of an apolitical science: the pursuit of objective scientific truth, unbiased and uncontaminated with political judgments. Just as politics should not determine the goals and methods of science, so science should not guide public policymaking. The ideal of apolitical science envisioned an international community of objective researchers dedicated to the pursuit of truth by the scientific method in their laboratories and classrooms, freely exchanging information about their findings. As individuals, scientists were politically heterogeneous. A few, including Einstein, were pacifists. Even fewer in America were socialists. Some sought highly personal goals, like Arthur Compton, who pursued a lifelong ideal of demonstrating that the teachings of Christianity were compatible with scientific research. Many scientists were skeptical of the role of governments and military establishments in promoting scientific research. The links between the federal government and science in America were few and weak, and emphasized applied science rather than basic research.

But the ideal of apolitical science was shattered by the grim history of the 1930s. The rise of fascism in Italy, the Nazis' crackpot idea of an "Aryan physics," the ominous 1939 victory of Fascist forces in the Spanish Civil War, and the Nazi–Soviet pact of the same year, all gutted scientists' skepticism about cooperating with the governments of the democracies. As the science community embraced the cause of the democracies against fascism, it shed its internationalist and apolitical ideals, as well as its reluctance to become politically involved. World War II merely ratified the abandonment of this apolitical idea, and created a scientific "establishment" in the United States and Great Britain.

The Russian physicist Pyotr Kapitsa observed these trends during a visit to Great Britain in 1966, and noted its darker side. Since 1938, science had left behind "forever the happy days of free scientific work which gave us such delight in our youth. Science has lost her freedom. Science has become a productive force. She has become rich but she has become enslaved, and part of her is veiled in secrecy."[16] This new condition of the scientific estate naturally caused stresses within the community of American science, particularly among the Manhattan Project workers, some of whom watched the emergence of nuclear policy with misgivings while others remained complacent. The leaders of the nuclear establishment like Bush, Conant, the Compton brothers, Fermi, Lawrence, and (during the war) Oppenheimer raised few criticisms of nuclear-related political decisions. The decision made by political and military leaders, with the acquiescence of the Scientific Panel and the Interim Committee, to drop atomic bombs on Hiroshima and Nagasaki, only enhanced the growing cleavage between establishment leaders and restive critics, who numbered not only the unknown, younger figures at the Met Lab but such senior figures as Bohr, Szilard, Franck, and Einstein.

The use of nuclear weapons against Japan was not the only issue troubling the scientific communities at Chicago, Oak Ridge, and Los Alamos. Resentment among the Chicago group about secrecy and the army's security regime had been festering since 1943. Security became even more intrusive toward war's end, if for no other reason than that the army was enlarging and improving its security apparatus. After V-J Day many of the scientists found the continuation of secrecy intolerable, and were in a position to make their irritation felt because they were now free to walk off the job and take research positions at universities or in industry. This irritation surfaced in the press less than a month after Hiroshima. On September 1, 1945, a prominent segment of the Chicago group, which now included Fermi and Nobel laureate Harold C. Urey, who won the prize in 1934 for his work in isolating heavy water, gained national attention for its complaints. Samuel K. Allison, associate director of the Met Lab, stated in a widely headlined speech that the army's security restrictions would soon reduce the nuclear scientists to studying nothing more important than the color of butterfly wings. Fermi warned that "we cannot work for the government. Unless research is free . . . the United States will lose its superiority in scientific pursuit."[17] A flustered General Groves sent his assistant, Colonel Kenneth Nichols, to Chicago to suppress such free expression of opinion, but he could not stem the tide. The scientists were determined to gain a voice in nuclear policymaking.

The secrecy issue was actually a cluster of problems. Scientists resented ham-handed military prying. They feared that secrecy would throttle the breath of scientific inquiry itself. Procedures such as badges, security checks, and censorship were not only a nuisance, but also seemed pointless once there was no longer a Nazi or Japanese enemy to worry about. And, most sinister of all, the scientists were beginning to fear that the army was deliberately lying to political leaders and the public about vital consequences of nuclear research. Groves, in his crude way, dramatically highlighted the problem.

Nuclear scientists were beginning to gain firsthand experience with the biological effects of radiation. Harry Daghlian, a Los Alamos physicist, received a massive dose of radiation when fissile material in his hands went critical in August 1945. He died of acute radiation sickness after twenty-four days of excruciating pain. His grim experience was repeated in May 1946 when Louis Slotin, a Canadian physicist at Los Alamos who had been Daghlian's supervisor, was exposed to another burst of deadly radiation caused by two hemispheres of U-235 going critical in his hands. He lingered in pain for nine days before death relieved him. The army quickly covered up both men's deaths.[18] Yet Groves, at a congressional hearing after Daghlian's death, stated that he had heard that death from radiation was "very pleasant."[19] Army personnel and scientists had only begun to investigate the biological consequences of nuclear warfare by organizing an Atomic Bomb Casualty Commission as occupation forces moved into Japan after V-J Day. Yet the army and navy sent troops into radiation-hot areas at both bomb sites dangerously soon after the blasts.

All the sources of scientists' dissatisfaction tended to blend together. They were alarmed by the army's determination to control the future direction of nuclear research, a fact first disclosed to the Chicago group when Colonel Nichols, in the course of his scolding for Allison's "butterfly wings" speech, mentioned that such talk might jeopardize the bill currently in Congress for organizing the postwar control of nuclear energy. The policies of Groves and other brass threatened to abolish traditional scientific control over the substance of research. A continuation of these wartime policies by postwar legislation would have strangled the freedom of scientific interchange. However this issue might eventually be resolved, the question of the army's role in nuclear research was becoming urgent.

As the Franck report demonstrated, the scientists were also giving serious thought to international control of nuclear power. Not all the Chicago group, much less those at Oak Ridge, Los Alamos, and elsewhere, agreed with the position adopted by Franck. But, like Bohr and Szilard, those who did found themselves impelled toward political activism. The nonscientific question of the postwar relations among the United States, Great Britain, and the Soviet Union quickly became an inseparable part of the more abstract issue of international control of nuclear power. The scientists had no knowledge of the Hyde Park aide-mémoire of September 18, 1944, in which FDR and Churchill had ratified the Anglo-American partnership and excluded the Soviet Union. The chill of the Cold War had not yet set in, and scientists remained hopeful about the prospects for postwar cooperation among the Allies.

But the frustration of having strong feelings about these issues —secrecy and security, military control of nuclear research, international control of nuclear weapons—coupled with an inability to voice those feelings, drove some of the Chicago group to the partially unfounded conclusion that the scientific community was split between the establishment consisting of Bush, Conant, the Comptons, and Oppenheimer, on the one hand, and the concerned Chicago group on the other. As the physicist John H. Manley noted to Groves in August 1945, a fault line was beginning to appear "between those [scientists] who had done most of the work and those who formulated policy."[20] Even before Hiroshima, Eugene Rabinowitch circulated a memorandum among his Chicago colleagues, recommending that "an organization of those who have made up their mind about certain basic problems and decisions to be made, should be created on the [Manhattan] Project, with the intention of spreading it beyond the Project limits to scientists at large."[21] Rabinowitch had in mind both lobbying—he actually used the word, something unthinkable before the war—and educating the lay public so that fundamental nuclear policy decisions could be made democratically by an informed electorate.

In the two months after Hiroshima, emotional pressures on the nuclear scientists intensified, and they found it necessary to organize in order to promote the policy views that they felt so strongly about. The bombing of Hiroshima produced a mixed reaction: elation, pride, relief, foreboding, and perhaps guilt. But the bombing of Nagasaki three days later produced largely negative feelings. Rabinowitch stated that Met Lab scientists were horrified, and Allison, who was associate director at Los Alamos, publicly denounced it to the press. Alice K. Smith, a wartime member of the Los Alamos community and subsequently premier historian of the scientists' movement, describes the subsequent emotional reaction:

> Revulsion grew, bringing with it—even for those who believed that the end of the war justified the bombing—an intensely personal experience of the reality of evil. It was this, and not a feeling of guilt in the ordinary sense, that Oppenheimer meant by his much quoted, and often misunderstood, remark that scientists had known sin.[22]

Laboratory scientists at Chicago, Oak Ridge, and Los Alamos were also learning to mistrust the men who supposedly spoke for them in Washington. Edward Teller recalled the unquestioning faith that scientists originally had in their spokesmen:

> [Oppenheimer] conveyed to me in glowing terms the deep concern, thoroughness, and wisdom with which these questions were handled in Washington. Our fate was in the hands of the best, the most conscientious men of our nation.

Because of that sort of reassurance, Teller went on, he implicitly trusted Oppenheimer's recommendation that he not circulate Szilard's petition that the bomb not be dropped on Japan without advance warning, a decision Teller later regretted.[23] But this innocent trust gave way after Hiroshima to a more normal reluctance among scientists to acquiesce in the views of an elite. Again, Alice Smith: "Scientists tend to recognize authority on an ad hoc basis, and the fact that men like Conant, Bush, and Oppenheimer had done a good job during the war, was not adequate reason for accepting their opinions about what should happen next."[24]

The nuclear scientists had far less reason to accept military opinions as expressive of their views. As if to reinforce their mistrust of the military, Groves made some incautious remarks at ceremonies honoring him in New York City on September 20, 1945, that insultingly criticized the scientists' estimate of the duration of America's nuclear monopoly: "The more they talk, the shorter the time seems to get, but they are thinking of science and theory and not of building and operating a plant."[25] In November 1945, army occupation forces seized five Japanese cyclotrons and dumped them in the Pacific, an act of senseless looting that appalled American scientists. They would have been even more angered had they known that the order to destroy the cyclotrons had gone directly from Groves to General Douglas MacArthur's command. Secretary of War Robert Patterson defended the action on the bizarre grounds that the War Department had to deny nuclear research materials to its enemies. The defeated, bombed-out, occupied Japan of 1945 was scarcely an enemy, and Patterson's rationale only served to convince scientists that the army had to be excluded from control of nuclear research.

The scientists' determination to speak out was also stimulated by two publications that appeared just after Hiroshima. On August 11, Niels Bohr published an influential piece in the London *Times* entitled "Science and Civilization," in which he repeated the gist of his message to Roosevelt and Churchill, and called upon scientists to enlighten nonscientists about the issues facing the world in the atomic age. On the same date, coincidentally, Groves authorized publication of the official in-house history of the Manhattan Project, written by Project physicist Henry D. Smyth.[26] The scientists were surprised by the amount of secret data about production methods that the official history disclosed. By an irony, in view of later official hysteria about leaks of "atomic secrets," the Smyth report was, in the estimate of David Lilienthal, the "principal breach of security since the beginning of the atomic energy project"[27] and one authorized by Groves himself, not some obscure physicist with leftist views on social questions. It only increased the scientists' pique that the same authority that approved release of the Smyth report was trying to censor their opinions.

Accordingly, at the Manhattan Project's principal nuclear research facilities—the Met Lab, Oak Ridge, Los Alamos, and the Manhattan District's labs at Columbia University in New York City—nuclear scientists cautiously but deliberately organized to express their views formally. By midautumn 1945, four organizations existed at these installations to coordinate the scientists' presentation of their policy positions to political leaders in Washington, to interested private groups, and to the public at large: the Atomic Scientists of Chicago, the Association of Oak Ridge Scientists, the Association of Atomic Scientists at Los Alamos, and the New York group, SAM, from its wartime code name, "Substitute Alloy Materials."[28]

The scientists' organizations appeared not a moment too soon. For on October 3, 1945, the day before the Chicago and Oak Ridge associations formally organized themselves, President Harry S Truman delivered his first major address on atomic energy, and thereby provided some confirmation to rumors beginning to circulate among the scientists: the army was about to steal a march on the scientific community by railroading an atomic energy bill through Congress.[29]

Back in 1944, Bush and Conant had come up with the idea of a regulatory commission controlling production and research in the nuclear field. But the military preempted the actual drafting of postwar control legislation. George L. Harrison, president of the New York Life Insurance Company and deputy to Secretary of War Stimson on the Interim Committee, instructed two lawyers with the War Department, Kenneth C. Royall and William L. Marbury, to draft an atomic energy bill. The War Department bill provided for a five-member commission, largely insulated from political influence, and a professional staff run by an administrator and deputy. Section 1 of the bill declared, with what has proved to be unwitting irony in the perspective of nearly forty years, that the misuse of nuclear energy, "by design or through ignorance, might inflict incalculable disaster upon the Nation, destroy the general welfare, imperil the national safety, and endanger world peace."[30] To forestall this, the bill created a government monopoly over the development of nuclear energy, a monopoly that the military would inevitably dominate. The commission created by the bill would own all nuclear facilities and materials. Functionally, it would direct and control all nuclear research; no one could carry on such research without the commission's permission or ultimate supervisory control. Finally, the commission would determine its own security procedures. Penalties for violation of the security provisions were draconian: $100,000 and/or ten years, increased to $300,000 and thirty years if the transmission of information was made with an intent to endanger the United States.

The day after Truman's address, the War Department bill was introduced in the House by Andrew Jackson May, an undistinguished Kentucky Democrat whose congressional career was soon to end because of influence-peddling charges, and in the Senate by Edwin C. Johnson, a conservative Colorado Democrat. It was thereafter known as the May–Johnson bill. May, chairman of the House Military Affairs Committee, held a one-day hearing at which only the new secretary of war, Robert P. Patterson, as well as Groves, Bush, and Conant testified. All spoke favorably of the bill, though the two scientists had reservations about it that they did not then express publicly. Patterson had assured House Speaker Sam Rayburn that the May–Johnson bill enjoyed the support of "the leading physicists" and represented a "consensus of the [Interim] Committee, the interested departments, and the scientists and representatives of industries most directly associated in the program."[31] The scientist members of the Interim Committee and the Scientific Panel offered no objections to the bill; in fact, Oppenheimer, Fermi, and Lawrence warmly endorsed it in an October 11, 1945, telegram to Patterson. Congressman May, whom the scientists correctly perceived to be a cat's-paw of those pushing the War Department bill that bore his name, tried to close the hearings before the site organizations' protests could be heard. "The War Department discovered the weapon," he growled at the hearing. "Why can they not keep the secret?"[32] Members of the newly formed scientists' organizations were dismayed. They felt betrayed, believing that the leadership was misstating their views and assuring politicians of the scientific community's support for a bill that the scientists had not yet even seen. When they did get copies of the bill to study the next week, their worst suspicions were confirmed. The physicist Herbert

Anderson lamented his previous faith in Oppenheimer. Lawrence, Arthur Compton, and Fermi had, he thought, been duped by the military. "Let us beware of any breach of our rights as men and citizens. The war is won, let us be free again!" he demanded.[33] Meanwhile, military surveillance of the dissident scientists seemed to provide a running confirmation of their fears that the security emphasis of the bill would stifle free exchange of ideas within the scientific community. *The New York Times* reported that military police investigated newspaper reporters who were talking to scientists at the Chicago laboratories.[34]

A consensus quickly formed among the concerned scientists that clustered around five related objections to the May–Johnson bill.

1. The security provisions would throttle scientific research and violate a cardinal ideal of prewar science: the unimpeded interchange of scientific information. Scientists' resentment at the army, voiced in Allison's "butterfly wings" speech, figured largely in this objection.

2. The powers of the administrator (who might well be a recently retired military man, possibly even Groves) were excessive, making him virtually a czar of nuclear science. Scientists' suspicions along these lines were bolstered by a legal analysis of the bill provided by Edward Levi of the University of Chicago law school (who became, many years later, attorney general of the United States in the Ford administration). Levi warned of the bill's potential for "rigorous control and direction of atomic research" and "censorship."[35]

3. The bill emphasized military aspects of nuclear power, to the exclusion of anticipated peacetime uses.

4. The May–Johnson bill implicitly threatened the cardinal objective of the scientists' movement: international control of nuclear power, especially in its security provisions, because it would have restricted the exchange of information essential to supervision by an international body.

5. The administrative role of the army threatened to continue military control of nuclear research on into peacetime, violating the normal path of scientific inquiry, continuing irrational military

security restrictions such as compartmentalization, and perverting the peaceful promise of nuclear energy. The chemist Sam Weissman recalled Oppenheimer's wartime fear that the bomb, if successful, would "become a secret of the military which they could use to control the government with after the war."[36]

Representatives of the site organizations hurried to Washington to lobby individual members of Congress. There, they found two invaluable allies: Barry Commoner, then a navy lieutenant who had been assigned to the staff of West Virginia Senator Harley Kilgore's Military Affairs Committee, who provided the priceless services that congressional staff have always been able to supply, including contacts and instruction on the realities of congressional politics; and James Newman, a young lawyer with the Office of War Mobilization and Reconversion, who happened to have considerable lay scientific expertise. In the east, they also found interested media contacts, including the popular Mutual Radio Network commentator Raymond Swing, and *The New York Times* military analyst Hanson Baldwin. Further, the experience of working together pushed the representatives of the site organizations toward formation of a national organization, the Federation of Atomic Scientists, formed in November 1945. Acquiring office space and a secretary, as well as full-time scientist-lobbyists, the Federation then was in a position to reach out beyond the scientific community to interested lay organizations: church, women's, and labor groups on the liberal end of the political spectrum who were sympathetic to some of the scientists' objectives, especially international control of nuclear energy. Representatives from the American Association of University Women, the CIO, the National Farmers Union, the League of Women Voters, and even the Disabled American Veterans eventually federated into the National Committee on Atomic Information, a vigorous, influential, and useful adjunct of the scientists' organizations. Thus leagued, scientists and liberals challenged the May–Johnson bill, and by midwinter stopped it dead in its tracks.

Scientists and liberals were not the only ones who would find May–Johnson objectionable in the fall of 1945. Congressmen not as wedded to the Pentagon as May saw that the bill virtually abandoned all political and congressional control over the development of nuclear power to the proposed commission. The commission's members were insulated from the influence of the president, a point that ultimately proved the undoing of May–Johnson when President Truman was forced to take a closer look at the legislation he had seemed to endorse in advance in his October 3 speech. Influential voices in the executive branch, most notably Newman, the reconversion board attorney, and Secretary of Commerce Henry Wallace, criticized the bill for its excessive emphasis on military applications for nuclear power. Wallace counseled Truman that "it is important to place much more emphasis on the peacetime development of atomic energy. We must recognize that the development of atomic energy for industrial purposes may soon be of much greater concern to the nation and have greater effect on our economy and our way of life than the atomic bomb."[37]

The men voicing these objections shortly found a positive alternative to May–Johnson. In October, the Senate established a special committee on atomic energy legislation, chaired by the Connecticut Democrat, Brien McMahon. Recruiting Newman as special counsel to the committee, McMahon authorized him to draft an alternate bill, which was eventually to bear McMahon's name informally and to become the Atomic Energy Act of 1946. As the issue was joined between the two bills, the War Department, in the persons of Secretary Patterson and General Groves, stubbornly backed May–Johnson, while the scientists, their liberal allies, and Secretary Wallace supported the McMahon substitute. Public debate in the winter of 1945–46 tended to emphasize the dangers of military control. Wallace darkly warned against the "possibility of military domination or dictatorship," while Herblock graphically illustrated the issue in the Washington *Post* by caricaturing the army sponsors of May–Johnson as a swarthy, crude gladiator.[38] But the army and its conservative allies did not lack for equally powerful issues to take to the public. In February 1946, the Canadian government announced that it had discovered and neutralized a Soviet spy ring in Ottawa. Later, American intelligence sources disclosed that Alan Nunn May, a British physicist who had wartime access to the Met Lab's work, had passed nuclear data—"secrets"—to Soviet agents through the Canadian ring.

Groves saw his opportunity in these disclosures and thumped away with flag-waving insistence on the primacy of national security and the military's role in preserving it: "Defense must come first and other things will have to come afterward until the international situation is resolved." Conservatives jumped eagerly into the fray with red-baiting. Congresswoman Clare Booth Luce called the commission proposed by the McMahon bill a "commissariat"; the entire bill, she added, displayed "a potentially revolutionary character" and "might have been written by the most ardent Soviet Commissar." J. Parnell Thomas, a member of the House Un-American Activities Committee who was eventually sentenced to prison on kickback charges, coyly suggested that "if you want to get the cue of who is pushing hard for the passage of [the McMahon] bill, read the *Daily Worker.*" Ernie Adamson, chief counsel of the House Un-American Activities Committee, accused the Oak Ridge site organization of advocating "world government" and added that the "security officers at Oak Ridge" feared for the security of the United States because of the McMahon bill's civilian emphasis.[39]

But such appeals to unreason failed. General of the Army Dwight D. Eisenhower and Fleet Admiral Chester Nimitz were untroubled by the civilian emphasis of the McMahon bill. Truman, though he understood nothing of the technical and scientific issues, was unalterably opposed to giving up his control of the commission, as the May–Johnson bill would force him to do. A swell of public support for the McMahon bill, orchestrated by the National Committee for Atomic Information and seconded by influential columnists like Marquis Childs, began to make itself felt in Congress. May was being ominously implicated in the influence-peddling charges that would eventually send him to prison. Though the McMahon bill underwent sweeping amendments in the House, including one that made its security provisions more drastic than the ones that first drew the scientists' fire in May–Johnson, it was the McMahon bill that was enacted in July 1946.

The Atomic Energy Act of 1946, as the McMahon bill was

formally titled, provided the first public statutory framework for the development and the control of nuclear power in the United States.[40] Its final form followed the lines of the McMahon bill, emphasizing civilian control of nuclear power, but it made significant concessions to the bill's opponents, especially in its security provisions. Its Declaration of Policy stated that considerations of national defense were paramount, but that the use of atomic energy should be aimed at improving the standard of living, promoting world peace, and "strengthening free competition in private enterprise," a curious notion in view of the de facto nuclear oligopoly already in place, and in view of the ownership, control, patent, and military application sections that followed.

The act created both the Atomic Energy Commission and the Joint Committee on Atomic Energy. The Commission was composed of five members eventually serving five-year terms, removable by the president only for inefficiency or misconduct, and required by the act to serve full-time, with no outside employment. A general manager served as the executive officer of the commission, coordinating divisions of research, production, engineering, and military applications.

The operative parts of the statute dealt with ownership, control, and military application. The AEC was the owner of all fissionable material to be produced in the future, as well as all existing nuclear facilities except for those too small to produce enough material for a bomb. The AEC could, however, license private organizations to produce fissionable material. It was charged with the production of nuclear weapons and all military research and development. To promote this governmental monopoly of nuclear materials and production, the statute prohibited the issuance of any patents on nuclear inventions, a source of distress to conservative Republicans at first, and dissolved all existing patents, with compensation. The AEC was empowered to issue regulations having the force of law concerning fissionable materials "to protect health or to minimize danger from explosions and other hazards to life or property."

The security provisions of the Atomic Energy Act were lethal, but ambiguous. It flatly banned dissemination of information concerning industrial applications until Congress declared that effective international safeguards were in place, but permitted dissemination of scientific and technical information "so as to provide that free interchange of ideas and criticisms which is essential to scientific progress." Assuming that was a workable distinction, the act went on to make the communication, acquisition, or stealing of restricted data with the intent to injure the United States "or to secure an advantage to any foreign nation" a capital offense, punishable by death, life imprisonment, or a fine of up to $20,000 and twenty years in prison. It also required an FBI security clearance "on the character, associations, and loyalty" of contractors, licensees, and employees of the AEC. These harsh security provisions were not only more extreme than the May–Johnson bill; they even outdid the severity of the long-repudiated Alien and Sedition acts of 1798, most particularly in their imposition of the death penalty in peacetime. For this reason, Alan Barth, an editorial writer for the *Washington Post,* warned that the act made "perilous the very interchange of ideas and information indispensable to scientific progress."[41] But the Federation of Atomic Scientists was willing to overlook these implications because of its relief that other provisions of the Act prevailed over the provisions of May–Johnson.

Finally, the act established an eighteen-member Joint Committee on Atomic Energy to oversee the AEC. Half its members were drawn from the Senate, half from the House. A seemingly routine and innocuous provision required that all bills in either house relating to atomic energy be referred to the committee. This became the source of the JCAE's unique and sweeping legislative powers.

The first Atomic Energy Act, as primitive as the nuclear "piles" that were its contemporaries, contained a clutch of unintended ambiguities. The Joint Committee, for example, was supposed to exercise an oversight function over the AEC, yet the act contained the potential, soon realized, for the Joint Committee to become the AEC's shield instead. The act's antimonopoly provisions and its verbal salute to free enterprise actually enhanced the power of a handful of prime nuclear contractors. Above all, it created a Commission that was to both promote and control the development of nuclear power, an incompatibility of function that became apparent when industry was brought into nuclear development in a big way in the mid-1950s.

5

"Super"

NUCLEAR POWER IN THE COLD WAR

AT THE BEGINNING OF 1947, the newly organized Atomic Energy Commission inherited what its official historians describe as "little more than the remnants of the military organization and facilities" of MED.[1] The Manhattan Project's physical facilities were scattered and their future uncertain. Would atomic energy remain primarily a military resource used to build bombs, or would it be redirected into nonmilitary avenues, toward medical, biological, industrial, and scientific applications? The leadership of the transitional Project was plagued with problems of low professional morale. Scientists left the Project in droves at war's end because they felt their mission was accomplished, or for better pay, or to return to the more congenial climate of academia, or because they resented the role of the army in overseeing security. The Cold War began to trouble the nuclear energy establishment. Security investigations intruded into the lives and professional work of scientists. The 1946 debates over military-vs.-civilian control of nuclear power had done much to enervate nuclear scientists; to their dismay, these debates were about to flare anew. Politically, the period between Hiroshima and early 1947 was a time of policy drift, marked by an absence of any clear directions from civilian political leadership about the future of nuclear power.

The sense of drift dissipated as the chill of the Cold War set in and American military policy underwent a revolutionary about-face from our traditional mistrust of standing armies.

116

Spurred by rising tensions in relations with the Soviet Union, the Truman administration presided over debates in the scientific and political communities on whether the United States should go ahead with development of a monstrous fusion bomb, first called Super and then, in the press, the H-bomb. Truman resolved these debates in favor of Super and produced a policy declaration, known as NSC-68, that committed the United States to both nuclear and conventional militarism. North Korea's invasion of noncommunist South Korea supplied a providential confirmation of Truman's new course. Back at home, the domestic Cold War, exalting considerations of "internal security" just as foreign policy exalted "national security," produced the synthetic drama of witch-hunts that journalists usually dubbed the atom-spy cases, which further insured nuclear power's short-term future as a military option. Nonmilitary potentials of nuclear power languished.

With passage of the Atomic Energy Act of 1946, formal military control of nuclear power's development came to an end. After V-J Day, General Groves superintended the organizational structure of the Manhattan Project on an interim basis. This arrangement continued until January 1, 1947, when the newly constituted Atomic Energy Commission took over. The five commissioners were a diversified lot, except, oddly, in their politics: four of them were Republicans, one an independent, an unusual pattern of choice for the normally partisan Truman. They were:

David E. Lilienthal, chairman: Former head of the Tennessee Valley Authority, he was one of the principal authors of the Acheson–Lilienthal Plan, a knowledgeable and independent public servant who had proven himself to be both politically adroit and an effective administrator.

Lewis L. Strauss: Strauss was later to succeed Lilienthal as chairman of the AEC, but at this time he was a partner in the investment banking firm of Kuhn Loeb and a rear admiral in the naval reserve. He demanded that he be addressed as Admiral Strauss. His wartime service consisted of administrative duties in the office of the secretary of the navy.

Sumner T. Pike: A Maine businessman and another investment banker, Pike served as a commissioner of the Securities and Exchange Commission.

William W. Waymack: Editor of the *Des Moines Register,* winner of a Pulitzer in journalism, and a supporter of the McMahon bill.

Robert F. Bacher: Bacher was a physicist who played a prominent role in development of the bomb at Los Alamos. He returned briefly to Cornell at war's end, but was recalled to government service as a member of Bernard Baruch's staff. As the only scientist member of the AEC, Bacher played an invaluable role in providing expertise to his lay colleagues. He was succeeded by other prominent nuclear scientists: Henry D. Smyth, the physicist who wrote the first official history of the Manhattan Project in 1945; John von Neumann, the mathematician whose work on computers was crucial to development of the H-bomb; Willard F. Libby; and Glenn Seaborg, Nobel laureate chemist and discoverer of plutonium.

The Atomic Energy Commission began its history as it ended it: in a blaze of controversy. Senator Kenneth McKellar, a "pinched, vindictive, and venomous man" who had served in Congress since 1917, launched a petty, personal attack on Lilienthal, the chairman-designate.[2] The Tennessee Democrat nursed a grudge against Lilienthal, who as TVA director had been instrumental in preventing a dam from being named after McKellar and who had thwarted some patronage appointments that McKellar sought. Vengeful to the point of obsession, McKellar sat in with the Joint Committee on the confirmation hearings and was given free rein by JCAE chairman Bourke Hickenlooper in his attempt to discredit Lilienthal. For weeks, McKellar pored over reports of the House Un-American Activities Committee seeking some clue that might disclose Communist affiliations in Lilienthal's past. At one point, McKellar demanded to know the exact birthplace of Lilienthal's parents. When Lilienthal informed him that it was Pressburg, in Czechoslovakia, McKellar shot back that that place is "under the domination of Russia, is it not?" Other conservatives joined in with variations on the theme. New Hampshire Republican Styles Bridges launched into an attack on Lilienthal's "extreme New Dealism" and concluded "as with all left-wingers, it is indicated Lilienthal is sympathetic toward Russia, which is Communist-controlled." Ohio's Robert Taft denounced Lilienthal as "too soft on issues connected with communism and Soviet Russia." He voiced suspicions that Lilienthal had permitted communists to work for the TVA and complained that the Acheson–Lilienthal Plan would have permitted the Soviets to acquire the bomb.[3] But when McKellar finally blurted out, "Your sympathies are very leftist, are they not?" Lilienthal's response, an extemporaneous paean to democracy, impressed uncommitted senators and newspaper editors, and gave his candidacy a powerful boost.[4]

Then the stale issue of military control of the atom reentered. Michigan's GOP Senator Arthur Vandenberg wanted the Military Liaison Committee, which he had inserted into the Atomic Energy Act, to play a greater role in the day-to-day work of the AEC. Eugene Millikin, a right-wing Colorado Republican, improved on that by suggesting that the committee sit in on all meetings of the Commission. Taft even recommended that in view of the crises then building up in Greece and Turkey, the basic design of the Atomic Energy Act be scrapped and the development of nuclear power be returned entirely to military control. But in the end, after wearing debates on the Senate floor, reason prevailed. The Senate abandoned talk of modifying the law, and confirmed Lilienthal as well as all the other nominees.

One of the AEC's first postwar responsibilities, and one that was to contribute mightily to the eventual emergence of nonmilitary applications of nuclear power, was the transformation of the Manhattan Project's physical plant into the National Laboratories and other scientific facilities. In a sharp break with the pre–World War II past, the United States undertook to conduct research under its own auspices, in laboratories that were federal property, by scientists and engineers who were on the federal payroll. The University of Chicago operation had already been removed to Argonne, Illinois, during the war; this was the beginning of the Argonne National Laboratory, the site of the country's earliest research reactors, CP-2 (the rebuilt version of CP-1) and CP-3. Walter H. Zinn, active in the Manhattan Project, provided dynamic leadership for Argonne. By 1947, the AEC determined to center all research on reactor development at ANL.

Things did not go so smoothly at the Clinton Laboratories at Oak Ridge, which were undergoing a crisis of morale caused by the change in its industrial leadership. Monsanto Chemical Company withdrew from its contract to manage the laboratories, and a proposal to have the University of Chicago take over direction foundered because Lilienthal distrusted Chancellor Robert M. Hutchins's attitudes toward nuclear research. Lilienthal's belief that academic research was being overemphasized at the expense of industrial research led him to substitute Union Carbide and Carbon Corporation as the contractor responsible for running what was to become Oak Ridge National Laboratory. Union Carbide soon became one of the nation's largest nuclear contractors. Although ORNL began as an industrial research laboratory, academic research was not neglected there. A regional partnership of universities, the Oak Ridge Universities Association, established a research consortium that enabled their scientists to participate in the activities of the federal facility. ANL subsequently adopted this arrangement for the Argonne Universities Association.

The third of the National Laboratories, Brookhaven, emerged in quite a different way. Its nucleus was the Columbia University–based group of Manhattan Project scientists. They selected an unused army barracks on Long Island, organized the Associated Universities, a group that would provide scientific personnel for the laboratory, and presented a fait accompli to the newly formed AEC in 1947.

The towering figure of Ernest O. Lawrence dominated a fourth major facility, the Berkeley Radiation Laboratory, which never became a National Laboratory. Maintained under the auspices of the University of California, it became the Lawrence Radiation Laboratory, and was later joined by an institution designed for weapons research at Livermore, California, some thirty miles away, which became the Lawrence Livermore Laboratory. At these institutions, Lawrence nursed his dreams of monster cyclotrons and Edward Teller incubated the Super project.

Though the three National Laboratories and the Lawrence labs constituted the main centers of nuclear research in the United

States in the late 1940s, other facilities comprised important parts of the nuclear network. Los Alamos, under the direction of Norris Bradbury, Oppenheimer's successor, became the Los Alamos Scientific Laboratory, but its mission remained exclusively devoted to weapons development. Sandia Laboratory near Albuquerque was also devoted to weapons research, but with an industrial slant. Hanford remained a production facility. The Knolls Atomic Power Laboratory on the Mohawk River near Schenectady, New York, a General Electric installation, undertook reactor research. Westinghouse's Bettis Laboratories, near Pittsburgh, played a major role in the development of propulsion reactors.

During the first years of the AEC, a body known as the General Advisory Committee played a policymaking role that virtually rivaled that of the AEC itself. This was due largely to the great prestige of the scientist members of the Advisory Committee. Chaired by Oppenheimer, the committee as it existed until 1950 included Conant, Fermi, Cal Tech president Lee DuBridge, Isidor Rabi, and Glenn Seaborg, among others. Meeting for the first time in January 1947, the GAC was joined by directors of other atomic energy laboratories—Walter Zinn from Argonne; Lawrence from the Radiation Laboratory at Berkeley; Wigner, then head of the Clinton Laboratories at Oak Ridge; Norris Bradbury, director of Los Alamos; and Frank Spedding of the Ames Laboratory at Iowa State College (now University). Their task was to formulate a basic research agenda for nuclear power in the United States. The GAC debated the relative merits of weapons development versus civilian reactors, with Oppenheimer stressing the potential of reactors for transforming the image of atomic energy from Hiroshima to peaceful applications, and Fermi militantly demanding expanded weapons production, including research on a thermonuclear bomb. In the end, the Fermi view prevailed, and the GAC's recommendation for priority in weapons was instrumental in committing the AEC to the same view, which in turn was the basis for President Truman's policy decision to make weapons the highest priority of the American atomic energy program. This trend exemplified what the official historians of the AEC have termed "the inexorable shift . . . from the idealistic hopeful anticipation of the peaceful atom to the grim realization that for reasons of national security atomic energy would have to continue to bear the image of war."[5] The 1946 hopes of many that atomic energy could be diverted from the arms race to peaceful applications wilted in the chill of the Cold War.

Shortly after its organization, the AEC reported to President Truman that there were no nuclear weapons assembled for immediate use, and that the number for which components were available for assembly was quite small. The AEC left the number blank in its written report, and the exact number was supplied orally by Lilienthal to the president. Truman seemed shocked, and therefore receptive to the GAC–AEC recommendation that it pursue weapons testing, manufacture more bombs, and develop sources of raw materials, especially uranium. Coinciding, as it did, with the president's enunciation of the Truman Doctrine, this basic policy recommendation committed the AEC primarily to a military orientation that it never lost.

Mounting Cold War tensions drove policymakers to seek American military superiority over the Soviet Union, but America's drastic demobilization in 1945–46 resulted in a vast numerical inferiority compared to the 4-million-man Red Army. Moreover, the Soviet forces had the advantage of being at or near the confrontation points in Europe, while American forces, except occupation troops in Japan and western Germany, were stationed in the United States. The United States reduced its army eightfold, from 8 million to one million men. The navy was going into mothballs, its personnel being reduced from 3.5 million to less than a million. George C. Marshall expressed the American dilemma pungently:

> When I was Secretary of State I was being pressed constantly . . . to give the Russians hell. . . . At that time [1947], my facilities for giving them hell—and I am a soldier and know something about the ability to give hell—was 1 1/3 divisions over the entire United States. That is quite a proposition when you deal with somebody with over 260 and you have 1 1/3.[6]

Given this seemingly irreversible disparity of ground forces, American policymakers from Truman down found it comforting to retain the Truman–Byrnes assumption that nuclear weapons could offset Soviet advantages, and they pushed for more and bigger bombs. The AEC was charged with supplying them.

Organizationally, military emphasis was built into the structure of the AEC from the beginning. One of its four operating divisions was military applications. A military liaison committee, consisting of six officers, was appointed by the Department of Defense to participate in the AEC's weapons work, particularly weapons testing. The armed services retained for themselves the intelligence function of the Manhattan Project, rather than transferring it to the AEC. The army placed intelligence and other nuclear-related functions in a new military agency, first called the Armed Forces Special Weapons Project, and later the Defense Atomic Support Agency, providing yet another link between the AEC and the Defense Department. The ties were so close that an incoming secretary of defense is supposed to have asked, after being shown the Department of Defense organization chart, "Where is the AEC?"[7]

The military did more than shuffle organization charts. As if to assert military predominance in nuclear development, in the summer of 1946 the navy set off two fission shots, code-named Operation Crossroads, on the Bikini atoll in the Marshall islands, then a United States protectorate. Shot Able was atmospheric, shot Baker underwater. Neither had any legitimate scientific purpose. Their only point was to enable the navy to elbow a place for itself alongside the army at the nuclear trough. American nuclear scientists, by then organized into the Federation of Atomic Scientists, protested to no effect, objecting not to fallout but to the pointlessness of the exercise. They accused their government of saber rattling to emphasize its position at the United Nations debates on international control of atomic power. Then, in the midst of the Berlin blockade in the spring of 1948, the Defense Department conducted a joint series of three test explosions code-named Sandstone on the Eniwetok atoll, the last to be conducted under military auspices before the AEC took over the responsibility for atmospheric testing in 1951. Sandstone demonstrated that many World War II–era components of nuclear weapons were already obsolete, and indicated the need for more research reactors, an accelerated program of materials testing, and other engineering research and design.

In 1948, the AEC had to surmount yet another challenge to civilian control of nuclear power. In varying degrees, Secretary of Defense James Forrestal; General Kenneth Nichols, who was Groves's successor as head of the Armed Forces Special Weapons Project; and Donald F. Carpenter, new civilian head of the Military Liaison Committee, all favored transferring "custody" of the stockpile of nuclear weapons from the AEC to the armed forces. Lilienthal and the AEC successfully fended off this challenge once again, persuading Truman to order that custody of nuclear weapons was to remain in civilian hands, that is, the AEC. The Commission then turned to more realistic questions of military application—this time not for bombs, but for propulsion.

Military interest in nuclear power as a source of propulsion dated from the last year of World War II, when an alert army air corps colonel, Donald J. Keirn, sought entry into the Manhattan Project to determine the feasibility of using nuclear power for aircraft propulsion. By 1946, this interest had developed into a full-blown, long-lived project known as NEPA: Nuclear Energy for the Propulsion of Aircraft. The idea of using a nuclear reactor as an engine to propel aircraft by heating air to create a jet force grew increasingly fantastic as time went on, and the air force was never able to surmount such obvious difficulties as the danger of dispersing radioactive material in a crash, or the weight problem caused by essential core shielding. Despite this, NEPA, later known as Project Kiwi, persisted stubbornly until the Kennedy administration killed it in March 1961. In its early years, though, nuclear power seemed feasible enough for both aircraft and rockets to merit a substantial air force commitment to research on the project. The military rationale for the nuclear-powered aircraft was that the air forces of the world, including that of the United States, were in danger of becoming too defense-oriented through the development of fuel-guzzling, high-speed defense fighters, leaving the long-range strategic bombers, necessary to deliver atomic bombs, at a disadvantage relative to the fighters that would be attacking them. This possibility particularly worried

General Curtis LeMay, a leading proponent of strategic air power.

The navy was also interested in nuclear power for propulsion. Unlike the air force, naval nuclear had a bright future, but the navy was a Johnny-come-lately to the field and could do little more to promote its interests than send a team of observers, headed by Captain Hyman Rickover, to Clinton Laboratories to learn about reactor technology. But the navy group, like its chief, was intense and hard-working, and established a reputation now legendary for its dedication to exploiting nuclear power for naval propulsion. Even before the AEC was organized, Rickover had cooperated with General Electric to design a propulsion reactor for a destroyer escort, the smallest of naval warships. He was confident that GE could develop a sodium-cooled reactor for a surface vessel by 1948 and for a submarine by 1950. Though this timetable proved overly optimistic, the Rickover/GE interest marked the remote beginnings of nonmilitary nuclear power in the United States. Rickover's dedication paid off when the navy launched its first nuclear-powered submarine, the *Nautilus,* in January 1954.

These beginnings were destined to remain remote, however. The military emphasis that the Truman administration and the AEC itself imposed on America's nuclear program virtually excluded any serious attention to nonmilitary applications. Such interest as there was in reactors having no direct military potential was continuously forced to the bottom of the AEC's list of priorities. The Commission had to allocate resources (funding and people) among four different types of reactor programs:

1. Production: reactors whose primary purpose was manufacturing plutonium for nuclear weapons

2. Propulsion

3. Experimental and research: small reactors designed to test the behavior of materials, provide neutron sources for scientific experiments, or material for medical and industrial use

4. Power: reactors designed to heat steam, which would turn conventional turbines that would power generators to produce electricity

In addition, hybrids were possible, the most likely combination being production and power. The January 1947 GAC report to its parent body, the AEC, did survey the potential for nonmilitary applications. It stressed the need for research reactors and for developing reactors as a source of power. But the report recognized that the uncertainty of foreign sources of uranium ore would be a barrier to expanded reactor development. In 1947, the United States' principal source of uranium ore was the Shinkolobwe mine of the then Belgian Congo (now Zaire), which was projected to be played out by 1952. The Union of South Africa was another potential source, but it was then still a member of the British Commonwealth, and developing difficulties with the United Kingdom over technical cooperation, coupled with British resentment at the policy of exclusion embodied in the Atomic Energy Act, made South Africa a questionable source. The deposits of the Colorado plateau were just beginning to dribble in, and could not provide a sufficient short-term supply. Recovery of fissionable materials from wastes at Hanford might help eke out the supply.

To cope with these difficulties in the long term, the GAC proposed that the AEC heavily promote the breeder, a reactor designed to produce a greater fuel output than the fuel fed into it. The theoretical basis of the breeder was that the fission of uranium or plutonium produced fractionally more than two neutrons. If one of these neutrons was used to bombard another nucleus to keep the chain reaction going, the second, and the occasional third, might be "captured" by fertile material to create a new atom of fissionable material. For this reason, ANL director Walter Zinn promoted research on a fast breeder at his National Lab, while GE worked on an intermediate breeder at Knolls.

But after nearly a year's deliberation, the AEC in 1948 reached a highly pessimistic conclusion on the development of power reactors. It stressed the engineering difficulties in the way of breeders, such as high operating temperatures and the behavior of materials in the unprecedented physical environment of nuclear reactors. From this, it concluded that power reactors would be feasible, in the sense of being competitive with fossil-fuel-fired power plants, only by the development of cheap, low-grade uranium ores. The Commission also recognized that the capital cost of a nuclear power plant would always remain higher than a conventional plant. It concluded that it would not "be possible under the most favorable circumstances to have any considerable portion of the present power supply of the world replaced by nuclear fuel before the expiration of twenty years."[8]

Nevertheless, AEC Commissioner Bacher and General Manager Carroll Wilson kept alive some interest in nonmilitary reactor research and development in 1948. Wilson solicited industrial consultation in October 1948, and met with Oliver Buckley, president of Bell Telephone Laboratories and a member of the General Advisory Committee; Crawford Greenewalt of DuPont, who had played an important role in DuPont's participation in the Hanford activity; and Eger Murphree of Standard Oil Development Company, another Manhattan Project veteran. Nothing immediate came of this consultation: Greenewalt thought that Wilson had underestimated difficulties in developing reactors. But industry had established an interested presence in deliberations on nonmilitary nuclear power at the very beginnings of AEC activity in that area.

Another damper on reactor development was the problem of safeguards. The AEC in 1948 established a reactor safeguard committee, a remote ancestor of the Advisory Committee on Reactor Safeguards created by statute in 1957. The first safeguards committee, chaired by Edward Teller, debated siting problems for a high-flux experimental reactor at Argonne. Generally adopting a conservative approach in the early years, the committee refused to approve a reactor larger than 1,000 kilowatts,* demonstrated a preference for remote siting as a safety technique, and expressed concern over the handling of radioactive wastes in populated areas.[9]

These relatively feeble stirrings of interest in civilian reactors were quickly blighted by a threat to American security that vindicated the wartime warnings of Bohr and Szilard. On August 29, 1949, at a place called Semipalatinsk in Siberia, the Soviets ex-

*An extremely small unit. For comparison purposes, most power reactors under construction in the late 1970s had a capacity of approximately 1,000 megawatts (1 megawatt = 1,000 kilowatts).

ploded their first atomic bomb. Some days later, a specially equipped American B-29 bomber on an air sampling mission over the Pacific detected radioactive debris from the explosion and relayed the news to Washington. President Truman publicly announced the end of America's nuclear monopoly and simultaneously restated his desire for the establishment of a "truly effective, and enforceable" system for the "international control of atomic energy." But in spite of the president's statement, which was enthusiastically seconded by Eugene Rabinowitch, the editor of the *Bulletin of Atomic Scientists,* and Linus Pauling, then the president of the American Chemical Society, Washington undertook no major new effort in the area of disarmament.

The shock to American pride was profound. President Truman, in the best position of any American to know the truth, could scarcely bring himself to believe that "those Asiatics" were capable of building an atomic bomb. He required Lilienthal, Bacher, and others to sign a statement asserting that they believed that the Soviets had actually detonated a nuclear weapon. Even at the end of his presidency, three years later, Truman still had difficulty believing it. He then stated to an interviewer that "I am not convinced Russia has the bomb. I am not convinced that Russians have achieved the know-how to put the complicated mechanism together to make an A-bomb work."[10] This attitude, widely shared, intensified the Cold War, as frightened, angry conservatives hunted the traitors who had given the "secret" of the bomb away. Such a mentality fueled the arms race. It reinforced the military orientation of nuclear power, among other things boosting work on the navy propulsion reactor to a high priority. Above all, the Soviet bomb forced the Super debates to a resolution.

The principle of Super dated back to theoretical work done in the 1930s by Hans Bethe on thermonuclear fusion processes that take place under the conditions of high temperature and pressure in the interiors of the stars. For this work he received the physics Nobel in 1967. When fission explosions made it seem possible that stellar temperatures and pressures could be reproduced on Earth, Fermi, Teller, and a few others began thinking about the possibility of an uncontrolled fusion reaction involving deuterium or tritium, both heavy forms of hydrogen; hence the popular name, "hydrogen bomb." These might be made to fuse, producing helium nuclei and vastly greater amounts of energy than was possible by the fission of heavy elements. But only a handful of men, led by Teller, worked actively on fusion reactions at Los Alamos during the war, because the scientific community's energies were directed toward the fission bomb, then closer to realization. After the war, a small group continued to develop fusion, though Teller had left Los Alamos for an academic appointment at the University of Chicago. Their work necessarily had to be theoretical rather than experimental, because they could rarely have access to the conditions of high temperature and pressure necessary for study of behavior of light atoms in the fusion process. Because of this theoretical bias, mathematics played a central role in the development of Super, since calculations had to depend on probability theories rather than laboratory experiments. John von Neumann and his Polish associate, Stanislaw Ulam, played key roles here as the foremost mathematicians associated with the project.

The Soviet bomb injected an urgent note into the ongoing debates over the future of nuclear weapons. This debate was carried on at two levels. The first, the public level, had little to do with the technical potential of a fusion weapon, and was concerned rather with the old problems of secrecy, international control, and espionage. Largely a recap of the arguments of three years earlier, the public debates did not even include Super as a topic until Colorado Senator Edwin Johnson, a member of the JCAE, leaked it in November 1949, and James Reston ran the story on page one of *The New York Times* in January 1950. By that time, it was too late to influence the real decisionmaking process. The second debate was carried on in secrecy, and never involved more than a hundred individuals: the members of the General Advisory Committee, its parent organization the AEC, some AEC and JCAE staffers, a few high-echelon Defense Department officials, and some scientists at Los Alamos and Berkeley not formally connected with any of these government organizations.

Among those insiders who knew something about Super, momentum built up quickly in favor of going ahead with the monster weapon. AEC commissioner Strauss reacted in a panicky way to the news of the Soviet bomb, demanding a "quantum jump" in weapons like Super to offset the Soviet gains.[11] Strauss approached Truman through Admiral Sidney Souers, an intelligence and security consultant to the AEC and first executive secretary of the National Security Council. Truman responded with interest. Meanwhile, Ernest O. Lawrence, as always a high-technology hawk on defense issues, and his colleague Luis Alvarez stopped at Los Alamos to confer with Teller and Ulam. Then they flew on to Washington, where they peddled Super to Defense and AEC officials, Senator Brien McMahon, who was now chairman of the JCAE, and the AEC commissioners. Lilienthal thought that Lawrence and Alvarez were "drooling" over Super. Lawrence also used General Kenneth Nichols as an intermediary to persuade the Joint Chiefs of Staff to demand the weapon. Thus a formidable lobby of scientists, military men, and civilian officials were backing Super even before there was any assurance that it could be built.

Some scientists doubted that they could build a fusion weapon compact enough to be delivered to its target.[12] Fissionable materials, which would be essential for the project, were scarce. Since American scientists had already developed nuclear weapons twenty-five times more powerful than the Hiroshima bomb, Super's doubters argued that it made more sense to step up "conventional" nuclear development rather than spend scarce dollars and even more scarce uranium and plutonium on what might turn out to be a futile effort.

These disagreements were funneled first to the AEC and then to the General Advisory Committee, which at that time still included all its original members: Oppenheimer (its chair), Conant, DuBridge, Fermi, Rabi, Seaborg (absent in Sweden), and several lesser-known scientists. After two days of intensive debate, the GAC recommended to the AEC that Super not be developed. The GAC condemned Super as a weapon not usable

> exclusively for the destruction of material installations of military or semi-military purposes. Its use therefore carries much further

than the atomic bomb itself the policy of exterminating civilian populations.

In separate opinions elaborating on the reasons for the full committee's recommendation, Conant, joined by five others including Oppenheimer, warned that Super was potentially "a weapon of genocide" because of its massive explosive force ("its use would involve a decision to slaughter a vast number of civilians") and its greater radioactive contamination. It "represents a threat to the future of the human race which is intolerable." In a separate opinion, Rabi and Fermi were more emphatic: Super "is necessarily an evil thing considered in any light." As a genocidal weapon, Super "cannot be justified on any ethical ground."[13] The GAC therefore recommended that the United States publicly renounce any intention of developing the weapon. The only division among committee members came at this point. Some believed that the United States ought to undertake an unconditional self-denying commitment. Others felt that self-denial ought to be contingent upon a similar pledge by the Soviets. The committee acknowledged that the Soviets might proceed to develop a super bomb no matter what the United States did. But at least a majority of its members, Oppenheimer included, thought there was actually little danger in this. If, on the one hand, the Soviets did develop "the super," they could attack the United States only at the risk of large-scale retaliation by America's nuclear forces. On the other hand, if the United States denied itself a thermonuclear capability, perhaps the Russians would too. The risk seemed worth the gamble because the alternative was to place unimaginable destructive power in the hands of military and political leaders not only in the United States and the Soviet Union but ultimately in a number of other countries as well.

The firm and nearly unanimous position of the General Advisory Committee proved to be the only real obstacle to Super, though.[14] The AEC was divided and equivocal, due in large measure to the fact that Lilienthal had some weeks earlier submitted his resignation and no longer had the stomach for a fight. Tired and dispirited, he watched Super's advocates burrow inerrantly toward key decisionmakers. The AEC endorsed the GAC's recommendations, but only by a 3–2 vote, and Strauss, one of the minority, worked harder than ever for Super. Much more influential was Senator McMahon, now dogmatic on the need for Super and hysterical at the thought of the Soviet bomb. McMahon saw the issue in apocalyptic terms: "If we let the Russians get the Super first, catastrophe becomes all but certain—whereas, if we get it first, there exists a chance of saving ourselves." The decision to renounce Super, McMahon said, "might well mean unconditional surrendering in advance—by the United States to alien forces of evil."[15] McMahon was becoming dangerously rabid on Super: Lilienthal recorded him as advocating preventive war with the Soviet Union: "Blow them off the face of the earth, quick, before they do the same to us—and we haven't much time."[16]

A few scientists other than the Lawrence–Teller–Alvarez nexus also backed Super. Karl Compton and, surprisingly, Harold Urey, both supported it. The JCAE, strongly influenced by McMahon, was also moving, without information or deliberations, toward backing Super. Not surprisingly, the Joint Chiefs of Staff and the Department of Defense backed it. In a position paper, the Joint Chiefs argued simplisticly that the United States should develop all weapons necessary to thwart communist aggression. They brushed aside moral arguments as "foolhardy altruism." It was "folly to argue whether one weapon is more immoral than another," they countered, thus entirely missing Rabi's and Conant's point about genocide.[17]

But, as the sign on Truman's desk said, "The buck stops here," and the president would have ultimate responsibility for the decision. Though there was probably never any doubt in his mind about Super, he first referred the question to a special subcommittee of the National Security Council that had previously been organized to coordinate military requirements with AEC programs, consisting of Secretary of Defense Louis Johnson, Lilienthal, and Secretary of State Dean Acheson. With Johnson supporting the Joint Chiefs/JCAE position, and Lilienthal backing the GAC view, the swing vote on the NSC subcommittee would be Acheson's. Already deeply committed to the views that made him the cold warrior par excellence, Acheson backed Super. In later autobiographical reminiscences, he dismissed the position of the GAC scientists. He was, he recalled

> not so much moved by the power of its logic (which I was never able to perceive—neither the maintenance of ignorance nor the reliance on perpetual goodwill seemed to me a tenable policy) as by an immense distaste for what one of them . . . described as "the whole rotten business."[18]

Though Acheson respected both Lilienthal and Oppenheimer, and had little use for Louis Johnson, he nevertheless supported the Pentagon view. He was convinced that only overwhelming power would deter the Soviets from attempts to expand their sphere. Whether or not the United States went ahead with thermonuclear research, he was satisfied that the Soviets would. Oppenheimer and Lilienthal were both, he believed, laboring under the delusion that Stalin was reasonable.

A minority of one on the NSC subcommittee, Lilienthal acquiesced in a recommendation that Super be developed. He did, however, manage to arrange an interview with the president at which he expressed grave reservations about the hydrogen bomb project as well as the dangerous emphasis the United States was placing on weapons of mass destruction as the underpinning of its foreign policy. But Truman, fuming that Lilienthal had gone soft, refused to hear him out. On January 31, 1950, he announced his decision to develop this new and terrifying weapon.

The nuclear arms race has a tragic quality of the inevitable about it. Though for many months the secret debate over Super raged in scientific and political circles, in retrospect it seems clear that President Truman could not have made any decision other than to authorize the development of thermonuclear weapons. The logic of the Cold War required it. Save for a very few Soviet experts—particularly George Kennan, who was rapidly shedding his earlier hard-line attitudes, and Charles Bohlen—the entire foreign policy establishment, including Secretary Acheson, assumed that the Soviets were unalterably committed to our destruction. If the United States did not proceed with the H-bomb, they would, and if they developed it first they would use it. Given this set of assumptions and the fear that underlay them, the only reasonable course was to maintain United States superiority. And so began a new, more deadly phase in the history of the arms race, for as Oppenheimer and Lilienthal had tried to point out, this weapon was something far different, far more devastating than the nuclear weapons that preceded it. Later, an aging Winston Churchill would put it most eloquently:

> There is an immense gulf between the atomic and the hydrogen bomb. The atomic bomb, with all its terror, did not carry us outside the scope of human control or manageable events in thought or action, in peace or war. But . . . [with] the hydrogen bomb, the entire foundation of human affairs was revolutionized.[19]

At the same time that he directed work on Super to proceed, President Truman asserted cryptically that "we shall also continue to examine all those factors that affect our program for peace and this country's security."[20] Vague though this may have seemed at the time, it nonetheless announced the beginning of a profound reversal in the traditions of American strategic policy. In reaction to the various foreign policy crises of the preceding two years, and in anticipation of the costs of developing Super, just one item in a long list of new weapons systems, the Truman administration was about to embark on a program of massive rearmament and budget-busting military spending. Embodied in the National Security Council study paper of 1950 known as "NSC-68," the new Truman strategic policy provided an essential underpinning to the 1947 Truman Doctrine, which committed the United States to the role of world policeman. Super was to be the most potent item in the policeman's arsenal of weapons.

From the time that he took over the State Department in 1949, Dean Acheson was troubled by the obvious lack of coordination between American foreign and military policy. Beginning in 1947 with the Truman Doctrine, the United States had undertaken a long-term struggle with the Soviets to establish global supremacy, but the armed services languished with budgets that seemed hopelessly inadequate. The army and navy were both badly under strength. Even the air force, which then had sole responsibility for delivering atomic bombs if there should be a war, was not well prepared. The backbone of the Strategic Air Command was the B-29 Superfortress. But this World War II relic did not have the range to strike at the Soviet Union from bases in the United States. In fact, at that time, the only bases from which B-29s could fly against the Soviets were in Great Britain. Moreover, this slow-flying bomber was becoming increasingly vulnerable to modern jet interceptors being built by the Russians.

Acheson believed that the United States would have to add to its military strength both in conventional forces and in its nuclear striking power. But many obstacles stood in the way. First, there was the conventional economic wisdom of the time. Edwin G. Nourse, the chairman of the president's Council of Economic Advisers, like many other conservative economists, warned that the nation could not afford to spend significantly more than was being allocated for national security. Too much nonproductive military spending, he feared, would produce serious economic dislocations. Like Nourse, Secretary of Defense Louis Johnson was also opposed to increased military spending. When he was appointed to replace James Forrestal as the head of the Defense Department, Johnson was told by President Truman that he must do everything possible to keep the lid on spending. Johnson took the president at his word and so cowed the military that even members of the Joint Chiefs of Staff were reluctant to attack budget allocations that they believed were too restrictive. Finally, Acheson had to contend with the president himself, who was intent upon maintaining a balanced budget and meeting all domestic obligations before allocating a penny for the military.

But Acheson had certain advantages, too. In the first place, only he knew the extent of the revolution he was contemplating: the force levels he had in mind would require tripling the defense budget overnight. Others could only guess at his intentions. Too, before he actually began to act, one of the most formidable obstacles to success conveniently disappeared when Nourse resigned as chairman of the Council of Economic Advisers to be replaced by the old New Dealer and Keynesian economist Leon Keyserling. Concerned by the 1949 recession and the rising level of unemployment the nation was experiencing, Keyserling offered what was to become the standard prescription for economic problems of this sort. The government should spend to stimulate economic growth and reduce unemployment. As he began planning for rearmament, Acheson did not have to concern himself about opposition from the council. In fact, Keyserling became an ally of Acheson by issuing dire warnings about the dangers of international communism and urging increased spending for national defense.

Other developments were to prove even more helpful to Acheson. Though neither the final collapse of the Nationalist regime in China nor the Soviet atomic test came as total surprises at the State Department, they did present Acheson with an opportunity to press for a reexamination of America's military posture. It was clear, he later wrote, that "changes in power relationships were imminent." Thus, at Acheson's urging, the president directed the State and Defense Departments "to undertake a reexamination of our objectives in peace and war and of the effect of these objectives on our strategic plans in the light of the probable fission bomb capability and possible thermonuclear bomb capability of the Soviet Union."[21] As Acheson, one of the most skilled bureaucratic infighters of his generation, well understood, it was a long way from making a study to winning congressional and presidential approval for rearmament. But the first important step had been taken.

Having won presidential approval for a study of America's defense needs, Acheson turned the job over to his policy planning staff. Again fortune smiled. Until recently the policy planning unit of the State Department had been headed by George Kennan, who had become completely out of sympathy with the developing militarization of American foreign policy, and who certainly would not have produced the report that Acheson needed. But a short while before, Kennan had resigned, to be replaced by Paul Nitze. Acheson and Nitze, an investment banker when not employed by the State Department, shared the same world view and were both advocates of a massive peacetime military establishment.

The president's order called for a joint study to be conducted by the state and defense departments. A coterie of Defense Department planners, including Major General James H. Burns and General Truman Landon, participated in the committee's deliberations. But the burden of the work was borne by Nitze and a few of his State Department intimates. The State Department personnel on the committee were clear about what they hoped to accomplish. Their Defense Department co-workers, however, went from meeting to meeting with no direction whatsoever from Secretary of Defense Johnson. In his memoirs, Acheson suggests that Johnson was not involved or even well informed regarding the progress of the joint study because communication between the two departments hardly existed at that time. But the evidence suggests that Johnson, who strongly opposed increased defense spending, was deliberately kept in the dark and that Acheson was involved in one of the more impressive end runs in the history of bureaucratic politics.

It was not until after the joint state–defense study committee had produced a document recommending a massive expansion of America's military strength that Secretary Johnson discovered what was going on. There followed an angry confrontation between Acheson and Johnson after which the secretary of state again outmaneuvered his cabinet colleague by winning endorsements for the study of each of the service secretaries as well as the members of the Joint Chiefs of Staff. In the end, Johnson too was forced to add his endorsement to the plan. He really had little choice in the matter. The alternative was to have his name conspicuously absent from a document all others approved when it went to the president.

Ultimately, the paper produced by a joint State–Defense Department task force was presented to the National Security Council where, designated National Security Council working paper #68, it took its place as one of the most important statements in the history of American foreign policy. It was an extraordinary piece of work, presenting an astonishingly overdrawn, not to say outlandish, evaluation of Soviet intentions and capabilities. The authors of NSC-68 contended that "the Soviet Union, unlike previous aspirants to hegemony, is animated by a new fanatic faith, antithetical to our own, and seeks to impose its absolute authority over the rest of the world." As the leader of a "worldwide revolutionary movement" and "the inheritor of Russian imperialism" the Soviet Union would not, indeed could not, rest until the United States had been destroyed.[22] This threat to the continued existence of the republic, the paper made plain, was both immediate and extreme.

Though the authors of NSC-68 sounded overwrought when describing the Soviet menace, they reverted to standard, nearly emotionless bureaucratese in describing how the United States might respond to it. In the style characteristic of national security managers then and now, they laid out four options. Two of these, however, were never seriously considered. There was no support among the members of the NSC for a do-nothing approach to the Soviet threat. Nor did the "Fortress America" concept advanced by Republican conservatives, including Senator Robert A. Taft of Ohio and former President Herbert Hoover, produce any enthusiasm. This idea called for the United States to withdraw from Europe and Asia and concentrate its interests in the Western Hemisphere. State and Defense Department officials agreed that any such move would create a vast power vacuum that could only be filled by the Soviet Union. The end result, they were certain, would be that the world balance of power would shift decisively against us. Acheson, Nitze, and Johnson were unwilling to take the risks entailed by this option.

The first of the two options seriously considered was a preventive war against the Soviet Union. Air Force General Nathan Twining, chairman of the Joint Chiefs of Staff from 1957 to 1960, was not himself on the National Security Council at the time. But he was obviously privy to the debate over NSC-68 and he discussed it in his 1966 book *Neither Liberty Nor Safety*. According to Twining, "pre-emptive action" was vigorously advocated by "some very dedicated Americans." They argued that since the Soviets were bent upon our destruction and ultimately the United States would fight "to preserve our way of life," action should be taken before the enemy developed "nation-killing capabilities." Twining recalls that someone at the meeting— probably one or more of the Joint Chiefs—proposed that an ultimatum be delivered to the Soviets demanding "a stop to international Communist infiltration and subversion" and that they "replace the Iron Curtain with an open door." The advocates of preventive war assumed the Soviets would reject this demand, thus freeing the United States to take action.[23]

A majority on the National Security Council rejected the preventive war option. Some opponents struck a moral pose, arguing that the United States could not sully its international reputation by striking first. Evidently that was still the sort of thing that only Japanese did. More to the point, however, many "sincerely believed that the Red Army could quickly neutralize and capture Western Europe even if we used our small existing stock of nuclear weapons in a direct attack upon the U.S.S.R."[24] This certainly must have seemed so to Secretary Acheson, who, in recalling his opposition to the preventive war option, made no reference whatsoever to ethical considerations. He rejected the idea because, as he put it, such an approach would solve nothing and only complicate matters immeasurably.

The National Security Council adopted as its recommendation a fourth possibility, one supported by Acheson and Nitze. The deterrent strategy that had been central to American foreign and military policy since the beginning of the Cold War would be continued. But in order to make it credible, American conventional and nuclear forces would be vastly expanded. Only by preparing for any military contingency, the authors of NSC-68 believed, could the United States hope to deter Soviet expansionism short of war. The cost of preparedness would undoubtedly be high. But any other course would ultimately prove more costly.

In April 1950, the president approved NSC-68 and its fourth option, thus committing himself in principle to an arms race with the Soviets. He refused to approve the specific programs recommended in the document, however, preferring instead to wait for cost estimates. Winning presidential approval was an important step forward on the road to rearmament. But for Acheson, Nitze, and other supporters of the program, many obstacles still loomed. It was certain to be difficult to persuade Congress and the American public to foot the bill for a massive, costly militarization of American foreign policy, and to sustain the new level of expenditure year after year. The joint state–defense working group that had drafted NSC-68 foresaw this; hence the nearly hysterical tone of the paper as well as the grotesquely oversimplified caricature of Soviet purposes it contained. Acheson and other State and Defense Department planners were interested in selling rearmament, not in engaging in a debate about the true nature of Soviet Communism. Thus, as Paul Y. Hammond has explained:

> The simplification of the political dimensions of the Communist bloc can . . . be attributed to the Truman Administration's efforts to popularize its rearmament plans and to unite foreign policy factions within the executive branch and Congress behind a common program.[25]

The authors of NSC-68 succeeded in eliciting the terrified reaction they sought. Certainly when Charles Murphy, the president's special counsel, read the paper he was stunned. "What I read," he later recalled, "scared me so much that the next day I didn't go to the office at all."[26] Instead Murphy remained at home reading and re-reading the paper. At length, he concluded that the United States had no choice save to rearm, and quickly.

The authors of NSC-68 had deliberately avoided attaching cost estimates to their proposal because they feared alienating the president, who remained committed to a balanced budget. When Truman approved their policy recommendations he still had no idea how much it would cost and was unwilling to have his hand forced by Congress until the program had some price tag attached to it. Meanwhile, during the spring of 1950 elements of the federal bureaucracy outside the State and Defense Departments gained access to NSC-68. Frank Pace, the director of the Bureau of the Budget, was particularly critical of the plan because it would have a disastrous impact on efforts to balance the budget. This gave some members of the Joint Chiefs of Staff second thoughts and they too began to withdraw support. For a time, NSC-68 was nearly sitting dead in the water while the Budget Bureau took pot shots at it and the Joint Chiefs waffled. Meanwhile, an increasingly concerned president demanded cost estimates. Advocates of rearmament were stymied. Their program, one later recalled, was "being nibbled away by the ducks."[27]

The Korean War changed everything. Literally overnight, opposition to rearmament withered on the vine. Ironically, Frank

Pace, who had led the opposition to NSC-68, moved over to the Army Department where he became one of its greatest advocates. There is an old adage in Washington that goes, "Where you sit is where you stand." Pace exemplified that adage perfectly. As President Truman later explained, the North Korean attack "made danger clear to everyone" and paved the way for a substantial upgrading in American military might. Years after the event, Secretary Acheson was still almost gleeful as he recalled how doubtful it was "whether anything like what happened in the next few years could have been done had not the Russians been stupid enough to have instigated the attack on South Korea." Noted another high State Department official, "Thank God Korea came along."[28]

The journalist I. F. Stone has contended that the Truman administration, operating through the South Korean government, actually provoked the Korean War in order to justify rearmament. While it is true that some members of the administration had considered manufacturing a crisis of sorts, the evidence in support of Stone's thesis is very thin and entirely circumstantial. The impetus for the Korean War came from North Korea. Having recognized that, however, it is equally important to note that administration leaders were quick to take advantage of the North Korean attack. A new national intelligence estimate of Soviet intentions reflecting the unstable atmosphere in Washington quickly replaced the old and outdated one. American foreign and military policy were to be based on the assumption that the Russians were preparing for a military confrontation with the West and that the year of "maximum danger" was 1954. By then, policymakers believed, Stalin would have accumulated a substantial stockpile of nuclear weapons and would be in a position to exploit his superiority in conventional forces.

Not too long before, Secretary of Defense James Forrestal had criticized President Truman for his unwillingness to run a deficit in the interest of higher defense budgets. The president was too much "a hard money man," the ex-Dillon Reed banker complained. The emotionally disturbed Forrestal, who ended his life by leaping from the sixteenth floor of Bethesda Naval Hospital, was not present for the metamorphosis, but Truman's budget balancing days were over, killed on the 38th parallel. Truman was buoyed by encouraging words from economist Leon Keyserling, who assured him that large-scale defense spending would not only produce full employment but would simultaneously pay for itself by stimulating economic growth and federal revenues. Truman gave the Pentagon carte blanche.

By July 1952, the once-understrength United States Army had built to a full complement of twenty divisions and eighteen regimental combat teams. A navy "second to none" showed the flag on all of the oceans of the globe, complemented by three marine divisions and three marine air wings. The air force, building toward a goal of 143 wings, already had 95 operational. With 3,636,000 men under arms, the United States again matched the Soviet Union in the size of its military establishment.

The United States also retained its quantitative and qualitative superiority in nuclear striking power. In 1952, the U.S.A. exploded its first thermonuclear device, an early H-bomb, having a force equivalent to ten million tons of TNT. The Soviet thermonuclear weapon exploded the next year had a force level only 1/20th that of its American counterpart. Not until 1955 would Soviet scientists produce a bomb comparable to the American. Nor could they keep up in delivery systems. They had nothing to compare with the nuclear-capable B-47 jet bomber. Stationed at overseas bases in Europe and North Africa, 1,400 B-47s gave the United States a weapons system against which the Soviets had little chance of defending themselves. The giant eight-engined B-52, flown for the first time in the early 1950s and made operational in the middle of the decade, added substantially to the growing strategic imbalance by providing the United States with an intercontinental capability that had until that time been almost wholly lacking. Finally, the United States began a program of research and development in the area of rockets and missiles. According to a 1951 memo written by Deputy Secretary of Defense Robert Lovett, the United States was making progress in the development of strategic missiles, tactical ground-support missiles, and submarine-launched missiles as well as missiles for air defense. The arms race was in full swing, with the United States leading the way.

The reality of American military superiority was not, however, reflected in the national psyche. On the contrary: just at the time when the United States reached a pinnacle of its power, international dominance, and relative invulnerability to Soviet challenge, the nation plunged into a crisis of fear. Frustrated in Korea and terrified by the Soviet bomb, many Americans vented their anger on domestic scapegoats, who could conveniently be blamed for the perceived Soviet threat. Sharing their president's scrappy attitudes toward the Soviet Union, some Americans developed the World War II–era security mania into a witch-hunt for those subversives who "gave away the atomic secret." The old conspiracy syndrome, dating back to the Protestant Reformation in England, that linked a foreign aggressor with internal subversives in a mortal threat to the most fundamental values of society, surfaced again.

Nuclear policy and the hunt for subversives were more than tangentially related. Because nuclear power was so awesome, and totally shrouded in secrecy, many thought it only natural that those who would want to betray the United States could most profitably do so by giving away nuclear secrets to the Soviet Union. Unfortunately for the country, evidence of such nuclear espionage actually did surface coincidentally with the Super debates, and nuclear policy became tangled in the net then being cast by Richard Nixon, Joe McCarthy, the FBI, and the House Un-American Activities Committee.

By 1950, the United States had created for itself a formidable security apparatus, staffed with civilian and military secret police, fed by professional informers, supplemented with concentration camps (never actually used) waiting to receive political radicals when a spasm of fear should seize the country. Back in 1936, FDR had authorized the FBI to gather information on subversive activities in the United States. Two years later, Congress created the House Un-American Activities Committee (HUAC), which indiscriminately denounced leftists and the New Deal throughout the war. In 1945, it became a permanent House committee, providing a platform for J. Parnell Thomas, the staunch proponent of military control of atomic power in the 1946 debates, as well as the Mississippi racist John Rankin and Richard Nixon among others. Congress also reenacted the 1917 Espionage Act and extended its prohibitions to peacetime activities, and then enacted the Smith Act, which forbade advocating the overthrow of the government of the United States by force or violence.

In 1946, the Canadian government announced that it had broken up a Soviet espionage ring in Ottawa. Documents turned over to the Canadians by a defecting Soviet cipher clerk revealed that Alan Nunn May, a British physicist who had worked in the Montreal laboratory that comprised the Anglo-Canadian branch of the Manhattan Project, transmitted data on nuclear power to Soviet contacts during the war. This revelation coincided with a sharp increase in Soviet–American hostility over Poland and American pressure on the U.S.S.R. to remove its troops from northern Iran. The confrontation frightened Americans, and briefly revived rightist efforts on behalf of the May–Johnson bill.

In 1947, Truman established a Federal Loyalty and Security Program to vet federal employees, but this did little to appease the voracious appetites of the Republican right, back in power after the 1946 off-year elections and determined to link the New Deal with communism. The sensational Alger Hiss revelations (1948–50) fed those appetites the red meat they demanded. Meanwhile, HUAC and comparable committees in the United States Senate kept themselves in the headlines with investigations of supposed communist influence in Hollywood, labor unions, and academia. Wisconsin Senator Joe McCarthy began the brief but spectacular career that gave his name to the era by his unsupported allegations of communist penetration in the federal government. At the same time, foreign troubles agitated Americans: the tensions of the Berlin blockade in 1948–49, the "fall of China" when Chiang Kai-shek's Kuomintang forces disintegrated and Chiang was forced to flee to Formosa, leaving mainland China to Mao Tse-tung and his Communist forces; and, most ominous of all, the U.S.S.R.'s successful detonation of its atomic bomb in August 1949.

For those Americans who, like their president, could not bring themselves to believe that the Soviet Union could develop an atomic weapon on its own, an alternative explanation soon presented itself. In early February 1950, the British announced that

Klaus Fuchs, a German émigré scientist who had worked at Los Alamos during the war and later became head of the division of theoretical physics in the British nuclear establishment at Harwell, was a Soviet spy, passing all information coming through his hands to Soviet agents. Shortly after, the FBI began rounding up Americans allegedly linked to Soviet espionage at wartime Los Alamos.

Fuchs fingered Harry Gold as his courier, Gold named an army engineer enlisted man, David Greenglass, as another member of the Los Alamos cell, and Greenglass in turn identified Julius and Ethel Rosenberg, two minor New York Communists, as the persons who recruited him into spying for the Soviet Union. The federal government tried the Rosenbergs for conspiracy to violate the Espionage Act, despite the fact that, whatever they might have done (if anything), they did for an ally, not an enemy. They were convicted and put to death in the electric chair at Sing Sing in June 1953.

The Fuchs–Rosenberg connection gave the American right just the explanation it needed for much that was frustrating about the Cold War: first the Soviet atomic menace, then the stalemate of the Korean War, then the Soviet H-bomb. How could the might of American power find itself so thwarted and menaced around the world? Surely, only by treason within, betrayal that turned on slipping the Soviets the secrets of atomic power. So the hunt for other traitors went on. Julius Rosenberg was, after all, merely an insignificant New York electrical engineer, as even his most avid accusers recognized. There must have been someone else more important, someone at least of the stature of Fuchs, responsible for the Soviet bomb—or, if not responsible, at least available for scapegoating.

So the search for "the Alger Hiss of science" continued.[29] In 1948, HUAC began poking around the Berkeley Radiation Laboratory, sniffing the trail of a dozen scientists who had flirted with Communist associations before the war and who had some remote connection with sensitive wartime scientific work. The Senate Internal Security Subcommittee probed Philip Morrison, a Los Alamos physicist, but did not succeed in getting him fired from his academic post. HUAC had somewhat better luck with

Edward U. Condon, briefly deputy director at Los Alamos in 1943. Before he himself was sent to prison, HUAC chairman J. Parnell Thomas sniped at Condon through leaks about his associations with organizations that promoted Soviet–American scientific contacts. Though Condon was elected president of the American Physical Society and the American Association for the Advancement of Science, HUAC kept after him, trying to link him to the minor 1930s Communists it had uncovered in Berkeley. Finally, Nixon, then vice-president, got Condon's security clearance revoked, and Condon resigned as director of research with Corning Glass. The State Department similarly harassed Linus Pauling, Nobel laureate in chemistry (1954), about his passport applications, presenting the absurd spectacle of the mightiest nation on earth afraid to let one of its most distinguished chemists travel abroad to scientific conferences. In the same period, Oveta Culp Hobby, a Texan appointed by President Dwight D. Eisenhower as the first secretary of the Department of Health, Education, and Welfare, blocked a research award to Pauling for political reasons. Not to be outdone, the Internal Security Subcommittee questioned him throughout the remainder of the decade about his activities in the international peace movement. Not until he received his second Nobel, this time for peace, in 1962, was Pauling free of such petty harassment.

But the witch-hunters' really big score came in the security-clearance hearings of J. Robert Oppenheimer, conducted in 1954. Oppenheimer's prewar Communist contacts were intimate —his brother Frank, a physicist, had been a party member, as well as his fiancée, Jean Tatlock. His wife, Kitty, had previously been married to a Communist who died fighting with the Abraham Lincoln Brigade in Spain. Oppenheimer, as he himself laconically admitted, had "probably belonged to every Communist-front organization on the West Coast."[30] These associations did not present any serious impediment to Groves's accepting him as the head of the most security-sensitive scientific position in the war effort. But Oppenheimer had a fatal talent for making enemies: sometimes by a tendency to be curt or sarcastic toward persons he found tiresome, sometimes by opposition to projects he thought scientific folly. His persistent opposition to the development of Super, retracted too late, made Edward Teller an enemy, and, behind Teller, the air force. Oppenheimer's skepticism about a monster linear accelerator project of Ernest O. Lawrence earned the enmity of Lawrence and Luis Alvarez. Finally, Oppenheimer's abrupt manner, indicative of an attitude that did not suffer fools gladly, alienated Lewis Strauss, soon to be AEC chairman, and General Kenneth Nichols, Groves's second-in-command of the Manhattan Project and later general manager of the AEC.

William L. Borden, a former director of the JCAE's staff and a man Herbert York describes as "a fanatic on the subject of nuclear weapons,"[31] played a key role in the formulation of the JCAE's position on Super. Borden had been a vehement advocate of defense buildup since the end of World War II, particularly nuclear weapons, and he strongly favored not only Super but a package he called "the ultimate weapon system—the thermonuclear weapon carried by a nuclear powered airplane."[32] Borden was troubled by the role that Oppenheimer had played in opposing Super. His suspicions festered, and in 1954 he wrote to FBI Director J. Edgar Hoover that "More probably than not, J. Robert Oppenheimer is an agent of the Soviet Union." Borden's review of the FBI investigative reports on the scientist, a stack four and a half feet high, persuaded him that Oppenheimer was a "hardened Communist" who had "gone underground" during World War II.[33] President Eisenhower promptly ordered that a "blank wall" be erected between Oppenheimer and classified information. Within a year, Oppenheimer had lost his security clearance after a political trial that came as close as anything in the American experience to the Dreyfus affair.

Strauss requested that Oppenheimer resign his AEC consultant's appointment; Oppenheimer refused. Consequently, the AEC appointed a special three-man hearing panel, known as the Gray Board after its chairman, former Army Secretary Gordon Gray, to pass on Oppenheimer's loyalty. The board, by a 2–1 vote (the only scientist member of the panel dissented), found Oppenheimer to be loyal but recommended that his security clearance be revoked because of his opposition to Super and because of personal defects of character. The decision was affirmed by the

AEC itself in a 4–1 vote (again, the dissenter being the only scientist member of the board, Henry D. Smyth), with Chairman Strauss taking a vindictive pleasure in writing out the findings that Oppenheimer had "placed himself outside the rules which govern others," had disregarded security procedures, and had displayed "fundamental defects in his character."

Oppenheimer was eventually exonerated by the decision of the Kennedy and Johnson administrations to award him the Fermi Medal in 1964, and the American scientific community today looks back on the show trial only with a shudder. The accusation that started the proceedings, that Oppenheimer was a Soviet espionage agent, was thoroughly discredited, and is now believed by none but the lunatic fringe. But conservatives generally behaved like the anti-Dreyfusards of two generations earlier; Senator Hickenlooper, chairman of the JCAE at the time of Oppenheimer's hearings, together with all his Republican colleagues on the JCAE, refused to attend the Fermi Medal presentation, calling the rehabilitation of Oppenheimer "disgusting."

As the first decade of the atomic era drew to a close, Americans could count few blessings that nuclear fire had brought them. They found themselves in an endless, costly arms race whose every escalation left them less, not more, secure. America's vaunted nuclear might proved useless as an instrument that might force the Soviets and other Communist nations like China and North Korea to behave according to American expectations. The nonmilitary promise of nuclear power seemed more remote than ever. Nuclear power was beginning to appear more a curse than a blessing.

6

"Massive Retaliation"
EISENHOWER'S STRATEGIC POLICIES

THE TRUMAN ADMINISTRATION'S strategic initiative, embodied in NSC-68, presented a potential dilemma to the incoming Republicans in 1953. After having indiscriminately accused Democrats of being "soft on Communism" and being responsible for the frustrations of what their spokesmen liked to call "this mess in Korea," the triumphant Republicans were scarcely in a position to reverse the militarization resulting from Truman's rearmament policy. Yet at the same time, the Republicans entertained a devout, if not superstitious, dedication to a balanced budget. They, too, could count—probably better than the Democrats— and they realized that rearmament was going to be costly. Consequently, it fell to Dwight D. Eisenhower and his advisers to formulate a strategic policy that scaled down the voracious demands of NSC-68 to fiscal reality. Eisenhower's response to this challenge provided the basis for his weapons policy, a policy much more sober than the intoxicated spree demanded by NSC-68.

By 1953, defense expenditures had skyrocketed to a record $50.4 billion, quadrupling the $13.5 billion level of only three years before. In calendar year 1950, national security expenditures had accounted for 5.2 percent of the gross national product. By 1953, that figure had risen to 13.5 percent. Leon Keyserling, the head of the president's Council of Economic Advisers, had advised the White House in 1949 that a full 20 percent of GNP could be diverted to defense purposes without causing serious dislocations in the economy. But this had not proven entirely correct. Although economic growth occurred and government revenues increased, they did not keep pace with the Defense Department's insatiable appetites. A budget deficit of over $4 billion appeared in the 1951–52 fiscal year, rising to $9.5 billion for 1952–53. Meanwhile, unmistakable signs of inflation turned up in the statistics regularly churned out by the government's economy watchers.

During the 1952 presidential election, the Republicans attacked the administration for running a deficit, warned about the dangers of inflation, and promised that they would win total victory in the struggle against "international Communism" while at the same time reducing defense spending. This was good politics in 1952. Following General Douglas MacArthur's dismissal as commander-in-chief of America's forces in the Far East and the Truman administration's decision to settle for a stalemate in Korea, popular support for the war and for massive defense budgets waned together. In a move that reflected this shift in public attitudes, Congress lopped a whopping 9 percent from President Truman's $50.9 billion defense budget request for 1953.

The Republican attack on unbalanced budgets was more than mere political rhetoric. It reflected the real concerns of Dwight Eisenhower himself as well as those fiscal conservatives who were his principal economic advisers. Thus Arthur F. Burns, the first chairman of Eisenhower's Council of Economic Advisers, saw a relation between excessive government spending and the inflationary tendencies already at work within the economy. Burns warned of the dangers posed by an inflation rate of even 1 percent annually. "Such a slow but persistent rise in the price level," he said, "is bound to deal harshly with the plans and hopes of millions of people in the course of a generation."[1] At a minimum, Burns argued, the administration should strive to balance the federal budget. Budget surpluses, however, should be the ultimate objective.

Because the Truman administration had kept spending for domestic programs to a minimum, Eisenhower would be forced to find methods of reducing defense expenditures to achieve a balanced budget. But the new president was no more willing to jeopardize the nation's security in the name of the budget than he was to weaken the economy in the cause of defense. Eisenhower, no less a committed cold warrior than his predecessor, believed that a weak economy was just as dangerous to the nation's security as the perceived Soviet threat. "Our military strength and our economic strength are truly one," he said. And neither could "sensibly be purchased at the price of destroying the other."[2]

Here lay the fundamental difference between the Truman and Eisenhower approaches to the problem of defense spending. Truman had surrendered completely to those urging a massive military buildup. Although it was quite out of character for him, Truman ignored the cost, hoping that his economic advisers were right in their belief that government spending would create economic growth that in turn would produce the increased tax revenues needed to meet expanded government obligations. Like Truman, Eisenhower was an instinctive economic conservative and budget balancer. But unlike Truman, perhaps because he had once worn five stars on his shoulders, he was not panicked by military leaders who claimed national security would be jeopardized if one or another of their programs was not funded. The new president felt intuitively that there had to be limits to defense spending. When unbalanced budgets and inflation threatened the health of the economy, Eisenhower believed it necessary to compromise between an ideal military posture and what the country could in reality afford. Early in his first term, he told Congress that "in providing the kind of military security . . . our country needs, we must keep our people free and our economy solvent. We must not create a nation mighty in arms that is lacking in liberty and bankrupt in resources."[3]

Eisenhower attacked the problem of reducing defense expenditures on several fronts. First, he was convinced that simple improvements in the administration of the Defense Department could produce significant cost savings. The Truman administration's helter-skelter approach to national defense planning had funneled too much money into the economy too quickly. By spending vast sums in order to achieve instant readiness, the national government encouraged waste while fueling inflation. Moreover, Eisenhower believed that once appropriate force levels had been achieved and weapons procurement completed, there would necessarily follow a falling off in defense spending that would produce deflationary pressures and the threat of recession. To avoid these economic dangers, the president decided at the outset to adopt a strategy for "the long haul," one that would be economically supportable for decades to come. This necessarily implied reduced spending levels for national defense to avoid deficits. In April 1953, he told a White House press conference: "We reject the idea that we must build up to a maximum attainable strength for some specific date theoretically fixed for a specified time in the future. Defense is not a matter of maximum strength for a single date. It is a matter of adequate protection to be projected as far into the future as the actions and apparent purposes of others may compel us. It is a policy that can, if necessary, be lived with over a period of years."[4]

At the same time, Eisenhower was determined to require the different branches of the military services to agree on a unified military strategy for the United States. Under the Democrats there had been no clear policy. Thus, while the air force was planning for a nuclear war, the army and navy were preparing for a conventional conflict on the assumption that nuclear weapons would not be used. Sherman Adams would later recall that when Eisenhower moved into the White House, the various branches were planning "for short wars, for police actions like the Korean war, for peripheral wars, for infantry wars, for air war and for completely destructive atomic attacks."[5] According to Secretary of the Treasury George Humphrey, there seemed to be six strategies, two for each branch of the services. And of course their budgets reflected this fact.

But what sort of military strategy should the United States adopt? As a former commander of NATO, Eisenhower was convinced that western Europe could not be defended against the Red Army by conventional military forces. The allies were either unwilling or unable to commit sufficient forces to the task, and the United States could not project enough strength across the Atlantic to make up the deficiency. To make such an attempt would be to waste men, money, and resources in a hopeless endeavor. Nor was Eisenhower satisfied that the Truman administration had been wise in making a large-scale conventional commitment in Korea. The Soviets could easily precipitate similar crises in other trouble spots, but the United States could not respond as it had in Korea without risking economic and military exhaustion. Soviet leaders would have to be placed on notice that any future Korea-style aggression would produce American retaliation against the Soviet Union itself.

Once Eisenhower had decided that there were to be no more limited wars and that Europe could not be defended by conventional means, there seemed little reason for retaining all of the 3.4 million men and women then serving in the armed forces. He instructed the Joint Chiefs of Staff to organize a new military strategy based on reduced conventional force levels, one that would rely heavily upon nuclear striking power to deter Soviet aggression. When members of the JCS objected, claiming that such a strategy would endanger national security, Eisenhower quickly overruled them. Subsequently, the president reorganized the Joint Chiefs of Staff, replacing those who had served in the Truman period with officers more willing to work within the constraints he had established. Under the leadership of Admiral Arthur Radford, the reorganized JCS then worked out a policy to comport with administration requirements. By abandoning the idea that any future war could be fought without recourse to nuclear weapons, Radford and his colleagues were able to recommend a 600,000-man force reduction for the armed services and substantially lower funding for defense. The army and the navy bore the brunt of administration budget cuts. Because the United States would rely upon its nuclear striking power and because in 1952 the only available delivery system was the manned bomber, the air force fared better. But even this branch was reduced in strength. The president authorized a 137-wing air force, down from the 143 wings earlier approved by President Truman. To compensate for the fact that fewer American soldiers would be available for the defense of western Europe, remaining forces would be equipped with tactical nuclear weapons. In the event of a nuclear war, the "joint strategic capabilities plan" drafted by the military and approved by the president called for an all-out attack on the Soviet Union and its satellites. Daniel Ellsberg, who reviewed the plan for the Defense Department in 1961, noted that if the plan had been implemented "we would have hit every city in the Soviet Union and China in addition to all military targets."[6] The Joint Chiefs estimated enemy fatalities from the initial strike at from 360 to 425 million.

The press immediately and appropriately dubbed the administration's strategy "The New Look." Paris designers had only just decreed their own New Look, requiring the hemlines on women's coats, skirts, and dresses to drop. Now defense expenditures and hemlines would come down simultaneously. "Our economy program . . . is based on more effective defense for less money," Charles Wilson, the new secretary of defense, explained. "We believe that Uncle Sam's big old pocketbook has been open just too wide. Crash programs and easy spending can no longer be justified, if they ever could. It is reasonable to expect the Defense Department to spend the money available to it in the same frugal, objective way that the people themselves have to spend what money they have left over after they pay their big taxes."[7]

The New Look, like any military strategy, depended for its effectiveness on its credibility. Potential aggressors would have to believe that the United States was prepared to use its nuclear muscle. This was particularly difficult because of the inhumane nature of nuclear and thermonuclear weaponry, as well as the general revulsion with which such weapons were viewed in the international community. Aware of the credibility problem, the Eisenhower administration was at pains to emphasize that it was deadly serious. Whenever the issue came up, President Eisenhower himself was quick to affirm the legitimacy of nuclear weapons and his own determination to use them if necessary. Technology had fundamentally changed the nature of warfare, he insisted, "and because America's most precious possession is the lives of her citizens, we should base our security upon military formations which make maximum use of science and technology in order to minimize numbers of men."[8]

But it was Secretary of State John Foster Dulles who focused national and international attention on the New Look. In January

1954, while addressing a meeting of the Council on Foreign Relations, Dulles announced that when responding to aggression the United States would "depend primarily upon a great capacity to retaliate, instantly, by means and at places of our own choosing."[9] It seemed clear from what the secretary said that there were to be no more Koreas—no more peripheral wars. He also seemed to imply that the administration was prepared to retaliate with an awesome display of nuclear might to any sort of Communist aggression wherever it took place.

Writing in *The New York Times* just a few days after Secretary Dulles gave his celebrated speech, James Reston interpreted "massive retaliation" to mean that "in the event of another proxy or brushfire war in Korea, Indochina, Iran or anywhere else, the United States might retaliate instantly with atomic weapons against the USSR or Red China." Several weeks later, Vice-President Richard Nixon seemed to confirm that view when he told a *Times* reporter: "Rather than let the Communists nibble us to death all over the world in little wars we would rely in the future primarily on our massive mobile retaliatory power which we could use at our discretion against the major source of aggression at times and places that we choose." But as Secretary Dulles himself subsequently tried to make clear, the administration did not intend to implement massive retaliation in so mindless or inflexible a way. Writing in *Foreign Affairs* magazine in April 1954, Dulles denied that the administration would respond massively to any and all provocations. He was even willing to admit that situations might arise in which the United States would not be able to react appropriately; that given the limited resources at the government's disposal, certain foreign policy setbacks might have to be accepted. While admitting this much, however, neither Dulles nor Eisenhower was prepared to state precisely what set of circumstances might call forth nuclear lightning. It was vital to the success of the strategy, Dulles explained, that no one knew "in advance precisely what would be the scope of military action if new aggression occurred. . . . That is a matter as to which the aggressor had best remain ignorant. But he can know and does know, in the light of present policies, that the choice in this respect is ours and not his." By keeping this nuclear sword of

Damocles forever suspended, Dulles and Eisenhower hoped to maximize its deterrent effect.

Massive retaliation became the subject of intense controversy almost immediately. George Humphrey, the influential secretary of the treasury, supported the policy down the line. "That and that alone, I am sure is what kept peace in the world," he later wrote. "And all the rest of these soldiers and sailors and submarines and everything else, comparatively speaking, you could drop in the ocean, and it wouldn't make too much difference."[10] Others who strongly disagreed believed that massive retaliation lacked credibility. Robert Oppenheimer pointed out that the Soviets would soon rival the United States as a nuclear power and that, under the circumstances, initiating a nuclear war would be suicidal. "We may anticipate a state of affairs in which the two Great Powers will each be in a position to put an end to the civilization and life of the other, though not without risking its own," Oppenheimer wrote. "We may be likened to two scorpions in a bottle, each capable of killing the other, but only at the risk of his own life." The respected British military strategist B. H. Lidell Hart reacted to Secretary Dulles's speech with incredulity. Lidell Hart doubted that "any responsible government" would "dare to *use* the H-bomb as an answer to local and limited aggression." Contrary to the administration's claims, he believed that the extraordinary destructiveness of thermonuclear weapons made limited wars more rather than less likely. "The value of strategic bombing forces has largely disappeared," he wrote, "except as a last resort." In a widely read article published in 1956, William Kaufmann of the RAND Corporation added his voice to the growing chorus attacking massive retaliation. "If the Communists should challenge our sincerity, and they would have good reasons for daring to do so," Kaufmann wrote, "we would either have to put up or shut up. If we put up, we would plunge into all the immeasurable horrors of atomic war. If we shut up, we would suffer a serious loss of prestige and damage our capacity to establish deterrents against further Communist expansion." Kaufman thought it wholly "out of character for us to retaliate massively against anyone except in the face" of extreme provocations such as Pearl Harbor.[11]

But Dulles was hard to convince. Both Robert Bowie and Gerard Smith, his successor as head of the State Department's policy planning staff, worked assiduously to convince the secretary that in the face of growing Soviet nuclear capabilities, massive retaliation would have to go. Dulles saw the point but feared the effect that abandonment of massive retaliation would have on the NATO allies. Eventually, however, he became convinced. Smith recalls the day in November 1958.

> I accompanied him to the Pentagon where all the hierarchy from Secretary of Defense and chairman of the Joint Chiefs on down had assembled. Dulles, in a most solemn manner, recalled that he had been the father of the massive retaliation doctrine—it had served the nation well, he said, deterring aggression for years. But he had reluctantly concluded that it was a wasting asset. With increasing Soviet nuclear forces, it would become less credible in the foreseeable future and the U.S. military should start preparing plans and weapons systems for alternative strategies.[12]

But that, as Eisenhower and Dulles well knew, was easier said than done. They had adopted massive retaliation in the first place because the open-ended commitment to the development of conventional military forces made originally during the Truman administration seemed economically unsupportable. According to Eisenhower, it would have "required massive defense units of such size and capacity that no matter how universal and threatening the danger or how many the local 'disturbances,' we could quickly defeat them by conventional means." Eisenhower was determined not "to turn the United States into an armed camp."[13] The president was grappling with a dilemma for which there was no completely satisfactory answer. The nation had assumed global commitments that it did not have the resources to honor. The nuclear option left gaps, to be sure. But the conventional military option was also, to quote Eisenhower, an "unrealistic solution." Little wonder then that defense planners found no resolution to the Republican dilemma. Thus, despite its shortcomings, massive retaliation remained official strategy throughout Eisenhower's eight years in office.

Between 1953 and 1955, President Eisenhower reduced the

defense budget by 20 percent and in 1956 produced his first budget surplus. But in accomplishing his economic purposes, the president alienated the military. The army, its strategic significance and mission sharply reduced as a result of the New Look's emphasis on air power and nuclear weaponry, was in open revolt. Among those most critical of the United States's new defense posture were Army Chief of Staff Matthew Ridgway, his successor, Maxwell D. Taylor, and the army's head of research and development, General James Gavin. In June 1955, embittered by his failure to influence the formulation of defense policy and unwilling to preside over the further deterioration of the army, Ridgway resigned. The following year he published his memoirs. Serialized in the *Saturday Evening Post,* Ridgway's *Soldier* was a biting criticism of Eisenhower's overemphasis on air power and the nuclear option. Gavin and later Taylor followed Ridgway's example. Both resigned, both wrote critical books, and both took their fight for increased military spending on conventional forces to the public.

Many air force officers were equally dissatisfied with the New Look. According to Air Force General Nathan Twining, chairman of the JCS from 1957 to 1960, "the Eisenhower Administration failed to make full commitment of United States national prestige in Asia and the near and Middle East. The developing problems of Africa and South America were likewise accorded insufficient attention."[14] Twining, who seems to have believed that any challenge to the international status quo no matter where could be resolved by a show of force, was also out of sympathy with Eisenhower's unsuccessful attempts at nuclear disarmament. But the final straw for Twining was the president's decision to create the National Aeronautical and Space Administration, which made it more difficult for the air force to militarize outer space. During Eisenhower's years in the White House, Twining bitterly declared that "there was a tendency to allow a gradual erosion of U.S. military posture through partial accommodation to those American pressure groups who were working for unilateral disarmament, the abolition of nuclear weapons, and the denial of the medium of space for military operations."[15]

At first glance it may seem strange that the air force, most lavishly funded of all the services, felt it was being shortchanged. But air force doctrine held that the United States should maintain nuclear superiority over the Soviets at all costs. As the Kremlin developed a nuclear capability of its own, air force leaders pressed the administration for a major expansion of American strategic nuclear capabilities. In an early version of counterforce strategy, they insisted that the Strategic Air Command should develop the capacity to destroy the Soviet bomber force on the ground in a single preemptive strike while maintaining enough strength in reserve to attack and destroy Soviet society in a follow-up attack if the Soviets did not surrender following this first strike. The costs of such a strategy would have been astronomical. According to one estimate, expanding and maintaining the Strategic Air Command alone would have required $30 billion annually.

The president was by no means ready to undertake such a policy, because he was convinced that it would have undermined his domestic economic program. Moreover, it had begun to dawn on him as well as several of his advisers that strategic superiority in the nuclear age was a goal of diminishing significance. There are indications that Eisenhower himself was aware of this as early as 1953. In any event, it is certain that by the following year the Pentagon was at work on a plan designed to enable the administration to avoid an expensive and largely senseless quest for strategic superiority. The new policy, dubbed "sufficiency," emerged in vague form in March 1955, when the president told a press conference offhandedly that once you "get enough of a particular type of weapon" it may not be important "to have a lot more of it." By the spring of 1956, the policy had become official. On May 4, in responding to a reporter who asked if it wasn't important to maintain superiority in bombers he replied: "No! I say it is vital to get what we believe we need. That does not necessarily mean more than anybody else does. We have to get what we need." Eisenhower refused to play what he described as "the numbers racket."[16] He explained that there "comes a time . . . when the destructiveness of weapons is so great as to be beyond imagination, when enough is certainly plenty, and you do no good, as I see it, by increasing these numbers." Secretary of

Defense Charles E. Wilson, testifying before Senator Stuart Symington's 1956 Senate air power hearings, argued that "the quality of our retaliatory force is now becoming increasingly more important than its size." Admiral Arthur Radford, chairman of the Joint Chiefs, went down the line with the administration. The most complete official statement of the doctrine of sufficiency was provided by Secretary of the Air Force Donald Quarles. His essay, entitled "How Much is Enough?" appeared in *Air Force Magazine* in September 1956. Here Quarles explained:

> The buildup of atomic power in the hands of the two opposed alliances of nations makes total war an unthinkable catastrophe for both sides. Neither side can hope by a mere margin of superiority in airplanes or other means of delivery of atomic weapons to escape the catastrophe of such a war. Beyond a certain point, this prospect is not the result of *relative* strength of the two opposed forces. It is the *absolute* power in the hands of each, and . . . the substantial invulnerability of this power to interdiction.[17]

With the air force committed to limitless growth and the administration advocating sufficiency, friction was inevitable. It first developed as a result of the 1956 "bomber gap" controversy. Despite the fact that Eisenhower refused to be drawn into a pointless quest for nuclear supremacy, at no time during his administration did the Soviets ever really threaten to draw even with the United States in nuclear striking power. But Russian scientific and technological achievements sometimes appeared menacing. In 1953, the Soviets exploded their first thermonuclear device and two years later followed with a second experiment that matched the explosive force (10 megatons) of America's 1952 "Mike" shot. At Moscow's May Day parade in 1954, the Soviets allowed U.S. Air Force observers to glimpse several medium range Badger jet bombers, as well as a single Bison, a nuclear-capable intercontinental jet bomber. A year later, in June 1955, Bisons were seen flying in squadron formations at a Soviet air show. We now know that in all no more than ten Bisons appeared that day. But Soviet leaders had them fly in wide circles so that the same planes appeared repeatedly over the reviewing area in order to create the impression that they had a large force of intercontinental jets. They didn't. In fact, hard at work on a program to develop intercontinental range ballistic missiles, and without resources to squander on alternative delivery systems, they had no intention of procuring a large bomber force. Soviet leaders evidently thought, however, that their security would be enhanced if the West believed that they had matched the United States in the number of strategic bombers they possessed. During the next several years Soviet leaders would consistently attempt to convince the West that they were stronger than was actually the case. They succeeded beyond their wildest imaginings.

The appearance of long range Soviet jet bombers offered critics of the New Look their first real opportunity to take the offensive. Charging that the administration had allowed a dangerous "bomber gap" to develop, Democrats in Congress, including senators Hubert Humphrey, Stuart Symington, and Henry Jackson, encouraged air force leaders to join in the attack. At Senator Symington's well-publicized Senate air power hearings that opened in April 1956, a parade of air force generals testified that America was in danger of losing its nuclear superiority. On the basis of some highly questionable intelligence estimates, generals Curtis LeMay, Nathan Twining, and Thomas White all claimed that the Soviets were outproducing the United States in terms of medium range and intercontinental jet bombers and that by 1960 they would be in a position to carry out a successful surprise attack. The only appropriate response, according to those spokesmen for air power, was to begin augmenting America's bomber force as quickly as possible. Commenting on this testimony, Harland Moulton, formerly of the Arms Control and Disarmament Agency, has written:

> Considering the fact that Air Force officers knew they were testifying before a friendly majority on the Symington committee and that appropriations for new weapons systems were at stake, it is difficult to determine whether the unduly pessimistic estimate of the Soviet bomber threat was completely candid, or whether the estimates were colored by other, more overriding considerations. In any event the estimates of the Soviet threat given in public by Air force military officers during the 1950's were consistently high

by wide margins—on both bombers and missiles—and those made
by civilian defense officials were more nearly accurate.[18]

The president knew that there was no bomber gap, and that he
was being pressured by air force officers who viewed the arms
race as fundamentally a competition among the three branches
of the military services. And he was furious. Shortly after the air
power hearings finished, he explained to a friend that "when each
service puts down its minimum requirements for its own military
budget for the following year, and I add up the total, I find that
they mount at a fantastic rate. There is seemingly no end to all
of this." Yet he did not think that "getting tough" with the military was any real answer. "I simply must find men who have the
breadth of understanding and devotion to their country, rather
than to a single service, that will bring about better solutions than
I get now."[19]

The president bent only slightly to the pressure applied by the
Democrats and the air force during the "bomber gap" controversy. He agreed to a supplemental air force appropriation of
almost $1 billion and increased procurement of the new B-52
bomber from seventeen to twenty planes a month. There was no
strategic justification for even this concession, however. In 1956,
the Soviets had only a tiny force of no more than 150 intercontinental bombers. In contrast, the United States had deployed a
force of some 1,400 B-47 bombers, still retained the propeller-
driven intercontinental B-36 bombers, and was deploying the
first of 600 B-52 bombers that were to become the backbone of
the Strategic Air Command. Moreover, data gathered as a result
of secret U-2 photoreconnaissance flights over the Soviet Union
indicated that the situation was not likely to change in the immediate future. Air force claims to the contrary notwithstanding,
Soviet aircraft plants were not turning out bombing planes in
large numbers. Nor were hangars and runways being constructed
to accommodate them.

A far more serious challenge to President Eisenhower's insistence on an economically sound defense policy came in the summer and autumn of 1957. On August 4, Radio Moscow announced that Soviet scientists had successfully fired a ballistic

missile with intercontinental range. Then on October 4, 1957, a Soviet rocket successfully placed Sputnik, the world's first artificial earth satellite, in orbit. Two more Sputniks, one weighing 1,120 pounds, and the second 2,925 pounds, soon followed. Not only had the Soviets preceded the United States into space, they had in the process demonstrated that they possessed a booster rocket of extraordinary power, one that might well be capable of delivering a nuclear warhead to a target thousands of miles away.

Even in the face of the Soviet Union's "space spectacular," President Eisenhower remained characteristically calm. Despite Nikita Khrushchev's claims to the contrary, the president did not agree that America's manned bomber force had suddenly become obsolete. It was one thing to launch a single missile into space, but something else entirely to deploy a large force of such weapons. A national intelligence estimate done shortly after Sputnik suggested that the Soviets would be unable to deploy more than a tiny force of perhaps ten ICBMs by early 1959, and no more than one hundred by 1960. Meanwhile, the United States missile research program was proceeding nicely. First-generation intermediate range missiles were almost ready for deployment in Europe and full-scale tests of the Atlas, an intercontinental range missile, were scheduled for 1958.

Satisfied that the United States was in no immediate danger and convinced that our own missile research was about to pay off, Eisenhower at first made a deliberate attempt to denigrate the importance of Sputnik. Rear Admiral Rawson Bennett, Chief of Naval Operations, called the satellite "a hunk of iron almost anybody could launch." A few days later, responding to demands by *The New York Times* and other newspapers that the United States enter the race for the control of space quickly, White House aide Sherman Adams told reporters, "the Administration is not interested in serving a high score in an outer space basketball game." Defense Secretary Charles Wilson joked in a similar vein. "Nobody is going to drop anything on you from a satellite while you are asleep," he told newsmen, "so don't worry about it."[20]

This was an ill-advised approach to what most agreed was a serious problem. *The New York Times* castigated the president for "putting domestic budgetary and political considerations ahead of security" and demanded a "maximum effort" to match a Soviet achievement that threatened a "radical change in the military balance of power." It seemed likely, the *Times* alleged, that the Soviets would now move swiftly to construct a fleet of intercontinental ballistic missiles capable of raining death on the United States. America was in a "race for survival" and what was needed was leadership from the White House. In their influential column, Joseph and Stewart Alsop described Sputnik as the "worst single piece of news of the post-war years," a confirmation of their oft-stated view that the United States was losing the nuclear arms race. The Alsops, who saw an exact analogy between Hitler's Germany and the Soviet Union of the 1950s, compared Eisenhower with Neville Chamberlain and warned of "American-made Munichs." Eric Sevareid contributed his own apocalyptic vision for the benefit of frightened American television viewers. The time was not far distant, he intoned in his measured, grave style, when Russia "can stand astride the world, its military master."[21] Nikita Khrushchev, who seemed on the verge of turning Sevareid's prophecy into reality, added fuel to the hysteria when he claimed that the Soviet Union was already mass-producing ICBMs.

With the media and the general public frightened by Sputnik and the "missile gap," congressional Democrats moved to the attack. After a briefing at the Pentagon on the military significance of the Soviet satellite, the Senate majority leader, Lyndon Johnson, launched a headline-making investigation into the administration's military policies. The chief administration spokesman to appear before the Johnson committee was Secretary of Defense Neil McElroy, who emphasized that whether or not a missile gap existed, there was certainly no deterrent gap. The United States had in its inventories approximately 1,700 medium and intercontinental range bombers capable of raining devastation on the Soviet Union. The air force and navy also deployed another two or three thousand fighter-bombers and other aircraft capable of attacking Soviet targets with nuclear weapons. In contrast, the Soviets had no more than two hundred bombers capable of attacking targets in the United States. But McElroy seemed considerably less sure of himself when testifying about the missile race. He admitted that it was unclear whether Washington or Moscow was ahead in the development of these weapons. This country, he continued, "must accelerate our programs if we are ahead, and to get ahead if we are not ahead."[22]

This statement, which was hardly reassuring coming as it did from the secretary of defense, seems to have been McElroy's inept way of trying to explain that the United States and the Soviet Union were involved in not one but a number of technological "races" in missile development. He implied that the power that first deployed significant numbers of reliable ICBMs —neither side had at that point—would be the "winner." But the committee, dominated by Democrats Johnson, Symington, and Henry Jackson of Washington, wasn't interested in an analysis that suggested the jury was still out on the question of the missile race. Seeking partisan political advantage, it produced a spate of prominent witnesses from business, industry, the scientific community, academia, and education, all of whom expressed dismay, shock, and fear at what the Soviets had accomplished. The physicist Edward Teller, by this time a regular at such extravaganzas, testified that in orbiting an earth satellite, the Soviets had demonstrated that they had booster rockets and guidance systems that came close to meeting the standards required for an operational intercontinental ballistic missile. Vannevar Bush, still a respected spokesman of the scientific community, warned against "smugness and complacency." Bush thought the United States was behind in the missile race and urged that immediate steps be taken to protect the Strategic Air Command against an ICBM attack that might catch all of America's retaliatory strike force on the ground. The mass of testimony pointed toward a single conclusion well articulated by Senator John Kennedy, Democrat of Massachusetts. Already a presidential aspirant, Kennedy charged the administration with seeking "economic security at the expense of military security."[23]

To no one's surprise, the military also turned on the administration. Between 1953 and the orbiting of Sputnik, General James Gavin, head of research and development for the army, had become increasingly disillusioned with administration defense policy. When Sputnik sailed into orbit, Gavin concluded that the administration had allowed the Soviets to develop a significant lead in missile technology. For Gavin this was the last straw. He resigned from the army and in testimony before Senator Johnson's committee warned that the Soviets could now be expected to practice a brand of international blackmail that he labeled "Sputnik diplomacy." In a little while, he predicted, Americans would "live and conduct . . . international negotiations under a canopy of fear."[24]

With Sputnik decorating the night sky and Congress anxious to fund projects that promised to help America "catch up," other military leaders broke with the administration in a scramble for money and control of missile programs. Thus, even though the administration had sound scientific and technological reasons for opposing it, Secretary of the Army Wilber Bruckner urged Congress to fund the army's Nike Zeus antiballistic missile system. Meanwhile, Army General John Medaris, the chief of the Redstone Arsenal,[25] and Dr. Wernher Von Braun, head of missile research at Redstone, both declared that national security, which they insisted depended upon "the control of space," was being endangered by a parsimonious administration that refused to appropriate sufficient funds for the army's missile research. Air force spokesmen were equally emphatic. The former commander of SAC, General Curtis LeMay, a man given to strong cigars and even stronger language, charged that the administration had consistently turned a deaf ear to requests for the expansion of the manned bomber force but that now it was "absolutely necessary." Unless the United States expanded its retaliatory forces, LeMay railed, by 1959 the country would fall behind the Soviets in nuclear striking power. Worse, if not dispersed, the Strategic Air Command's forces would be vulnerable to a devastating first strike by fleets of Soviet ICBMs. General Thomas White, echoing LeMay's arguments regarding the manned bomber force, simultaneously urged a speedup in air force missile development programs as well as the space program, which he envisioned as falling under air force control. He was particularly critical of the administration's decision to soft-pedal the air force's Titan missile program, even though he understood that the second generation Minuteman missile, already in the planning stages, would quickly make the liquid-fueled Titan obsolete.

One month after the first Sputnik was orbited, the missile gap controversy heated up still further as a result of the findings of the Gaither commission. Headed by H. Rowan Gaither, the chairman of the board of trustees of the RAND Corporation, this blue-ribbon presidential commission had originally been established to evaluate a proposal made by the Federal Civilian Defense Administration to build blast shelters to protect the civilian population against nuclear attack. The price tag placed on this project by the FCDA was $40 billion. On its own initiative, however, the committee expanded its inquiries to include a vast range of defense-related questions. Although its report was classified (and remained so until 1973) and was intended only for the use of the president and the National Security Council, most of the committee's findings were leaked to the press, thus turning the report into an important element in the case then building against the administration.

The Gaither commission's recommendations represent the first serious post-Sputnik attempt by opponents of massive retaliation to recommend an alternative strategy. In preceding years, a number of different individuals ranging from Army Chief of Staff Matthew Ridgway to numerous academic strategists including Henry Kissinger and the RAND Corporation's Raymond L. Garthoff had focused attention on the inadequacies of massive retaliation. As early as 1954 a national debate over whether the United States needed conventional forces capable of fighting limited wars was already under way. The members of the Gaither commission now joined in, insisting that America's conventional force levels should be dramatically increased.

But with Sputnik and the Soviet Union's demonstrated ICBM capability very much on their minds, the commission members went well beyond this. Strategists of the pre-Sputnik era generally assumed that the balance of terror was stable. Neither side could launch an attack—defense analysts called it a first strike—without suffering a devastating retaliatory blow. But the intercontinental missile seemed to have changed all that. Missiles fired from bases in the Soviet Union would take a mere thirty minutes to reach targets in the United States. And because the administration had not yet deployed radar capable of detecting such an attack, incoming missiles would hit without any warning.

The Gaither commission emphasized the overriding importance of building a strategic nuclear force capable of surviving an initial Soviet attack and retaliating. If the Soviets should decide to attack, the commission reasoned, the primary targets would be America's Strategic Air Command bases, which were soft—that is, vulnerable to such a blow. They therefore recommended that the administration act immediately to disperse SAC bombers, to construct blast shelters to protect them, to implement a vast civil defense program, and to establish an early warning radar network to detect incoming missiles. In addition, the commission recommended the deployment of 600 Atlas and Titan ICBMs rather than the 80 the administration had in mind. It also urged the deployment of 240 rather than 60 IRBMs at overseas bases.

During the next few years, prominent defense analysts, including Bernard Brodie and the RAND Corporation's Herman Kahn, elaborated on the Gaither commission's conclusion that the guided missile had fundamentally altered the strategic balance. But it was Albert Wohlstetter who had the greatest impact. In a January 1959 article, "The Delicate Balance of Terror," which appeared in *Foreign Affairs* magazine, Wohlstetter challenged the conventional wisdom that held that neither superpower could launch a first strike because each side possessed a large retaliatory capability. The survivability of strategic forces and the proper mix of systems to retaliate effectively, Wohlstetter pointed out, was far more important to an effective deterrent than merely having large numbers of weapons in the nation's inventory. Wohlstetter envisioned the possibility of a Soviet counterforce strike that would destroy much of the Strategic Air Command and the small force of American IRBMs on the ground. Remaining U.S. forces would of course retaliate. But the effectiveness of the American second strike would be limited by insufficient numbers of bombers and missiles, Soviet air defenses, and civil defense precautions. Noting that the Soviets had just recovered from a war that claimed the lives of twenty million people, Wohlstetter thought it at least conceivable that they might be tempted to pay that price again in order to defeat and perhaps destroy the United States. To avoid such a disaster and insure the continued stability of the balance of terror, he argued, the United States would have to take a variety of steps. His recommendations emphasized the creation of a "survivable" retaliatory strike force and a mix of active and passive defensive measures intended to protect the civilian population as well as the economic base in case of nuclear war.

Under unremitting attack in the media, by Congress, defense academics, and the military, Eisenhower tried to recoup some eroded credibility. He realized that his first reaction to Sputnik —to downplay its significance in order to head off a panicky overreaction—had proved to be a mistake. He now set out to regain lost ground. On November 7, 1957, in a television address to the nation, Eisenhower sought to assure the public that America's nuclear deterrent was just as effective as before. While admitting that the Soviets enjoyed a lead in missile development, he maintained that "the overall military strength of the free world is distinctly greater than that of the communist countries." Some might talk about a "missile gap" and a "space gap" but there was no "deterrent gap."

Simultaneously, Eisenhower and other members of his administration took pains to point out that missile research in the United States had not been neglected. On the contrary, ICBM research was well advanced and had the highest priority. The Atlas, a "first generation" missile, was almost ready for testing and the air force had already begun development of the more sophisticated Titan missile. Two IRBM programs, the air force's Thor and the army's Jupiter, had made rapid progress. When deployed at forward bases in Europe, these IRBMs would serve the same purpose as Soviet missiles that might be aimed at the United States. The president insisted that everything necessary was being done to develop the missile forces of the United States and that increased funding would not, and could not, speed up the process.

In counseling moderation, the president cautioned: "We must apply our resources at that point as fully as the need demands. This means selectivity in national expenditures of all kinds. We cannot on an unlimited scale have both what we must have and what we should like to have." Secretary of the Treasure George Humphrey was more cogent. "The real danger of Sputnik," he warned, "is that some too eager people may demand hasty and sensational action regardless of cost and relative merit in an attempt to surpass" the Soviets. "Americans," he continued, "must never lose their sense of balance and proportion."[26]

Eisenhower gave similar advice to the National Security Council as they gathered to consider the Gaither commission's recommendations. "We must neither panic nor become complacent," he told the assembled policymakers. "We should decide what needs to be done, and do it—avoiding extremes." Impressed by the view that survivability had become the crucial test of an effective deterrent, Eisenhower agreed to accelerate the dispersal of the strategic bomber force (already under way), ordered a speedup in the deployment of the ballistic missile early warning system, implemented plans designed to get bombers into the air more quickly in an alert, and gained congressional authorization to place a percentage of B-52 bombers on airborne alert in the event of a major crisis with the Soviets.

Eisenhower was far less enthusiastic about the $40 billion proposal to build a civil defense system. But it was John Foster Dulles who led the attack against the shelter scheme. The secretary of state erupted into a tirade, accusing the Gaither commission of exaggerating the danger and taking a narrow, purely military approach to a complex political problem. Warning that the United States could spend too much on defense and thereby devastate its economy, Dulles pointed out that the Kremlin had "made its greatest gains—its greatest seizures of territory and people—in 1945–50, when it had the ravages of war to repair and when only the United States had the atomic bomb."[27] He warned that if the United States began building a massive system of shelters, it would be tantamount to announcing that we had abandoned deterrence in favor of a first strike strategy. And if we did that, especially at a time when the western European nations could not afford such programs, we could "write off" the NATO alliance. That was the end of the discussion. Eisenhower sat back in his chair, grinned, and quipped, "You *are* a militant Presbyterian, aren't you?"[28]

But not even President Eisenhower, the most trusted leader of the postwar era, could calm an American public stampeded into fear by the Soviet Sputnik. Widespread belief in the fictive missile gap refused to disappear and, in the Kennedy administration, became the justification for an enormous expansion of America's strategic nuclear capabilities. It is therefore important to ascertain, to the degree possible, exactly how many missiles the Soviets did deploy during these last frenzied years of the 1950s. The United States intelligence community was even then using early electronic eavesdropping devices, the U-2 photoreconnaissance plane, and, beginning in August 1960, the Discoverer space satellite to gather information about military developments inside the U.S.S.R. As a result, American intelligence officers were able to state with a relatively high degree of confidence that between August 1957 and April of the following year, the Soviets conducted only ten tests of the long range SS-6 missile. Four of these were unsuccessful. Missile tests were then completely halted for almost a year, evidently because Soviet technicians had run into problems. As late as September 1959, when the first American Atlas missiles became operational, American intelligence had not located a single operational Soviet ICBM. In July 1960, the latest in a long string of national intelligence estimates still reported "the total absence of observed operational sites."[29] At the time that Eisenhower left the White House, the Soviets evidently still had no operational ICBMs save for those at two test sites.

The administration was of course unwilling to explain how it was gathering its information, but it was not shy about spreading the word. In an interview given to *U.S. News & World Report* in January 1959, Secretary of Defense McElroy stated categorically that the United States had no evidence that the Soviets had operational ICBMs. He went on to predict that they would at most have no more than one or two operational by the end of the year.

But such statements, whether they came from the Defense Department or the White House, had little effect. Eisenhower was kept on the defensive and forced to make concessions during each of the remaining years of his presidency. The original ballistic missile program of the United States called for the deployment of from twenty to forty missiles. Before Sputnik, the Eisenhower administration had already revised these figures upward. But according to Desmond Ball, "at no time before 1958 did the ballistic missile policy group seriously recommend to the Air Force that more than about 200 missiles be sent to operational sites."[30] After Sputnik, Eisenhower made significant surrenders to his congressional and air force critics. By the end of his administration, he had authorized the construction and deployment of 255 Atlas and Titan ICBMs as well as 450 silo based and 90 mobile Minuteman missiles. He also approved the construction of 19 Polaris type submarines each armed with 16 missiles. In all, Eisenhower approved a strategic missile force that approached the 1,100 mark.

During this period of missile-gap mania each of the military services, supported by their prime contractors and congressional friends, entered into a scramble to grab off research and development money that suddenly became available as Congress panicked after Sputnik. Herbert York, director of defense research for the Pentagon, was able to scratch some of the more technologically unrealistic proposals. He killed off Bambi, a scheme to surround the earth with myriad small satellites programmed to destroy missiles leaving the earth's atmosphere, and the Aerospace plane, a weapon intended to fly directly into orbit from a normal ground takeoff. Then again, a number of very questionable programs were funded. One was the B-70, a manned bomber that was built only to be scrapped during the Kennedy administration in favor of the more reliable and cost-effective Minuteman missile. One copy, a monument to the determination of the air force to keep its manned bomber program alive, resides today in the Dayton, Ohio, aerospace museum.

An even more bizarre example of a program that never should have been funded was the nuclear powered airplane, on the drawing boards since 1946. There were massive technological and scientific obstacles to overcome before a nuclear powered plane could be flown. No materials existed that could "stand up to the high-intensity nuclear radiation which necessarily existed throughout the interior of the reactor, resist corrosion by the very hot air which passed through the reactor at great speed," or be "guaranteed not to leak any of the highly radioactive fission products into the exhaust airstream" of the airplane. The shielding problem was equally perplexing. The material to be used obviously had to protect crew and cargo from the intense radiation generated by the reactor, had to be light enough to be flown, and also had to "be pierced in such a way as to allow large masses of air to pass through it at high speed without creating too large a radiation leak." Another problem that plagued project engineers was how to protect against the scattering of dangerous radioactive materials directly into the environment in the event of a crash.[31] In spite of the fact that after years of research none of these problems had been resolved, constant pressure from the Joint Committee on Atomic Energy, interested congressmen and contractors, and the air force kept the project alive. In 1957, after the orbiting of Sputnik, these pressures increased and remained intense for the remainder of Eisenhower's presidency. The message of those who fought hardest for a nuclear powered airplane was always the same and usually effective: if the United States did not develop one, the Russians would. Thus, in 1957, Congressman Melvin Price, a member of the JCAE, noted that while on a recent visit to Moscow, Soviet scientists had informed him that they were hard at work on a nuclear powered plane. He warned the president that "recent events including the launching of an earth satellite by the Soviet Union have lent urgency to the longstanding need for the United States to develop a flying capability in the field of nuclear-propelled aircraft."[32]

Air Force General Donald Keirn, head of the Aircraft Nuclear Propulsion Project, was even more emphatic. His fertile imagination conjured up "a fleet of enemy high-speed aircraft continuously patrolling the air space just outside our early warning net, capable of air-launching a devastating missile attack, followed by high-speed penetration or attack against our hardened installations."[33] Though this vision smacked more of *Star Trek* than the technological realities of 1957, *Aviation Week*, the principal organ of the aerospace industry press, nevertheless sought to convince the American public that Keirn's fantasy had come true. In a story that seemed authoritative, if only because it was datelined Washington, the magazine alleged that a "nuclear powered bomber" had already been "flight tested in the Soviet Union" and that the test had been witnessed by numerous foreign observers. The magazine accompanied this piece of startling "intelligence" with what were supposed to be detailed drawings of the plane and followed with a scathing editorial blaming the administration for this terrible setback.

> [The] appearance of this nuclear powered military prototype comes as a sickening shock to the many dedicated U.S. Air Force and Naval aviation officers, Atomic Energy Commission technicians, and industry engineers who have been working doggedly on our own nuclear aircraft propulsion program despite financial starvations, scientific scoffing, and top level indifference, for once again the Soviets have beaten us needlessly to a significant technical punch.[34]

Senator Richard Russell, Democrat from Georgia, commenting on this report in *Aviation Week,* told a television audience that it was "an ominous new threat to world peace" that followed "in tragic sequence the Russian success of last fall in launching the first earth satellite."[35]

Ten days after the *Aviation Week* article appeared, President Eisenhower, who presumably had better sources of intelligence than *Aviation Week* could command, denied the validity of the story. "There is absolutely no intelligence to back up a report that Russia is flight-testing an atomic-powered plane," he said. Meanwhile, a careful evaluation of progress on America's nuclear powered plane, done at the request of the director of defense research, "revealed that during all this political maneuvering, while there had been substantial progress in the rate of spending money, there had been precious little progress toward solving the basic problems which had been recognized by 1948, well over a decade before."[36] Nevertheless, in spite of the fact that ten years of research had led nowhere, funding for the project was continued, though at a reduced level, until 1961 when Defense Secretary Robert McNamara finally abandoned the project.

The "missile gap" controversy raged through most of Eisenhower's second administration. Although he never gave up the struggle, President Eisenhower was not entirely successful in resisting pressure for increased defense spending. Thus defense expenditures in 1960 were 20 percent higher than the level established in 1955 and 1956. And what did this increased emphasis on defense produce? On the positive side, it led directly to the creation of the National Aeronautics and Space Administration and the programs for manned space flight. The president's Science Advisory Committee, the Advanced Research Project Agency of the Defense Department, and the Office of the Director of Defense Research and Engineering were also important bureaucratic agencies that grew up in the period. On the negative side, it produced a strategically destabilizing "missile gap" of another sort, as the United States pulled rapidly ahead of the U.S.S.R. in the number of strategic weapons it deployed. Moreover, not one of the expensive new programs spawned by inventive technocrats, military men, and their industrial patrons after Sputnik produced anything significant. "Surprising as it may seem," Herbert York wrote in 1970, "the wild outburst of ideas inspired by Sputnik and the missile gap psychology has produced nothing of direct value to our current strategic posture more than twelve years later." It may even be that these new programs were detrimental to the defense effort. York believes that the sudden artificially induced demand for scientists and engineers stretched human resources too thin and led to "excessive job switching" and other forms of instability in the aerospace industry as salaries spiraled upward. The confusion thus created, he believes, helps to explain "the relatively low level of reliability of some of our early missiles and space launchers."[37]

Finally, when considering the negative effects of "missile mania" there is what Eisenhower referred to in his 1961 farewell address as "the military-industrial complex." This powerful force includes not only representatives from business and the military, but also academia, the scientific community, organized labor, and Congress. The complex was not born in the Eisenhower years, but it reached maturity during that time. The hysteria that followed Sputnik produced "a still bigger defense industry and hence a still bigger political constituency in support of weapons development. This, in turn, strengthened those elements of the Congress that automatically endorsed any weapons-development program, and tipped the congressional balance of power still further in that direction."[38] A powerful engine for the perpetuation of the arms race thus matured more rapidly than would otherwise have been the case, in the hysterical atmosphere created by the Soviet space exploit.

7

"Atoms for Peace"

THE DREAM OF PEACEFUL APPLICATIONS FOR NUCLEAR POWER, 1953–1957

STRATEGIC POLICY WAS NOT THE only area of Eisenhower's innovation. He was also responsible for reviving the languishing interest in nonmilitary applications of nuclear power. Where Truman and the early AEC had seemed obsessed with the arms race and competition with the Soviets, Eisenhower's less rigid approach to arms policy enabled his administration to take a broader view of nuclear power's potential. Responding to ideological and partisan pressures, Eisenhower launched an initiative in foreign affairs, known as "Atoms for Peace," that resulted in the hesitant beginning of the civilian nuclear power industry. By the time Eisenhower left office in 1961, the United States had established a beachhead in the international competition to market power reactors. It had brought the private sector into reactor development by revising the statutory basis of America's entire nuclear power program and by exempting the infant industry from financial responsibility for accidents that it might cause. But this generous exemption did not relieve the industry from the reactor accidents and controversy that dogged it from its earliest days.

Though it is difficult if not impossible to prove, many observers of the nuclear power industry conclude that a principal impetus for the development of civilian nuclear power was a sense of guilt over the role of science in the atomic destruction of Hiroshima and Nagasaki, followed by a desire to redeem science itself,

177

by diverting military applications to peaceful uses. In this vein, to cite one example, Daniel Ford maintains that

> instead of reflecting on the horrors visited upon Hiroshima and Nagasaki or on whether the bombs should have been used in the first place, news reports [in 1945] helped to alleviate the nation's feelings of repulsion and guilt by focusing public attention on the more congenial aspects of "the new force."[1]

Whether or not guilt spurred interest in nonmilitary nuclear power, nuclear scientists and lay commentators revived dreams of the atom's miraculous potential as an energy source that outdid H. G. Wells's Professor Rufus. Robert M. Hutchins, for one, anticipated Lewis Strauss's dream of electricity "too cheap to meter" when he predicted that nuclear-supplied "heat will be so plentiful that it will even be used to melt snow as it falls. . . . The central atomic power plant will provide all the heat, light, and power required by the community and these utilities will be so cheap that their cost can hardly be reckoned." George Gamow, a physicist with a knack for popularizing scientific subjects in writing for mass audiences, outdid Hutchins in anticipating "the miraculous 'K-ration' fuel, a small package of which will be enough to fly a huge passenger airliner across the ocean. We may also prepare ourselves for a trip to the moon and to various planets of our solar system in a comfortable rocketship driven by atomic power."[2] Others lyrically prophesied a transformation of our entire civilization through energy derived from small atomic pellets.

These hopeful visions, commonplace in 1946, were frozen in the chill of the Cold War, but they never entirely disappeared from the minds of scientists, despite their Buck Rogers quality. Meanwhile, at a much more mundane level, the organizational and industrial beginnings of civilian nuclear power appeared in the waning days of the Lilienthal AEC. Scattered flutterings of interest from electric utilities, chemical companies, and nuclear contractors in the military program coincided with a crucial diversion of the navy's nuclear propulsion program. These combined to create a weak impetus for nonmilitary research, which was stifled by the secrecy provisions of the Atomic Energy Act of 1946.

As AEC chairman, Lilienthal had never lost hope that nuclear power might prove to have some nonmilitary applications. Shortly before leaving the AEC, he contacted an acquaintance in industry, Philip Sporn of American Electric Power, who in turn persuaded the AEC to establish an advisory committee comprised of executives from some utilities, to investigate and make recommendations to the AEC on nuclear power's potential industrial applications. At first, Sporn's group took only the modest step of recommending greater declassification of technical data. But in 1949, Lawrence R. Hafstad, director of reactor development for the AEC, suggested to a friend in Dow Chemical Company that only the actual prototype development of nuclear reactors would bring industry into the atomic mainstream. Another chemical executive, Charles Thomas of Monsanto, expressed an interest in a power demonstration project, possibly involving a reactor then being constructed at Oak Ridge. Finally, several weeks after his retirement from the AEC, Lilienthal published an influential article in *Colliers* magazine, advocating commercial development of nuclear power. All these various contacts between the AEC and industry led the Commission to request proposals from industry for study projects using then-restricted data. Hafstad, meanwhile, managed to exploit the military emphasis dominant in the Korean War period to achieve nonmilitary goals when he argued that national defense would benefit from an expansion of the nation's supply of electrical power, to be provided by nuclear power reactors.

Monsanto, joined by Union Electric Co., a St. Louis–based utility, proposed a dual-purpose reactor that would produce both plutonium and electrical power. Comparable proposals came from a joint Dow Chemical–Detroit Edison team, from Commonwealth Edison of Chicago, and from another joint team, Pacific Gas & Electric and Bechtel Corporation, a civil engineering firm specializing in construction of power plants and other energy related projects. These early expressions of interest produced extremely powerful vested interests in what was to become the nuclear power industry. Commonwealth Edison and PG&E are today two of the nation's largest nuclear utilities; Bechtel is a leading builder of nuclear power plants; Dow and Monsanto have long been involved in defense-related nuclear projects. The nuclear-industrial complex was beginning to take shape. In the winter of 1951–1952, these four study groups formally asserted their interest to the AEC in pursuing reactor development, especially along hybrid-reactor lines, that is, reactors for both power and plutonium production. They also urged further AEC-funded studies. None recommended a single reactor design, but all hoped to see the development of some kind of nuclear reactor that would produce electricity to be fed to the national grid.

Late in 1951, a team from Argonne demonstrated that generation of electricity by a reactor was possible. At the AEC's National Reactor Testing Station (NRTS) in Idaho Falls, Idaho, they constructed EBR-1: Experimental Breeder Reactor number one, which they brought to criticality in August 1951. Walter Zinn, head of Argonne, then conducted an experiment on December 20 that established the power potential of nuclear reactors. From heat produced in a natural uranium blanket surrounding the core of EBR-1, Zinn connected a load dissipator to the station's generator and thereby produced enough electricity to light four 25-watt bulbs. In the log, Zinn noted the historic occasion laconically: "electricity flows from atomic energy."[3] Ironically, in the same month, the General Advisory Committee, meeting in Washington, reaffirmed its conclusion of three years earlier that nuclear power had a dubious economic future.

A third momentous impetus to civilian nuclear power took place in 1950, when the navy proposed what was in effect a triple-hybrid reactor: one that would be designed as a shore-based prototype of a propulsion reactor for a large surface vessel, such as an aircraft carrier, but that could also be used, after it served its experimental purpose, to produce both plutonium and electricity. The navy assigned Rickover to the project, and by 1952 Westinghouse began work on it.[4] But the Eisenhower administration, fulfilling the president's campaign promise to balance the budget by cutting federal expenditures, terminated the carrier project early in 1953. The whole issue meanwhile had been caught in the swirl of political and ideological controversy that surrounded the emergent debate over private versus public power. The priorities for the triple hybrid—plutonium production, engineering data, generation of electric power—had been shifting, as had the criteria for selection of a site for the carrier prototype. By 1952, the AEC began to show a strong interest in making power production a high priority. Simultaneously, the four industry study groups were expressing their interest in developing power reactors. This produced an incipient clash— should the first nuclear reactors be built by private industry or the federal government? This fanned the embers of the smouldering controversy that had burned during the 1930s over TVA. Utility executives and Republicans, including Eisenhower and the officials of his administration, feared "socialism" if the federal government developed nuclear power. Challenging them were many Democrats, as well as some lower-echelon officials in TVA and the Department of the Interior, who thought that nuclear power was too portentous for humankind to be left to a monopoly of private utilities.

Meanwhile, initiatives for development of power reactors began coming from the Eisenhower administration, which insisted on commercial development of nuclear power under private auspices. The administration even suggested to the AEC that the carrier prototype it was then killing be redirected toward the development of a power reactor. AEC commissioner Thomas Murray revised this suggestion and presented it again to the administration as an AEC proposal in May 1953. The AEC was concurrently recommending that the Atomic Energy Act of 1946 be revised, and it used the opportunity of recycling the carrier project as a concrete example of the benefits to be derived by letting private industry exploit the power of the atom. The JCAE also began to display an interest in the industrial applications of nuclear power. JCAE hopes were piqued by a letter from Walker Cisler, president of Detroit Edison, one of the companies involved in the study groups, expressing an interest in building a power reactor.

With the Republican victories in the fall of 1952, the GOP wrested control of the White House and both houses of Congress. The federal government was now dominated by the most intensely business-oriented administration since the 1920s. In Lewis Strauss, former AEC commissioner, now Eisenhower's personal adviser on nuclear matters and future AEC chairman, American capitalism enjoyed an aggressive advocate of its viewpoint. Many Republicans read the 1952 election results, as they had earlier hopefully looked for favorable portents in the auguries of the 1946 elections, as a sign that the American people were turning away from the New Deal with its "socialistic" experiments like public power and TVA.

By the beginning of 1953, it was apparent that the policy framework for the development of nuclear power embodied in the Atomic Energy Act of 1946 had become obsolete and counterproductive. One of the 1946 act's basic premises, the need for secrecy pending establishment of an effective system of international control of nuclear power, was an egregious failure. The possibility of effective international control was probably dead even in 1946. By 1953, the Soviet Union had become a nuclear power and it was an open secret that the British would soon become one. The French had constructed their first atomic pile in 1946 and there was a strong movement within the French government to develop a French atomic bomb. The Soviet test of a thermonuclear weapon was on the horizon.

The Atomic Energy Act of 1946 also impeded other objectives of American foreign policy. By effectively stifling the growth of a nonmilitary nuclear power industry, through its secrecy requirements, it kept American manufacturers from competing in the international market to sell nuclear reactors. Potential American suppliers worried about the British lead in developing power reactors. Calder Hall, a hybrid power-production reactor that came on stream in 1956, suggested that the British might capture the market provided by several European nations, especially Italy and Switzerland with their high electricity costs. The United States was handicapped from pursuing policies that would strengthen its partners in the NATO alliance by promoting European economic and political integration. American policymakers were also looking for some dramatic gesture to offset the Soviet achievement of developing nuclear weapons, particularly some accomplishment that would enhance America's sought-after reputation as a peace-loving nation facing an aggressive and militaristic U.S.S.R.

Probably the greatest failure of the 1946 act was its perverse encouragement of the very proliferation of nuclear knowledge and capability that the United States sought to limit, while at the same time it weakened the prospects for international control. The British were shocked and embittered at the secrecy provisions, which had rudely terminated the wartime partnership in an insulting and humiliating manner.[5] Determined to go it alone, British scientists created their own nuclear establishment at the Harwell laboratory and at the Windscale reactor, which went critical in 1950. Calder Hall's very existence served as a goad to American proponents of civilian nuclear power. Wartime fears of British rivalry in the nuclear industry seemed about to be realized, as much because of as in spite of the Atomic Energy Act of 1946. Political leaders in both Democratic and Republican administrations also felt a need to secure reliable foreign sources of uranium. Belgium's long-term control of Congolese mines was beginning to look doubtful as European colonialism waned, while the Canadians, sharing Great Britain's resentment of America's high-handed treatment of them in 1946, had pursued a go-it-alone nuclear policy that struck a discordant note in Canadian–American relations. Within the United States itself, some industry projections suggested that the nation would need more electricity before the end of the century than extant fossil fuel power plants could supply, and American pride recoiled at the idea of having to import reactor technology.[6]

President Eisenhower and his advisers were also keenly conscious of the value to be derived from a dramatic American propaganda initiative in the field of nuclear power. If the United States could establish some sort of lead in the development of nonmilitary nuclear applications, it would cast the Soviet Union, soon to be exploding a thermonuclear weapon, in a bad light. Additionally, it would divert attention from the crescendo of opposition to American atmospheric testing of fission and fusion weapons, giving American policy a civilian gloss that had previously been wholly lacking. The time was ripe for a thorough overhaul of American nuclear policy.

The president announced this new initiative in an address to the United Nations on December 8, 1953, that embodied his Atoms for Peace program. After a grim review of the destructive potential of the world's nuclear arsenals, Eisenhower suggested that "this greatest of destructive forces can be developed into a great boon, for the benefit of all mankind." To realize the biblical dream of turning swords into plowshares in the nuclear field, the president proposed that the United States, the Soviet Union, and Great Britain contribute uranium and other fissionable materials to a stockpile administered by a proposed International Atomic Energy Agency. The IAEA would "devise methods whereby this fissionable material would be allocated to serve the peaceful pursuits of mankind," particularly in the fields of agriculture, medicine, and power production. It would stimulate research into peaceful applications and generally promote disarmament.[7]

Atoms for Peace and its daughter idea, the "peaceful atom," proved to be remarkably long-lived images of policy. As metaphors, they survived long after their substantive fallacy had become obvious. Their basic assumption that the military and civilian applications of nuclear power could be separable, and that certain uses of nuclear power could be developed for peaceful purposes, held sway for almost a quarter century. In making these hopeful beliefs the foundations of American nuclear policy, Eisenhower reversed what had been until then the AEC's operating assumption, articulated by its first chairman, David Lilienthal, in 1947: "This must always be remembered: atomic-energy research and development—whether for the uses of war and destruction or for beneficent and creative purposes—is virtually an identical process: two sides of the same coin."[8] But Atoms for Peace formally enunciated the dogma that military and civilian applications were separable. Like other dogmas, it continued to be cherished by its believers as an article of faith long after it had ceased to be tenable as a matter of common sense or observation.

Atoms for Peace was a protean slogan, serving foreign policy objectives as well as domestic ones. Harold Green, a staff attorney with the AEC, explained in 1957 with a candor that has since gone out of fashion: "The rapid development of atomic power has become a primary element in the cold war, and it is regarded as of paramount importance that the United States, rather than the Soviet Union, be able to take the lead in bringing nuclear power to those areas of the world which are desperately in need of cheap power." "American industry," he added, must "be able to compete effectively with industry of other nations in the race for overseas nuclear markets."[9]

Atoms for Peace was in fact nothing less than a coherent global strategy for protecting western Europe from Soviet domination. Conceived as an "atomic Marshall Plan," Atoms for Peace was integrated with the emergent policies of Euratom, the European nuclear cooperative comprising France, the Federal Republic of Germany, Italy, and the Benelux countries. Behind the protection of America's military nuclear shield, the western European community was to develop an industry dependent on electricity produced by nuclear power, a brilliant solution for the coal- and oil-short nations of Euratom. Ultimately this grand scheme failed, due partly to the inflow of cheap Middle Eastern oil and partly to the reluctance of all NATO partners to see the United States undertake centralized energy planning for western Europe.[10]

The glittering generalities of the Atoms for Peace address would have to be supplemented by specific statutory and administrative policy before the promise of peaceful applications could be realized. The AEC enthusiastically turned its hand to the task, discarding the 1946 act's inconvenient framework. In an effort to rid the nation of nuclear isolationism, AEC staffers drafted bills designed to make it easier for the AEC to share nuclear information both with foreign nations and with American firms. New York Republican congressman Sterling Cole, new chairman of the JCAE and a nuclear enthusiast, plus Iowa Republican Senator Burke Hickenlooper, cooperated to substitute for these "administration bills" a revised bill known as the Cole–Hickenlooper bill, which was to become the 1954 Atomic Energy Act. The new statute did not altogether overturn the old; rather, it was a complex, tangled, and inconsistent clutch of compromises and evasions that marked a determined, if stumbling, effort to create a statutory framework in which civilian nuclear power might develop in the United States and be exported into the international market. In the words of one early commentator, the act was a "technically and economically premature statute" consisting of "an extraordinary bundle of ambiguous compromises, awkward contradictions and errors in drafting."[11]

In the preamble, Congress set forth its reasons for amending the McMahon Act. Because "atomic energy is capable of application to peaceful as well as military purposes," the revised statute declared, "the development, use, and control of atomic energy shall be directed so as to promote world peace, improve the general welfare, increase the standard of living, and strengthen free competition in private enterprise."[12] To achieve these ends, the existing statutory framework for nuclear power was modified in five ways:

1. The federal government should promote nuclear research and development.

2. This in turn required a less restrictive dissemination of unclassified data: Section 141 provided that "the dissemination of scientific and technical information in relation to atomic energy should be permitted and encouraged so as to provide that free interchange of ideas and criticism which is essential to scientific and industrial progress."

3. It provided a new scheme for the government's control of the use and production of nuclear energy.

4. It encouraged private industrial participation in the development of nuclear power.

5. It promoted international cooperation in nonmilitary applications.

The 1954 act discarded almost completely the 1946 act's provisions for governmental monopoly and absolute secrecy, except as to weapons. In their place, it provided for a system of control to be achieved through government ownership of "special nuclear materials" (essentially, fissionable materials such as plutonium and the isotopes U-233 and U-235) and through licensing the private ownership and use of "source materials," that is, ores, and the "utilization and production facilities" that would put them to use. Thus industry would be brought into the nuclear business, but with regulation preserved through the licensing system and subsequent supervision of the licensed industries. In an effort to preserve competition, the Act explicitly made the antitrust laws applicable to the nuclear industry. The AEC would similarly license medical research-and-development applications.

The Act attempted to deal with other problems of nuclear power. One section permitted the president to direct American participation in an "international atomic pool," the statutory green light that Eisenhower had promised in his Atoms for Peace address. The old secrecy-security restrictions were mitigated somewhat, both by statute and by later AEC regulations. In place of the absolutist either/or system established in the 1946 act, where data was either wholly secret or wholly open, the 1954 act created a new category of "restricted data" but encouraged liberal declassification of information out of that category. It imposed more severe penalties than the 1946 act (death, life imprisonment, $20,000 fine, 20 years imprisonment) for communication of such data with an intent to injure the United States or to secure an advantage for foreign powers, but moderated their severity by a new felony offense—disclosure of restricted data to unauthorized persons—which carried only a maximum fine of $2,500. The Act also permitted some dissemination of restricted data in the interests of international control. The AEC moderated the security system further by regulations establishing gray areas of information—data in this less sensitive category would not be as rigidly concealed—and by a new security classification, the "L clearance," which supplemented the old top-secret "Q clearance" by permitting access to less sensitive data. Declassification was speeded and liberalized by a new statutory test, that declassification would impose no "undue risk," rather than the older and more stringent test of "no adverse effect."[13]

The 1954 act reversed the old patents policy by permitting patenting of nonmilitary inventions, preserving, however, the primacy of national over private interest by permitting the AEC to declare certain patents and the inventions they represented to be "affected with a public interest," in effect confiscating them with payment of a suitable royalty fee. The statute also tried to abolish the controversial "cost-plus" contracts that the AEC had continued to use after the war.

The 1954 act provided only a framework within which change might take place. The success of the AEC in achieving meaningful change would depend on how skillfully Congress, the administration, and the AEC itself managed to finesse a lion in the path of nonmilitary nuclear applications: the controversy of public versus private power. It was here that the compromises of the statute were weakest. The 1954 act prohibited the AEC from getting into the power business itself by building reactors and selling their electricity, but it did permit the AEC to sell electricity produced incidentally to the operation of research and development or production facilities. It also authorized public-power bodies like TVA or the Bonneville Power Administration to apply for licenses to operate reactors, like any other utility. (Under the umbrella of these provisions, TVA has become one of the country's largest nuclear utilities.) Finally, it continued the policy of statutory preference in licensing and in sale of surplus electricity to "public bodies and cooperatives or to privately owned utilities providing electric utility services to high cost areas." But if Congress thought that these provisions would steer nuclear power through the Scylla and Charybdis of public vs. private power, such hopes were soon dispelled by the hurricane winds of the Dixon–Yates controversy, which blew the AEC right into the dispute that the 1954 act tried to avoid.

Dixon–Yates was a complex, squalid, and partisan controversy of no enduring significance—merely a symptom of the underlying conflict of public vs. private power. Democrats had been smarting ever since the Republicans had made political capital out of the charge of corruption in the 1952 presidential campaign, based on nothing more serious than mink-coat favors to a subordinate official of the Truman administration. In late 1950, as part of its program of expanding production facilities for weapons material, the AEC had approved construction of a huge gaseous diffusion plant at Paducah, Kentucky, in the extreme western tip of the state, on the Mississippi River near the junction of the Missouri–Illinois–Kentucky borders. This plant greatly increased the demand the AEC was making on TVA for electricity in the Tennessee Valley region. So in early 1954, Eisenhower suggested that the AEC release power back to TVA, and get its power from private utilities. In October 1954, the AEC approved a contract that would permit two private utilities, the Dixon–Yates group (named after the presidents of the two utilities), to build a power plant in West Memphis, Arkansas, that would feed power into the TVA system to supply Memphis with electricity. Public-power Democrats sensed an opportunity to turn the corruption charge back on the GOP, alleging improper favoritism in awarding the contract. Their campaign cry in the fall 1954 elections was "Nixon, Dixon, and Yates," though the vice-president had nothing to do with the affair. Democrats claimed that the Eisenhower administration and AEC Chairman Lewis Strauss were using the Dixon–Yates contract as a means of trying to gut public power in the TVA region. The charge of corruption took on a little substance in January 1955, when the JCAE, dominated by Democrats, many of whom were public-power advocates and some of whom were in a vindictive frame of mind, disclosed that an official of Dixon–Yates's financial agent, the First Boston Corporation, simultaneously served as a consultant to the Bureau of the Budget on the Dixon–Yates contract. Though this was not exactly an instance of massive corruption, it made the whole transaction suspect, and Eisenhower canceled the contract in July. Memphis, meanwhile, had announced that it was building its own power plant, and the controversy trailed off. But, in AEC Commissioner Eugene Zuckert's apt metaphor, it left the AEC politically "deflowered."[14]

Dixon–Yates was symptomatic of an intense political and ideological struggle under way within the AEC, and between the AEC and the JCAE, which was echoed in struggles between the new Democratic Congress and the Republican administration. AEC Chairman Strauss, a self-made millionaire who had come into public service out of investment banking, was almost fanatically dedicated to the expansion of both civilian and military nuclear power. His personal creed on the matter approached extremes, as when he suggested in a 1955 *Reader's Digest* article that God Himself had given humankind nuclear power. "My faith tells me that the Creator did not intend man to evolve through the ages to this stage of civilization only now to devise something that would destroy life on this earth."[15] Such an attitude deprived him of the critical distance and skepticism of his predecessor, Lilienthal, and placed him in the camp of nuclear True Believers that included his successors Glenn Seaborg and Dixie Lee Ray. Strauss's dogmatic dedication to nuclear power was exceeded only by his fervent espousal of the cause of private power, which he saw as a citadel of free-enterprise capitalism besieged by the armies of socialism marching under the banner of public power.[16] His closed ideologue's mind guaranteed a confrontation with public-power Democrats.

The confrontation was not long in coming. Democrats on the JCAE, led by California Representative Chet Holifield, one of the most prominent and effective nuclear advocates in Congress in the entire postwar period, called for "nuclear TVAs" as the only way to realize the nonmilitary potential of nuclear power. The Atomic Energy Act of 1954 seemed to have squelched the idea of nuclear TVAs, but that did not prevent congressional Democrats from pushing the Holifield viewpoint. They incorrectly accused Strauss and the AEC generally of foot-dragging in promoting reactor development and backed the Gore–Holifield bill of 1956, named after its sponsors Holifield and Democratic Senator Albert Gore of Tennessee. This bill would have appropriated $400 million for the construction of demonstration reactors by the federal government in partnership with industry. The bill died in the House, and its defeat marked the high point of the public versus private power controversy, though the dispute sputtered on inconsequentially a few years longer. The basic compromise policy outlined in the 1954 act prevailed: prohibition of direct federal involvement in building reactors, permission for public agencies to build and operate reactors, reliance principally on private utilities to develop nuclear power, and a lavishly generous outlay of federal subsidies to nuclear industry.

Despite this policy consensus favoring private power, by an historical irony the first commercial reactor in the United States proved to be just what the Democratic backers of the Gore–Holifield bill had demanded: a federally funded demonstration reactor built in partnership with private industry. The genesis of the Shippingport, Pennsylvania, reactor can be traced back to President Eisenhower's budget stringency, which had the effect of killing further development of one of Hyman Rickover's projects at Bettis: the prototype propulsion reactor for a large surface vessel. It occurred to some that this prototype might be recycled for nonmilitary use. In June 1953, the AEC adopted guidelines for such a project, specifying that it be a pressurized water reactor, which had the long-term effect of committing the United States to light-water reactors, as opposed to heavy-water or liquid-metal types. It also bent reactor development in the direction of the engineering, results-oriented approach favored by Rickover, rather than an academic, experimental approach that might have been followed if the National Laboratories were directing the project. Rickover set fall 1957 as the target date for bringing this power reactor on stream, and assigned responsibility for design of the reactor to Westinghouse. The AEC required that a utility operate the plant.

After the Soviet Union tested its first thermonuclear device on August 12, 1953, AEC Commissioner Thomas Murray sought to turn the Soviet threat to America's advantage. He saw the Westinghouse project as an offset to the U.S.S.R.'s propaganda coup because it projected an image of the United States as the proponent of peaceful applications for nuclear power. In a speech to utility executives in October 1953, Murray maintained that electric power generation would be as significant as purely military projects in the arms race with the U.S.S.R. But he recognized that nuclear-generated electricity would not be competitive in cost with electricity derived from fossil fuels, so he suggested a government–industry partnership in nuclear development, an implicit promise of governmental subsidy for the new power source.

These ideas impressed Phillip Fleger, president of Duquesne Light Company, a Pittsburgh utility. Fleger wanted his comparatively small company to participate in the proffered partnership for a variety of reasons: it would be good publicity for Duquesne, it would forestall a governmental monopoly in the development of nuclear power, and it would patriotically contribute to various foreign policy objectives. Westinghouse was pleased to have Duquesne aboard, since Westinghouse corporate headquarters were in Pittsburgh and Duquesne was an old customer. Westinghouse brought in Combustion Engineering, Inc., to build the pressure vessel and Babcock & Wilcox to build the generators. Stone & Webster of Boston was the architect-engineer for the plant.

In September 1954, President Eisenhower, in Denver, used a neutron source, which press accounts dubbed a "radioactive wand," to activate remotely a bulldozer that began groundbreaking on the site of the nation's first commercial power reactor at Shippingport. Work progressed on schedule, thanks in part to Rickover's firm hand and in part to the determination of AEC Chairman Strauss that the United States try to maintain a competitive posture with Great Britain in nonmilitary nuclear development. Strauss wanted the United States to enjoy the prestige of being the first nation to construct a purely "civilian" reactor, and the British Atomic Energy Authority was expected to bring the Calder Hall reactor on line in 1956. Shippingport was not quite the world's first electricity generating reactor, however. The dual-purpose Soviet reactor (plutonium production plus power) at Obninsk, a little unit (5 MWe) as reactors go, went on line in 1954, and the larger (50 MWe) British dual reactor at Calder Hall began supplying power to the British grid in 1956. But Shippingport was the world's first reactor devoted exclusively to the generation of electricity, with no plutonium production on the side. Because of—or despite—Rickover's legendary insistence on rigid conformity to specifications and high standard of quality control, Shippingport began generating appreciable amounts of electricity by Christmas 1957. It was decommissioned in 1982, following years of controversy over its routine operating releases of radioactivity.

In its day, Shippingport enabled Westinghouse and the AEC to provide a massive education program for American engineers through seminars and technical reports. Its initial success as an engineering project stimulated later reactor development, proving the technical (but not economic) feasibility of nuclear power as an alternative to fossil fuels. It established light-water reactors as *the* American reactor. There was great symbolic significance in the choice of a full-size replica of Shippingport's pressure vessel as the centerpiece of the American exhibit at the Geneva conference on the peaceful uses of nuclear power in 1958. With Shippingport, nonmilitary nuclear power emerged as a partner with military nuclear power.

But in the crucial years of 1954–57, Shippingport was the only bright spot in the picture for nuclear-power advocates. Elsewhere, they met only obstacles and frustration, culminating in a challenge so severe that, for a time, the power reactor program was stopped dead in its tracks.

The troubles began, by another great historical irony, with the reactor that had produced the world's first nuclear generated electricity: EBR-1 at the National Reactor Testing Station in Idaho. On November 29, 1955, NRTS officials were testing the behavior of EBR-1's core under deliberately induced, abnormally high temperatures.[17] The problem they were investigating is this: in a fast breeder, with a core of highly enriched fuel, a disruption in the configuration of the core, such as that produced by a partial melt of the cladding containing the fuel, would make the core more radioactive, inducing higher temperatures, which would then make it more radioactive yet, and so on into a dangerously escalating, reinforcing cycle of temperature/radioactivity buildup. At the conclusion of the test at the Idaho station, the operator tried to shut down the reaction using the control rods, a relatively slow procedure, rather than the scram mechanism, which would have shut down the reactor instantaneously. The fuel melted and slumped to the bottom of the containment vessel where coolant resolidified it. About half the fuel had melted; the core was destroyed.

Curiously, no one informed AEC chairman Strauss. Word of the meltdown did not enter public debates until a newspaper reporter asked Strauss about it in April 1956, four months later. Strauss professed ignorance; later in the day, the AEC issued a press release admitting the occurrence. News of the EBR-1 meltdown could not have come at a worse time. For at that moment, the AEC was beginning licensing procedures for one of the most ambitious reactor projects to date, the Fermi-1 300 MWe fast breeder. The Fermi reactor proved to be such a multiple disaster for the nuclear power industry that nuclear advocates might well wish that Detroit Edison and its chairman, Walker Cisler, had never developed an enthusiasm for a commercial breeder.

As one of the first steps in its program to promote private development of nuclear power under the revised policy of the 1954 Atomic Energy Act, the AEC created what it called the Power Reactor Demonstration Program, which constituted the carrot half of a carrot-and-stick approach to persuading industry to make a commitment to nuclear development. The program was a series of enticing subsidies so generous that even such an unquestioning nuclear enthusiast as Senator Clinton Anderson, Democrat of New Mexico, condemned it as an effort to "force-feed atomic development" at the expense of the American tax-payer.[18] These subsidies included free nuclear fuel for reactors, reimbursement for private research and development costs, and federally funded research and development in the National Laboratories. Lest the appeal of this carrot prove inadequate, the stick of nuclear TVAs loomed in the background.

Responding to the AEC's beckoning, Detroit Edison formed a consortium of some twenty firms, two thirds of them utilities, the rest nuclear suppliers, called the Power Reactor Development Corporation.[19] PRDC supplier-members included Westing-house, Babcock & Wilcox, and Combustion Engineering. In November 1954, Detroit Edison invited some leading physicists, among them Argonne's Walter Zinn (who had supervised the building of EBR-1), and Hans Bethe to a symposium on the problems of fast breeders. These consultants were not encouraging: they warned that a meltdown might preclude the control rods from shutting down the reaction, leading to disastrous results. Similar doubts beset the Advisory Committee on Reactor Safeguards nearly two years later. (The ACRS was a body of scientists and engineers or other technical experts that advised the AEC on safety issues. Until safety investigations became routine to the point where they could be handled by AEC staff, the ACRS was involved in every request for reactor construction permits.) In June 1956, the ACRS declared that not enough was known to be able to assure that a fast breeder could be safely operated near a major American city. The Fermi site was thirty miles south of Detroit and Windsor, Ontario, and twenty miles north of Toledo.

Undeterred, the AEC in August 1956 issued a provisional construction permit to PRDC. This touched off a political and legal explosion whose tremors are still being felt today. Relations between the AEC and the Joint Committee had been deteriorating ever since Lewis Strauss became AEC chairman in July 1953. This was the result partly of policy disagreements and partly of a conflict between two powerful personalities, Strauss and the JCAE's Senator Clinton Anderson. Following the passive period that characterized its first three years of existence, the JCAE in the years 1950–53 aggressively promoted greater military nuclear development, demanded increased production of fission bombs, urged development of the Super, sought greater production of fissionable material and the opening of more uranium mines. Though the JCAE constantly nagged and prodded the AEC, relations between the AEC and the JCAE remained cordial until 1953. After a transitional period, those relations ran rapidly downhill in the partisan conflict over Dixon–Yates. Truman appointees on the AEC, especially Murray, complained to the JCAE that too much power was becoming centralized in the hands of Chairman Strauss. Moreover, the potential for conflict between Strauss's dual roles of AEC chairman and nuclear adviser to the president was beginning to surface. Strauss, for his part, often refused to respond to queries from the JCAE about administration nuclear policy, invoking the doctrine of executive privilege (the confidentiality of communications between the president and his subordinates in the executive branch). The discontent of congressional Democrats with Strauss's policies produced the Gore–Holifield bill, as well as a great deal of public carping about Strauss's biases.

Into this soured political atmosphere, with JCAE Democrats impatient and frustrated, and Strauss maintaining an attitude of galling aloofness, the PRDC controversy came to Washington. Michigan's Democratic governor, Mennen "Soapy" Williams, asked the AEC for assurances that Fermi-1 would pose no safety problems for the Detroit metropolitan area. The AEC declined to reveal the results of its safety studies to Williams. After it issued the provisional construction permit, the JCAE's chairman, Senator Anderson, wired Williams, commiserating with him and condemning the AEC's refusal to let him in on the safety deliberations. Anderson asserted that the AEC had "violated established legal principles by the confusion of its development and promotion functions with its regulative and quasi-judicial functions." Going further than his JCAE colleague, Congressman Chet Holifield wrote President Eisenhower, asking that the president persuade the AEC to rescind its provisional permit in light of the unsettling ACRS report. To Governor Williams, Holifield prophetically wired that "once large sums of money are spent for construction, pressures to have reactor operated will be overwhelming."[20]

More to the point, Anderson and the JCAE took two momentous steps in the summer of 1956 to impede the construction of Fermi-1. First, Anderson urged United Auto Workers union president Walter Reuther to intervene in the AEC licensing proceedings to attempt to halt construction on safety grounds. The UAW did so, and provoked an eleven-month struggle. Though it ultimately lost, the UAW established the principle that nonparties in regulatory hearings have the right to participate as "intervenors." This effectively opened AEC hearings to public participation. Previously, such hearings had been held behind closed doors, with only the AEC's decision, not the testimony, printed in the *Federal Register.* Now AEC hearings became public forums, open to unions, environmentalists, and activists of all sorts, much to the AEC's chagrin. The new role of intervenors also turned AEC hearings into legalistic struggles, where administrative hearings were replayed in the courts after dissatisfied parties or intervenors sought to have a judicial authority overturn some regulatory rule. So it was in the Fermi-1 case: after the AEC's Atomic Safety and Licensing Board affirmed issuance of the construction permit, the union intervenors secured a reversal by the United States court of appeals for the District of Columbia circuit. Now it was the PRDC's turn: it appealed to the United States Supreme Court, which by a 7–2 decision sustained the AEC and the PRDC. Justices Hugo Black and William O. Douglas dissented sharply, Douglas condemning the AEC's procedures as "a lighthearted approach to the most awesome, the most deadly, the most dangerous process that man has ever conceived."[21] The utility and the AEC won this battle, but they had begun to lose the long war of attrition waged by intervenors against nuclear power.

While Anderson was sending angry telegrams to Michigan, he also forced the AEC to embark on a full-dress investigation of reactor safety problems. The AEC commissioned the Brookhaven National Lab to prepare this review. The resulting document, technically titled "Theoretical Possibilities and Consequences of Major Accidents in Large Nuclear Power Plants," but more popularly known as WASH-740, was released in March 1957.[22] Oddly, the AEC expected that the Brookhaven report would mollify the general public if not Fermi-1's opponents, because it stated that a nuclear disaster was extremely improbable, no more likely than one chance in 100,000 per reactor year, maybe as little as one chance in a billion. But those were not the figures that caught the headlines. Rather, the press picked up on estimates of the worst-case damages: 3,400 deaths, 43,000 injuries, $7 billion property damage. Another contemporaneous study, commissioned by PRDC and carried out by the Engineering Research Institute at the Ann Arbor campus of the University of Michigan "made even WASH-740 look like soothing bedtime reading," in Walter Patterson's words.[23] Conjuring up an even worse "worst case" than WASH-740, but an entirely credible one, the Michigan study estimated 133,000 fatalities, followed by 425,000 long-term physical or genetic injuries. These estimates staggered the nuclear power industry, not so much by their apocalyptic scenes of death, suffering, and radioactive hell, as by their implications for that most prosaic of topics, liability insurance.

When the original Atomic Energy Act was amended in 1954, proponents of civilian nuclear power were aware that there might be an insurability problem lurking in the future, and utility executives suggested to Congress that the federal government, rather than the utilities, insure the operation of nuclear reactors. But no such provisions were included in the 1954 act, and industry was left to its own devices. Even before the 1956 estimates of casualties and damage became publicized, utilities interested in going nuclear learned that they could not cover their potential losses by buying insurance. Insurors refused to underwrite nuclear reactors for two perfectly sound reasons: there was no operating experience to guide actuarial calculations; and the possible scope of a nuclear catastrophe was far beyond the capacity of any insuror, or group of insurors, to cover. As Herbert Dennenberg, former insurance commissioner for the Commonwealth of Pennsylvania later remarked, "Nobody but God could write the insurance policy we need on nuclear plants."[24] Herbert W. Yount, vice-president of Liberty Mutual Insurance Company, agreed in testimony before the JCAE. Alluding to the possibility of an accident running into billions of dollars, Yount speculated:

> It is a reasonable question of public policy as to whether a hazard of this dimension should be permitted, if it actually exists. Obviously there is no principle of insurance which can be applied to a single location where the potential loss approached such astronomical proportions. Even if insurance could be found, there is serious question whether the amount of damages to persons and property would be worth the possible benefit accruing from atomic development.[25]

And even if underwriters could somehow cover losses, no utility could afford to pay the premiums for such massive coverage. This was not a merely speculative or academic problem. After Shippingport, nine other reactors were proposed in the first two rounds of solicited proposals under the Power Reactor Development Program. Unless the insurance problem could be solved, the newborn industry faced infanticide.

Lawyers came to the rescue of beleaguered actuaries, engineers, and management. Harold P. Green, the JCAE staff attorney, glimpsed the outlines of a solution. The international objectives of the nuclear power program and the novelty of the technology "preclude reliance upon forces of the marketplace as determinants of the rate of nuclear growth," he wrote. Nuclear development would require an "aggressive program of Government intervention," even though such activity "cannot be justified on conventional economic grounds."[26] The necessary unconventional solution was shortly proposed by the JCAE, which urged Congress "not to treat this as an insurance problem but to treat it as an indemnification problem."[27] What the JCAE meant by this was not the conventional third-party liability indemnity contract, under which, say, the federal government would make good all losses beyond those the industry and its insurors could cover, but rather an "indemnity" in a more literal and unusual sense of the term. The nuclear power industry would be released from liability for all damages above a specified and relatively trivial amount. The loss was to be borne by the victims. Arthur Murphy, another nuclear attorney, explained the thinking that underlay this proposal. The "atomic industry should be protected against the possibility of overwhelming losses from liability in the event of a catastrophic accident."[28] Murphy, like other nuclear spokesmen, did not see any need to protect victims fully from those overwhelming losses. Harold L. Price, the director of the AEC's Division of Civilian Applications, was even more candid. In testimony given at 1956 hearings on the insurance problem, he told the JCAE that the AEC had "not approached this from the standpoint of disaster insurance to protect the public. . . . We are trying to remove a roadblock that has been said to interfere with people getting into this program."[29] With this approach in mind, the ingenuity of staff attornies for the AEC and the JCAE created the most generous subsidy of all to the nuclear power industry: the 1957 Price–Anderson Act.

This statute required utilities to obtain $60 million in private coverage, and provided an additional $500 million in federal coverage which, of course, was paid for by the American taxpayer. This ratio of coverage was to be altered over the years, with the private contribution increasing and the federal liability correspondingly shrinking.[30] But $560 million was the ceiling on total liability, less than a tenth of WASH-740's estimate of property damage alone. And WASH-740 proved to be an unrealistically conservative estimate. The statute also contained a ten-year statute of limitations, a particularly vicious provision from the viewpoint of potential cancer victims, because cancer latency often exceeds ten years. Price–Anderson was renewed in 1965 and again in 1975, when the statute of limitations was extended to twenty years, still an insufficient period. In keeping with Congress's eagerness to exempt the nuclear industry from liability for any disasters it causes, all homeowners' liability policies today contain clauses excluding coverage for injuries caused by nuclear accidents.

Antinuclear activists in the 1970s, hoping that the demise of Price–Anderson would doom the industry, sought to have the statute declared unconstitutional, alleging that its shift of the burden of liability from tortfeasor to victim deprived potential nuclear victims of property without due process of law and denied them the equal protection of the laws. Though this claim was upheld in a United States district court, the Supreme Court disagreed, holding that the substitution of statutory remedies for those available under the common law did not deprive potential victims of property, for two reasons: first, the statutory remedies were more certain, if less adequate; and second, Congress had promised vaguely to take "whatever action is deemed necessary and appropriate to protect the public from the consequences" of a nuclear catastrophe.[31] As a matter of law, this was an extraordinary conclusion—when is a tortfeasor relieved of liability when some third party promises to provide unspecified relief?—but it was in keeping with the Supreme Court's disinclination to challenge Congress on nuclear matters. The Court's opinion notwithstanding, the potential uncompensated losses of nuclear accident victims constitute a massive subsidy to the industry.

With the two major nuclear events of 1957—Shippingport coming on stream and enactment of Price–Anderson—the civilian nuclear power industry made its debut. Though not economically viable, the use of nuclear power for the generation of electricity was a technological reality, and seemed to offer some hope for a redemption from Hiroshima and Nagasaki.

8

"Sunshine Units"

THE FALLOUT CONTROVERSY, 1953–1963

THOUGH ANTINUCLEAR ACTIVISM seems a phenomenon of the 1970s, its roots go back much further than that. Originating with popular worry over atmospheric weapons testing, the basis for later antinuclear activism was laid in the 1950s, as Americans gradually became aware that American and Soviet fallout was raining strange and invisible poisons down on them.

From 1946 through 1949, the AEC conducted five nuclear weapons tests at the remote Bikini and Eniwetok island chains in the South Pacific. Protection for military personnel was inadequate from the beginning. Radiological safety officers at the 1946 navy Bikini tests complained that ships' commanders permitted their crews to be exposed to radioactive fallout without protection. The Pentagon's Defense Nuclear Agency today shrugs off criticism of those procedures, contending that the test procedures were "generally within established radiation exposure limits."[1] The South Pacific sites soon proved to be undesirable from the viewpoint of the military and the AEC, however. Extended lines of supply, the accessibility of the test sites to Soviet surveillance, and emergent opposition to nuclear testing among the nations of the Pacific basin all stimulated the AEC to seek potential locations within the continental United States for nuclear weapons testing. After exploring five candidate sites, the Commission settled on the Las Vegas–Tonopah Bombing and Gunnery Range, a vast, roadless, uninhabited tract of some 1,350 square miles in the southern part of Nevada, northwest of Las Vegas. At first, this place seemed to have little to recommend it. Original reports described it as suitable only for "a few relatively low-order detonations," and then only on an emergency basis.[2] But after the outbreak of the Korean War, President Truman quickly approved the Nevada site.

The Nevada option may have solved logistics problems, but it presented an inescapable biological danger: the fallout of radioactive debris on humans and the environment around the test site. To evaluate these, the AEC convened a conference of physicists, meteorologists, radiologists, and others at Los Alamos on April 24, 1950. There, army and AEC physicians recommended dangerously high levels of radiation, up to 25 roentgens,* as one-time dosage ceilings. They finally settled on a maximum dosage of 6 to 12 roentgens *outside* a 180° test sector having a radius of 100 miles. Las Vegas, Nevada, is about sixty-five miles from the Yucca Flats test site, the most irradiated, nuclear-blasted spot on the face of the earth.

Physicians accepted the high 1950 dosage ceiling in reliance on the "threshold theory" of radiation, which postulated that there was a minimum level below which radiation would have no permanent effects. In this view, humans could tolerate repeated subthreshold doses. In 1953, the AEC confidently trumpeted that

> Over a period of many years, a human being may safely receive a total amount of radiation which would cause a fatal illness if administered to his whole body within a period of a few minutes.

And:

> low levels of radiation produce no detectable somatic effect; that is, the body is able to repair the damage virtually as quickly as it occurs. Such low level exposure can be continued indefinitely without any detectable bodily change.[3]

*A roentgen (abbreviation R) is a measure of ionizing gamma and X-ray radiation. It has been superceded by a unit called the rem (roentgen equivalent in man), a biological measure of radiation, and the rad (radiation absorbed dosage), a measure of physical absorptance of radiation.

But despite this hopeful whistling-through-the-graveyard, the AEC did realize that fallout might pose some hazards. In 1953, it created the weirdly named Project Sunshine, a program to monitor the levels of the radioactive isotope strontium-90 deposited worldwide by fallout. AEC Commissioner Willard Libby supervised the work, which adopted an arbitrary level of 100 micromicrocuries as the maximum permissible concentration of Sr-90. Someone on the project had the bright idea of calling a specified amount of Sr-90 a "sunshine unit," a bit of unintended, ghastly humor that the AEC quickly disavowed, but never quite lived down.[4]

Department of Defense advisers calculated that the 1950 AEC dosage ceilings would permit test shots in the 25- to 50-kiloton range, but they added a recommendation that became of paramount importance throughout the period of atmospheric testing: "Not only must high safety factors be established in fact, but the acceptance of these factors by the general public must be insured by judicious handling of the public information program."[5] Public relations thus became an integral component of the continental atmospheric testing program through the entire twelve years of its duration from 1951 through 1963.

The AEC began its Nevada tests with the Ranger series in January 1951 at a site known as Frenchman's Flat, some sixty-five miles from the fringes of Las Vegas. To the AEC's puzzled surprise, one of the shots, a relatively modest 8-kiloton blast, broke storefront windows in Las Vegas. In July 1951, the AEC's Military Liaison Committee delivered its own bombshell. Army Colonel H. M. Roper recommended that military personnel—he had in mind an entire regimental combat team, 5,000 soldiers—be stationed near the test site at the time of explosion for purposes of testing the psychological effects of battlefield use of tactical nuclear weapons. The AEC approved, but insisted that support of the soldiers was the military's responsibility. The Department of Defense promptly began constructing a military encampment, Camp Desert Rock, near the tiny crossroads town of Mercury, which lay just outside the test range.

Though army planners were probably not aware of it at the time they made this recommendation, General Leslie Groves had been the first to come up with the idea of using a soldier for experimental or demonstration purposes. Two months after the Trinity explosion in 1945, Groves wanted to reassure American reporters that radioactivity posed no hazards at the New Mexico site, so he ordered Patrick Stout, an army counterintelligence agent, to descend into the blast crater to prove this. Stout did so and emerged seemingly unscathed, but he probably received about 100R dose. He died of leukemia in 1967.[6]

Throughout all subsequent tests, the army moved soldiers toward ground zero as soon as possible after the detonation. It pressured the AEC to permit soldiers to be stationed ever nearer ground zero at the moment of impact, moving them from seven miles out to four and then eventually as close as one mile (in trenches). The AEC, after some debate, reluctantly acquiesced. The monitoring of radiation in subsequent tests grew increasingly sloppy, as soldiers took over the task from AEC civilians. Soldiers soon were ordered to advance to ground zero immediately after detonation, rather than waiting for radiation to subside to permissible levels. The commandant of Camp Desert Rock wrote his soldiers afterward, with unintended irony, that "for the first time in our history, troops successfully attacked directly toward ground zero immediately following the atomic explosion. You can remember, with a sense of pleasure and accomplishment, that you were one of those troops, a real pioneer in experimentation of the most vital importance to the security of the United States."[7]

Chafing under the AEC-imposed restriction of 3R dose for ground personnel at the test site, AEC health physicists insisted that air force personnel flying planes through mushroom clouds on radioactive sampling missions be allowed a dosage of twenty or more roentgens. Once that ceiling had been established, Navy Captain John C. Hayward demanded a doubling of the ceilings for ground personnel, arguing that the 20R+ level for pilots demonstrated that humans could sustain greater exposure than the "conservative" AEC limits. The AEC again gave in, washing its hands of the matter by warning the military services "of the hazards in order that they may be fully aware of the responsibility which they assume."[8] In this way, responsibility for the fate of those men now known as the "atomic soldiers" passed from AEC civilians to military commanders eager to get on with human experimentation.

Eugene Zuckert, an AEC commissioner from 1952 to 1954, later recalled that Defense officials "knew the implications" of using soldiers in this way. "The AEC was not in a position to recommend that normal limits be observed," Zuckert went on, though he did not explain why.[9] Presumably, in this era of rampant McCarthyism, a publicly aired disagreement between military brass and AEC civilians would appear to be something worse than unseemly. The AEC, only seven years old and still elbowing to establish itself in the bureaucratic structure, might have seemed unpatriotic if it raised quibbles about the irradiation of American infantrymen. With AEC resistance thus neutralized, according to Defense Department estimates somewhere between 250,000 and 500,000 soldiers, sailors, marines, and airmen, plus some unknown number of civilians, were used as experimental subjects of weapons tests between 1945 and 1963. The crudity of these figures is symptomatic of the lack of care with which the military services approached the whole matter.

Despite the AEC's concern for its public relations, protests over atmospheric testing began coming in almost immediately, first at a trickle, then swelling to an irresistible tide. The AEC and the Defense Department responded with soothing assurances and cover-up. From the outset, a pattern developed that continues to the present: lay people or scientists would protest some facet of official nuclear policy; the AEC (or NRC, JCAE, Department of Defense, etc.) dismissed the objection as unfounded and poured on a public relations rebuttal; the protests continued to mount; and eventually the AEC gave way, implicitly admitting the validity of the protester's views by lowering dosage ceilings.

When 1952 press reports revealed that soldiers were being deliberately exposed to nuclear test shots, Helen Dodds of Lexington, Kentucky, wrote President Eisenhower, objecting to the practice and demanding trenchantly "if the men running this experiment say there is no danger, then why do they build such elaborate shelters for themselves, farther away from the explosion area than the troops which have no protection?" Air Force

Colonel H. C. Donnelly replied reassuringly that "in none of the many military maneuvers has there been an instance of injury to personnel as a result of exposure to the atomic weapon, and you may rest assured that under present policies, the chances of any such injury in the future are so extremely remote that they are negligible."[10] Mrs. Dodds's objections could be shrugged off because she was a laywoman, but scientific criticism a year later was another matter.

The path of fallout was demonstrated dramatically in 1953 by a peculiar happenstance. During a heavy rainstorm on the Troy–Schenectady–Albany area of New York State two days after a 43-kiloton shot at Yucca Flats, Professor Herbert Clark of Rensselaer Polytechnic Institute noticed abnormally high readings on laboratory Geiger counters. Close investigation revealed substantial radioactivity throughout the region, but especially around places where rainwater collected, such as a nearby reservoir. Dosages were approximately 2 roentgens, a third of that in the vicinity of the test site some 2,700 miles away. The New York State studies marked the first systematic measurement of fallout in the continental United States by persons outside the nuclear establishment. A month later, heavy fallout from another shot descended on the town of St. George, Utah, a small city of some 4,500 inhabitants 150 miles due east of the Yucca Flats. Area sheepmen complained that the tests were killing their sheep. All these various complaints caused the AEC considerable concern —not that people were being endangered by radioactivity, but rather that public resistance might interrupt the scheduled tests. Eugene Zuckert worried aloud that "in the present frame of mind of the public, it would take only a single illogical and unforeseeable accident to preclude holding any future tests in the U.S."[11] Zuckert's anxiety reflected AEC plans for testing a fusion weapon —the hydrogen or H-bomb, as the press was soon to call it—at the Nevada site. AEC officials considered the problem serious enough to buck it up to President Eisenhower, who smoothly recommended that in press releases the AEC omit mention of words like "thermonuclear," "fusion," and "hydrogen." "The President," noted AEC Chairman Gordon Dean, "says keep them confused as to 'fission' and 'fusion.' "[12] Who was "them": the

Soviet leaders or the people of the United States? Neither Dean nor Eisenhower clarified the ambiguity.

Despite their 1953 worries, the AEC ordered a fusion test shot to be carried out at Bikini in the South Pacific. On March 1, 1954, this test, code-named "Castle-Bravo," announced to the world that the United States had developed a deliverable version of "Super," the decade-old ambition of Edward Teller. Castle-Bravo and other 1954 tests produced such massive fallout in the northern hemisphere that "in Washington [D.C.] you could swipe a Kleenex over a car top and cause a Geiger counter to respond readily."[13]

But it was the Marshallese Islanders and others unlucky enough to be in the vicinity of Castle-Bravo who were lethally contaminated. Residents of Rongelaap, an island about 100 miles east of Bikini, received beta burns and other symptoms of radioactive poisoning following a total exposure of around 175R. The navy transported them by helicopter to American facilities at Kwajalein for medical treatment, but many of them developed long-term symptoms of radiation poisoning, including leukemia and cancer of the thyroid. The crewmen of a Japanese tuna trawler in the vicinity, the *Lucky Dragon,* were even more badly exposed to radioactive ash that fell on their vessel, and one of them, Aikichi Kuboyama, died of radiation poisoning seven months later. The United States at first tried to cover up the *Lucky Dragon* incident, sequestering the victims and declaring the site off limits. AEC Chairman Strauss tried to anesthetize American guilt by peddling the crackpot idea that the Japanese crewmen of the *Lucky Dragon* were a "Red spy outfit" conducting surveillance on American testing.[14] The United States paid Kuboyama's widow and children the equivalent in yen of about $2,500. As for the Rongelaap Islanders, the AEC blithely declared that "the medical observations to date indicate that there is no reason to expect any permanent aftereffects on the general health of these people."[15] By 1977, half the islanders had developed thyroid nodules or hyperthyroidism, a product of radio-iodine in the fallout ash that fell on Rongelaap in a blanket an inch thick. Some responsible critics have contended that the exposure of the Marshallese people was not accidental, an unanticipated result of an unpredictable wind shift, but rather was deliberate, a laboratory experiment on remote, expendable, nonwhite people.[16]

The *Lucky Dragon* incident created the first broadly based popular peace movement in Japan. Every prefectural legislature and both houses of the Japanese parliament passed peace resolutions demanding a halt to nuclear testing. Nationwide peace movements collected 33 million signatures demanding that nuclear weapons be outlawed. Though these movements have fallen victim to internal political disputes, the peace movement in Japan today is a child of the weapons-testing program of the 1950s. Resistance to atmospheric testing was not confined to Japan. India demanded a halt to the tests. Americans got their first popularized lesson in the dangers of fallout from Ralph Lapp's book, *The Voyage of the Lucky Dragon*.[17] Lapp told the story of the Japanese fishermen in understated, sympathetic detail, humanizing the cold and empty statistics churned out by the AEC. Lapp had originally come to the story of the *Lucky Dragon* through his 1954 calculations of fallout in the South Pacific, which he published in a series of articles in the *Bulletin of the Atomic Scientists* between 1954 and 1957. His book could not have appeared at a worse time from the AEC's viewpoint, coinciding as it did with sensational hearings on the dangers of fallout that the AEC was forced to conduct in 1957.

Years later, the consequence of continental testing for American citizens was revealed dramatically. In 1980, *People* magazine disclosed that of some 220 cast and crew members who filmed a 1956-release film, *The Conqueror*, on location near St. George, Utah, ninety-one had come down with cancer, an unheard of 41 percent morbidity rate. Of these, forty-six had died of the disease by 1980. Among the victims were John Wayne and Susan Hayward, the stars of the film; Dick Powell, its director-producer; as well as lesser-known Hollywood figures including Pedro Armendariz (who killed himself when he learned he had terminal lymphatic cancer), Agnes Moorehead, and Jeanne Gerson (who has survived both skin and breast cancer, at the cost of a mastectomy and chemotherapy). These victims and their children believe that their exposure to the windblown radioactive dust at the filmsite induced these cancers. Dick Powell's son, Norman, spoke of the nameless victims of fallout: "These poor folks, with no celebrities among them, are just quietly dying out there and nobody cares. But with the high number of casualties among a Hollywood cast, maybe someone will sit up and take notice." Someone did. The *People* article quotes an unnamed scientist on the staff of the Defense Nuclear Agency as saying: "Please, God, don't let us have killed John Wayne."[18] The victims and survivors of *The Conqueror*'s cast have begun a class action suit against the United States government for damages. The "poor folks with no celebrities among them" have also begun litigation against the United States government. Twenty-four of the "downwind people"—as the residents of Utah, Nevada, and Arizona in the path of fallout are called today—are seeking $7.5 million for actual damages to themselves, their families, and their property, with eventual claims expected to run into the hundreds of millions of dollars. As might be expected, the federal government denies that fallout caused the injuries of the downwind people.

The AEC responded to spreading criticism of its test program with a stepped-up propaganda campaign. In 1953, it categorically proclaimed that "the radioactivity released by fallout has proved not to be hazardous."[19] The AEC's willful optimism persisted even after data began coming in on the sheer quantities of fallout. John Bugher, head of the AEC Division of Biology and Medicine, said after the Castle-Bravo tests that the amount of strontium-90 "now present over the United States would have to be increased by the order of one million times before an increased frequency of bone [cancer] from this cause could be recognized."[20] Fortunately for humanity, Bugher's level has never been attained; if measured by the deposition of fallout in the South Pacific, that quantity of strontium-90 would doom the entire human race. The AEC compounded this computational error by assuming that strontium-90 would be ingested by humans only in the form of amounts deposited in animal bones that had been splintered off in the meat cutting process. Apparently the concept of a food chain did not occur to AEC scientists. It came as a surprise to them when independent biologists pointed out that human uptake of strontium-90 would occur through drinking milk produced by cows who had grazed contaminated grass.

Behind its brave public front, the AEC was growing increasingly worried about public fears of fallout. Elvin Stakman, the director of its Biology and Medicine Advisory Committee, demanded "maximum speed in the development of [nuclear] weapons. Speed is essential to survival. In emergencies such as this some risks, immediate and long term, must be accepted. These risks should be frankly and publicly acknowledged. However, the policy of minimizing these risks must be continued."[21] The Commission nervously began to acquire some experimental data on fallout levels by contracting with the U.S. Public Health Service to monitor offsite radioactivity in 1954. But public disclosure of the PHS findings was the last thing the AEC desired. As part of its contractual arrangement with the PHS, the AEC prohibited any dissemination of findings without its approval and stipulated that such unauthorized publication would subject PHS personnel to the criminal penalties provided in the Atomic Energy acts.[22] Statutes intended to prevent leakage of atomic "secrets" were now being used by an agency of the United States government to prevent American citizens from learning about dangers to them created by their own government.

The AEC thrashed about desperately for ideas that might mitigate fallout or allay public fears about it. Willard Libby, formerly an AEC commissioner, in 1956 wrote in the influential journal *Science,* published under the auspices of the American Association for the Advancement of Science, that "world-wide health hazards from the present rate of testing are insignificant."[23] Another scientist-commissioner, Henry Smyth, author of the 1945 history of the Manhattan Project known as the Smyth report, recommended that the AEC compare fallout levels to normal radiation from medical X rays. This began another familiar pattern, the use of a meaningless and misleading comparison to minimize the dangers of radiation. This technique is still in use at present, as nuclear proponents compare normal running releases from a reactor favorably to dental X rays, cosmic radiation encountered by living in Denver, flying in a 727 from San Francisco to New York, the normal background radiation encountered in brick or stone buildings, and even a freshly plowed field.

Incompetence and recklessness of commissioners and staffers

were not the worst of the AEC's problems in 1955. Pressures were mounting worldwide to stop American, Soviet, and British atmospheric tests, the great majority of which were American, just at the time when the United States and the Soviet Union were planning a massive expansion of atmospheric shots. The United Nations General Assembly created a commission, the United Nations Scientific Committee on the Effects of Atomic Radiation, to determine the dangers of fallout. Albert Einstein and the British philosopher-mathematician Bertrand Russell issued the Russell-Einstein manifesto, "An Appeal for the Abolition of War."[24] In it they warned that nuclear war threatened the human race itself because of the dangers of fallout. "If many H-bombs are used there will be universal death—sudden only for a minority, but for the majority a slow torture of disease and disintegration." In biblical language, they called on their fellow scientists to "choose continual progress in happiness, knowledge and wisdom. Shall we instead choose death because we cannot forget our quarrels? We appeal as human beings to human beings: remember your humanity and forget the rest." From this grew the Pugwash conferences, held annually at Pugwash, Nova Scotia, where American and Soviet scientists meet to discuss issues relating to nuclear arms. In 1956, Norman Cousins, editor of the *Saturday Review of Literature* and a preeminent independent commentator on American public policy, organized the Committee for a Sane Nuclear Policy (SANE). Though impeded by the chill of the later Cold War years and by lingering McCarthyite suspicions of peace and disarmament initiatives, these movements posed a formidable challenge to the arms race.

As if these weren't enough, pressures were building up inside the American nuclear establishment, too. But they tugged the AEC in opposite directions. The more immediate threat came from Senator Clinton Anderson, a New Mexico Democrat who was then chairman of the JCAE. Anderson and AEC Chairman Lewis Strauss regarded each other with a venomous hostility. Anderson had gone out to the Nevada test site to witness one of the shots in the "Teapot" series. But the test officials, moved to caution by the controversy blowing up over fallout, delayed the shot because of unfavorable weather conditions that would de-

posit higher than normal fallout on St. George and other locali-
ties off-site. Each day for a week, Anderson rose early to watch
the test, only to be told it had been canceled. He finally left,
returned to his Washington office, and sent Strauss a letter of
unambiguous pique, suggesting that perhaps the Nevada test site
would be usable only for "very small yield devices . . . leaving all
substantial shots for the Pacific," where weather conditions
would not delay them.[25]

At the same time, the AEC was beginning to encounter intense
local opposition to a continuation of Nevada testing from off-site
residents, as well as criticism of its atmospheric testing policies
from within the AEC itself. An AEC staffer warned them that
"people in the vicinity of the Nevada Proving Ground no longer
have faith in the AEC," and William Ogle of the Los Alamos
Scientific Laboratory objected at the beginning of the Teapot
series: "we should not put any large, single dose onto those
people [St. George] again." A Nevada legislator introduced a bill
to stop nuclear testing in the state.[26]

Nothing deterred, the AEC determined to press on. Commissioner Thomas Murray warned that "we must not let anything
interfere with this series of tests—nothing." Commissioner Willard Libby insisted that "people have got to learn to live with the
facts of life, and part of the facts of life are fallout." Suspecting
that the residents of southern Utah might not take so detached
a view of the matter, John Bugher created a new word to shrug
off their concerns: "St. George is hypertensified. It is not a question of health and safety with St. George, but a question of public
relations."[27] The next day, the people of St. George got the
fallout from a 43-kiloton blast and an even more massive public
relations barrage from the AEC.

Worse was yet to come, from the AEC's standpoint. In 1955,
Strauss and the AEC were caught red-handed in suppressing a
scientific investigation of the genetic impact of fallout. Hermann
I. Muller, the University of Indiana geneticist and Nobel laureate,
submitted a paper on gonadal damage caused by the radioactive
fission products deposited by fallout to the first United Nations
conference on the peaceful uses of the atom. Because he discussed Hiroshima, the AEC forced the conference to exclude the

paper. When investigative reporting by the *Washington Post* disclosed Strauss's hand in the matter, Strauss first apologized, then stated in a television interview that "some irresponsible statements that had been made on the subject [Hiroshima] were liquidated in the course of the conference."[28]

Strauss soon discovered that scientific criticism could not be "liquidated" by AEC censorship. In 1956, a British physician, Dr. Alice Stewart, began publication of her extensive work on fetal damage caused by X rays of pregnant women. She concluded that only a minute amount of radiation, such as that received in one X-ray exposure, could cause abnormalities in a fetus. Her findings were a massive blow to the threshold theory of radiation, which postulated that there was some level of dosage below which radiation would cause no long-term injuries. A corollary of the theory stated that subthreshold doses could be accumulated in repeated exposures without damage. Nobel laureate Linus Pauling entered the controversy in the mid-1950s, publishing both scientific and polemical papers demonstrating the dangers of the radioactive isotope carbon-14. AEC Commissioner Willard Libby, who had received the Nobel in chemistry in 1960 for his work on radiocarbon dating by carbon-14, denied that the isotope posed any problems. Pauling estimated that as of 1957, 10,000 people received lethal doses of radioactivity from fallout fission products and organized a petition drive that netted signatures of 11,000 scientists throughout the world demanding an end to atmospheric testing. In response, Eisenhower's secretary of Health, Education, and Welfare, Oveta Culp Hobby, terminated HEW funding for one of Pauling's research projects, and pressured his institution, Cal Tech, to drop him from the project.

Pauling's Cal Tech colleague, geneticist E. B. Lewis, concentrated on another hot isotope, iodine-131, ignored by the AEC because of its short half-life, eight days. Lewis demonstrated that iodine-131 was site-specific in the human body: it collected in the thyroid, and thus would be particularly dangerous to children. He and Pauling focused attention on leukemia, extrapolating from the Japanese experience to predict a great increase in that and other forms of cancer as a result of fallout.

The United States Weather Bureau refuted another of Libby's scientific claims. The AEC chemist had earlier minimized fallout danger by claiming that fallout was dispersed uniformly over the earth's surface by high-altitude winds. Weather Bureau soil sampling demonstrated this to be false. Fallout concentrated in the more heavily populated northern hemisphere, especially in the breadbasket of the midwestern United States. Thence it became easy to trace the pathways of radioactive elements, particularly strontium-90, up the food chain to humans. Sr-90, too, is site-specific, concentrating in bones and teeth. A Harvard biochemist, Herman Kalckar, suggested an ingenious, devastatingly dramatic way to test Sr-90 levels in humans: measure its content in baby teeth that had fallen out. This produced the famous 1958 baby-tooth survey.

The survey was conducted by yet another potent scientific foe of the AEC, the Committee on Nuclear Information, first organized at Washington University in St. Louis. At first, CNI's sole purpose was to correct false and misleading AEC propaganda with accurate, experimentally based data, and to explain scientific issues in terms comprehensible to lay people. CNI undertook the baby-tooth survey in St. Louis, which, as might be expected, revealed Sr-90 concentrations undreamed of by the AEC. CNI published a monthly newsletter, *Nuclear Information,* which in time became the respected journal *Environment,* today one of the most reliable sources of scientific reporting on nuclear matters. Scientists elsewhere replicated the activities of CNI, and founded a national organization, the Scientists' Institute for Public Information, headquartered in New York. SIPI went on to provide a constant counterpoint of truth and reason to the AEC's uninformed propaganda. Through it and CNI, many prominent scientists, including Barry Commoner, René Dubos, and Margaret Mead, entered the arena of nuclear controversy. Even the AEC's own Biological and Medical Advisory Committee estimated that fallout to date would produce between 2,500 and 13,000 genetic abnormalities.[29]

This scientific criticism was no laughing matter to AEC officials, especially when it was seconded by popular resistance from laypeople in Nevada, Utah, and Arizona, who complained of dying livestock, human skin burns and loss of hair, and of other-wise inexplicable rises in the incidence of leukemia in the path of fallout. The AEC responded in two ways: propaganda and red-baiting smears. To soothe off-site residents, the AEC sponsored films with titles like "A is for Atom," "Atomic Energy," and "Atomic Tests in Nevada," hoping that a judicious combination of elementary scientific information and government lying would quell fears in the southwest. The AEC hired public health offi-cials, college professors, and scientists for something called the "Off-Site Radiological Safety Organization" (Rad-Safe for short) to address public gatherings. The culmination of this effort was a pamphlet, *Atomic Tests in Nevada*, printed for distribution in the affected areas. "You people who live near the Nevada Test Site," it explained mordantly, "are in a very real sense active partici-pants in the Nation's atomic test program." The AEC seemed oblivious to the fact that the readers knew that fact all too well, and that was precisely why they were complaining. Proclaiming that "no one outside the test site has been hurt in six years of testing," the AEC flatly stated that all its findings "have confirmed that Nevada test fallout has not caused illness or in-jured the health of anyone living near the test site."

But there was a little problem. Some of the more sophisticated "active participants in the Nation's atomic test program" had bought their own Geiger counters to determine for themselves just what dosage they were involuntarily getting, and their read-ings expectably showed that they were getting dangerous levels. So the AEC pamphlet cooed that "we can expect many reports that 'Geiger counters are going crazy today.' Reports like this may worry people unnecessarily. Don't let them bother you. A Geiger counter can go completely off-scale in fallout which is far from hazardous."[30] The suspicions of Utah laypeople were vin-dicated over the pseudoscientific guessing of AEC officials by a 1979 study reported in the *New England Journal of Medicine* that concluded: "A significant excess of leukemia deaths occurred in children up to 14 years of age living in Utah between 1959 and 1967. This excess was concentrated in the cohort of children born between 1951 and 1958, and was most pronounced in those residing in counties receiving high fallout."[31]

During the climactic 1957 test series, the Department of Defense produced a television film for the general viewing public. One of its scenes depicts an uneasy group of soldier-observers waiting for a test shot. The narrator's voice-over says with the unconscious irony typical of AEC propaganda of the time: "In the minds of men who are about to become part of an awesome experience, fundamental questions remain." A solicitous army chaplain approaches a soldier: "What seems to be the trouble, soldier? You look a little bit worried." The soldier admits he is. "Actually, there's no need to be worried," the chaplain reassures him, "as the Army has taken all necessary precautions to see that we're perfectly safe here." The chaplain enthuses lyrically about the fireball he and the trooper are about to witness: "You look up and see the fireball as it ascends up into the heavens. It contains all of the rich colors in the rainbow. And then as it rises up into the atmosphere, it turns a beautiful, pale yellow, and then assembles into the mushroom. It's a wonderful sight to behold."[32]

Propaganda constituted the high road of AEC response to criticism; the low road was a smear campaign directed against the critics. When in 1955 two University of Colorado Medical Center scientists warned that their state was getting dangerous doses of radiation, Colorado Governor Edwin C. Johnson urged that they be arrested. He ranted: "This is a phony report. It will only alarm people. Someone has a screw loose someplace and I intend to find out about it." An International News Service writer, Jack Lotto, wrote a syndicated column informing readers that "a big Communist 'fear' campaign to force Washington to stop all American atomic hydrogen bomb tests erupted this past week." The *Los Angeles Examiner* ran this under the headline "On Your Guard: Reds Launch 'Scare Drive' Against U.S. Atomic Tests." Nevada Senator George Malone artfully suggested that "it is not impossible to suppose that some of the scare stories are Communist-inspired." The syndicated conservative columnist David Lawrence wrote that "evidence of a world-wide propaganda campaign is accumulating. Many persons are innocently being duped by it and some well-meaning scientists and other persons are playing the Communist game unwittingly by exaggerating the importance of radioactive substances known as 'fallout.' " After Linus Pauling collected eleven thousand signatures in his 1957 petition campaign to stop atmospheric testing, another widely syndicated conservative columnist, Fulton Lewis, Jr., hinted darkly that behind Pauling was a well-funded organization. Picking up the cue, the House Un-American Activities Committee called Pauling before it and grilled him on the source of his funds.[33]

Neither ploy stifled criticism. On the contrary, attacks on atmospheric weapons testing, and on the AEC itself, only increased, even from within the nuclear establishment. JCAE Democrat Chet Holifield, a zealous nuclear backer, condemned what others were calling the AEC's "body-in-the-morgue"[34] attitude toward fallout danger:

> The AEC's approach to the hazards from bomb test fallout seems to add up to a party line—"play it down." As custodian of official information, the AEC has an urgent responsibility to communicate the facts to the public. Yet time after time there has been a long delay in issuance of the facts, and oftentimes the facts have to be dragged out of the agency by the Congress.[35]

Holifield's attitudes were apparently shared widely on the Joint Committee. It scheduled hearings on fallout that lasted from May through June 1957. These hearings were remarkable for the extremes to which AEC officials would go in denying reality. At one point, Ralph Lapp was permitted to question Merril Eisenbud, a New York AEC official, on the latter's 1955 assertion that fallout could be a million times greater without danger to human health. For illustrative purposes, Lapp used the fallout levels of the 1953 Troy–Albany rainout, which Eisenbud estimated at 10 milliroentgens (one-hundredth of a roentgen). Lapp observed: "I have done a little arithmetic. Let us take ten milliroentgens, as Mr. Eisenbud estimates, and we multiply [it by Eisenbud's million, producing] ten thousand roentgens." At this point Senator Clinton Anderson, a JCAE member, exclaimed: "Ten thousand roentgens would kill everybody in sight!" "Yes," replied Eisenbud. Anderson could only ask incredulously, "So that would mean there would not be any immediate danger if you kill everyone in sight?"[36]

Despite such morbidly funny moments, the JCAE hearings ultimately proved inconclusive. Nothing inhibited the AEC from conducting the greatest round of tests up to that time, both at the continental test site and at Eniwetok in the South Pacific. In 1957–58, the United States conducted a total of 86 known shots in the atmosphere, and 15 underground or underwater. (For comparison purposes, in the entire thirteen years of testing, it had set off 124 atmospheric shots and 4 underground or underwater.) At both places, the "atomic soldiers" (a phrase widely used today by the men and their widows) were again used in human experimentation.

At the Eniwetok tests, code-named "Hardtack," the army assigned a sergeant, Orville Kelly, to organize a squad of enlisted men to observe the shots from the island of Taipan. They faced the blast protected only by goggles. Between shots, Kelly had to take radiation readings throughout the surrounding environment. At one point, he gashed himself on coral, had to swim through 400 yards of radioactive water, and contracted an infection that did not heal for two years. Fourteen years later, he learned he had lymphoma, a cancer of the lymph glands. He founded the National Association of Atomic Veterans, an organization that lobbies and campaigns for Veterans Administration benefits to men who got cancer and other disorders as a result of being nuclear guinea pigs. Kelly died in 1980, after being the only atomic veteran to date to be awarded veteran's liability compensation for the cancer that the VA concedes was "probably" caused by his exposure to twenty-two Hardtack shots.[37]

At the Nevada tests, the Defense Department reached new extremes in its use of soldiers to test the effects of radiation. By 1957, the army had developed a new tactical concept, the "pentomic division." World War II–era divisions in the American army consisted of three infantry regiments (each approximately 5,000 men) together with supporting artillery batteries. But as military planners tried to envision the use of tactical battlefield nuclear weapons after 1951, they thought a five-regiment division, with more soldiers scattered over the battle site, might minimize casualties; hence the peculiar neo-Greek coinage, pentomic ("five-atomic"). To try this concept out, the army proposed to deploy unprecedented numbers of ground troops around the 1957 "Smoky" test shot series. At the same time, the AEC wanted to go for larger shots than it had detonated in Nevada, up to 74 kilotons.

The air force proposed yet a third innovation for the Smoky series. It was about to deploy "Genie" antibomber missiles throughout the United States, and was concerned about the public relations problems that would come up when the civilian population suddenly found this new weapon in its backyards. Colonel Barney Oldfield came up with an ingenious gimmick to reassure civilians. He discovered five air force officers willing to stand directly underneath an air blast of a small weapon (2 kilotons) at approximately 20,000 feet. They did so, and survived, much to the relief of the military.

Perhaps encouraged by this bizarre experiment, the army prepared ground troops for maneuvers and direct exposure to a nuclear blast. One aspect of this preparation was a lecture to assembled troops designed to reassure them about their personal safety. Defense Department psychologists had discovered that the soldiers' chief worry was that they might become sterile. A psychologist tried to reassure them: "Well, if you hold your balls up on a stick, that would probably do it." But the enlisted men's common sense ignored this elephantine attempt at humor, so the lecturer tried some laymen's science. Beginning with the suspect threshold theory, he assured troops that they could take a 25R to 50R dosage without damage, and possibly even survive a dose of 200R. He went on reassuringly:

> But don't worry. The National Academy of Sciences has estimated that it would take as much as 30 to 80 roentgens of radiation directly on the reproductive organs to cause as many mutations in offspring as would occur spontaneously. The Academy has also reported that low doses of radiation have not been proven to shorten life expectancy. Even doses up to 100 roentgens, spread over many years, have not been shown to shorten human life.
>
> All of this brings us to one critical question. How much radiation is safe? We can't say for sure what is absolutely safe, but what we do know is that you can get quite a bit of radiation without any

real significant risk of danger. We've set a permissible radiation dose limit for these tests at five roentgens. That corresponds with the limits that atomic energy workers live with. Each of you will be issued a radiation film badge when you enter the test site. Later, these badges will be analyzed to determine exactly how much radiation you've received and the amount will be entered into your records.

Remember this, no observer has ever been injured by test activity at the Nevada Test Site, though there have been construction and traffic accidents. We're taking every possible measure to make sure we maintain this clean record.

The guinea pigs sensibly remained skeptical. One said:

The Army was just trying to blow smoke up our butts. I wondered if they actually think people are that dumb. Sure they said we'd be completely monitored at all times, but hell, nobody believed them. Nine chances out of ten the monitor was just some PFC assigned to the detail who didn't give a damn.[38]

The dogfaces' skepticism did not deter army tactical planners. Smoky went off as scheduled, with paratroopers from the 82nd Airborne being directly exposed—no trenches, no foxholes—to a 44-kiloton blast less than three miles away. AEC scientists at the same time were no closer than seven miles and wore protective garb. Corporal Russell Jack Dann recalls one of his comrade's, Corporal Chuck Newsome, comments at the time. Noticing Dann shivering, Newsome said, "Don't you worry, pal. You'll warm up just as soon as them old gamma rays start runnin' through ya." But Newsome's humor evaporated when he learned the size of the shot that he was about to be exposed to: "This is what we suffered three weeks [of desert training] for? To get zapped like those Japanese?"[39] The men stayed at their duty post. When the shot went off, they held their hands in front of their eyes, and recall seeing their bones through the flesh, as in an X ray.

A decade later, some members of the JCAE expressed sober second thoughts when it was disclosed that the AEC had been using *them* as experimental subjects. In 1959, the AEC had promoted the irradiation of human food, in hopes of devising techniques to preserve food that would replace canning and freezing.

As part of this promotion, JCAE members dined at annual "Irradiated Food Luncheons." But in 1968, the Food and Drug Administration warned the army that some irradiated ham might be carcinogenic, mutagenic, and harmful in other ways. The worried members of the JCAE asked the secretary of the army, Stanley Resor, to explain when the first of these "hot" luncheons was held. But apparently Resor had left the room. Representative Craig Hosmer, a California Democrat and nuclear proponent, observed, "He is gone now." Representative William Bates worriedly responded: "He is gone and the question is, are we going to be gone." Representative Melvin Price (of Price–Anderson) lamented, "We were guinea pigs." But canny Vermont Republican Aiken commented, with Yankee shrewdness:

> I sent my bacon to the leading radiologist in the state. He ate it, and so far as I know he is still doing business. I didn't eat it myself. It might be all right, but why take a chance when you have a good radiologist to take a chance for you?[40]

Indeed. So might have AEC officials responded: Why take chances when you can put American soldiers in a field laboratory?

The increasing tempo and size of American test shots provoked ever more urgent resistance. Scientific criticism became more pointed, while civilians near the Nevada test site refused to be seduced by AEC blandishments about the safety of nuclear power. In vain did Edward Teller claim that atmospheric fallout either had no effect or a beneficial one.[41] AEC chairman Strauss intoned: "Let us keep our sense of proportion in the matter of radioactive fallout. . . . The dangers that might occur from the fallout involve a small sacrifice when compared to the infinitely greater evil of the use of nuclear bombs in war."[42] Willard Libby echoed him: "Are we willing to take this very small and rigidly controlled risk, or would we prefer to run the risk of annihilation which might result if we surrendered the weapons which are so essential to our freedom and our actual survival?"[43] But as Libby well knew, the risks were not all that rigidly controlled. Some scientists urged development of what the press called a "clean" nuclear weapon: one that minimized radioactive fallout. Libby stoutly opposed the idea in 1958 because, as he said, "there was a desire by the military for some degree of off-site radiation for troop training purposes."[44] Radiation exposure of the atomic soldiers thus was not an unwanted, regrettable side effect; by 1958, it had become an objective of the atmospheric testing program.

John Gofman offers the following judgment on the role of scientists in all this:

> It should have been clear to me, even then [1950s,] that both atmospheric bomb-testing and nuclear power constituted experimentation on involuntary human subjects, indeed on all forms of life. . . . I feel that at least several hundred scientists trained in the biomedical aspect of atomic energy—myself definitely included—are candidates for Nuremberg-type trials for crimes against humanity through our gross negligence and irresponsibility.[45]

Libby, Teller, Strauss, and other test proponents were about to be overwhelmed by events outside the United States, though. In 1957, Great Britain detonated its first thermonuclear weapon. In response, a British disarmament group, the Campaign for Nuclear Disarmament, called for a public protest march from London, beginning Good Friday, 1958, to Aldermaston, headquarters of U.K. nuclear weapons research, arriving on Easter. From five to ten thousand people participated, to the chagrin of the British and American governments. It was then that CND adopted the symbol ☮ that became a universal sign of peace in the next decade, formed by the semaphore signalman's positions for N and D: nuclear disarmament.

Then, even more astonishingly, the Soviet Union announced a unilateral halt to its own atmospheric testing program in March 1958, thereby scoring an immense propaganda coup. AEC and defense officials nevertheless insisted on completing the scheduled Hardtack series in the Pacific and Nevada that summer, testing every conceivable type of weapon available in the nuclear armory of the time. At the completion of Hardtack in 1958, the three nuclear powers began a voluntary moratorium that lasted until 1961. This did not inhibit France, however, from joining the nuclear club by detonating three atmospheric explosions in 1960. The moratorium came to a rude halt when the Soviets set off a monstrous 50 *megaton* blast in October 1961.

But the uncharacteristic Soviet act of spring 1958 may well have been prompted by something more than desire for a propaganda advantage. (It certainly had nothing to do with a concern about fallout.) Though not disclosed until almost two decades later, sometime late in 1957, the U.S.S.R. suffered some sort of massive nuclear catastrophe in the Chelyabinsk region of the southern Urals, near the industrial city of Sverdlovsk. The exiled Russian biochemist who revealed this event to the world, Zhores Medvedev, implies that the self-imposed ban was forced on Soviet leaders by damage or destruction of the nuclear facility at Kyshtym in the Chelyabinsk region.[46]

Western authorities remain in disagreement over the causes and scope of the Urals disaster. They also remain silent about it. Medvedev himself, in the most widely accepted speculation about the accident, suggests that some sort of explosion occurred at a nuclear waste dump that spewed radioactive contaminants into the atmosphere and dispersed them throughout the region. Contemporary rumors in the U.S.S.R. itself attributed the catastrophe to an accidental explosion of a nuclear weapon. The CIA, in its official version, classifies the incident as a relatively small reactor blowdown. Others have speculated that an earthquake disrupted a reactor or a waste dump.

Similar disagreement exists on the scope of the injuries and damage. Medvedev can only offer vague speculation:

> The hospitals and clinics in [Sverdlovsk and Chelyabinsk] were filled with thousands of evacuated inhabitants, who were held for observation. After a time, when symptoms of radiation sickness began to appear in more distant areas, the evacuation zone was enlarged and people began to be placed not only in hospitals but also in sanatoria and "houses of rest" (vacation facilities) which were re-equipped as hospitals. Hunting and fishing were prohibited throughout the southern and central Urals and for several

years the sale of meat and fish in private markets and collective farm markets was not permitted without special inspection for radioactivity.[47]

The CIA knew about the accident at the time it happened, from U-2 spy plane overflights that were regularly undertaken to monitor Soviet nuclear facilities in the region, from refugee reports, and from information leaked out by Russian "friendlies" in the U.S.S.R. But the agency declined to disclose what it knew of the event, despite the loss of whatever propaganda advantage might accrue to the United States from a Soviet nuclear blunder, because it feared that news of this remote nuclear disaster might aggravate American or British public opinion about their own nations' nuclear programs. Great Britain had just experienced the Windscale reactor accident and Americans were edgy about fallout. Moreover, the United States' first civilian reactor, Shippingport, had just gone on stream. Hence American authorities concealed their intelligence data on the disaster until they were smoked out nearly twenty years later by publication of Medvedev's disclosure in a *New Statesman* article in November 1976. Even then the nuclear establishment in the U.K. and the United States ridiculed and belittled Medvedev's revelation. East–West rivalries are readily overshadowed by the common interests of all nuclear nations in protecting their programs from public skepticism.

The CIA was probably correct in assuming that disclosure of the Soviet accident would have been more damaging than helpful to the American nuclear program, because the debate over a nuclear test ban was intensifying in 1957. To deal with the rising level of public resistance, President Eisenhower appointed Harold Stassen as his personal adviser on disarmament in 1955. The National Academy of Sciences, with the financial subvention of the Rockefeller Foundation, began a comprehensive and, they hoped, definitive scientific study of the consequences of fallout. An intense debate pitted Cold Warrior politicians and scientists on one side against test-ban proponents on the other. Advocates hoped to halt somatic and genetic threats resulting from fallout, and, more broadly, to reverse the nuclear arms race, possibly even to begin down the path of disarmament. Hubert Humphrey in the United States Senate and Adlai Stevenson on the campaign trail in 1956 called for a test ban. Albert Schweitzer broadcast an influential appeal for a halt to weapons tests, but it was virtually blacked out in the United States. Nevil Shute's depressing novel about nuclear doomsday, *On the Beach,* reached mass audiences in 1957. Critics compared it to *Uncle Tom's Cabin* in its combination of supposed technical inaccuracy and popular appeal.

On the other side, Edward Teller, Ernest O. Lawrence, and Willard Libby led that segment of the scientific community demanding that atmospheric testing continue. They insisted that the dangers of fallout, whatever they might be, paled into insignificance before the threat of Soviet aggression. Other ban opponents resorted to McCarthyite tactics. The New York *Daily News* editorialized the test ban advocates were "as nutty as so many fruitcakes." The Reverend Daniel Poling, a widely read minister, condemned the test ban movement as part of the "insidious and far-reaching menace of atheist Communism in its world-wide peace drive." Pennsylvania Democrat Francis Walter, chairman of the House Un-American Activities Committee, proclaimed that behind the movement, "the black hand of the Communist conspiracy remains clearly visible."[48]

At the scientific level of debate, the crucial question was whether the threshold theory was valid, or whether, as geneticist E. B. Lewis insisted, the effects of radioactivity were "linear": every exposure to radioactivity had a long-term and cumulative effect, with each subsequent dose piling on what had gone before rather than being rebuffed by the supposed "threshold." If linearity proponents were correct, or even merely closer to the truth than threshold advocates like Libby, then all atmospheric testing, being cumulative, was dangerous. Like pregnancy, it would be misleading to speak of just a little bit of it. This esoteric question penetrated down to public discourse through the 1958 furor over strontium-90 levels in milk. Test ban advocates emphasized that the principal consumers of milk, children, are also the most susceptible to thyroid risks. They pointed out that a nursing mother could even transmit contaminated mother's milk to her infant. The Public Health Service began systematic monitoring of Sr-90 levels and found them higher than the AEC had anticipated. This struck an emotional chord so profound that McCarthyite hysteria lost its potency. The Libby–Teller formula —small radiation risk, large U.S.S.R. nuclear threat—appeared unconvincing.

No agency of the United States government has ever conceded that radiation standards were nothing more than guesses made in ignorance of actual facts and in the absence of scientific experimentation. In private, though, government scientists did concede the point. During debates of the National Advisory Committee on Radiation in 1958 on the danger of radioactivity levels in Los Angeles resulting from the binge of Soviet and American atmospheric tests, Lauriston Taylor of the National Bureau of Standards admitted that current standards "carry the implication that we know what we are talking about when we set them. But in actual fact, they really represent the best judgment we would exercise now in the total absence of any real knowledge as to whether they are correct or not."[49]

Ignorance, acknowledged or not, did not deter nuclear proponents from action, though. In 1959, the National Council on Radiation Protection, a private group of government and industry scientists that followed the AEC line, raised standards for the maximum permissible concentrations of Sr-90, doubling it for nuclear industry workers and raising it 25 percent for the general population. In justifying its action, one commission member explained that "the nation's security may demand the exposure of people to higher levels of radiation than those just established by the International Commission" on Radiological Protection.[50] The JCAE's Chet Holifield echoed this line in hearings the same year before his radiation subcommittee, held expressly for the purpose of calming public fears rather than for understanding the real danger of fallout. Holifield opened the hearings by declaring that he did "not intend to be swayed by emotional arguments," but he went on to insist that "the national defense is important enough that if there is some risk involved, we must take that risk."[51]

The anomalous status of the NCRP, a body having rule-making powers but not subject to governmental control, troubled some federal officials. President Eisenhower created a federal agency, the Federal Radiation Council, in 1959 to provide "advice" to the president and "guidance" to federal agencies on radiation standards. The FRC proved to be a classic case of setting the fox to guard the chickens. Two of the six FRC members were the chairman of the AEC and the secretary of defense. Its first executive director was a health physicist, Paul C. Tompkins, who had been at the Met Lab, Oak Ridge, and the Navy Radiological Defense Labs. The FRC did move against Sr-90 concentrations in 1960, when it reduced permissible concentrations of the isotope in milk and tacitly rejected the threshold theory by jettisoning the concept of "maximum permissible exposure." But what the FRC gave with one hand it took away with the other. In place of the old maximum-dose criterion, it substituted something called a "radiation protection guide." The new substitute invited evasion because it was defined as the "dose which should not be exceeded without careful consideration of the reasons for doing so."[52] Under the new standard, there was virtually no limit to dosage levels. The "protection" it offered was obviously for military activities, not for their human victims.

The tactic of abolishing crime by repealing criminal statutes continued to characterize FRC and AEC response to the fallout controversy. After Soviet resumption of atmospheric testing in 1961, the controversy shifted from strontium-90 to another radioactive isotope, iodine-131, which also goes up through the food chain into milk and concentrates in the thyroid, where it induces cancer. Harold Knapp, a staff member of the AEC's Division of Biology and Medicine, completed studies in 1962 that demonstrated the carcinogenic potential of I-131 from fallout. The AEC ordered an in-house review of Knapp's studies. The committee assigned to this task included John Gofman, a physician specializing in cancer and also a physical chemist who in 1943 had participated in the original isolation of plutonium. Gofman recalls that when he was asked to review the Knapp findings, an AEC official, one of a group of six, told him, "We must stop that publication. If we don't stop that publication, the credibility of the AEC will just disappear, because it will be stated that we've been lying." Gofman objected, and the official repeated: "We can't afford to have him publish that evidence." Gofman realized then that he was being used "to help with a coverup."[53]

The four scientist members of the Knapp review committee, including Gofman, endorsed Knapp's findings; the lone dissent came from the only committee member who was not a scientist, Oliver Placak, head of the AEC's Rad-Safe operation at the Nevada site. The AEC suppressed the first version of the Knapp report, and had the second classified secret. When the third version was finally published in 1963, the AEC made a point of insisting that the review affirming it was "not unanimous," neglecting to explain the bias of the lone and unqualified dissenter. Not satisfied with that, the FRC in September 1962 finally declared that the radiation protection guides it promulgated earlier did not apply to fallout.[54] In 1969, Paul Tompkins explained the rationale of these actions with respect to I-131: "We had to take our choice between that much iodine or a predictable level of malnutrition from pricing the milk off the market."[55] This was a scare tactic, because feasible means existed to prevent contaminated milk from reaching the market without prohibitive cost increases.

The question of linearity versus threshold also reentered the debate on fallout in 1962 when Ernest Sternglass, a Pittsburgh physicist, determined that the linear thesis was confirmed by the research of Alice Stewart. Sternglass attempted to publish his findings in *Science,* the prestigious publication that serves the entire American scientific community, but was rebuffed by its editor, Philip Abelson, who had ties to the nuclear community. On a later submission, Abelson relented and published the article in June 1963.[56] The nuclear establishment was to hear a great deal more from Sternglass, Knapp, and Gofman in the decade to come.

Though the scientific façade of the AEC was crumbling, the American public learned little about it, due in large measure to the spectacular events that occurred during the first two years of the Kennedy administration: the erection of the Berlin Wall, the Bay of Pigs invasion, and the Cuban missile crisis in October 1962. This last event, which all Americans realized carried the United States and the Soviet Union far toward the nuclear brink, proved to be the decisive stimulus for an end to atmospheric testing. On July 31, 1963, the U.S.A., U.S.S.R., and U.K. signed the Partial Test Ban Treaty, banning atmospheric testing. France and China, refusing to adhere, insulted the conscience of civilization by continuing atmospheric testing. But the atmospheric ban did not halt contaminations. Fifteen to eighteen of the subsequent underground tests produced what the AEC called "venting": accidental eruptions of fallout from underground. Nevada and Utah residents continued to have fallout dropped on them, though at greatly reduced levels.

The fallout issue largely lay dormant for the remainder of the decade, and when it did reemerge late in the 1960s, it was overshadowed by America's involvement in the quagmire of Vietnam. But problems of fallout lingered, as did the long-lived radioisotopes themselves, to further discredit the AEC and becloud the future of nonmilitary applications of nuclear power.

9

"Mutually Assured Destruction"

STRATEGIC DOCTRINE IN THE KENNEDY ADMINISTRATION

DURING HIS LAST YEAR IN OFFICE, Dwight Eisenhower seemed to be plagued, like Job, with unrelenting troubles. Sputnik had greatly enhanced Soviet prestige, and Premier Nikita Khrushchev took advantage of this to expand his nation's influence, especially in the Middle East, an area of great sensitivity to the West. America's role as the leader of the NATO alliance, shaken by the 1956 Suez crisis, was being directly challenged by President Charles de Gaulle, who had already begun to make France the leader of a European coalition aligned with neither of the superpowers. Latin American hostility toward the United States, once again on the rise after the CIA-engineered coup that overthrew the Guatemalan government in 1954, flared as a result of administration moves to destabilize Fidel Castro's regime in Cuba. In far-off Southeast Asia, ominous guerrilla warfare troubled Laos and Vietnam. In Africa, the Congo was aflame. Anti-American rioting in Japan and the humiliation caused by the U-2 affair added to Ike's already overflowing cup of woes.

At home, the administration was under attack not only because of foreign policy problems but also for the president's conservative attitude toward defense spending. If the rest of the world seemed to be turning against the United States, some thought it was because we were growing perceptibly weaker. The young Massachusetts senator, John Kennedy, charged that the administration had traded national security for false economy while permitting "the power and strength of the United States to decline in relation to the Communist world."[1] Democrats sensed that foreign policy and national security issues would be crucial during the 1960 presidential campaign. Lyndon Johnson repeatedly denounced the administration for its failure to close the missile and space gaps. Missouri's Stuart Symington set the tone for his abortive run at the presidency by calling for new and decisive leadership to make America great again.

Kennedy, the eventual winner in the 1960 Democratic sweepstakes, challenged Americans with a rhetoric that was extraordinarily effective. Russia and China, he warned, were on the verge of conquering the entire Eurasian land mass. Only the United States stood between them and the onset of a new dark age. If America should falter, he believed, "the whole world . . . would inevitably begin to move toward the Communist bloc."[2] During the presidential campaign, Kennedy gave great emphasis to one theme in particular, the need to strengthen America's defenses. "As a power which will never strike first," he said, "we require a retaliatory capacity based on hidden, moving, or invulnerable weapons in such force as to deter any aggressor from threatening an attack he knows could not destroy enough of our force to prevent his own destruction."[3]

Kennedy believed that the struggle against international Communism would be fought and decided in the underdeveloped nations of the world. He viewed Soviet accomplishments in space as providing Khrushchev with a dangerous propaganda edge in this competition. Unhappily, most Americans did not fully appreciate the "world-wide political and psychological impact of the space-race," he argued. "Dramatic Soviet achievements were helping to build a dangerous impression of unchallenged world leadership generally and scientific pre-eminence particularly."[4] Before the United States could seize the initiative in the Cold War, it would first have to reestablish a reputation for technological superiority. An aggressive new approach to the related problems of space and national defense in the nuclear age seemed essential.

In spite of his own deep concerns, during his 1960 run for the presidency Kennedy was careful not to overemphasize the missile gap. It had been almost three years since the first Sputnik was launched. In the interim, national defense estimates of Soviet ICBM strength had consistently declined. They declined once again during the campaign. Though suspicious of information provided by the Republican administration, Kennedy did not want to risk the possibility of hammering away at the missile gap only to be proven wrong on the eve of the election. And so the missile gap, a pressing concern in his own mind, remained only one among a number of issues that he emphasized.

Kennedy was far more strident in denouncing massive retaliation, still the official nuclear strategy of the United States. As early as 1954, he had pointed out to his Senate colleagues that the strategy lacked credibility, and urged not cuts but increases in spending for both conventional and strategic forces. Later in his book, *The Strategy of Peace*, he argued that the greatest danger to the United States did not come from a direct nuclear attack, but from "Sputnik diplomacy, limited brushfire wars, indirect non-overt aggression, intimidation, subversion, [and] internal revolution." In such situations, he declared, massive retaliation had not worked in the past and would not work in the future. "We have been driving ourselves into a corner," he exclaimed, "where the only choice is all or nothing at all, world devastation or submission."[5]

In 1960, Kennedy was more convinced than ever that massive retaliation was a dangerous anachronism. Nuclear weapons had revolutionized warfare. It troubled him that so few people really understood the nature of the change. "When that day comes, and there is a massive exchange, then that is the end, because you are talking about . . . 150 million fatalities in the first eighteen hours."[6] Kennedy was nearly obsessed by the thought that as the superpowers dueled like players at a vast gaming board, one miscalculation by either side might plunge the world into thermonuclear holocaust. He recalled a conversation between two German leaders surveying the ruins of their once-great empire in the aftermath of World War I. One asked the other how it had come to pass. "Ah, if only one knew," came the reply. "If this planet . . . is ever ravaged by nuclear war," Kennedy told Theodore Sorensen, "if the survivors of that devastation can then endure the fire, poison, chaos and catastrophe—I do not want one of those survivors to ask another, 'How did it all happen?' and to receive the incredible reply: 'Ah, if only one knew.' "[7] Such lugubrious thoughts led others to take up the struggle for nuclear disarmament or at least to seek a reduction in tensions with the Soviets through diplomacy. They did not have the same effect on Kennedy, however. He was too much the Cold Warrior for that. And so he set out to find military options short of a nuclear Armageddon that might allow him to pursue an aggressive Cold War policy and that would in the event of a direct confrontation with the Soviets offer military options short of a nuclear spasm.

In his search for such a flexible military strategy, Kennedy found an outspoken ally in retired Army Chief of Staff Maxwell Taylor, whose book, *An Uncertain Trumpet,* published in 1959, was extremely critical of the Eisenhower administration's military policies. Taylor charged that by reducing America's conventional military forces to skeletal size while emphasizing nuclear striking power, the government had denied itself the military flexibility that was essential if it was to respond appropriately to the many Cold War challenges it faced. The nuclear deterrent was important, to be sure, but it was only one component in an effective military policy, and was not useful in crises of less than the gravest importance. Time and again, Taylor told a congressional committee in 1960, Eisenhower's defense secretaries promised that the government would "maintain flexible mobile forces capable of coping with lesser situations in the world." Yet in spite of the fact that the administration recognized the need for both nuclear and conventional forces, the budget was never sufficient to provide them. Taylor explained that this issue had produced sharp division within the JCS itself until it "was a clear split right down the middle . . . crying for decision."[8]

Following his hair's-breadth victory in the November election, Kennedy made the decision Taylor called for, organizing a new military strategy based on the principle of flexible response. Kennedy questioned none of the basic foreign policy assumptions that had grown up during the postwar years. He believed that a monolithic international Communist conspiracy was bent upon world domination. He was also satisfied that the single most important component of American foreign policy should be military strength. And like Taylor, he did not believe that in the struggle to contain Soviet expansionism the nuclear option would of itself prove to be particularly effective. The Soviets would not confront the United States directly. They did not want nuclear war any more than we did. Instead they would nibble away at the peripheries of Western strength. Yet so long as the United States failed to provide funding for effective conventional military forces, there could be no appropriate response, for while "each Soviet move" would "weaken the West," none would "seem sufficiently significant by itself to justify our initiating a nuclear war which might destroy us."[9]

To implement these strategic assumptions, Kennedy chose Robert McNamara, the 44-year-old president of the Ford Motor Company, to be his secretary of defense. It was an inspired choice. Both men shared a proclivity for spelling things out, for developing meticulously defined policies. Each sought a large, well-organized military establishment that utilized resources with a minimum of waste. Most significantly, both were determined to get away from the all-or-nothing policy of massive retaliation. McNamara abhorred the idea that there was only one way to do anything—especially fight a war with the Soviets. Because the world was an unstable and unpredictable place and the stakes were so high, he constantly sought a variety of possible approaches to potential problems.

While at Ford, the hard-driving Californian's great strength had been his ability to rationalize the production process through the application of modern management techniques and personal leadership. Demanding and "utterly merciless in criticism of error or in achieving a goal," Robert McNamara seemed to some the archetypal corporate manager. He was born "fully programmed when somebody flipped a switch at the Harvard Business School," quipped one bitter Pentagon colonel.[10] No secretary of defense, either before or since, has so shaken the American military establishment. From the moment he took over at the Pentagon, it was clear that McNamara was going to be extraordinary. Each of his predecessors had, without exception, played the role of mediator, attempting to resolve the disputes that invariably arose to set one branch of the service against another. Military planning as well as weapons research and development had been left to the generals and admirals. McNamara, however, made it clear at the outset that his would be a qualitatively different regime. He intended to be "a leader, not a judge." He had come to Washington, he said, "to originate and stimulate new ideas and programs, not just to referee arguments and harmonize interests." He would use "deliberate analysis to force alternative programs to the surface, and then [make] explicit choices among them."[11]

The members of the Kennedy administration arrived in Washington eager to get things moving. They viewed the previous few years as a period of drift during which the Soviets seized the initiative in world politics while Eisenhower and his aged, irresolute advisers stood paralyzed, overcome by lethargy. They saw themselves as a second wave of New Dealers come to the nation's capital to solve problems, not wallow in indecision. As Under Secretary of State Chester Bowles later complained, the Kennedy people were "sort of looking for a chance to prove their muscle." They were "full of belligerence."[12] Of course, from inside the charmed circle things looked rather different. "Euphoria reigned," wrote Arthur Schlesinger, Jr. "We thought for a moment that the world was plastic and the future unlimited."[13]

The keynote of those early New Frontier days was action. This was nowhere more apparent than in the Office of the Secretary of Defense (OSD). The new regime reflected the secretary's own impatience with mediocrity and incompetence. McNamara's men at the Pentagon wanted data and were not easily impressed by uniforms, no matter how dazzling the stars and ribbons that decorated them. Military commanders soon discovered that this new breed, the "defense intellectual," was not easily co-opted by the VIP treatment that had for so long worked so well on junketing congressmen. Alain Enthoven, who worked in systems analysis during these years, later recalled an early visit to an air force base in Germany where a large number of senior officers were gathered while the commanding general explained to Enthoven the briefing sessions planned for him. Enthoven listened impatiently for a time and then blurted out, "General . . . I don't think you understand. I didn't come for a briefing. I came to tell you what we have decided."[14]

Puzzled military officers wondered at first what "cost effectiveness" and "systems analysis" meant. The more they learned, the less they liked it, for they soon realized that these were tools that would be used to challenge their expertise and corrode their power. Inevitably then, as the secretary and his staff began to reorder priorities and centralize decisionmaking in a department where feudal baronies were as common as once they had been in fourteenth-century Germany, they bruised egos and made enemies. Soon the military began to fight back. *The Army, Navy, Air Force Journal* charged that "the professional military leadership of the nation is being short-circuited in the current decision making process at the Pentagon."[15] General Thomas D. White, having fled into retirement in 1961, complained that he was "profoundly apprehensive of the pipe-smoking, tree-full-of-owls type of so-called professional defense intellectuals who have been brought into this nation's capital. I don't believe a lot of these often overconfident, sometimes arrogant young professors, mathematicians, and other theorists have sufficient worldliness or motivation to stand up to the kind of enemy we face."[16] General Curtis LeMay, even less enthusiastic, groused: "Today's armchair strategists, glibly writing about military matters . . . can do incalculable harm." Claiming expertise "in a field where they have no experience, they propose strategies based upon hopes and fears rather than upon facts and seasoned judgments."[17]

Some of the friction that developed between the civilians at OSD and the military was unnecessary, the result of impatience and intolerance on both sides. But a good deal of the antagonism stirred up by McNamara and his associates was the result of their effectiveness in reforming a department that could only be considered an organizational and managerial nightmare. For example, although Eisenhower had tried to keep a tight rein on overall defense allocations, budgeting within OSD "had several important defects, the most important of which," according to Enthoven, "was the almost complete separation between planning and decision making on weapons systems and forces on the one hand, and budgeting on the other." The various services made decisions regarding the size of the military as well as weapons development based on their own conception of what national security required and without any concern for costs. But the administration and Congress allocated funds "based on estimates of the burden the economy could or should bear." Often the result was a yawning gap between what the services felt they needed and what they were allocated. "The process by which the conflicting interests were resolved was unsystematic and wasteful" and "led to unbalanced programs."[18]

Nor did the various services show any interest in coordinating their research and development programs. On the contrary, each seemed determined to establish its claim to participate in the development of glamorous weapons such as ballistic missiles, while ignoring other important but less "sexy" projects. The resulting tendency toward waste and redundancy was the despair of Eisenhower's director of defense research, Herbert York, who struggled with little success to hold the line against ambitious military officers who saw the missile race as a competition between the army, navy, and air force. York later explained that of the six separate missile development programs undertaken during his years at the Pentagon, at least three had no justification whatsoever save to boost the salaries and reputations of certain well-known scientists. Wernher Von Braun, whose success at promoting himself with the media made him the best-known weapons expert in the country, and whose Jupiter missile project was an expensive waste of time, talent, and money, was York's particular bête noire.

The different services were no more cooperative when it came to developing war plans. Alain Enthoven's first full-scale briefing session by the navy serves as a case in point. The purpose of the briefing was to explain to the civilian staff at OSD the navy's plans in the event of a war with the Soviet Union. The briefing ended without a single mention of air force plans. Under questioning, the navy's briefing team was forced to admit that the navy had no idea what its sister service intended. There had been no coordination even on the basic question of targeting. A similar air force briefing was only slightly more impressive.

The two services might almost have occupied separate worlds.
Nor had the military planners done any serious thinking about
the nature of the nuclear war they might one day be called upon
to fight. They therefore had no conceptual framework for developing the sort of weapons that would be most useful in a nuclear
war. Research and development were being carried out in a completely unplanned and uncoordinated way with predictable results. McNamara soon discovered that the various services were
still developing weapons systems that could only be used in a first
strike mode, even though it was an absolute certainty that in a
half-dozen years the Soviets would have a survivable second
strike capability that would make a first strike tantamount to
suicide. McNamara, Enthoven, and others were even more
amazed to discover that Soviet capabilities notwithstanding, the
air force's strategic goal, its raison d'être so to speak, was to
achieve a "credible first strike capability"—an absolute impossibility no matter how much money was lavished on technology.

In his attempt to cut through this thicket of waste and create
a coordinated, flexible military establishment for the United
States, McNamara had the advantage of advice from a small but
extremely able group of scientist-bureaucrats who helped immeasurably in deciding which weapons systems were important
to national security, and which could be scrapped. In the late
1950s, at the height of the hysteria over the missile gap, a number
of scientific advisers and advisory committees were attached to
the executive branch. The Advanced Research Projects Agency,
the President's Science Advisory Committee, the office of Special
Assistant to the President for Science and Technology, and the
Director of Defense Research and Engineering all sprang into
being as part of a national response to the Soviet space shot.
Moreover, scientists charged with responsibility for research and
development were appointed to high-level administrative positions in the various service bureaucracies. McNamara, unwilling
to lose this valuable scientific establishment, invited these non-
political appointees to remain. A substantial number of them did,
including Herbert York, under secretary of the air force, Joseph
Chayet, and James Wakelin, Jr., assistant secretary of the navy for
research and development. Jerome Wiesner's appointment as

President Kennedy's special assistant for science and technology assured continuity in the office. Wiesner, who had worked closely with his two predecessors, James Killian and George Kistiakowsky, held views quite similar to theirs. Nor did it make any difference when, several months later, Harold Brown replaced Herbert York at Defense.

With the aid of these experts, McNamara was able to make informed decisions about which weapons systems would be deployed, which should be encouraged by funding for research and development, and which were to be dropped. He quickly decided to place heavy emphasis on the weapons capable of surviving a first strike, especially the Polaris submarine and Minuteman land-based missile, systems favored by Eisenhower.

Whenever McNamara decided against continued funding for a system, he ran the risk of arousing substantial opposition both from the service affected and from interested congressmen and senators. In some cases this opposition was muted or ineffective. He was, for example, able to kill off one hoary white elephant, the nuclear airplane, with little trouble. He was just as successful in abandoning Dyna-Soar, "a kind of hypersonic manned aircraft designed to be boosted up to very nearly orbital speed by a large rocket, skip along the top of the atmosphere, pass over its target, and then fly back down to its home base."[19] Herbert York viewed Dyna-Soar as nothing more than a toy for the jet jockeys at Edwards Air Force Base where rocket planes were then being tested. The principal reason that the air force supported the project, he thought, was to be certain that air force pilots would be at the controls of the spacecraft they saw coming along in the not too distant future. York pointed out that the cost of building the system would be far in excess of air force estimates, that it would take a long time to make this first piloted space plane fly, and that it had absolutely no military utility—"that its ostensible purposes could all be achieved more readily and more cheaply by [missiles]."[20]

Killing a partially developed system was not always so easy, though. McNamara had considerable difficulty in abandoning the Nike Zeus, an antiballistic missile system that the army wanted to deploy but that the technical experts at the Pentagon judged to be ineffective. He had even more trouble discontinuing Skybolt, an air-to-ground missile that the air force as well as the British wanted in order to prolong the life and utility of manned bombers. His decision to discontinue funding for the B-70 bomber produced a major conflict, with the civilians in OSD arrayed against the air force and its many friends in Congress.

The B-70, designed to attack predetermined targets while flying at altitudes in excess of 70,000 feet and at speeds greater than 2,000 miles per hour, was a pilot's dream and the air force's hope for preserving its role into the 1980s. But the very qualities that made the B-70 so appealing to air force generals made it hopelessly obsolete. Soviet surface-to-air missiles, guided by sophisticated radars, made it extremely difficult to penetrate air defenses by flying at high altitudes and great speed. It was clear even then that the successful bombers of the future would need to fly at low altitudes in order to elude radar, and that a variety of devices designed to confuse radar would be more important than speed in helping the plane reach its target. Worse, because of its speed, the B-70 had none of the flexibility that defenders of the manned bomber force liked to attribute to that particular weapons system. As Alain Enthoven explained, the plane flew so fast that it "could not look for new targets or targets of uncertain location." In fact, it had no "capability beyond preplanned attacks against previously identified and located targets—a mission that could more effectively be performed by missiles." From a management point of view the B-70 was a bad investment, combining all of the disadvantages of the manned bomber and the missile with some that were uniquely its own.

By the time McNamara left office, he had scuttled an impressive array of costly but questionable weapons projects. What emerged was the outline of a reasonably cost-effective strategic weapons program. First there were the Minuteman and Titan missiles deployed in hardened silos and immune from a first strike by the then relatively inaccurate Soviet missiles. Next came the submarine-launched ballistic missiles. Submerged and constantly in motion, these missiles were also immune from attack and capable of retaliating devastatingly in the event of a first strike Soviet attack. Finally there were the bombers of the Strategic Air Command, one third of which were always on fifteen-minute alert. Although a Soviet strike would destroy some SAC bombers on the ground, many would be airborne in time to join in the retaliation. Together these separate components made up the elements of the so-called "Triad" upon which the Kennedy administration would depend to deter a Soviet nuclear attack.

Roger Hilsman, Kennedy's assistant secretary of state for Far Eastern affairs and a frequent critic of McNamara, nevertheless thought him "a brilliantly efficient man" and credited him with rebuilding "the whole armed services, for the first time in its modern history giving the military establishment a coherent, flexible strategy, a rational weapons policy, and an effective cooperation among the services."[21] But, all of his successes notwithstanding, McNamara failed to achieve one of the administration's fundamental objectives. Kennedy, keenly aware that nations sometimes stumble unintentionally into war, had instructed McNamara to prepare military options short of an all-out nuclear exchange in the event of a war with the Soviets. Yet McNamara was never able to provide them. This was not for lack of trying, however.

In 1961, Europe still seemed to be that point on the globe where American and Soviet differences were most likely to boil up into a conflict. During the 1950s, the Truman and Eisenhower administrations had sheltered western Europe from the potential of a Soviet invasion with a nuclear umbrella. Any move against the West by Warsaw Pact forces would have brought down on the Soviet Union and eastern Europe an all-out American nuclear strike at a time when the Soviets were ill-prepared to retaliate. But with the Russians developing a survivable second strike capability, and the Kennedy administration anxious to establish military options other than "surrender or suicide," the search was on for new approaches.

One possibility was to fight a limited war for Europe using tactical nuclear weapons. Though the Eisenhower administration had armed NATO forces with these weapons, most strategists thought it would be impractical to use them. Europe was a small, densely populated continent, and some of these so-called tactical weapons were only a little less powerful than the bombs that had destroyed Hiroshima and Nagasaki. Moreover, most strategists agreed that once tactical nuclear weapons had been used in combat, there would be no stopping the escalation to strategic nuclear war. Henry Kissinger, at the time professor of political science at Harvard, at first took exception to this general view. In his 1957 study, *Nuclear Weapons and Foreign Policy,* Kissinger argued that a limited nuclear war for Europe was possible, provided that the rules of the game were carefully laid out in advance and agreed upon by both sides. Even Kissinger soon changed his opinion, however. In *The Necessity for Choice: Prospects of American Foreign Policy,* published in 1960, he rejected the views he had expressed three years before.

McNamara and Kennedy were no more enthusiastic about the prospect of fighting a limited nuclear war in Europe than most of the strategists. McNamara in fact found it impossible to envision "large scale ground operations with the exchange of . . . thousands . . . of nuclear warheads between the two sides." It seemed "inconceivable" to him that military commanders would be able to "send troops through an area in which there may have been literally hundreds of nuclear bursts." The defense secretary wondered whether those who proposed such scenarios had ever really been exposed "to . . . the destructive power of nuclear weapons."[22] More significantly, both the president and the secretary were utterly convinced that such a war could not be limited, that escalation to the point of a full-scale strategic nuclear exchange would soon follow.

Since tactical nuclear weapons could not be used for the defense of western Europe, and the administration remained intent upon reducing the peril posed by continued reliance on massive retaliation, there seemed only one logical conclusion: Europe would have to be defended with conventional forces. But was that possible? From 1949 on, American thinking on the subject had been conditioned by the view that the large, well-trained and equipped Red Army had such superiority over Western forces that there was no possibility of stopping it by conventional means. But a series of Defense Department studies begun in 1961 produced an entirely different conclusion. The more the OSD staffers studied the question, the more completely convinced they became that a conventional defense of Europe was feasible, and that the overwhelming superiority of the Red Army was a myth. In fact, they pointed out, even excluding the growing number of forces being employed by the United States in Southeast Asia, NATO allies actually deployed more men than did the Soviet Union and the other Warsaw Pact nations. The Kennedy administration concluded that it would be both desirable and feasible to develop the option of fighting a nonnuclear war for Europe in the event of a Soviet invasion. In the words of Theodore Sorensen, Kennedy

> refused to concede that the Warsaw Pact nations in the Soviet Alliance were automatically more powerful in conventional strength than the members of NATO, who had a hundred million more people, twice as large an economy, one-half million more men in uniform, and the capability of placing in time more combat forces on the ground in Central Europe and more tactical bombers in the air.[23]

Most of western Europe's leaders were distinctly cool to the idea of fighting a conventional war on the continent. They believed western Europe was too small to survive any sort of war. In their view, NATO was designed not to fight a war but to deter one by making it clear to the Soviets that an invasion would be met by all-out nuclear retaliation. A serious conventional buildup would undermine the credibility of this nuclear threat, lowering the threshold for a third major European war by indicating to the Soviets that the West was prepared to fight with conventional weapons only. To an administration bent on finding some method of surviving the next war, this seemed utterly insane. McNamara noted repeatedly during the long debate over the defense of Europe that "one cannot make a credible deterrent out of an incredible action."[24] Nevertheless, having the experience of two world wars to draw upon and aware of how much more destructive another war using modern conventional weapons would be, European leaders preferred to stick with the bluff rather than increase the possibility of war by admitting that they would even consider fighting a nonnuclear contest for Europe.

Because the allies remained wedded to the strategy of massive retaliation, attempts by the Kennedy administration to create military options short of an all-out nuclear spasm raised questions in European chancelleries about America's reliability in the event of a Soviet invasion. According to Arthur Schlesinger, General Lauris Norstad, NATO commander in 1961, warned the president "that every document we submitted stressing conventional warfare cast doubt on our nuclear resolve" and weakened our claim to continued leadership of the alliance.[25] These differences came out into the open in May 1961, during talks between Kennedy and Charles de Gaulle. The French president pointed out that circumstances had changed dramatically since the late 1940s. Because the United States was now vulnerable to a nuclear strike, her willingness to come to the aid of an ally in the event of a Soviet attack was in question. European security, de Gaulle insisted, could only be insured by European countries "not without the United States but not exclusively through the United States" either.[26] Kennedy insisted that the American commitment to the defense of Europe was firm, but de Gaulle remained unconvinced. He doubted that the Russians believed any more than he did that the United States would risk annihilation in order to defend another country. He even questioned whether American policymakers themselves believed it. No one, not even an American president, could know what he would do until the time came for decision. But in de Gaulle's judgment, America would use nuclear weapons "only when its own territory was actually threatened."[27]

Whatever else may be said of de Gaulle, given his frame of reference he was behaving rationally and sensibly. Nobody could know whether an American president would commit the United States to a suicidal course in defense of an ally. Writing in 1959, Henry Kissinger made exactly the same point. "The defense of Europe cannot be conducted solely from North America," he wrote, for no matter how firm "allied unity may be, a nation cannot be counted upon to commit suicide in defense of a foreign territory."[28] And why, after all, was the administration so anxious to find a conventional method of defending Europe? Clearly it was because massive retaliation, which Kennedy himself had described as suicidal, had become an extraordinarily unappealing option.

Secretary McNamara nevertheless continued to hammer away at the NATO allies, until at length the two sides agreed upon a compromise.[29] The nuclear option was to be retained in the event of a Soviet attack, but conventional options were also to be included in the overall strategy for the defense of Europe. This compromise, however, was a hollow victory for McNamara. In the first place, neither the western Europeans nor the United States proved willing to develop a NATO force truly capable of withstanding a conventional Soviet attack. Moreover, President de Gaulle soon removed French forces from NATO control and began to develop a small but potent independent nuclear capability. This force, which eventually came to constitute 300 bombers, missiles in hardened silos, and 5 missile-firing submarines, made it clear that whatever NATO did, France would rely as a last resort upon a nuclear deterrent and that if there was to be a war for Europe it would not be limited, nor would it necessarily be fought with conventional weapons. Administration attempts to create a variety of military options short of nuclear war in the event of a Soviet attack on western Europe had proven unavailing.

Repeatedly, during his short period in office, John Kennedy commented on the dangers posed by nuclear weapons. He seemed particularly concerned lest through some error or miscalculation the superpowers accidentally trigger a nuclear war. Yet in many ways the president's actions seemed to belie his words. At the time of his inauguration, the American intelligence community had been unable to locate any operational Soviet ICBMs, save for two at test sites. To counteract this slowly growing Soviet missile force, Kennedy inherited 5,000 nuclear-capable aircraft and approximately 1,100 missiles either already deployed or being built. In spite of the fact that President Eisenhower had left the United States with a sufficiency of strategic weapons, the Kennedy–McNamara administration more than doubled the size of the Minuteman force and increased the Polaris submarine fleet from 19 to 41 boats. The principal result of this was a dramatic escalation of the nuclear arms race.

One explanation offered for this seemingly pointless buildup emphasizes the importance of campaign rhetoric in decisionmaking. According to this view, the young president came to power claiming that Eisenhower's defense policies endangered national security. He had been emphatic about the importance of reversing the missile gap. He could not then abandon these themes immediately following his election. To have done so would have left the impression that he had campaigned on a phony issue or, worse, that he didn't know what he was talking about. Therefore, although he realized that from a strategic point of view more missiles were unnecessary, he plunged ahead and in the process fueled the arms race as had nobody before him.

Appealing though this cynical view of decisionmaking in the republic may be, it rests on shaky foundations because it requires us to believe that Kennedy actually felt bound by commitments made during the campaign. Yet one has only to recall Dwight Eisenhower's promise of total victory over international Communism, Lyndon Johnson's campaign as the peace candidate in 1964, or Richard Nixon's promise, repudiated within a week of taking office, that as president he would reestablish clear-cut nuclear superiority over the Soviet Union, to realize how unimportant campaign promises can seem to a sitting president. During the 1960 campaign, Kennedy made many commitments he had no intention of keeping. For example, when speaking in San Diego, a city in the throes of a recession caused in part by Eisenhower's cutbacks in the B-70 bomber program, he chastised the retiring president for the cuts and told the crowd: "I endorse wholeheartedly the B-70 manned aircraft." In Fort Worth, while speaking to workers at the Convair plant, he endorsed the B-58 bomber program, and on at least two occasions argued that the government ought to "step up our production of Atlas missiles."[30] None of these weapons systems survived the first year of the Kennedy administration. And the many recommendations that Kennedy did make to Congress during those first months in office more than protected him against the charge that he was not living up to his campaign rhetoric. It is most unlikely, then, that the huge buildup in strategic nuclear forces under Kennedy had anything at all to do with such considerations.

If political rhetoric cannot account for Kennedy's decision to expand the missile forces of the United States, economic considerations probably played a greater role. In 1961, the American economy was in the midst of a serious recession. Unlike Eisenhower, Kennedy was not averse to running deficits in the interest of stimulating productivity and reducing unemployment. Nor did he have that fear of inflation which in recent years has been so characteristic of Republican presidents. On the contrary, very early in his presidency Kennedy decided that the government would have to take a number of steps to reinflate the economy. Aware of this, economist Seymour Melman has argued that

> having just concluded that an infusion of capital funds was needed in order to raise American economic activity to a higher level, the White House decided that an outlay of capital for missiles, as well as other military forces, was necessary. This particular form of economic stimulation was carried out through the period 1961–1963.[31]

Melman is undoubtedly correct in arguing that the White House saw increased spending on the missile force as falling in with its overall plan to increase federal spending and thus revive the economy. This does not necessarily prove, however, that Kennedy was therefore motivated by economic considerations when he ordered the buildup. It is far more likely that at first strategic and later political considerations were primary and that administration leaders considered the economic impact of the program something of a bonus, an important and welcome side effect.

One of McNamara's priorities on taking over at the Pentagon had been to find an alternative to the old strategy of massive retaliation. A new approach to nuclear war soon came to his attention, one that seemed to provide the sought-for options short of all-out attack. At a briefing given for McNamara, Enthoven, and another Defense Department official, Marvin Stern, William W. Kaufmann of the RAND Corporation explained counterforce strategy to the neophyte secretary of defense. The concept had first emerged two years earlier and was the product of a study done at RAND and headed by Kaufmann himself. But the air force, which had commissioned the study in the first place, soon all but abandoned the idea. "Air Force jealousies and interservice rivalries," Richard Fryklund has written, "almost strangled the epochal new strategy in its cradle."[32] Now McNamara and his whiz kids would bring it back to life.

In the event of a Soviet first strike, Kaufmann believed that it was possible to limit damage to the United States while providing policymakers with a range of options short of all-out retaliation. Damage from an attack could be limited by having in place a civil defense apparatus designed to save a substantial portion of the American population, and by deploying an effective antiballistic missile system capable of intercepting and destroying a number of missiles before they could reach their targets. The strategy also called for a program of offensive damage limitation. After absorbing the Soviet strike, the United States would respond by attacking not Soviet population centers but military targets— particularly air bases and missile-launching facilities, thus making it difficult for the Soviets to launch a follow-up strike. While keeping a large "counter-city" missile force in reserve, the government could then seek to end the contest before it became necessary to attack Soviet cities. In order to be certain that in the chaos of a thermonuclear exchange it would be possible to control the use of one's own forces and establish a dialogue with the Soviets, special care would be taken to secure command and control facilities in this country and, at least in the early stages of the war, not to attack similar facilities inside the U.S.S.R. Of course if diplomacy failed, the administration would then be forced to launch a full-scale strike against Soviet population centers and accept Soviet retaliation. But counterforce strategy did seem to offer options short of total spasm. By announcing this strategy in advance, moreover, the Soviets would be given considerable incentive to adopt a similar strategy. After all, everyone understood that total nuclear war amounted to national suicide. Kaufmann suggested a method of fighting a nuclear war and surviving.

One vital component of counterforce strategy was civil defense, a half-forgotten idea whose time, it seemed, had come around again. World War II's bombing raids taught Allied leaders the need for protecting civilian populations of cities from aerial onslaught, and shortly after the war Pentagon planners gave some thought to building "blast shelters" to shield urban

Americans against bombing. The idea was soon abandoned, though. Who, after all, was going to bomb the United States in 1946? However, the unexpectedly severe patterns of local radioactive fallout that followed the hydrogen bomb tests of 1954 demonstrated that radiation might prove to be a more lethal threat than blast, and so civil defense planners turned to another option: evacuation. A strategy of evacuating cities depended on the assumption that Soviet bombers would need ten to twelve hours to reach their American targets. In 1957, Sputnik dispelled that assumption, and for the next three years civil defense planning languished, as Pentagon officials concluded, sensibly enough, that neither blast shelters nor evacuation constituted a rational defense against intercontinental ballistic missiles.

But with McNamara's enthusiasm for counterforce, civil defense thinking revived, principally as a means of demonstrating to Soviet leaders that the United States was serious about its defense posture. Air Force General Lyman Lemnitzer, chairman of the Joint Chiefs of Staff, insisted that civil defense "bears an essential relationship to military strength. . . . It provides further unmistakable evidence of serious determination on our part."[33] Credibility being the high-priority issue that it was after President Kennedy's 1961 confrontation with Nikita Khrushchev in Vienna, such a rationale proved persuasive, and in that same year, Kennedy approved a limited though enthusiastic revival of civil defense planning. The key to Kennedy-era civil defense was "insurance": the idea that some limited and inexpensive preparations might save perhaps ten million lives in a nuclear war. The administration supported efforts to identify and mark suitable shelter sites, such as the basements of large buildings in cities, and the familiar yellow-and-black radiation logo began to appear in the cities, directing persons to shelter areas. Civil defense authorities also stockpiled some of these areas with barrels of water and cartons of survival crackers.

The administration's support touched off a civil defense craze that lasted a little over a year. Private enterprise snatched at the opportunity, and offered either prefabricated or custom-built backyard bomb shelters. Priests and ministers speculated aloud on moral questions surrounding the appearance of shelters: Is it justifiable to shoot someone trying to break into your shelter? (A surprisingly large number of clergy saw no moral complications with that recourse.) When homeowner enthusiasm seemed to flag, public and private civil defense enthusiasts tried to stimulate sales by reminding them of Nikita Khrushchev's 1956 boast, "We will bury you."

But the common sense of the American people prevailed, and the craze soon died. Few were willing to invest thousands of their dollars and dig up their backyards, just to enhance the credibility of an insecure administration worried about its image. Government officials themselves gave the American public little reason to invest money and confidence in the civil defense program. As ever throughout its history, civil defense was starved for appropriations, with Kennedy budgeting only a relatively small $700 million for it annually. This was in keeping with the initial Kennedy "insurance" rationale, which stressed low costs, in the public sector at least. Even at a more personal level, administration officials demonstrated that they shared the public's skepticism. None of the members of the National Security Council, nor Vice-President Lyndon Johnson, nor Attorney-General Robert Kennedy, nor Assistant Secretary of Defense Steuart Pittman, who was in charge of civil defense when it became housed in the Department of Defense, bothered to build a home bomb shelter for their own families.

More knowledgeable critics seconded the attitude of the man in the street. They pointed out that, whatever its value as protection against blast and radiation, a backyard shelter would be useless against the igniting and suffocating effects of a fire storm. They also noted that any truly serious American commitment to civil defense would suggest to Soviet planners that we were considering a preemptive first strike or some nuclear blackmail of our own. In this they were inadvertently seconded by one of the nation's foremost civil defense supporters, Hudson Institute figure Herman Kahn, who had argued in his book *On Thermonuclear War* that the earlier civil defense strategy, evacuation, would give the United States greater leverage to "regulate" Soviet behavior.[34] The leaders of the U.S.S.R., who are not fools, responded as we might have expected: they viewed the American civil defense program not as an affirmation of a determination not to be bullied, but as another mulish escalation of the arms race, to be met by a Soviet counterescalation.

In the civil defense debate of 1961–62, defense planners confronted for the first time one of the most perplexing and ironic dilemmas of the arms race. In a world of ICBMs, what appears on its face to be purely defensive, like a civil defense system or an ABM, turns out on second thought to be provocative because it signals the enemy that you may well be preparing for a first strike. The reasoning, born of counterforce thinking, goes that you are doing your utmost to beef up your survival capability because you expect to launch a first strike and are willing to pay the price, as Kahn was, of absorbing the enemy's retaliatory strike. Further, such "defensive" systems, as Kahn also noted, enhanced your ability to blackmail the enemy. But McNamara and Kennedy were not yet in a position to ponder these dilemmas, nor even to take a sober and critical look at the follies of bomb shelters.

Despite the flawed thinking so obvious in hindsight, Defense Department planners turned enthusiastically to translating Kaufmann's study into policy. Eisenhower's strategy had called for an immediate attack on all cities and important military bases in the Soviet Union, China, and the satellites. Now, planning became more complex as targets in the Soviet Union were separated from those in other "enemy" countries, while Soviet military facilities were separated from Soviet cities on target lists. What emerged was a strategy that offered the president five broad options, which together constituted a primitive ladder of escalation. In the initial stages of a war, the president could respond to a Soviet strike by attacking missile-launching sites, air bases, and submarine pens inside the U.S.S.R. If the war continued, he might next order attacks on air defense systems that were some distance from Soviet cities but along routes to be used by American bombers. If it still proved necessary, he could then order attacks on air defenses near cities and go on to strike at Soviet command and control facilities. Finally, if all else failed, he could use America's strategic reserves to launch a full-scale attack. Because the strategy focused on military targets and sought to avoid attacks on population centers, it soon came to be known as the "No Cities doctrine."

It was obvious that to implement such a strategy the United States would require a very large and flexible strategic nuclear force. In the spring of 1961, a subcommittee of the National Security Council undertook to answer the inevitable question, How much was enough? According to Alain Enthoven:

> The study group developed a list of all strategic targets and, using the best available intelligence and their own judgment, projected the growth of these target lists over the next ten years. They then estimated the performance and operational characteristics of the various available weapons systems and calculated how many would be needed for destruction of 75 percent and 90 percent of the targets in each of the next ten years.[35]

The study group recommended a force of 150 Minuteman missiles for 1963, expanding to a full 2,000 by 1971. This missile force would be supplemented by 60 Titan missiles, 150 RS-70 bombers (a variation of the B-70) each armed with 18 cruise missiles, from 230 to 370 Skybolt missiles deployed aboard B-52 bombers, and a force of from 40 to 47 Polaris-type submarines. The administration did not embrace all of these recommendations. The B-70 and the Skybolt were both killed by Secretary McNamara. But he gladly authorized expansion of the Polaris and Minuteman programs.

To an administration haunted by the prospect of conflict and anxious for a strategy that would provide a range of options between the extremes of acquiescence and obliteration, counterforce strategy seemed perfect. In his January 1962 State of the Union message, Kennedy announced: "We have rejected any all-or-nothing posture which would leave no choice but inglorious retreat or unlimited retaliation."[36] In the following month Secretary McNamara elaborated on the theme. "Our new policy," he told members of the American Bar Foundation, "gives us the flexibility to choose among several operational plans, but does not require that we make any advance commitment with respect to doctrine or targets. We shall be committed only to a system that gives us the ability to use our forces in a controlled and deliberate way, so as best to pursue the interests of the

United States, our allies and the rest of the free world."[37] In June, McNamara went a step further, spelling out his No Cities doctrine in detail in a speech delivered at the University of Michigan's commencement ceremony. In part he said:

> The U.S. has come to the conclusion that to the extent feasible basic military strategy in a possible general nuclear war should be approached in much the same way that more conventional military operations have been regarded in the past. That is to say, principal military objectives, in the event of a nuclear war stemming from a major attack on the Alliance, should be the destruction of the enemy's military forces, not of their civilian population . . . we are giving a possible opponent the strongest imaginable incentive to refrain from striking our own cities.[38]

Reaction to the Ann Arbor speech came swiftly and was almost universally negative. In western Europe, it fed already established fears that Washington was having second thoughts about protecting the NATO allies against a Soviet attack. Worse, McNamara seemed to be lowering the threshold to war by making it seem that nuclear war was survivable. *Pravda* denounced the No Cities doctrine as "monstrous" while Soviet leaders declared that they had no intention of cooperating with what they characterized as an American attempt to make nuclear war feasible. Marshal V. D. Sokolovskii attacked the No Cities doctrine as a first strike strategy pure and simple, and accused the United States of planning a preemptive war. "A strategy which contemplates attaining victory through the destruction of the armed forces," he wrote, "cannot stem from the idea of a 'retaliatory' blow: it stems from preventive action and the achievement of surprise."[39]

The domestic response was no more favorable. High-ranking naval officers, sensing that counterforce strategy would provide the air force with a significant edge in the battle of the budget, were quick to challenge the validity of the new doctrine. Admiral Arleigh Burke told the Senate Armed Services Committee that:

> Many of these missile bases are right close to our cities, right close, so are many of our other bases. So an attack on our major bases would necessarily destroy a great many cities and a great many of our people. When those missiles start coming over you do not

know whether the intent of the enemy was to hit or not to hit a city
if he hits it. The same thing is true with the Russian military
installations.[40]

Other critics of the new strategy pointed out that the concept of
deterrence was based on the assumption that nuclear war was
both unthinkable and unwinnable. But the No Cities doctrine
denied this premise, undermining the validity of a deterrent
strategy. Clearly, McNamara was planning to survive a nuclear
war. Worse, counterforce suggested to some that he had abandoned deterrence altogether in favor of preparations for a first
strike against the Soviets. Assuming that the United States did
intend to use its forces only in retaliation for an attack, what sense
did it make to target missile silos and air fields in the Soviet
Union? If the Soviets had already attacked, these silos and bases
would be empty. The only conclusion that one could logically
draw from such a targeting policy was that the Defense Department was planning a preemptive strike against Soviet nuclear
installations. That was certainly not the message that McNamara
meant to send to Moscow, but it illustrated again the emerging
dilemmas of strategic planning in the nuclear era.

McNamara was stunned by the criticism. He later explained to
Stewart Alsop that he and other planners were so habituated to
thinking only in terms of deterrence and the development of a
second strike damage-limiting capability that it had occurred to
none of them that the strategy they were developing might be
interpreted in any other way. A far-fetched explanation, it is
nevertheless probably true. One aide, while defending his chief
from the swarming critics, argued that "Bob still wasn't thinking
for himself. He was listening to his Whiz Kids and accepting too
much of what they said at face value." Even this loyalist was
forced to admit, however, that "he should have known there
could be no such thing as primary retaliation against military
targets after an enemy attack. If you're going to shoot at missiles,
you're talking about first strike."[41]

McNamara began to back away from the No Cities doctrine
almost immediately. But before he had completed his retreat and
fully reoriented his thinking, a crisis developed in Soviet–Ameri-

can relations. The Cuban missile confrontation of 1962 not only threatened to produce the nuclear war McNamara hoped to avoid but also suggested that his critics were correct in predicting how the Soviets would react to a counterforce strategy. On the morning of October 15, 1962, National Security Adviser McGeorge Bundy came to the White House for a hastily arranged meeting with the president. The day before, Air Force Major Rudolf Anderson, while on a routine reconnaissance flight over western Cuba, had photographed the unmistakable beginnings of Soviet medium and intermediate range missile installations. Once operational, these weapons would command targets in all but the extreme northwestern corner of the United States.

Although there are a number of possible explanations for Khrushchev's daring gamble, it is most likely that he was attempting to redress a dangerous imbalance in strategic nuclear forces that had come about as a result of the American buildup in nuclear striking power. McNamara's Ann Arbor speech, the 1961 commitment to civil defense, and the expansion of American missile forces may well have suggested to Soviet strategists that the United States was preparing for a preemptive war. Even if this were not the case, the United States held such a commanding lead in nuclear striking power that it was now in a position to practice nuclear blackmail. Indeed, Kennedy already had. Late in 1961, in the midst of the third crisis over Berlin since 1948, Under Secretary of Defense Roswell Gilpatric issued this statement:

> The fact is that this nation has a nuclear retaliatory force of such lethal power that an enemy move which brought it into play would be an act of self-destruction on his part. . . . Our forces are so deployed and protected that a sneak attack could not effectively disarm us. The destructive power which the United States could bring to bear even after a Soviet surprise attack upon our forces would be as great as—perhaps greater than—the total undamaged force which the enemy can threaten to launch against the United States in a first strike. In short, we have a second-strike capability which is at least as extensive as what the Soviets can deliver by striking first. Therefore, we are confident that the Soviets will not provoke a major nuclear conflict.[42]

Shortly after this blatant proclamation of American nuclear superiority, the president sent an armored column crashing down the
Autobahn through East Germany into Berlin. The message was
unmistakably clear to those who invented Sputnik diplomacy. If
Russian interests were to be advanced, or even protected, something would have to be done to erase the strategic imbalance that
threatened to immobilize Soviet foreign policy.

But why not simply build several hundred strategic missiles
just as the Americans had? This proved to be impossible. In the
first place, any significant reallocation of resources for the purpose of the rapid deployment of strategic missiles would have
damaged an already strained economy. Moreover, strategic missiles that the Soviets could deploy at that time were unwieldy,
inaccurate, and unreliable. They were so large that they could
only be transported in sections on railroad cars and deployed
along railroad right-of-ways. Worse, they could not be stored in
hardened silos, but had to be fired from a vulnerable aboveground launch site. Finally, they were liquid-fueled and like the
early Atlas undoubtedly took a long time to prepare for firing.

Khrushchev might have attempted to reverse the nuclear imbalance by building and deploying these missiles. But the cost
would have been excessive and the benefits marginal. Another
option seemed more feasible—to deploy in Cuba a substantial
number of medium and intermediate range missiles already in
the strategic rocket force's inventory. Such a quick fix would
temporarily redress the dangerous strategic imbalance without
damaging the Soviet economy. It would also gain time for the
development of more advanced strategic missiles based in hardened silos or at sea—the sort of weapons that would provide the
Soviet Union with a survivable second strike capability similar to
the one the United States already possessed.

Actions taken by the Kennedy administration during the
Cuban missile crisis, which took place in mid-October 1962,
demonstrated that the No Cities strategy had been abandoned.
Counterforce doctrine held that by announcing before a clash
that the United States would not attack Soviet population centers, the Russians would be encouraged to follow suit and thus
limit the devastation. But during the 1962 crisis, SAC bombers

were deployed at municipal airports all along the Gulf Coast, leaving the Kremlin no choice but to launch immediate attacks on these population centers in the event of a war. Nor did the president's televised address to the nation on October 22, 1962, reveal any commitment to the new strategy. Kennedy demanded that the Soviets remove their missiles from Cuba, announced a naval blockade of the island, and warned Premier Khrushchev that the United States would regard any nuclear missile fired from Cuba against the United States or any other nation in the Western Hemisphere as "requiring a full retaliatory response upon the Soviet Union."[43] This was massive retaliation pure and simple.

By the end of 1962, McNamara was hinting publicly that a change in nuclear strategy was in the wind. In November, he admitted to columnist Stewart Alsop that the Soviets would soon develop the same sort of survivable nuclear retaliatory capability that the United States already possessed. When they did, America's nuclear superiority would become largely meaningless. McNamara did not seem disturbed by this prospect, however. On the contrary, he almost welcomed it. "When both sides have a sure second-strike capability," he told Alsop, "then you might have a more stable balance of terror. This may seem a rather subtle point," he continued, "but from where I'm sitting it seems a point worth thinking about."[44] These remarks, coming only weeks after the missile crisis, suggest that dramatic changes were taking place inside the Department of Defense. For more than a year, McNamara and his aides had devoted themselves to developing the capability to wage nuclear warfare. But the events of 1962 had forced them to reconsider their purposes. McNamara's remarks to Alsop reveal a man no longer thinking in terms of fighting and surviving a nuclear war but attempting instead to reduce to an absolute minimum the possibility that nuclear weapons would be used at all. Counterforce was in disrepute. McNamara now had deterrence on his mind.

In his renewed search for the best possible nuclear strategy, McNamara took up a position between extremes. He continued to reject massive retaliation because it left policymakers no option in the event of war save to initiate an attack that would lead to the total destruction of the Soviet Union, the United States, and much of the rest of the world. But he also turned away from those who continued to insist on seeking full nuclear superiority and a counterforce capability. "Damn it," he snapped at one particularly insistent air force general, "if you keep talking about ten thousand missiles, you are talking about pre-emptive attack. Why don't you just say so?"[45]

The Cuban missile crisis also killed off the boomlet for civil defense. Throughout the tense two weeks of crisis, no national leader, least of all the president himself, mentioned civil defense or recommended that Americans scurry to bomb shelters and begin munching survival crackers. Tacitly the American government confirmed what man-in-the-street skepticism had known all along: the very concept of civil defense was a preposterous contradiction, useless and dangerous. The Soviets were not impressed by civil defense preparedness, much less intimidated. McNamara came to realize that the Soviets could offset even the most costly American civil defense schemes simply by increasing the numbers and megatonnage of their retaliatory strike force.

Early in 1963, McNamara began to refute those who insisted that the nation could survive a nuclear war. In a speech before New York's exclusive Economic Club, he contended that such a conflict would be "highly destructive to both sides" under "all foreseeable circumstances." Two years later in testimony given before Congress, he pointed out that even if the government spent an astronomical $25 billion to protect the civilian population, "no foreseeable defense program within the assumed cost restraints could reduce fatalities to a level much below 80 millions."[46]

McNamara had little trouble convincing Congress and the public that civil defense was a dangerous and futile idea. He was less successful with military planners who continued to harbor fantasies about winning a nuclear war. "The Pentagon is full of papers talking about the preservation of a 'viable society' after nuclear conflict," he once complained. "That 'viable society' phrase drives me mad. I keep trying to comb it out, but it keeps coming back."[47]

In January 1964, more than a year after the missile crisis,

McNamara at last unveiled the Defense Department's latest nuclear strategy. It was based on the assumption that the development in the Soviet Union of a survivable second strike force made it impossible for the United States to develop a first strike capability, and that even an elaborate civil defense program could not reduce fatalities in a first strike much below eighty million. From this McNamara concluded that a strategy that emphasized deterrence but included certain "damage limiting" characteristics appeared to be "the most practical and effective course for us to follow." To that end, he explained, the United States should maintain "a clear and convincing capability to inflict unacceptable damage on an attacker, even were that attacker to strike first." However, in the event that the deterrent failed and a nuclear exchange actually did take place, the United States should be in a position "to limit damage to our populations and industrial capacities." This involved the destruction of the enemy's "war-making capability so as to limit, to the extent practicable, damage to this country and to our allies."[48] Put simply, this meant that the United States would include on its list of potential targets military installations as well as population centers inside the Soviet bloc.

McNamara called the first element of the new strategy "mutually assured destruction" (MAD) and defined it as "the capability to destroy the aggressor as a viable society, even after a well planned and executed surprise attack on our forces." The second aspect, which he was at pains to emphasize was of far less overall importance, he called "damage limitation," i.e., the capability to reduce the impact of the enemy attack by both offensive and defensive measures and "to provide a degree of protection for the population against the effects of nuclear detonations."[49]

This, McNamara's last attempt to articulate a credible nuclear strategy for the United States, bears none of the hallmarks that are normally associated with policy formulation during his tenure in the Defense Department. Maddeningly imprecise, it was an improvisation—a flawed one at that, for it begged the essential question. In 1961, the secretary had set out to devise a method of fighting a limited nuclear war in the event that the deterrent failed. MAD, which placed overwhelming emphasis on deterrence, was McNamara's admission that it couldn't be done.

McNamara had a facility for making his judgments seem precise even when they were not. He was in excellent form when describing the force levels that would provide the United States with a true assured destruction capability. First, he argued that to attain this goal the United States would have to be able to absorb a first strike and still destroy 50 percent of the Soviet Union's industrial capacity while killing 25 percent of her population. (He later increased his estimate of required industrial destruction to 70 percent.) To accomplish this, the nation would require a force of 1,000 Minuteman ICBMs as well as 41 missile-firing submarines in addition to existing bomber forces. To those who read his carefully worded statements, it appeared that the figures he reeled off were derived from elaborate Pentagon studies. In fact, they were improvised, little better than guesswork. Just as MAD itself was an improvisation, the force levels that McNamara described as necessary to implement the strategy were inflated and not the product of careful study.

In 1961, key figures in the administration, including Kennedy and McNamara, thought in terms of a substantial increase in the number of strategic nuclear weapons in the American arsenal. Counterforce strategy required that. But when MAD replaced counterforce, administration leaders did some serious rethinking about "how much was enough." White House staffers, including Jerome Wiesner, George Rathjens, Carl Kaysen, and Arthur Schlesinger, claim that President Kennedy believed 800 Minuteman missiles would do. McNamara probably agreed, but insisted that the political pressures were such that he "could not live in the Pentagon" with fewer than one thousand.[50] He and his aides had a "gut feeling" that a recommendation of fewer than a thousand missiles would touch off a revolt of the generals similar to the one Eisenhower had experienced and neither McNamara nor Kennedy wanted any part of a "public conflict with the Joint Chiefs and . . . Congress."[51] McNamara's deputy, Roswell Gilpatric, has even claimed that McNamara feared the administration would lose such a battle; that a decision to deploy fewer than a thousand Minuteman missiles "could be overridden on the Hill." According to Gilpatric, McNamara thought it "better to shorten sail ahead of time rather than to catch the blast in full rig."[52]

In the end, neither economic nor strategic considerations determined the size of the American missile force. The numbers were produced as a result of bargaining involving the Defense Department, the White House, the navy, and the air force. Negotiations between the Defense Department and the navy were actually almost pro forma. The Navy Department's original goal, set during Eisenhower's years as president, was to deploy 45 Polaris-type submarines. At that time, however, only 19 boats had been authorized. A National Security Council study done early in the Kennedy administration recommended that the navy deploy anywhere from 41 to 47 boats. The navy then, for purposes of bargaining, increased its estimated need to 50 boats. When Secretary McNamara approved 41 boats, the navy acquiesced, probably because the four extra boats it actually sought didn't seem worth a fight.

Though the navy proved accommodating, McNamara had his hands full with the air force. During Eisenhower's presidency, air force leaders had insisted that a minimum of 1,450 Minuteman missiles were essential. In 1961, with a new and presumably more sympathetic administration in power, the air force quietly doubled that figure. It is not clear exactly how many missiles air force planners really thought were essential. But dreams of three thousand missiles turned out to be wishful thinking. The myth of the missile gap had been exploded, reducing at least temporarily the air force's clout in Congress. Moreover, the strategy of mutually assured destruction required many fewer weapons than counterforce doctrine.

The question of how many Minuteman missiles would be deployed was finally resolved during a meeting held at President Lyndon Johnson's ranch on December 22, 1964. Present were Johnson himself, McNamara, Air Force Chief of Staff General Curtis LeMay, and Kermit Gordon, director of the Bureau of the Budget. At that time, McNamara was committed to a maximum of 1,000 missiles while LeMay was holding out for 1,200. Johnson allowed the two men to wrangle for some time and then asked Gordon (whom he knew favored a figure of 900 missiles) for his opinion. Once Gordon became involved, LeMay and McNamara both tore into him. With the two former antagonists on the same side, Johnson then intervened to arrange one of his famous "compromises." One thousand Minuteman missiles would be deployed.

The decision to deploy 41 Polaris boats and 1,000 Minuteman missiles then, had less to do with the strategic than with the political requirements of the Johnson administration. McNamara acquiesced in these numbers because he believed that to have insisted on fewer would have opened the door to a rebellion in the military and on Capitol Hill that might well have produced even higher force levels. Lord Solly Zuckerman, chief scientific adviser to Britain's minister of defense from 1960 to 1966, has recently explained the defense secretary's actions in this way: "In other words, McNamara felt himself bound to put his stamp of approval on what was already in train, presumably in hopes that by so doing America's nuclear build-up would come to an end." Zuckerman has also noted that many civilians in the Defense Department were dismayed by what seemed to them the outlandishly high force levels attained under MAD. "Don't you see?" one particularly unhappy assistant secretary told Zuckerman at the time. "First we need enough Minutemen to be sure that we destroy all those Russian cities. Then we need Polaris missiles to follow in order to tear up the foundations to a depth of ten feet. . . . Then, when all Russia is silent, and when no air defenses are left, we want waves of aircraft to drop enough bombs to tear the whole place up down to a depth of forty feet to prevent the Martians recolonizing the country. And to hell with the fallout."[53]

The events of 1962 convinced McNamara and Kennedy to give up their search for a method of fighting and surviving a nuclear war and instead to concentrate on developing a credible deterrent nuclear strategy. At the same time, the missile crisis made it clear that nuclear weapons alone could not serve as a reliable deterrent. During those tense October days, Khrushchev and Kennedy were undoubtedly more cautious than they otherwise might have been because of the high stakes game they were playing. Yet, in the last analysis, though war would have been suicidal, both leaders realized that had the circumstances of the crisis been only somewhat different, war might well have ensued.

Both leaders recognized the necessity for a major effort designed to reduce political tensions as well as the danger posed by the very existence of nuclear weapons. Khrushchev seized the initiative. On October 28, the same day on which he defused the crisis by agreeing to withdraw the missiles from Cuba, he indicated that his government "should like to continue the exchange of views on the prohibition of atomic and thermonuclear weapons, on general disarmament and other problems relating to the relaxation of international tension." Kennedy responded quickly and affirmatively, saying that "perhaps now, as we step back from danger, we can make some real progress in this vital field."[54] The two leaders agreed to begin by renewing their efforts to achieve a comprehensive nuclear test ban agreement.

Negotiations for a ban on nuclear testing actually began in 1959 during the Eisenhower administration. But the collapse of the Paris summit conference in May of 1960 temporarily brought them to a halt. Early in his administration, Kennedy reinvigorated the idea of a test ban treaty through public statements and by establishing the Arms Control and Disarmament Agency (ACDA). But the young president was unable to unite his administration in pursuit of an agreement. McGeorge Bundy, Kennedy's national security adviser, remarked in 1964 that "military men in all countries find it hard to approve any arms control proposal which is not either safely improbable or clearly unbalanced in their favor." This was certainly the case in the early 1960s when the Joint Chiefs of Staff opposed any agreement that might stand between them and the continued pursuit of military superiority over the Soviets. The military, aided by the AEC and their allies in Congress, proved a major obstacle blocking all progress toward a comprehensive nuclear test ban agreement.

In the summer of 1962, prospects for a comprehensive agreement were so bleak that White House aide Carl Kaysen and Assistant Secretary of Defense John McNaughton proposed the negotiation of a partial test ban agreement prohibiting only atmospheric testing. This idea was strongly opposed by the ACDA on the ground that only a ban on all testing would be of any real value in terms of true disarmament. The arms controllers also pointed out that a treaty that allowed unlimited underground tests would provide the Soviets with an opportunity to catch up with the United States in the one area (relatively small devices) where they lagged far behind. But to an administration frustrated by its failure to achieve support for a comprehensive ban and under unremitting pressure from groups distressed by mounting evidence indicating that continued atmospheric testing posed a major health hazard, the proposal had considerable political appeal. Kennedy did propose the negotiation of a partial test ban agreement. But nothing came of this prior to the missile crisis. And afterward, Kennedy believed—at least initially—that his position had been so strengthened as a result of the crisis that he might no longer have to settle for a partial agreement. So began the big push for a comprehensive test ban agreement.

While the political atmosphere seemed promising, a vehicle for negotiations was conveniently at hand. An eighteen-nation United Nations disarmament conference was scheduled to open within a month. But it remained to be seen whether the two superpowers could muster enough moral energy to break the deadlock that had paralyzed earlier test ban talks. In 1961, a ten-nation conference made up of the United States, the Soviet Union, and eight nonaligned nations had failed in a similar attempt to work out a formula for a ban on nuclear weapons testing. The crux of the dispute was a disagreement over methods of verification. Fearing that the Soviets would conduct clandestine tests, the United States insisted on as many as twenty annual on-site inspections. The Soviets, on the other hand, argued that seismic instruments alone could detect nuclear explosions and reiterated their conviction that the United States would use the inspections for espionage purposes.

The administration's position regarding the importance of on-site inspections came into serious question in July 1962, when the Defense Department published a seismic research study, Project Vela. Among other things, the Vela study found that methods already existed for substantially improving the detection capabilities of seismic instruments, thus making it more likely that clandestine nuclear tests would be detected. The study also undercut a basic objection against heavy reliance on seismic verification by demonstrating that there were many fewer earthquakes in the Soviet Union than had previously been thought. The Soviets believed that these findings, produced by the American Defense Department, proved that on-site inspections were unnecessary. This view was not shared by AEC scientists, however. Glenn Seaborg, the head of the AEC, objected that it was questionable whether seismic equipment could detect nuclear explosions under 15 kilotons and insisted that

> much could be accomplished by underground tests below 10 kilotons in the areas of (1) tactical weapons, (2) developing detonation mechanisms for large weapons, (3) developing pure fusion weapons [the neutron bomb], (4) tests of effects and vulnerability, and (5) experiments to verify new ideas that came out of the laboratories, with the consequent effect of keeping the laboratories strong.[55]

White House science adviser Jerome Wiesner was not so completely negative about the Vela study. Wiesner agreed that the United States should not completely abandon its insistence on inspections. But he told Kennedy that improved seismic detection could reduce the number of necessary inspections to around five annually. Kennedy, who faced the considerable task of convincing the Joint Chiefs as well as a doubtful Senate that fewer inspections would be safe, was willing to reduce the number of on-site inspections to eight. Even at that, from a purely political standpoint, he was probably stretching things.

When the UN disarmament conference convened on November 26, 1962, chances for progress seemed reasonably good. But negotiations soon bogged down, for the Soviets continued to oppose any on-site inspections whatsoever. After a month of futile talks, Khrushchev, who had evidently staked a good deal of his own political capital on his ability to negotiate a test ban treaty, tried for a breakthrough. On October 30, Soviet Deputy Foreign Minister V. V. Kuznetsov conferred with the head of the American delegation, Ambassador Arthur Dean. According to Kuznetsov, Dean had informed him that Kennedy would be willing to settle for from two to four annual inspections. Somehow

Khrushchev also got the impression that Kennedy insisted on the inspections only in order to placate the Senate, which would not approve a treaty that did not include them. Probably at great personal political risk, Khrushchev managed to convince the Politburo to take a major step in a conciliatory direction by abandoning its long-held opposition to on-site inspections. On December 19, he informed Kennedy that he would concede the principle and was "prepared to agree to two or three inspections a year."[56]

The significance of this Soviet concession should not be underestimated. Khrushchev obviously wanted a test ban treaty and made a major effort to achieve one. Unfortunately, however, he based his initiative on inaccurate information. We will never know whether Kuznetsov misunderstood Dean, or whether Dean, who later denied the Russian's story, was lying to protect himself from Kennedy's anger. At the time, however, it really did not matter. Kennedy found himself in a difficult predicament. He could not accept the Russian offer. But neither could he reject it without risking the future of the negotiations. So he made the best of a bad situation by informing Khrushchev that there had been a serious misunderstanding and that the United States would agree to no fewer than eight on-site inspections. Simultaneously he sent a personal emissary to the Kremlin with instructions to reassure the Soviet leader that he really was anxious to negotiate a treaty. For this purpose he employed the services of Norman Cousins, the editor of the *Saturday Review of Literature* and a well-known advocate of nuclear disarmament, who was already scheduled to journey to the Soviet Union for an interview with Khrushchev.

Observers have noted that Khrushchev's demeanor could range "from the cherubic to the choleric." He was definitely not in a cherubic mood when he met with Cousins. He told the American journalist that he did not believe Kennedy really wanted a treaty. Then he remarked:

> People in the United States seem to think that I am a dictator who can put into practice any policy I wish. Not so. I've got to persuade before I can govern. Anyway, the Council of Ministers agreed to

my urgent recommendation. Then I notified the United States I would accept three inspections. Back came the American rejection. They now wanted—not three inspections or six. They wanted eight. And so once again I was made to look foolish. But I can tell you this: it won't happen again.[57]

He told Cousins that he was under considerable pressure from his nuclear establishment to begin a new series of tests. "Why am I always the one who must understand the difficulties of the other fellow?" he griped. "Maybe it's time for the other fellow to understand my position." Then he relented. "You can tell the President," he said, "I accept his explanation of an honest misunderstanding and suggest that we get moving. But the next move is up to him."[58]

On returning to the United States, Cousins relayed this message to Kennedy, along with his personal view that though angered at this recent rebuff Khrushchev remained interested in pursuing the negotiations. Later, in a telephone conversation with the president, he suggested the chances for success might be substantially enhanced if the president were to make a "breathtaking offer to the Russians."

Cousins's advice had been anticipated by Britain's prime minister, Harold Macmillan, who wrote Kennedy at length on March 16, 1963. Making light of the technical objections to fewer inspections raised by AEC scientists, the military, and congressional conservatives, Macmillan urged Kennedy to "send some personal message to Khrushchev . . . or perhaps some emissary such as Averell [Harriman], or even your brother Bobby, who would . . . clear up any misunderstanding."[59] Kennedy agreed and the two Western leaders spent most of the next month drafting and redrafting an appeal to Khrushchev. They proposed reopening negotiations either at the UN or through "very senior representatives who would be empowered to speak for us and talk in Moscow directly with you."[60] Khrushchev, though still annoyed at having the ground cut out from under him, agreed to receive an Anglo-American delegation and Kennedy appointed Averell Harriman to head it.

Still pessimistic about chances for an agreement, Kennedy decided to take Cousins's advice about "a breathtaking offer." Theodore Sorensen set to work drafting a major policy address. Kennedy and Sorenson both realized that if the speech was submitted for approval to the various interested bureaucracies within the government, compromises on the wording would have to be made that would reduce its overall effectiveness. And so the address was prepared in secret, with only a few White House aides participating. Delivered early in June 1963 on the campus of American University, it was unlike any previous Kennedy speech. Gone was the toughness, the Cold War rhetoric. Instead a new, gentler and more humane Kennedy spoke of "not merely peace in our time but peace for all time." Nor was it to be a peace "enforced on the world by American weapons of war." To those who contended that peace was impossible until the Soviets changed their views, he responded with the hope that change would come. "But I also believe," he said, "that we must reexamine our own attitude—as individuals and as a nation—for our attitude is as essential as theirs." He then reminded his listeners that peace did not require all men to love each other, "it requires only that they live together in mutual tolerance."[61]

Although one Republican member of Congress attacked the speech as "a dreadful mistake," it was generally applauded, especially in Europe where the threat of nuclear war was taken most seriously. The Manchester *Guardian* regarded it as "one of the great state papers of American history." More important, Khrushchev pronounced it "the greatest" given "by any American President since Roosevelt."[62]

Kennedy succeeded in getting the negotiations started again, but he remained doubtful about the chances that they would produce a comprehensive test ban treaty. The administration's decision to lower the number of on-site inspections it would require had caused many in the Senate to grow increasingly skeptical. In March, Senator John Pastore of Rhode Island, the Democratic chairman of the JCAE, warned the president that "ratification of such a treaty could only be obtained with the greatest difficulty." Pastore confessed that he himself had "reservations as to whether such a treaty would be in the best interests of the United States at this time. This opinion," he continued, "is based upon expert testimony presented to the Joint Committee in a series of hearings over the past few weeks."[63] Later, while Harriman's instructions were being drafted, Senator Joe Clark of Pennsylvania conducted his own informal poll of the Senate and reported to the president that as things stood a comprehensive test ban treaty would fail by ten votes. Even this pessimistic estimate was based on the assumption that the Joint Chiefs would support the treaty. As preparations for the negotiations in Moscow went forward, this seemed more and more unlikely. The chairman of the Joint Chiefs, General Maxwell Taylor, explained that some of his colleagues would not support a comprehensive test ban treaty if one were submitted to the Senate. According to Taylor, certain unnamed AEC scientists had informed the chiefs that without an adequate inspection system the Soviets could, undetected, conduct about 80 percent of the weapons research they had intended to do without a treaty. Admiral George Anderson, naval chief of staff, was emphatic on the point. In testimony given before Senator John Stennis's Preparedness Investigating subcommittee, he stated categorically that the chiefs viewed a comprehensive test ban agreement as threatening to the nation's security.

British Prime Minister Harold Macmillan, a staunch advocate of nuclear disarmament and a man who believed that the West "ought to take risks for so great a prize," took a jaundiced view of the maneuverings of the AEC and the American military. He didn't believe that the opponents of a test ban were seriously concerned by the danger that the Soviets might cheat. He thought that "The real reason is that the Atomic Commission and the Pentagon are very keen to go on indefinitely with experiments (large and small) so as to keep refining upon and perfecting the art of nuclear weapons." Macmillan believed that American weaponeers were especially interested in developing a low-yield tactical nuclear weapon that could be used at a range of one thousand yards and that they were also anxious to get to work on warheads for an ABM system which he described then as "almost a fantasy"—and which remains one to this day. The prime minister was perhaps correct. Opponents of a test ban agreement would have found it not only convenient but politically effective to focus on the possibility of Soviet noncompliance rather than to reveal their own technological ambitions.

With the odds against winning Senate approval of a comprehensive test ban agreement lengthening almost by the hour, President Kennedy once again began to consider the possibility of an agreement to limit atmospheric testing only. At first the Soviets showed little interest. At a private luncheon that took place sometime early in June, Soviet Ambassador Anatoly Dobrynin told the State Department's Llewellyn Thompson that given the strength of the Senate's opposition, even a limited test ban agreement might not prove a politically realistic objective. Thompson shot back: "If the President is behind it, the Senate will fall in line." The American's rejoinder may have had some effect, for on June 10 Khrushchev told the British Labour party leader Harold Wilson, who was then in Moscow, that a comprehensive test ban agreement was probably not in the cards. Wilson also got the impression, however, that chances for a partial test ban agreement were reasonably bright. Three weeks later, on a visit to East Berlin, Khrushchev made it official—the Soviet Union would not "open its doors to NATO spies." Khrushchev did indicate, however, that in the interest of humanity he would be willing to sign an agreement "on the cessation of nuclear tests in the atmosphere, in outer space, and underwater."[64]

Less than two weeks after Khrushchev's Berlin announcement, the Anglo-American delegation arrived in Moscow. Shortly thereafter, hopes for a comprehensive test ban treaty faded and the negotiators settled for what they could get, a partial test ban agreement. The treaty, which allowed both sides to continue underground testing, was hardly a major disarmament achievement. Nor did President Kennedy describe it in that way. In a radio and television address delivered on July 26, 1963, he called the treaty "a step toward reason" and "an opening wedge" in what was to be an ongoing campaign for the limitation of nuclear weapons. "Let us, if we can, get back from the shadows of war and seek out the way of peace. And if that journey is one thousand miles, or even more, let history record that we, in this land, at this time, took the first step."[65]

The Partial Test Ban Treaty did not lead to a more comprehensive agreement. On November 22, 1963, the president was felled by an assassin's bullet. Whatever plans he may have had for the pursuit of further agreements with the Soviets died with him. Not long after this, Nikita Khrushchev was stripped of his power and sent into forced retirement. The new Soviet leaders proved less interested in negotiating limits to the arms race than in increasing the pace of weapons development in order to achieve nuclear parity with the United States. And though atmospheric testing ended, underground tests in both countries continued at an accelerated rate.

A disillusioned Alva Myrdal, winner of the Nobel peace prize for her long struggle for nuclear disarmament, has argued that the superpowers got exactly what they wanted in 1963. The health hazards associated with atmospheric testing had produced widespread opposition to the arms race, leading to "ban the bomb" movements in the United States and several European countries. By going underground, Myrdal believes that the nuclear powers deliberately denied the disarmament movement a formidable weapon in the struggle to end the arms race, thus clearing the way for new generations of even more deadly weapons. "The truth has since become irrefutably clear," she has written. "The Moscow treaty probably was never intended as a measure to curtail the development of weapons."[66]

Though for some this view undoubtedly has great appeal, such a devil theory fails to take into account the complex problems that even well-intentioned policymakers often encounter. A comprehensive test ban agreement would have been, as Myrdal suggests, a major accomplishment. But such an agreement could only have been achieved if the United States and the Soviets had settled the troublesome question of on-site inspection. Khrushchev was not a free agent. He had to reason, cajole, and above all compromise with the foreign ministry, the Strategic Rocket Forces, the Red Army, the KGB, and other members of the Politburo in order to win approval for even three on-site inspections. Kennedy's position was just as complex. He had to convince the Joint Chiefs, Secretary of Defense McNamara, the State Department, and two thirds of the United States Senate in order to succeed. It is not surprising that he could not reduce American demands to a level acceptable to the Soviets. Nor is it surprising that the Soviet position was firm. Negotiations must first succeed at home to establish a bargaining position acceptable to all elements in the government. Sometimes the compromises a national leader is forced to make to achieve domestic consensus make it impossible to arrive at an agreement once the talks begin. The political institutions by which we govern ourselves make it virtually impossible to achieve the kind of consensus necessary for an effective program of nuclear disarmament.

10

"Too Cheap to Meter"

THE COMMERCIALIZATION OF NUCLEAR POWER, 1957–1967

THE FRUSTRATIONS AND DISAPPOINTMENTS that the Kennedy administration encountered in the diplomacy of nuclear arms were notably absent in the growth of civilian nuclear power during the same period. The political conflicts of the Strauss–Eisenhower years dissolved, and power reactors seemed to establish their technological feasibility and market competitiveness with relative ease. Faster than even sanguine nuclear proponents dared predict in the 1950s, nuclear reactors came on stream and utilities rushed to place orders for nuclear plants.

The economics of America's first commercial nuclear power plant, Shippingport, were dismal: it produced electricity at a cost of 64 mills per kilowatt hour at a time when conventional coal-fired plants were producing at 6 mills per kilowatt hour.[1] But rather than daunting nuclear proponents, these figures only stimulated them to demand greater government support for the infant industry. The acrimonious dispute over reactor policy that had plagued Washington since 1955 lingered on, despite the defeat of the Gore–Holifield bill. Joint Committee Democrats, municipal utilities, and rural electric cooperatives continued to demand a more active federal role in developing commercial nuclear power, while in the AEC and in industry, the ideological stance of Lewis Strauss predominated. Strauss remained convinced that the federal role should be limited to removing impediments to wholly private reactor development (such as by

273

waiving antitrust bars to firms pooling nuclear know-how). The Edison Electric Institute, a trade association of utilities and firms involved in producing electric power, spoke for industry when it declared that

> at each stage of development of the new field [nuclear power], prime consideration [must] be given to the maintenance of our normal business system. Whatever we have in the way of productive capacity in this country can be credited to that system and . . . every effort should be made to protect and strengthen it. . . . Government controls and Government ownership of nuclear power plants will not serve to create this environment.[2]

Given the political climate of the Eisenhower years, with the administration's phobia of what the president called "creeping socialism," the program of Democrats and public-power advocates, calling for federally built nuclear reactors, sat dead in the water.

But a curious combination of Democrats and the infant nuclear industry circumvented this ideological deadlock in an extraordinary way, and thereby gave nuclear development a stimulus great enough to overcome the forbidding economics of Shippingport. The lone Democrat left on the AEC, Thomas Murray, heralded the new approach in 1957 when he called attention to the foreign-policy implications of domestic commercial reactor policy: "Industry's time schedule" for developing nuclear power, Murray argued, "is set primarily by this country's need for electric energy. But the time schedule required by the national interest is much shorter. It is set by the crisis in nuclear weapons and the world need for atomic power."[3]

A policy outline for exploiting that "world need for atomic power" was already in place: Eisenhower's Atoms for Peace proposal of 1953. The domestic deadlock over reactor policy was broken by American penetration of foreign reactor markets. American nuclear promoters found a transnational structure at hand, ready for their exploitation: Euratom. Beginning in 1955, the principal nations of western Europe, including Great Britain, France, Belgium, and Italy, began discussions looking toward formation of a "European Atomic Energy Community." Italy had the most urgent need for new sources of electricity, Great Britain the most advanced reactor development program, and France the most ambitious combined military-civilian program, thanks to Charles de Gaulle's desire for a French nuclear weapon, the centerpiece of what was to become the *force de frappe*. The Suez crisis in 1956 provided an exigent reminder of Europe's need for reliable long-term power supplies. A three-man commission, promptly called by journalists "The Three Wise Men" and headed by the president of the French National Railroad, Louis Armand, toured the United States, Canada, and Great Britain as well as several continental countries in 1957. They submitted a report titled *A Target for Euratom*, calling for a vast increase in European nuclear generating capability and recommending close cooperation with the United States in nuclear matters. The six members of the European Economic Community (the Common Market), accepted these recommendations when they ratified the Euratom treaty shortly afterward.

A Target for Euratom was an open invitation for American penetration of the European market. Four members of the U.S. Atomic Energy Commission supplied essential data and heavily influenced the report.[4] The struggle for the European market that it announced involved a competition among technologies as well as economies. The two principal American nuclear vendors, General Electric and Westinghouse, were promoting light water reactors —the boiling water reactor and the pressurized water reactor respectively. The British and French, by contrast, had constructed gas graphite reactors. (For the differences among these, see appendix 1, "Power Reactor Types.") The American vendors vigorously and optimistically predicted technical and economic success for their largely untried light water reactor (LWR). The European commission lacked technical advisers and operating experience to challenge American claims. Meanwhile, the United States was concluding bilateral agreements with individual nations and with Euratom, calling for construction of American LWRs, projected to equal a thousand megawatts of installed capacity in the 1960s. The United States government indirectly provided financial support to the American vendors through low-interest Eximbank loans, guarantees of supply and performance of enriched uranium fuel, and contributions to joint research and development programs. The total amount of America's subsidies for Euratom came to about half its budget.[5] Euratom thus became, in the evaluation of Irvin Bupp and Jean-Claude Derian, a "Trojan horse" by which American vendors captured the European market with LWRs.[6] The Trojan horse enjoyed immediate success, with orders promptly coming in for American reactors at Chooz, France, Gundremmingen, West Germany, and Garigliano, Italy. The principal German nuclear vendor, Siemens, thereupon lost its interest in gas graphite reactors and announced its conversion to light water. These events cemented the American vendors' hold on the European market, and enabled them to play off American and European developments against each other in a tour de force of marketing strategy. This stimulated a boom for American light water reactors that industry experts have since called the "Great Bandwagon Market."[7]

In November 1962, the AEC staff prepared a report, entitled *Civilian Nuclear Power: A Report to the President—1962,* and sent it to President John F. Kennedy.[8] In it, the AEC noted that the cost of nuclear-generated electricity was then at about 10 mills/kwh, and predicted that it would soon fall to nearly half that, 5.6 mills/kwh at Pacific Gas & Electric's projected Bodega Head reactor in California. By 1980, the AEC expected generating costs to fall further, to about 3.8 mills/kwh. (It is a revealing commentary on the reliability of such predictions that the actual 1980 generating costs were 2.3 *cents,* a 600 percent increase.) The report suggested that only modest government assistance, in the form of direct subsidies, would be necessary to carry nuclear power across the threshold of economic competitiveness with fossil fuel–fired plants. These optimistic predictions were based on a number of assumptions:

> 1. The future economic performance of essentially untried high-technology ventures could be predicted accurately, even where these predictions were for plants three times the size of any that might provide a base of operating experience, and even where auxiliary supporting industrial technologies were just as untried.

2. The scaling-up process would achieve significant economies of scale.

3. "Learning experience" would further reduce costs as engineers perfected designs and procedures on the basis of operating experience.

Each of these assumptions soon proved to be unfounded. Bupp and Derian sardonically observed in retrospect that "the distinction between empirically supported fact and expectation—often quite obviously self-interested expectation—was blurred from the beginning."[9]

Reality, however, promptly seemed to vindicate the optimism of the AEC report. In December 1963, Jersey Central Power and Light, a New Jersey utility, signed a contract with General Electric to purchase a 515 MWe boiling water reactor for a proposed power plant at Oyster Creek, New Jersey. Jersey Central justified its decision on the grounds that the nuclear plant would produce electricity more cheaply than a comparable coal-fired plant. The Oyster Creek contract proved to be historic: It seemed to announce to the world that nuclear generation of electricity had become competitive with fossil fuels. The rosiest dreams of the nuclear community seemed about to be realized. An entirely new power source had come into existence; it promised to deliver electricity more cheaply than people had dared hope a decade earlier; and it did so without the pollution, transportation problems, and labor controversies that bedeviled coal. Lewis Strauss's prediction of the 1950s now appeared to be within reach: nuclear plants would deliver electricity "too cheap to meter."[10]

The Oyster Creek contract was remarkable in several respects, all of which enhanced its dramatic impact. To begin with, it was a turnkey contract: that is, GE promised to deliver and build a power plant at a guaranteed price, adjusted only by an inflation escalator. The buyer need only turn the key to the front door, like a new homeowner carrying his bride across the threshold, walk in, start up the machinery, and begin producing electricity. The prime contractor assumed responsibility for the charges of subcontractors. All the risk lay with the nuclear supplier. The economics of this arrangement for the utility looked so promising that shortly the industry predicted that generation costs would immediately drop even below the low 1962 AEC figures; specifically, from something in the neighborhood of 6.0–7.5 mills/kwh to a breathtaking 4.3 mills for Oyster Creek. Bupp and Derian laconically comment on these figures: "In keeping with the standards of skepticism established during the debate on the 1962 AEC report, the fact that the latter figure was expectation and not accomplishment was not the object of widespread attention."[11]

Industry analysts have concluded that Oyster Creek, and probably at least the next five commercial reactors, were what retail merchants call "loss leaders": a product sold at or below cost to lure buyers into the store, where they will probably purchase something else. Oyster Creek validated the AEC's optimism; it pushed the Europeans along in their decision to abandon gas graphite and other reactor types for the American LWRs; and, above all, it presented claims of economic performance so impressive that the bandwagon effect began.

Within five years of the Oyster Creek order, American utilities alone had placed orders for seventy-five new nuclear plants having over 45,000 MWe generating capacity. Installed capacity (that is, reactors actually built and on line) by 1975 approached 100,000 MWe. The growth of nuclear power in the United States was proceeding along an exponential curve. Hope and reality, at first mutually reinforcing, became indistinguishable. Normally sober men spoke of a Promethean future. Alvin Weinberg, director of the Oak Ridge National Laboratory, hailed the "nuclear energy revolution" that would provide a "permanent and ubiquitous availability of cheap power."[12] Promise beckoned reality, then substituted for it, while reality elicited ever more dazzling expectations. In these unreal expectations, the engineering equivalents of watered stock, the Great Bandwagon Market in retrospect eerily resembles the Great Bull Market on Wall Street from 1927 to 1929.

In all this, utilities were taking a high risk, measured by the distance between actual operating experience and extrapolated estimates. This represented a revolutionary change in management practices. Previously the electric power industry considered even an extrapolation as low as 2:1 over experience as risky;

during the Great Bandwagon Market, this ratio moved recklessly up to 4:1. At the end of the Bandwagon era in the late 1960s, the ratio of ordered to operating capacity soared from 2:1 to 30:1.[13] More than ignorance, greed, and folly account for this. In the 1960s, nuclear power remained a "sexy" technology, in an era when few questioned either the premises or the promises of high technology. A talented and ambitious engineer or business-school graduate might well have regarded coal as a dull, frumpy, uninteresting career option. At a time when men dreamed of nuclear rocket and aircraft propulsion, when many saw nuclear power as the only sure and ultimate guarantor of our national existence, the glamour of the industry provided its devotees an unusually intense stake in its success. Engineers and scientists had an emotional commitment to achieving the success of nuclear power, something that went beyond the mere self-interest of the sort that aims at keeping the paychecks coming in. They were, in Alvin Weinberg's unforgettable phrase, the "nuclear priesthood," oddly reminiscent of the ancient Egyptian priestly caste that retained its power at the pinnacle of its society by reason of its monopoly of the arcane lore of astronomy and mathematics, which they used to predict the annual flood patterns of the Nile. Nuclear science and technology had been spectacularly successful, and few were prepared to hang crepe about its future.

Economic considerations played a role, too. Private utilities had been so frightened by Democratic talk in the previous decade of nuclear TVAs that they jumped on the bandwagon to prevent a public-power preemption of nuclear power. (TVA itself, the real TVA, placed orders for two large units, Browns Ferry 1 and 2, each 1,000 MWe, early in the Bandwagon era.) Finally, the vicious circle of industry basing its predictions on AEC assertions, and the AEC basing its claims on industry predictions, produced "a circular flow of mutually reinforcing assertions that . . . inhibited normal commercial skepticism about advertisements which purported to be analyses."[14]

Reality quickly intervened. Capital and operating costs did not fall as predicted; on the contrary, they rose stubbornly. Just as stubbornly, the AEC and nuclear vendors claimed that "stabilization" was just around the corner, that uncertainties would soon vanish, that experience, economies of scale, and engineering improvements would shortly set costs on a predictable, downward curve. Moreover, AEC economists masked or excused the failure of their predictions by claiming that competitive costs, especially for coal, moved in tandem with nuclear costs so that nuclear power still remained relatively competitive. But events on the other side of the globe would shortly relieve the nuclear industry of these frustrating uncertainties.

From 1971 through 1974, a series of shocks deranged the economics of electric utilities. The best remembered is the Arab oil embargo of 1973. After the outbreak of the Yom Kippur War, Egypt's Arab supporters in OPEC (the Organization of Petroleum Exporting Countries) declared an embargo on their oil exports to the United States and the Netherlands. The effect was instantaneous and dramatic: gasoline and heating oil prices shot up, long lines formed at gas stations, distributors and state governments were forced to experiment with various measures to restrict the purchase of gas, such as odd/even date purchase restrictions or minimum five-dollar purchase requirements. In 1970, the U.S. imported Arabian light crude at around $2/barrel; by the end of 1973, that price had jumped to nearly $12, a 600 percent increase. The Arab oil embargo struck Americans directly where they were most vulnerable: in their relationship with their autos.

Surging gas prices at the pump were symptomatic of a steady increase in all energy prices. Residual fuel oil was tied to the OPEC prices and it rose with them, hitting residents of the east coast hardest because of their dependence on imported oil for domestic heating. Coal and natural gas prices followed along, coal being stimulated by increased costs caused by enforcement of the Clean Air Act of 1970 and a brief mineworkers' strike. These rising fossil fuel prices saved the economic position of nuclear power.

A fundamental proportion underlies the economic competitiveness of fossil and nuclear generating plants. Relative to each other, fossil plants have low capital costs but high fuel costs and high operating-and-maintenance costs; nuclear plants present high capital costs but low fuel costs, plus low O&M costs. As one concrete illustration of this relationship, consider the following Bandwagon-era figures, compiled by the now defunct Federal Energy Administration in its 1974 "Project Independence Report."[15]

	NUCLEAR	COAL
fuel cost	2.50	5.56
O&M (incl. environmental costs)	1.50	2.75
fixed charge (at 70% capacity factor)	14.84	11.48
plant costs ($/kw of installed capacity)	455.00	352.00
projected construction time	10 yrs.	7 yrs.

Moreover, the capital costs were rapidly becoming unpredictable at the time of the 1973 oil embargo because of cost escalation and interest rates. Nearly half the capital cost of a 1,000 MWe nuclear plant, with costs estimated in 1974 and projected start-up in 1983, was attributable to interest and escalation (17 percent and 30 percent respectively).[16] Fossil plants would suffer from the same uncertainties of the capital markets, too, but their lower initial capital costs and shorter construction time made this component relatively less important.

The upshot of all this is that for nuclear generation to remain competitive with coal, nuclear fuel costs must remain low and stable. Where nuclear's capital costs shoot up, as they did in the decade 1963–1973, this rise must be offset by an equally drastic rise in fossil fuel costs. That is exactly what the Arab oil-exporting countries provided the United States in 1973. Had imported crude prices remained at their Garden-of-Eden 1970 levels, nuclear power would not have been near a competitive position with fossil fuel and the industry would have died at birth. As it is, only massive life-support systems, in the form of federal subsidies, have kept the infant breathing so far.

As the 1970s wore on, the economics of the nuclear power industry did not improve, and subsidies plus ballooning fossil fuel prices were necessary to keep nuclear in the game. Nuclear's position was mauled further when its fuel costs rose. In 1972, the spot market price for yellowcake, a form of processed uranium oxide, was unnaturally low, somewhere between six and eight dollars a pound. This came about largely because Westinghouse in the Bandwagon days had committed itself to numerous long-term contracts as a uranium-buying agent to supply yellowcake at low prices in order to provide an incentive for utilities to buy its pressurized water reactors.[17] This was a high-risk, economically irrational gamble, but Westinghouse persisted in it until by January 1975 it had gone 40,000 tons short on its commitments. By December of that year, yellowcake prices had risen five-fold, to somewhere around $35/lb. Claiming that it faced potential losses of $2 billion, Westinghouse announced in September 1975 that it would not honor its supply contracts, arguing that it was released from its contractual obligations by reason of "commercial impracticability" under section 2-615 of the Uniform Commercial Code. Twenty-seven utilities promptly sued, and the litigation provided one of the most significant modern episodes of commercial law development in recent times, both by reason of its magnitude and because it presented a dramatic opportunity to test the meaning of section 2-615. As of this writing, this litigation is still pending. But the sudden and shocking rise in fuel prices was simply another blow to an industry that could only look back wistfully on its Bandwagon era.

While the industry was undergoing its painful confrontation with market reality, the AEC was beginning to overcome its adversarial posture toward the JCAE and to establish policies for civilian nuclear power that were to have important long-term consequences. Under the Atomic Energy acts, the AEC had both promotional and regulatory roles. It had a mandate to develop and encourage nonmilitary applications, yet at the same time, its responsibilities for public safety and health created a tension in its functions that it never satisfactorily resolved. As early as 1961, when the Commission had been functioning only fifteen years, concerned observers of the regulatory process recommended that it be split, with one branch being responsible for promotion and operations, and the other for regulation, licensing, and standards.[18] Its military responsibilities only complicated this dual role, with disastrous results.

The AEC became part of what David Lilienthal, its first chairman, called "an atomic consortium, that is, groups of bureaucracies in private and public life that have a vested career interest in the status quo and that guard their reputations and privileges as zealously as any other 'establishment.' "[19] This establishment formed what political scientists informally call "the iron triangle":

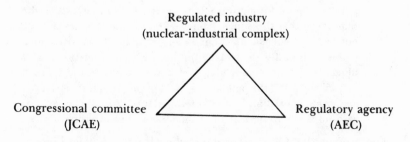

Regulated industry
(nuclear-industrial complex)

Congressional committee   Regulatory agency
(JCAE)   (AEC)

But the picture is more complicated than this simple diagram would suggest. For one thing, there is a fourth element, necessitating a quadrangular sketch: the research and academic groups, consisting of scientists and engineers at the National Labs and the other federal nuclear facilities, as well as the departments of nuclear and chemical engineering at the nation's larger universities. In fact, some of the universities, most notably the University of California at Berkeley, are themselves an inherent part of the establishment because of their position as academic contractors. (At one time, the Lawrence Livermore weapons laboratory and the Los Alamos Scientific Laboratory were both operated under Berkeley's auspices.) Industry itself is not a monolith, as the dispute between Westinghouse and its yellowcake buyers indicates. The increasingly close relations between the AEC and the JCAE, amicable to the point of being incestuous, succeeded the asperities of the Strauss era and blurred the distinctions between the two bodies. Still, the notion of the "iron triangle" provides a usable beginning for evaluating the AEC's policies and performance.

With unique rapidity, the AEC experienced "capture," a phenomenon long noted by observers of public administration. Nowhere was capture better outlined than by the prominent Boston corporation lawyer Richard S. Olney, shortly before he was ap-

pointed U.S. attorney-general and then secretary of state. Writing to railroad president Charles Perkins in 1892, Olney cautioned against industry efforts to abolish the recently created
Interstate Commerce Commission. The ICC, Olney explained,

> is, or can be made of great use to the railroads. It satisfies the
> popular clamor for a government supervision of railroads, at the
> same time that the supervision is almost entirely nominal. . . .
> Further, the older such a commission gets to be, the more inclined
> it will be found to be to take the business and railroad view of
> things. It thus becomes a sort of barrier between the railroad
> corporations and the people and a sort of protection against hasty
> and crude legislation hostile to railroad interests. . . . The part of
> wisdom is not to destroy the Commission, but to utilize it.[20]

The process that Olney described, whereby the regulated industry captures its regulator, took only a few years at most. The AEC,
conditioned over its first decade to serve its primary client, the
Department of Defense, found little difficulty adjusting to a captured role when it dealt with suppliers and utilities. It soon con-
formed to the "standard American pattern of providing clientele
interests with public agencies to further their own ends."[21]

Capture produced a persistent pattern of regulatory failure,
derived partly from what nuclear engineer Frank Dawson called
a "closed loop" of information flow.[22] Beginning with the wartime secrecy that was extended by the 1946 Atomic Energy Act,
the process of information flow concerning nuclear power has
always suffered from a circularity that deliberately excludes those
outside the nuclear establishment. In matters of economic performance, for example, the AEC in the Bandwagon days accepted
uncritically the estimates of capital costs and operating performance put out by GE, Westinghouse, and other vendors. Industry,
in turn, cited the published AEC figures as official confirmation
of industry's projections. When a rare skeptic, such as Philip
Sporn, president of American Electric Power Company, challenged the official optimism, industry and the AEC closed ranks
to dismiss his alternative estimates as excessively pessimistic.
When Sporn in 1963 compared coal and nuclear costs for his
utility, GE criticized his approach as "unduly conservative" and
the AEC chimed in: "Mr. Sporn could have been more optimis-

tic."[23] The relationship between the regulators and the regulated resembled more the picture of two cheerleaders in front of an apathetic cheering section.

In the long run, this proved harmful to both industry and the government. The AEC lost its credibility; even nuclear power's friends in Congress dismissed it as a flack for industry. Industry's data crumbled under the onslaught of reality, so that when industry and the AEC most needed credibility, in meeting the challenges of the 1970s, their past performance produced only skepticism.

Another offspring of industry–government incest was the AEC's enthusiasm for breeders in the 1960s. Accepting industry's assurances that light water reactors were successes from an engineering point of view and cost-competitive with coal, the AEC turned its attention from light water technology, including safety issues, and instead promoted the more glamourous breeder. The AEC diverted research and development funds to advanced breeder concepts, not to evaluating challengers to light water or to exploring in adequate depth the safety constraints that might have thrown roadblocks in front of the light water bandwagon.

This problem began when Milton Shaw took over direction of the Reactor Development and Technology division (RDT) of the AEC in 1965. An engineer, Shaw was an alumnus of Rickover's navy program, and brought to the AEC a sharp and abrasive emphasis on an engineering approach in place of a scientific one. He proclaimed to the JCAE that AEC laboratories under his administration had been "converted from a research orientation to one stressing disciplined engineering application." This was part of a larger AEC reorientation of direction, founded on the assumption that once light water reactors had become commercialized, they had to be weaned from federal support, and the federal research effort diverted to more exotic, next-generation concepts such as the breeder. (To this, the director of the Argonne National Labs angrily rejoined that Argonne's purpose was "not to build submarines but to produce knowledge.") An anonymous AEC research physicist complained that under Shaw, "the philosophy was that if something didn't solve a problem—particularly for the breeder—it wasn't going to be picked up in the budget."[24] "Engineering is the name of the game," boasted Shaw. "When he came in, science died," bitterly countered an AEC physicist.[25]

This new policy caused great distress at the National Reactor Testing Station near Idaho Falls, Idaho. NRTS was created in 1948 as a result of a dispute between Edward Teller on one hand and Enrico Fermi, Robert Oppenheimer, and Glenn Seaborg on the other. The latter three supported a proposal to locate three major reactors—a breeder, the materials testing reactor, and a propulsion prototype—at Argonne, whereas Teller maintained that such a concentrated installation near the nation's second largest city was too risky. Teller won out, and test reactors were located in the remote Idaho desert. For fifteen years, NRTS was managed by the nuclear division of Phillips Petroleum, but when Shaw took over he squeezed Phillips out in favor of Aerojet-General, a firm with heavy financial commitments to a gas cooled reactor that faced bleak prospects after the victory of light water. Since the AEC itself admitted that the NRTS contract was a lucrative subsidy, some suspected that the arrangement was a bailout for a bad Aerojet management decision. Whatever the merits of that suspicion, Aerojet's nuclear division never bit the hand that fed it. This change in management policy, coupled with erratic funding, left NRTS researchers suspicious of the competence and good faith of RDT's leadership under Shaw.

Until 1973, Congress funded the AEC's research programs, including both safety and the breeder, in a lump sum to be allocated as the AEC wished. Research funding stagnated, partly because of rising inflationary costs that drove up the expense of carrying out any sort of research and partly because the AEC under Shaw imposed new and extremely high standards on all research-reactor construction. The LOFT reactor (Loss of Fluid Test) is a case in point. Originally conceived as a sacrificial reactor for a loss of coolant accident, under Shaw, LOFT was rescheduled for testing standards of reactor design. This necessitated such high standards for components that vendors refused to bid. Consequently, NRTS had to cannibalize parts for LOFT, even from the then defunct nuclear powered merchant transport, the N.S. *Savannah*. NRTS engineers not surprisingly complained they had to build LOFT out of "scrap." Meanwhile, Shaw's enthusiasm for the breeder, in keeping with his next-generation emphasis, diverted funds from other research projects, including safety. RDT scientists called this "bootlegging."

In this climate of suspicion, NRTS and ORNL scientists began to accuse Shaw and eventually the whole five-man AEC of more sinister motives. In 1971, the AEC abruptly canceled an ORNL contract on loss of coolant accidents, citing funding problems. But ORNL scientists connected with the program maintained that the true motive for cancellation was that safety research "raised more questions than it answered." "In its haste to get on with developing the breeder," wrote Robert Gillette at the time, the AEC gave research scientists the impression that it was "methodically sidestepping grave uncertainties that still surrounded ordinary water-cooled nuclear power plants." "RDT is simply in bed with the vendors," claimed an ORNL researcher. "Everyone wants his merit badge for the breeder."[26] In the crucible of the early 1970s safety controversy, such allegations grew more heated. The Advisory Committee on Reactor Safeguards prodded RDT to sustain its research on safety issues, while at the same time Shaw seemed to be forcing research and funding in other directions. A NRTS researcher described the process:

> The more we worked this problem the more it fell apart in our laps. Everything we did to analyze the physical phenomena, to improve correlations, to better describe what happens during blowdown pushed our predicted temperatures higher toward melting and the margins of fuel safety lower.
>
> The more we got into this the more it became apparent that RDT was very unhappy with all this. The problems we were raising were upsetting their cozy relationship with the vendors and utilities, whose support they needed for the breeder. . . . It also became clear that Shaw and others just didn't believe a serious accident of this kind could happen, and that it was really worth working on. They'd say all the right things in public but in the small, executive session their enthusiasm would cool off.

An ORNL engineer commented that "what bothers me most is that after twenty years we are still making purely subjective judgments . . . in reactor safety. Purely by decree, some things, like the rupture of a reactor's pressure vessel, are ruled impossible. To decide these things without some objective measure of probabilities is, to me, almost criminal."[27]

Shaw compounded the problem by demanding that industry itself take on the burden of conducting safety research. This would have lessened the AEC's capability to verify industry results independently of industry-generated data. One AEC safety administrator commented that "this is like asking the agricultural chemical industry to tell us how safe pesticides are." Scientists objected strongly to Shaw's practice of sending all NRTS and ORNL research proposals to industry for review, rather than to more independent evaluators in the universities. Finally, the AEC inhibited communication by its research scientists about safety programs. It refused to let them speak with visiting German and Japanese reactor purchasers; it tried to scuttle a 1973 NRTS seminar on reactor safety issues, and finally consented to permit it only if it was off-site and held under the auspices of the Atomic Industrial Forum, the nuclear industry's trade association; and it prohibited safety staff from communicating with AEC regulatory staff about safety problems.[28] The consequence of all this in the 1970s was a meltdown of public confidence in the nuclear regulatory process.

Despite these difficulties, the nuclear power industry entered the decade of the 1970s buoyantly optimistic. In those halcyon days before the 1973 Arab oil embargo, analysts in government and industry predicted ever-rising demands for electricity by American consumers, and confidently assumed that nuclear reactors would provide most of the increased capacity necessary to meet those demands. Nuclear critics then were only a small cloud on the horizon, easy to dismiss as cranks. Industry–government cooperation had accomplished a more successful commercialization of nuclear power than optimists of the early 1960s had thought possible. America's nonmilitary nuclear future seemed bright and assured. Political leaders in the Johnson and Nixon administrations could therefore turn their attention to efforts to bring the nuclear arms race under control.

11

"Strategic Sufficiency"

TECHNOLOGICAL LEAPFROG AND THE FIRST SALT AGREEMENT

THE COALITION OF BUSINESS and governmental leaders who engineered the development of the nuclear power industry during the 1960s moved resolutely toward the achievement of a clearly defined purpose. During these same years, however, on the military side of the nuclear question, all was in flux. The Kennedy administration explored virtually every avenue open to it, except nuclear disarmament, in a vain attempt to resolve its nuclear dilemma. Rejecting what they regarded as the "surrender or suicide" policy of the Eisenhower administration, Kennedy and his associates first tried counterforce strategy in an attempt to use nuclear weapons in "discreet" ways, only to find that the new approach almost produced the war that nuclear weapons were supposed to deter. Following the Cuban missile crisis, the administration regrouped, began a diplomatic offensive designed to reduce Cold War tensions, and adopted an assured destruction strategy that emphasized deterrence rather than nuclear-war fighting capabilities, positing that neither side could win a nuclear war. But placing the emphasis on deterrence did not guarantee that a catastrophic war would not take place. So Kennedy settled for a policy that was intended to reduce to an absolute minimum the incentive either side might have for using nuclear weapons, by making it clear that retaliation would be swift and devastating.

A stable nuclear balance in which each of the superpowers has complete confidence in its retaliatory capability is fundamental to the strategy of mutually assured destruction. But such a balance is a fragile thing, constantly threatened by advances made in weapons technology. One such advance was the development in both the Soviet Union and the United States of antiballistic missile technology. The threat it posed to stability moved both Washington and Moscow to seek an arms control agreement that would head off an explosive escalation of the arms race.

By 1964, Robert McNamara had accepted the inevitability of rough equality (parity) between the strategic nuclear forces of the United States and the Soviet Union, and had abandoned thoughts of civil defense. He did these things in hopes of establishing a stable nuclear balance. But in such matters advancing technology is ever the enemy of what Albert Wohlstetter once called "the delicate balance of terror." During 1964, a number of different intelligence gathering agencies developed a keen interest in certain mysterious black buildings that had recently appeared on the outskirts of Moscow. Soon the Defense Intelligence Agency concluded that the Soviets were deploying the Galosh antiballistic missile (ABM) interceptor. Had the Kremlin developed the technology to mount a successful defense against a missile attack? The Galosh system as well as the Tallinn Air Defense System near Leningrad, which some thought could be upgraded to attain full ABM capabilities, suggested that this was a distinct possibility. Why else would the Soviets deploy the system? But if that was true, the credibility of America's second strike force was in question and stability was seriously threatened.

The appearance of Galosh provided the United States Army with a long-sought opportunity. In 1958, Neil McElroy, who was then secretary of defense, resolved a long drawn-out struggle between the air force and the army over control of ballistic missile defenses by assigning the army the responsibility for developing an antiballistic missile system. The army went enthusiastically to work. By 1960, weapons experts had made considerable progress on the Nike Zeus, enough to prompt the Department of the Army to urge the Eisenhower administration to approve production and deployment of what looked at the time to be a $15 billion weapons system. But the president, anxious to balance the budget, cut taxes in an election year if possible, and unresponsive in any event to pleas for the deployment of an unproven weapons system, refused.

The outcome of the 1960 presidential election gave the army another chance. Kennedy, who had trumpeted his support for increased defense spending prior to the election, intended to review the last Eisenhower budget before submitting it to Congress and seemed certain to recommend significant increases for defense. The military-industrial complex went quickly to work. First, the editors of *Missiles and Rockets,* an industry journal, devoted the entire January 30 issue to articles promoting the Nike Zeus. *Army,* the magazine of a pressure group named The Association for the United States Army, followed suit in February. At the same time, the army itself mounted an impressive last-minute public relations campaign. In March, twenty-nine reporters and editors were given a tour of the missile test center on Kwajalein in the Pacific where the major attraction was, not surprisingly, the Nike Zeus. This tactic produced invaluable nationwide publicity for the missile. The campaign was punctuated by periodic statements from various military leaders, including the army's head of research and development, trumpeting what they all described as the Soviet Union's huge commitment to its ABM program. Certain congressional leaders, meanwhile, added to the din, warning that if the Soviets developed an effective ABM system first, the United States would lie defenseless before a Soviet onslaught. Senators Strom Thurmond and Karl Mundt, along with congressmen John McCormack, George Miller, and Daniel Flood, all strongly supported the army's position. Flood, a member of the House Defense Appropriations Subcommittee, was particularly vehement, urging Kennedy:

> to loose the Zeus, to put it into immediate production, to hasten the day when U.S. and allied forces at last can stand armed and ready with the ballistic boxing gloves so desperately needed for defense against the ceaseless threat of Communist world-wide nuclear aggression.[1]

When Secretary McNamara refused to authorize production of the Nike, deciding instead to keep the system at the research and development stage, Congressman Flood exploded, denouncing both the secretary and Herbert York who, as the head of the Office of Defense Research and Engineering, had strongly opposed producing the missile. "I do not care what the Secretary of Defense says, or Dr. York, or any more of these long-haired flat-heeled jokers in science say," he railed, "you cannot go from development into deployment unless you have production in these things." When McNamara testified before Flood's committee, the congressman again attacked him. "I thought we had broken through this problem in this country . . . of wanting things to be *perfect* before we sent them to the troops."[2] McNamara's reply was simple and direct—the Nike Zeus didn't work.

Despite the congressional sound, fury, and political posturing, McNamara knew exactly what he was doing. On learning that experiments in antimissile technology were under way both in this country and in the Soviet Union, the scientists and engineers who designed America's offensive missiles became intrigued with the problem of developing penetration aids intended to confuse ABM defenses. They had created an impressive array of these "penaids," including metal fragments resembling children's jacks that showed up on radar screens as valid targets, penetrating balloons, chaff, and a method of disrupting radar by means of high-altitude nuclear explosions. The Nike Zeus design team had come close to solving the problem of "hitting a bullet with a bullet," or, as the colorful Nikita Khrushchev once put it, "hitting a fly in space." But the penetration aids changed the nature of the problem. An effective ABM system would have to distinguish between genuine warheads and decoys. There would be hundreds of possible targets to choose from, traveling at thousands of miles per hour. For this, Nike Zeus simply was not up to the job.

Reluctantly, the army went back to its research and with more than $3 billion in funding, produced the Nike X. When Galosh appeared in 1964, the new American system was still in the developmental stage. Nevertheless, counting on the political pressures always generated when the Soviets make what appears to be a weapons breakthrough, the army pressed the Office of the Secretary of Defense for authorization to begin deployment. Again,

McNamara refused. The Nike X was, he insisted, far from perfect. It did not always distinguish decoys from incoming warheads, its complex radar was unreliable, and it would be monstrously expensive to deploy.

But these technical objections were not at the heart of McNamara's hostility to the ABM, however useful they might have been in bolstering his testimony before congressional committees. Between 1961 and 1964, the secretary had given the whole question of nuclear strategy perhaps the most thorough review it has ever received. In the end, he opted for a strategy that emphasized deterrence as much as the importance of maintaining a stable nuclear balance. Each of the superpowers had a credible second strike capability and each therefore understood that war would be suicidal. Any weapon that threatened the credibility of this second strike capability threatened stability. And that was precisely what ABM systems did.

Perhaps just as significantly, McNamara had also concluded that no ABM system—even if technically perfect—could work. The Soviets could easily overwhelm the system by using chaff and other decoys to present false targets, by exploding a thermonuclear weapon at high altitudes over the central United States, which would create an electromagnetic surge that would wipe out computer memory banks across the continent, or by the use of multiple reentry vehicles designed to confuse ABM radars. McNamara was convinced that if the United States deployed the Nike X at a cost of about $40 billion, the only effect would be to intensify the arms race. In the end, both sides would have more weapons and be less secure than before the buildup.

This was precisely the pattern the nuclear arms race had followed from its inception. In the late 1940s, for example, the Soviets had spent lavishly on air defense systems. What had been the result? As Herbert York explained, the United States responded with "fancier, more complex, and more deadly bombers as well as . . . entirely new kinds of offense, the intercontinental ballistic missile and the submarine-launched ballistic missile." The Soviets countered in kind and both sides found themselves not less but more vulnerable. McNamara described this phenomenon as the action/reaction cycle. Many, including Gerard Smith, who later headed the American delegation during SALT, have made similar observations. Smith likes to compare the arms race to a game of ticktacktoe. "If one knows how to play it and makes no mistakes, one cannot lose. And if both sides know how to play it and make no mistakes, neither can win. After a while," Smith concludes, "at least for adults, it becomes a boring game."[3] More than that, it becomes an exceedingly dangerous boring game.

Of course the Soviets had acted first—and foolishly, McNamara thought—by deploying Galosh. But this did not mean that the United States ought to reply with its own brand of foolishness. The proper response, he believed, was to add to America's offensive capabilities, thus neutralizing Galosh and restoring stability. Nor would the government have to spend inordinate amounts to do the job. One of the penetration aids developed to confuse ABM defenses was the multiple independently targeted reentry vehicle (MIRV). In this system, the last stage of an offensive missile becomes in effect a space bus carrying not one but many separate warheads and decoy packages. Each of the "passengers" on the bus is independently targetable. As a result, one rocket launcher can send warheads against a number of different targets. McNamara proposed to neutralize Soviet ABM defenses (and demonstrate how easy it would be for the Soviets to do the same to the Nike X) by modifying the Minuteman missile to deliver three warheads and equipping missile-firing submarines with the MIRVed Poseidon missile. Each boat would then be capable of launching not 16 but approximately 160 warheads against Soviet targets.

The secretary of defense, never a man to avoid a fight, was determined not to allow the army to deploy its $40 billion white elephant, the Nike X. But pressures for production and deployment were mounting. In his 1965 defense posture statement to Congress, an annual rite performed by defense secretaries, McNamara could still successfully oppose deployment of the Nike X on the ground that it was plagued by technical bugs. But by 1966, the administration was in a much weaker political position. Congressional liberals were at odds with Johnson and McNamara over the war in Vietnam. Conservatives were equally unhappy at the way the administration was handling the war but for entirely different reasons. Simultaneously they were demanding deployment of the ABM, a new manned bomber, and a variety of other new weapons systems intended to keep America "ahead" in the arms race.

Before the end of the legislative year, supporters of the ABM program won an important victory: Congress appropriated an initial $167.9 million to begin deployment of the Nike X. McNamara was irate. "You don't even say what kind of a system we're supposed to deploy," he told one important committee chairman. But the unnamed congressman didn't care. "Just get it out there," he said.[4]

Because arms control has no natural constituency in Washington, it makes progress only when one or more high-ranking policymakers come to believe that the nation's security is better served by limiting weapons development than by going ahead. McNamara's opposition to the ABM is a case in point. After Congress made the decision to provide funds to deploy the Nike X, the secretary became convinced that the only hope of heading off a further escalation of the arms race was to convince the Soviets to cooperate in turning things around. But before he could do that, he had to convince President Johnson not to order deployment of the Nike X. Calling representatives of Western Electric, the prime contractor for the ABM system, to the Pentagon he extracted an admission from them that the missile was not yet ready for deployment. Armed with this, he journeyed to the Texas White House, where he convinced the president to delay the final decision on deployment, at least for the time being. Johnson was willing to go along with McNamara, but not indefinitely. Back in the late 1950s, while he was majority leader in the Senate, Johnson had taken full political advantage of early Soviet space shots by holding well-publicized hearings designed to prove that the Eisenhower administration had allowed a dangerous missile gap to develop. He had no intention of being victimized by an antimissile gap.

At the same time that McNamara sought to keep the president in line while fending off supporters of the ABM, he followed through on plans to replace older A-3 Polaris submarine-launched missiles with the newer MIRVed Poseidon. He also set in motion plans to MIRV a portion of the land-based Minuteman force. McNamara may have hoped this massive expansion of the number of deliverable warheads in the American arsenal would convince the Soviets that ABM systems simply could not work and that it would be better for both sides to agree not to develop such weapons. Yet in approving the development and deployment of MIRVed missiles, McNamara missed an obvious point. He was so fixated on the destabilizing impact ABM deployments would have that he failed to realize that MIRV too was one of those technologies that diminish stability and encourage an escalation in the arms race. It was an astonishing oversight. In making this decision, as one strategist has since observed, McNamara went a long way toward restoring the "first strike capability, which he was [committed] to avoiding." Moreover, as Herbert York, a leading critic of this new technology, subsequently pointed out, the introduction of MIRVed missiles would permanently destabilize the arms race. "MIRV makes it easily possible for *each* side to have many more warheads than the *other* side has missiles," he explained. If each side increased the number of warheads in its arsenal while improving the accuracy and reliability of its missiles, it would "eventually be able to wipe out better than ninety-five percent of the other side's silo based missile force in a surprise attack." During periods of political crisis, York concluded, having MIRVed missiles substantially increased the danger of all-out nuclear war. "Each side, believing the other could make a pre-emptive attack, would certainly be stimulated to consider doing so first." Use them or lose them, York was saying, might well become the motto of both superpowers.[6]

York was not the only weapons expert to caution against proceeding with MIRV development. Physicist Harold Brown, another member of the government's elite science bureaucracy and later President Jimmy Carter's secretary of defense, added his voice to a growing chorus warning of the dangers posed by MIRV. "Accurate MIRVs would tend to lessen the chance of land based missiles surviving an attack since one first-strike missile with accurate MIRVs would destroy several deterrent missiles in their silos. . . . Clearly," Brown continued, "an agreement to ban the deployment of MIRVs would be desirable in order to forestall erosion of the capability to deter."[7]

None of this had as yet occurred to McNamara, whose purpose was to do whatever seemed necessary to forestall the deployment of an American ABM system while trying to win presidential approval for an attempt to open arms control negotiations with the Soviets. As usual, when major national security issues are involved, it was necessary to arrive at a consensus among the various interested bureaucracies before talks could begin. For a time there seemed little basis for compromise. McNamara and Secretary of State Dean Rusk supported the idea of negotiation aimed at banning the production and deployment of ballistic missile defenses. The Joint Chiefs, on the other hand, were pressing for deployment. The president, meanwhile, viewed the question from an entirely different perspective. Morton Halperin, who was intimately involved in these internal negotiations, later explained that Johnson interpreted the ABM debate as a domestic political question and did "not appear to have seen any major national security stakes in the decision whether or not to deploy the ABM. Since it was an issue that generated intense passion in others" it was important to him, "but he does not appear to have seen any intrinsic importance in terms of . . . American security."[8]

With the president near a decision in favor of deployment, McNamara and his deputy, Cyrus Vance (who would later become secretary of state in the Carter administration) eked out a last-minute compromise. The Joint Chiefs agreed to support one serious attempt to convince the Kremlin to enter into arms control negotiations. In return, McNamara restored funds cut from the Defense Department budget that had been earmarked for the early deployment of the Nike system. These funds would be spent, however, only if the Soviets refused to negotiate.

All sides were satisfied with this arrangement. McNamara had succeeded in putting off the deployment of the ABM, at least for the time being. If the Russians behaved rationally, they would agree to talk. Otherwise, the Nike X would raise questions about the credibility of the Soviet deterrent and force the Kremlin to increase its offensive forces, which would place a serious strain on the Russian economy. The Joint Chiefs, betting the other way, were certain that the Russians would prove uncooperative, leaving McNamara no option but to agree to ABM deployment. As for President Johnson, he was satisfied because the arrangement, whichever way it turned out, would take him off the hook before an ABM gap developed to further tarnish a political reputation already battered as a result of the Vietnam war.

Although an agreement had been reached to seek negotiations before deploying the Nike X, the debate over the merits of the system continued, increasing in intensity through the first half of 1967. Army General Earl Wheeler, the chairman of the Joint Chiefs and a major proponent of the new system, made frequent public statements questioning Secretary McNamara's judgment and expertise. Wheeler claimed that the cost of deploying a system capable of defending America's fifty largest cities as well as the fixed Minuteman installations would be a mere $20 billion, hardly half what McNamara estimated the cost to be. He also disputed the secretary's claim that the Soviets would respond to an American ABM system by expanding their offensive missile forces. He further insisted that McNamara was wrong when he alleged that an ABM system would not reduce civilian casualties in the event of war. Between thirty and fifty million Americans could be saved, the general claimed, if the antimissile system was deployed.

Although McNamara found himself on the defensive, this was by no means an unequal contest. He fought back, managing to win a good deal of support in the press. Always aware that the ultimate decision was in the hands of the president, he took special pains to keep him in the fold by carefully educating him on the merits and demerits of the ABM system. Early in 1967, he organized an extraordinary meeting of policymakers and weapons experts at the White House. McNamara intended to resolve the ABM dispute in the presence and with the participation of the president himself. It was an impressive gathering. Johnson, McNamara, and the Joint Chiefs of Staff were joined by a galaxy of scientific talent including James R. Killian, Jr., George Kistiakowsky, Jerome Wiesner, Donald Hornig, Harold Brown, John S. Foster, Jr., and Herbert York. There, assembled at one time and in one room, were most of the scientific experts who had guided weapons development in the United States over the preceding two decades. After the ABM system had been discussed in great detail, the scientists and engineers assembled were asked a final, simple question. "Will it work and should it be deployed?" According to Herbert York, the "answer in relation to defending our people against a Soviet missile attack was No, and there was no dissent from that answer."[9]

Not even a definitive "no" could deter the Joint Chiefs, Western Electric, and their friends in Congress from continuing to fight for the ABM, however. On the contrary, the first six months of 1967 was a period of increasingly sharp recriminations as supporters and opponents of the ABM program sparred in Congress and the media. The debate became so heated that Senator Joseph Clark, one of McNamara's strongest supporters in the upper House, urged the creation of a special blue ribbon presidential commission to investigate the need for an ABM system. The United States, Clark charged, was being "victimized by weapons cultists" who stood to make hundreds of millions of dollars by the deployment of a "pointless and inefficient system."[10]

The issue would not be decided in Congress or by a special presidential commission, however. The Russians held the key. If they agreed to serious arms control talks, the American ABM could be killed through diplomacy. Otherwise, it seemed certain to be deployed.

In January 1967, secret talks began in Moscow between Ambassador Llewellyn "Tommy" Thompson and Premier Aleksei Kosygin. Thompson's early dispatches were mildly optimistic. He described Kosygin as "vaguely positive" and the talks themselves as polite. Thompson was never so optimistic as McNamara and Rusk, who both thought that the Thompson–Kosygin meetings might well produce the agreement they sought. These highly secret and infrequent tête-à-têtes between the American ambassador and the Soviet premier continued for some months without producing anything substantive. Nor did a subsequent meeting between Soviet ambassador Anatoly Dobrynin and McNamara. The Kremlin did not seem to be interested.

In June, with time running out, McNamara made one last bid to convince the Soviets to come to the bargaining table. The occasion was the summit meeting between President Johnson and Kosygin in Glassboro, New Jersey. McNamara attempted to convince the Soviet leader that deploying ABM systems would accomplish nothing positive, while it destabilized the strategic situation. Kosygin listened and was perhaps impressed by the secretary's obvious earnestness. But according to Henry Kissinger, he told President Johnson that he thought "the idea of limiting missile defenses was one of the most absurd he had ever heard." Time had run out for the secretary of defense.

Following the Glassboro summit, President Johnson made the decision to deploy the Nike X. But how extensive should the system be? Johnson had no firm convictions. Because he viewed the ABM question as a matter of domestic politics rather than national security, he would be satisfied with any pattern of deployment that would take the political play away from the advocates of ABM. General Wheeler, the other members of the Joint Chiefs of Staff, and their congressional allies urged the deployment of a "thick" system of defenses designed to protect America's urban centers. The rationale offered by advocates of this extensive program seemed to be that since the Soviets were doing it, we should too. "Monkey see, monkey do," muttered one McNamara loyalist at the Arms Control and Disarmament Agency. Another group within the defense establishment proposed the creation of a "thin" anti-China system designed to protect the United States against an accidental launch or an attack by the Chinese, who had only a few missiles in their inventories. Those who advocated this view realized that the ABM would be utterly useless against a full-scale Soviet attack but saw some virtue in taking out a little insurance against either an accident or a foolhardy attack launched by the Chinese.

The respected nuclear strategist Albert Wohlstetter spoke for a small number of defense intellectuals who believed the United States should deploy a thin anti-China system with the capability of protecting fixed, hard-site, land-based missile installations. Wohlstetter was among the first to realize that as Soviet strategic missile forces grew in numbers, they would also become more accurate, eventually threatening America's fixed land-based missiles. He sought to close what later became known as "the win-

dow of vulnerability" by defending missile sites with antiballistic
missiles. McNamara believed that the most appropriate response
to Galosh was to increase America's offensive strength. But
Wohlstetter warned of the dangers inherent in such an approach.
"Simply adding more vehicles is costly and more destabilizing
than active defense of hard points," he wrote. When the United
States increases the number of missiles in its inventories, it also
"increases its capacity to strike first."[12] The best response to the
growing Soviet offensive capability, he insisted, was "to protect
the hard-fixed elements" of this country's force with antiballistic
missiles. It had evidently never occurred to Secretary McNamara
that in adding to America's offensive nuclear forces he would be
building toward the counterforce capability that he sought to
avoid. Wohlstetter's point, therefore, impressed him.

On September 19, 1967, while speaking before the editors of
United Press International in San Francisco, McNamara announced Defense Department policy on the ABM. The secretary
devoted the first several minutes of this curious speech to the
dangers of the nuclear arms race, its mad momentum, the need
for stability, and how the action/reaction cycle had led both sides
to build more weapons than they needed. Many in the audience
undoubtedly thought they were listening to a speech explaining
why, in spite of all the pressure, the Johnson administration was
not going to deploy the Nike X. In reality, however, McNamara
was describing forces that neither he nor the president had been
able to control. That became apparent when he turned to the
immediate subject of his talk, the ABM. He abruptly announced
that the government would soon begin production and deployment of a thin anti-China ABM system which would have as a
"concurrent benefit: a further defense of our Minuteman sites
against Soviet attack [and] protection of our population against
. . . accidental launch of an intercontinental missile by any of the
nuclear powers."[13]

Exactly why McNamara opted for the thin anti-China system is
still a matter of debate. One high-ranking Defense Department
official, close to McNamara at this time, speaking not for attribu-
tion, claimed that he actually believed in the anti-China idea.
Others disagreed. "Bob had been whipped on the ABM," said

one of the nation's senior strategists. "But he was determined to give it the least possible chance for expansion. He chose deliberately the worst credible rationale for its deployment."[14] John Newhouse, whose book *Cold Dawn* is definitive on the origins of SALT, agrees with this latter point of view. "The truth is that the United States launched its ABM program because Washington . . . found itself caught up in a wave of ABM hysteria, and the decision, like so many others, was not measured. It was driven by essentially tangential concerns, among them: the failure to start immediate talks with the Russians; the pressure to appease members of Congress who insisted on emulating the Russian example; and understandable White House fear of ABM becoming a solid Republican issue in 1968."[15]

McNamara categorically rejected the view that this thin anti-China system was but the first installment on the more elaborate thick anti-Soviet system that some envisioned. And when General Wheeler chose to interpret early deployment in this way, McNamara was quick to rebut him. To the extent possible, he still hoped to restrain the arms race by assuring the Soviets that the American ABM in no way threatened the credibility of their deterrent.

In January 1968, the Johnson administration asked Congress for an initial $1.2 billion to begin construction and deployment of the ABM system. Naming the new program proved more difficult than convincing Congress to vote the appropriation. For a while, the Pentagon brass were stymied. John Newhouse has observed "that all the appropriate names had been adopted either for other weapon systems or for male contraceptives; and the latter, of course, would not do."[16] Ironically, it was the wife of a government official who was a critic of the Vietnam war and of almost everything military who suggested the name Sentinel.

There are many ironies to the fact that the administration should have decided to deploy Sentinel in 1968. In the first place, by that time the ostensible reason for an American antiballistic missile system had disappeared. Galosh, that imagined threat to the credibility of the American deterrent, had not been expanded. On the contrary, the Soviets had all but lost interest in the system and were moving at a snail's pace to complete the facilities around Moscow. Moreover, Tallinn, once touted as having ABM capabilities, was now known to be an air defense system, nothing more. Finally, the Chinese strategic missile program, which was the ostensible reason for deploying Sentinel, had slowed dramatically.

It was the bomber gap and the missile gap all over again. Basing its response on a worst-case assumption, the Defense Department had responded to Galosh by MIRVing its offensive missile forces and beginning the deployment of a thin ABM system. Now the threat of a Soviet ABM had disappeared. But MIRV and an American ABM were harsh realities. The arms race had reached a new level of intensity. As John Newhouse has observed, "MIRV and Sentinel were responses to threats that either had not materialized, would not materialize, or were not even threats at all." They "should have been held within the level of research and development. Neither bore much relation to the really significant buildup of enemy strength."[17]

In the spring of 1968, the Soviets added to the irony by finally signaling an interest in arms control talks. "It's too bad we waited so long," one Soviet arms controller later lamented. "If only we had gone ahead with talks when McNamara was pressing for them. Don't think we weren't studying the problem. It was just too soon. We didn't think we were ready."[18] Unhappily, by the time the Soviets did think they were ready, technology was again running out of control.

Why did the Soviets take so long before agreeing to talks? This important question will probably never be answered definitively. Yet certain points are reasonably clear. First, there was no difference of opinion inside the Soviet government on the desirability of achieving nuclear parity with the United States. It was only after parity was assured—sometime around 1967—that internal differences began to emerge. The prevailing view among Soviet military leaders, encouraged by the U.S. debacle in Vietnam, was that America's power was in decline relative to that of the Soviet Union. This, it was believed, would encourage U.S. leaders to adopt a more truculent and adventuresome foreign and military policy as they attempted with fewer resources to hold on to America's predominant position in the world. Red Army leaders placed no faith in the stated American interest in arms control and urged a policy of military superiority as vital to Soviet security in a threatening world. Writing on the eve of the opening of the second round of SALT in Vienna, one Soviet officer observed:

> Official Washington has given out not a few statements in order to convince American and world society of its interest in these negotiations. However, the facts speak otherwise. The closer comes the time for the beginning of the negotiations in Vienna, the more feverish becomes the activity of the Pentagon. The American military hasten to carry out the creation of new types of strategic weapons.

The development of MIRV technology in the United States seemed particularly threatening to the Russian military, an indication that Washington was seeking a first strike capability. As one Soviet officer pointed out, the great accuracy of America's MIRVed missiles "permits them to destroy in a first strike a large percentage of the intercontinental ballistic missiles deployed in hardened sites, so that only a few of them can be used for inflicting a retaliatory strike."[20]

Soviet arms controllers agreed that American power was waning. But they drew entirely different conclusions from this. Where the military believed that the United States would in the future become more dangerous, they argued that America was at the time badly divided between realists who sought détente with the Kremlin as well as a limit to the arms race, and aggressive imperialists who wanted to escalate the arms competition. Because at the time America's realists held the upper hand, they believed the time was right for serious arms control negotiations.

Nor did Soviet arms controllers find much that was appealing about the Soviet military's insistence on establishing military superiority. Like their counterparts in Washington, they believed that the search for superiority was endless and pointless. The wiser course was to secure parity and stability through bilateral negotiations. Remarked Andrei Gromyko:

> To the good-for-nothing theoreticians [all of them military men] who try to tell us . . . that disarmament is an illusion, we reply: "By

taking such a stand you fall into step with the most dyed-in-the-wool imperialist reaction [and] weaken the front of the struggle against it."[19]

In the spring of 1968, Soviet arms controllers and the more conventional hard-line militarists within the Soviet hierarchy finally reconciled at least some of their differences. Over the preceding several years and at great sacrifice, the Kremlin had managed to achieve nuclear parity with the United States and to create a credible deterrent. But new American technologies—ABM and MIRV—threatened that deterrent. The Soviet Union might of course continue to add to its arsenal. But as Foreign Minister Gromyko told the Supreme Soviet, escalation was pointless.

> What is involved here is above all the question of whether the major powers are to reach an agreement on checking the race for the creation of increasingly destructive means of attack and counterattack, or whether each power will seek to pull ahead in one area or another in order to achieve military superiority over its rival, which would compel the latter to mobilize still more national resources for the arms race. And so on ad infinitum.[22]

The course agreed upon by arms controllers and military men alike was to attempt negotiations for the purpose "of preventing a new round in the arms race without harming the security of the country, and releasing significant resources for creative objectives."

The Strategic Arms Limitation Talks might have opened in the summer of 1968. But with President Johnson poised to announce that the two countries had finally agreed to sit down and talk, the Soviets invaded Czechoslovakia, and for domestic political reasons the administration could not then proceed. SALT would have to wait for the new year and a new administration in Washington.

Richard Nixon's 1968 election victory forced another delay in arms limitation talks. A Republican was now in the White House, and a suspicious one at that. He had no intention of simply going forward with plans laid by his Democratic predecessor. "We will not make the same old mistakes," National Security Adviser

Henry Kissinger told a group of reporters in 1969. "We will make our own." The former Harvard political scientist and expert on nuclear strategy was commenting on Vietnam when he made this remark. But he might just as well have been speaking of any other aspect of foreign and military policy. The Nixon administration was in no rush to do anything until it had thoroughly surveyed the territory.

Together Nixon and Kissinger made a bold show of seeming to modify the policies of the Kennedy–Johnson years. Yet continuity rather than contrast was characteristic of their approach to the nuclear question. For example, during the election campaign, Nixon attacked the Democrats for allowing the Soviets to catch up in the nuclear arms race and promised that he would "restore clear-cut military superiority" over the Soviets. Yet hardly a week after taking office he abandoned that theme in favor of a policy he described as "strategic sufficiency"—an updated version of Eisenhower's post-Sputnik policy. Henry Kissinger has claimed that though the president wanted to pursue a more aggressive weapons policy he was frustrated by opponents of large defense budgets. It was the period of the Vietnam war and "all things military came under assault."[23] Kissinger paints a vivid picture of a government beseiged and at the mercy of a short-sighted yet powerful public and congressional opposition that hamstrung the president. But the facts are open to another interpretation. It may well be that Nixon abandoned the idea of nuclear superiority because, like McNamara, he realized that it was unattainable. Further increases in American strategic forces would only have encouraged the Soviets to add to their already impressive array of nuclear weapons. A Republican had replaced a Democrat in the White House but the action/reaction cycle was alive and well. Moreover, the existence of secure second strike capabilities in both the United States and the Soviet Union made superiority almost meaningless. In a moment of candor Kissinger himself once asked: "What in the name of God is strategic superiority? What is the significance of it politically, militarily, operationally at these levels of numbers? What do you do with it?"[24] Finally, had President Nixon actually sought nuclear superiority, it would have proven damaging to his basic foreign policy objective, which was détente with the Soviet Union.

At the beginning of the Nixon administration, mutually assured destruction remained the announced nuclear strategy of the United States. Not even those who endorsed MAD were exactly enthusiastic about it, however. Herbert York thought it "too frightful and too dangerous a way to live indefinitely" and insisted that something would have to be done before civilization went "up . . . in nuclear smoke." This former head of the Livermore weapons laboratory believed that it was essential for the United States to "find some better form of international relationship than the current dependency on a strategy of mutual assured destruction."

Less tolerant critics went a good deal further. No less a figure than Albert Wohlstetter lashed out at those in the strategic community who had the temerity to describe what amounted to a plan for the mass slaughter of civilians as a military strategy. They were, he insisted, making "murder respectable" while cloaking their true intentions in such "chaste phrases as 'countervalue attacks' and in all the unreflective vocabulary of the arms race."[25] Writing in *Foreign Affairs* magazine, Fred Iklé, another prominent strategist who would later head up the Arms Control and Disarmament Agency, was equally emphatic:

> The jargon of American strategic analysis works like a narcotic. It dulls our sense of moral outrage about the tragic confrontation of nuclear arsenals, primed and constantly perfected to unleash widespread genocide. It fosters the current smug complacency regarding the soundness and stability of mutual deterrence. It blinds us to the fact that our method of preventing nuclear war rests on a form of warfare universally condemned since the Dark Ages—the mass killing of hostages.[26]

Iklé, Wohlstetter, and others denounced MAD not only because it was immoral but because they viewed it as unrealistic, inflexible, or lacking in credibility as well. Henry Kissinger himself summarized this point of view very well indeed when he asked rhetorically what would happen if the deterrent failed "and

the President was finally faced with the decision to retaliate."
Would he be prepared to "take the moral responsibility for
recommending a strategy based on the mass extermination of
civilians?" Kissinger thought not. But if he guessed correctly,
how would the United States hold NATO together once "the
credibility of its strategy eroded?" Kissinger also wondered how
a president would react in the event of a limited Soviet nuclear
attack:

> Should a President . . . be left with a single option of ordering the
> mass destruction of enemy civilians in the face of the certainty that
> it would be followed by the mass slaughter of Americans?[27]

The strategic debate had obviously come full circle. Fifteen years
earlier Kissinger, Wohlstetter, William Kaufmann, and others
had raised similar objections to massive retaliation. Now it was
MAD that was suicidal and therefore lacked credibility. A president needed options short of all-out war. Some way had to be
found to employ nuclear weapons selectively.

MAD's critics were far more impressive in attacking the established doctrine than when they turned to constructing an alternative. Iklé, for example, reverted to an updated version of counterforce, arguing that it had become technologically feasible to
conduct methodical limited nuclear strikes against military, industrial, and communications centers, "the sinews and muscles
of the regime initiating war," while avoiding countervalue strikes
against population centers. Wohlstetter agreed, but was always
on firmer ground when pointing up the shortcomings of MAD.
Thus he noted that, on one hand, in the event of a military
showdown massive strikes against Soviet population centers
would do nothing to save the millions of Americans who would
die in the encounter. On the other hand, strikes against Soviet
military installations might. Wohlstetter thought it nonsense to
argue that we could "eliminate the possibility of nuclear war
simply by *assuring* that if it occurs it *will* be an unlimited catastrophe." "All out attacks would be acts of despair while limited
attacks offered some hope of war termination at a level of destruction that was something less than total and on terms of some
political value."[28]

During his first three years as Richard Nixon's national security adviser, either because he was too preoccupied with Vietnam and other foreign policy initiatives, or because he recognized a losing proposition when he saw one, Henry Kissinger managed to avoid becoming enmeshed in the search for a more credible nuclear strategy. But in 1972 he and several National Security Council staffers set to work on a scheme to develop a limited nuclear-war fighting capability. The work was well under way when James Schlesinger took over the Department of Defense in 1973. Schlesinger, who during the mid-1960s had worked as a strategist for the RAND Corporation, shared Kissinger's concerns about the credibility of MAD as well as the conviction that some method of fighting limited nuclear wars should be developed. Thus, in spite of the fact that the two men soon became political rivals, these differences had no effect on the evolution of strategy.

Neither Kissinger nor Schlesinger would ever publicly admit that what came to be known as the Schlesinger doctrine varied in any significant way from the strategy of mutually assured destruction. Both recalled only too well what had befallen McNamara after he announced the No Cities doctrine. Yet it is clear that by 1974 some very basic changes in America's nuclear strategy were being implemented. This latest approach to nuclear war, Schlesinger explained, was intended to reduce the possibility for uncontrolled escalation while attacking "meaningful targets with a sufficient accuracy-yield combination to destroy only the intended target and to avoid wide-spread collateral damage."[29] The new strategy was intended to be flexible, taking into account a wide array of potential dangers ranging from a limited Soviet first strike to an accidental launch. Because both superpowers had assured destruction capabilities, Schlesinger believed there was little likelihood that the Soviets would be foolhardy enough to risk a full-scale disarming first strike. But the strategy did not overlook that possibility either.

Kissinger and Schlesinger believed that they had improved on mutually assured destruction. The new approach, Kissinger later explained, "gave us at least the theoretical capability to use forces for objectives other than the mass extermination of populations." But the national security adviser, never shy when it came to self-advertisement, didn't push the point in this case. In 1979, he admitted that much remained to be done and that unless some more effective solution to the nuclear riddle was found, "the problem" would "sooner or later paralyze our strategy and our foreign policy."[30]

The Schlesinger doctrine was intended to provide the president with a range of nuclear options in the event of Soviet aggression in order to reduce chances for an uncontrolled escalation to all-out nuclear war by creating the possibility of fighting a limited one. But in developing the new strategy, Kissinger and Schlesinger inevitably lowered the threshold for the use of nuclear weapons while ignoring the warnings of those who believed that once nuclear weapons were introduced onto the battlefield, an all-out exchange would become inevitable. Alain Enthoven, who spent eight years in the defense department studying the problem, was quick to point out that he had never encountered a plan for a limited nuclear war in Europe that made any sense. Enthoven was particularly critical of those strategists who believed that battlefield nuclear weapons could be used effectively without risking a wider war:

> Tactical nuclear weapons cannot defend Europe; they can only destroy it. Studies and war games done in the 1960's showed repeatedly that even under the most favorable assumptions about restraint and limitations in yields and targets, between 2 and 20 million Europeans would be killed in a limited tactical nuclear war, with widespread damage to the economy of the affected area, and a high risk of 100 million deaths if the war escalated to attacks on cities. . . . Twenty years of effort by many military experts have failed to produce a believable doctrine for tactical nuclear warfare.[31]

British military men were of the same opinion. A few months before his murder at the hands of the Irish Republican Army, Admiral of the Fleet Lord Mountbatten, chief of Britain's defense staff from 1959 to 1965, told a Strasbourg audience: "In all sincerity, as a military man I can see no use for any nuclear weapons which would not end in escalation with consequences that no one can conceive." He was seconded by Air Marshal Sir

Neil Cameron who believed that the "notion of winning some sort of military success in an exchange of nuclear weapons is unreal. . . . So-called battlefield nuclear weapons are not means of winning military victories . . . the warfighting school of nuclear theorists has lost the argument in the West."[32]

General A. S. Collins, Jr., an American who, like his British colleagues, doubted that a nuclear war could be limited, pointed out another serious flaw in the Schlesinger doctrine when he observed that once NATO forces had used nuclear weapons in a limited or "discreet" way, "control of events passes to the other side." And there was nothing in Soviet doctrine to indicate that Russian military leaders accepted the concept of limited nuclear war. The late Marshal V. D. Sokolovskii, author of *Military Strategy*, harbored no illusions about what the use of nuclear weapons would mean. Clearly, once such weapons had been used, escalation would become inevitable. "The logic of war," he wrote, "is such that if a war is unleashed by the aggressive circles of the United States, it will immediately be transferred to the territory of the United States of America. All weapons: ICBMs, missiles from submarines, and other strategic weapons, will be used in this military conflict."[33] In an interview given to *The New York Times* on August 28, 1980, General Mikhail Milshtein indicated that nothing had changed since the publication of Marshal Sokolovskii's book. "Our doctrine regards nuclear weapons as something that must never be used," Milshtein explained. "They are not an instrument for waging war in any rational sense. They are not weapons with which one can achieve foreign policy goals. But if we are forced to use them, in reply to their first use by an aggressor, we shall use them, with all their consequences, for the punishment of the aggressor."[34] This Soviet insistence on what amounted to a strategy of massive retaliation made any notion of using nuclear weapons in so-called "discreet" ways utterly impossible. As Lawrence Freedman has explained in *The Evolution of Nuclear Strategy*, "If US policy was designed only as a reaction to a Soviet first strike (which according to Soviet policy would . . . be massive) it was futile. If it was intended as a first shot on our part it would be folly inviting a massive counter-value strike."[35]

Henry Kissinger admitted that the Schlesinger doctrine was far from perfect. Like McNamara before them, Kissinger and the secretary of defense had tried but clearly failed to develop a workable strategy for fighting limited nuclear wars. Yet in spite of this, Kissinger at least was unwilling to base all his future hopes on deterrence and diplomacy. A realist, he thought it a mistake not to take into account the possibility that some day the two great adversaries might fight. If they did, and if the United States had only nuclear weapons at its disposal, it would use them. The result might be the end of all life on the planet. Kissinger has continued to insist, therefore, that there is only one sensible way for the nation to proceed. "Achieving a more discriminating nuclear strategy, preserving at least some hope of civilized life," he wrote in 1979, "remains to this day one of the most difficult tasks to implement, requiring a substantial recasting of our military establishment."[36]

Because Kissinger realized the dangers implicit in using nuclear weapons in combat, he sought to convince the NATO allies to develop effective conventional forces. But he was no more successful than McNamara had been. The allies, who continued to view flexible response as a sign of America's disinclination to commit nuclear suicide on their behalf, and who feared that the Soviets might be encouraged by this to try their hand at conventional aggression, insisted that in the event of an attack, tactical nuclear weapons be used immediately against advancing Warsaw Pact forces. They enforced this demand, as they always had, by the simple expedient of failing to develop effective conventional forces. Kissinger thought he knew why. It was (and still is) assumed that once nuclear weapons have been used, there would be no stopping the swift escalation to full-scale exchange. And that, Kissinger believed, was western Europe's hope. The "real goal of our allies," he has since observed, "has been to commit the United States to the early use of *strategic* nuclear weapons, which meant a US–Soviet nuclear war fought over their heads."[37]

Distressed at his inability to convince the western Europeans to plan a conventional defense of the continent, Kissinger was no more satisfied by developments in Washington, where anti-Vietnam sentiment predominated in Congress and the Pentagon budget was a prime target. War or no war, Kissinger believed the United States needed to beef up its conventional forces. But the reverse was actually taking place and there was little or nothing the administration could do about it. As he explained to the president:

> We are in danger of sliding into a period of relying on massive retaliation even though it is absurd. Our general purpose forces must be looked at. We have to have forces in which we can believe. We must be able to project a credible power abroad in a situation where general nuclear war is no longer a likely or reasonable alternative.[38]

But if, as Kissinger thought, America's conventional forces were "the way we are seen by allies" as well as being the "contact and the reality," they were also diminishing in size and in the effectiveness of existing units.

Though Kissinger wrestled ineffectively with many aspects of the nuclear question, his efforts were not entirely unavailing. On the contrary, he brought the SALT negotiations, begun during McNamara's tenure in the defense department, to a successful conclusion. And if the first SALT treaty was not all that it might have been, it nevertheless did represent a significant step in the right direction.

The Soviets made their interest in an early beginning for arms control negotiations evident on January 20, 1969, inauguration day in Washington, when a spokesman for the Soviet foreign ministry indicated Russian readiness to "start a serious exchange of views" on a "mutual limitation and subsequent reduction of strategic nuclear vehicles," including "defense systems."[39] This swift Soviet opening was doubtless a bit unnerving to an administration still struggling to get its feet on the ground. But President Nixon sensed in the Soviet proposal a certain amount of anxiety which he thought might be turned to his advantage. He therefore decided to find out what the Soviets were willing to pay for an early beginning to talks. In April, several weeks after the initial Soviet proposal, Kissinger informed Anatoly Dobrynin that the president "was prepared to send a high-level delegation to Moscow . . . to agree immediately on the principles of strategic arms limitations" provided the Soviets would arrange a meeting in Moscow between North Vietnamese and American representatives for the purpose of bringing the war to a swift conclusion. Kissinger's offer sounded grand. But an agreement on principles was of course no agreement at all. It was clear that Nixon and Kissinger hoped to convince the Soviets to help extract them from a painful situation in Vietnam while paying little in return. When the Soviets showed no interest in this patently one-sided proposal, the administration abandoned all thought of an early opening for SALT. As far as the public knew, President Nixon had serious though unstated reservations about the initiatives undertaken by the Johnson administration and was in the process of subjecting the entire arms control issue to extensive review.

His public stance notwithstanding, there was never any doubt that the president would go ahead with the talks. He even thought he was ideally suited to win confirmation for an arms control treaty. He told Gerard Smith, the head of the ACDA and soon to be the leader of America's SALT delegation, "that because of his anti-communist record he believed he could bring the country to favor Soviet–American arms control to a degree not possible for any Democrat President."[35]

President Nixon had every incentive to work for an arms control agreement. In the first place, the defense budget was unpopular and under attack. It would have been impossible to win congressional support for new weapons systems. Moreover, the Joint Chiefs were not interested in adding to the number of older weapons already in their inventories. These systems, designed in the 1950s, were considered obsolete. More modern weapons were already on the drawing boards. But even with funding, it would take at least until the mid-1970s before a new land-based missile, the Ohio class of submarine with its Trident missiles, and the B-1 bomber could become operational. Given congressional attitudes, it might take even longer. In fact, an internal memorandum circulated at this time by Assistant Secretary of Defense David Packard argued that "an early freeze on offensive weapons was imperative because the squeeze on our defense budget would make it nearly impossible to maintain existing strategic forces, much less increase them."[41] In effect then, save for MIRV, a de facto freeze on the deployment of new weapons systems was already in effect in the United States.

The Soviets, meanwhile, following their own schedule, were replacing older missiles with the larger and more reliable SS-9 and were simultaneously increasing the number of missile launchers in their inventories. This was a matter of gravest concern in Washington, because the new MIRV technology would give the Kremlin the beginnings of a counterforce capability. A negotiated limit on the number of offensive weapons each side could retain would be in the interest of the United States. "In fact," as Gerard Smith has noted, "looking at projected rates of Soviet missile launcher construction in the light of the absence of any such U.S. programs, the Nixon Administration realized that there was no way, save by an arms limitation agreement, to prevent the USSR from achieving numerical superiority in offensive ballistic missile launchers."[42]

Nixon and Kissinger also realized that the United States would probably never be stronger relative to the Soviet Union than it was at that time. Here was another good reason to begin negotiations as soon as possible. In 1969, the United States could deliver 1,710 strategic nuclear warheads to enemy targets. Within two years, that number would more than double as the MIRVing process sped along. By the end of 1975, the United States would have between 6,000 and 7,000 deliverable strategic warheads. But this advantage would not long endure. Once the Soviets had deployed the new generation of "heavies" and mastered MIRV technology, they would quickly narrow the gap in warheads and then pull ahead. Neither Kissinger nor Nixon wanted to enter negotiations from an inferior position. Though parity was a fact of life, and counting warheads had become all but meaningless at the astonishing levels then being contemplated, the two men nevertheless believed that it was to their advantage to begin talks while the United States still held the advantage in the number of nuclear warheads it deployed.

The Republican leadership viewed prospects for a successful negotiation as rather bright. Soviet military leaders continued to view the American ABM and MIRV technologies as threatening to their hard-won deterrent. Also, it was becoming increasingly difficult for the Russian leadership to ignore mounting economic pressures at home. In order to achieve nuclear parity with the United States, the Soviets had been forced to divert badly needed resources from the domestic economy to the arms race. By the end of the decade as Soviet economic growth slowed, the Kremlin's leadership felt a growing need to provide increasing quantities of consumer goods and increased military budgets at the same time. Sooner or later something would have to give. Finally, as more than one arms controller has quipped, the Soviet Union was the only nation in the world entirely surrounded by hostile Communist states. Problems with the east European satellites and with China were a constant drain on Soviet resources. As Sino-Soviet relations hit rock bottom in 1969, the Kremlin became increasingly interested in détente with the West and even seemed to have envisioned some sort of alliance with the United States to keep China in check. The emergence of Leonid Brezhnev as preeminent among Soviet leaders was another indication that these stresses were having an effect, for throughout his career Brezhnev had placed heavy emphasis on the importance of improving economic conditions inside the Soviet Union while showing a considerable interest in easing tensions with the West.

Before negotiations could actually begin, the administration found it necessary to reconcile strong differences of opinion over just how MIRV and ABM fit into its developing plans. From the beginning of the debate, MIRV had been a political as well as a strategic issue, the focus of a good deal of attention on Capitol Hill and in the media. Senator Clifford Case, an opponent of MIRV development, tried unsuccessfully to add an amendment to an appropriations measure calling for an end to MIRV testing. Massachusetts's Edward Brooke introduced a resolution, cosponsored by forty of his Senate colleagues, urging the president to announce a temporary moratorium on MIRV testing. Over a hundred members of the House of Representatives signed resolutions urging the president to call a halt to MIRV tests pending the outcome of the arms control talks. And on two successive days, June 11 and 12, *The New York Times* ran editorials urging a similar course on the president. "One way to entice Mr. Kosygin into a MIRV test suspension would be to offer to suspend American MIRV tests—or even actually suspend them with the announcement that they would not be resumed so long as the Soviet Union refrained from testing its multiple warheads."[38]

Behind these arguments lay a simple, persuasive logic. If the United States MIRVed its missiles, the Soviets would perceive this as an attempt to develop a first strike capability. They would have no choice but to follow suit and in the end U.S. land-based missiles would—at least in theory—be vulnerable to a Soviet first strike. Once that happened, MIRV technology would inevitably be excluded from future arms control talks and the weapons race would take a giant leap forward. The only hope of heading off this dangerous escalation lay in acting unilaterally to suspend MIRV testing temporarily in hopes of negotiating a bilateral ban on the development of the technology. If this sounds like a familiar argument, it should. J. Robert Oppenheimer had employed exactly the same line of reasoning in 1950 in his vain attempt to head off the development of the H-bomb.

Gerard Smith, the head of the Arms Control and Disarmament Agency, was the most outspoken supporter of a MIRV ban inside the administration. He pointed out that MIRV technology had originally been designed to counteract the threat to the American deterrent posed by Galosh, the Soviet ABM system. But by 1969, it was clear that no Soviet ABM threat existed. But then, as Smith explained to Secretary of State William Rogers, if the MIRVing continued, by 1977 the United States would have deployed approximately 9,500 warheads and the Soviets would not be far behind. This, Smith pointed out, was "hardly a way to limit strategic arms."[44]

The Joint Chiefs of Staff and Secretary of Defense Melvin Laird, however, not only opposed a temporary ban on MIRV research; they insisted that MIRVing America's missile force was essential to national security and should not be the subject of negotiations. The defense establishment was determined that MIRV would not become a mere bargaining counter. In the event of a Soviet counterforce strike that destroyed a portion of America's land-based missiles, the military contended, those missiles remaining, if MIRVed, would have three times their current retaliatory capability. This was a curious argument. By the military's own admission, their great fear was that the Minuteman force would become vulnerable when the SS-9 was MIRVed with accurate silo-busting warheads. Yet instead of pursuing a negotiation that might ban MIRV and thus secure Minuteman, they preferred to proceed with the development of the technology. The Soviets were bound to follow suit and in the end both sides would find their land-based forces vulnerable. It would be the action/reaction cycle all over again, with the same depressing result—more weapons and less security.

Because the military's argument in favor of MIRV was so obviously flawed, we must explore the unstated reasons for insisting on adding this new technology to the nuclear arsenal. Military leaders wanted the technology for two reasons, although neither could be stated publicly. First, although assured destruction, a deterrent strategy, remained the policy of the United States, some in the military had never abandoned the hope of achieving a first strike counterforce capability. MIRV seemed to offer the opportunity to achieve this long sought after goal. For years the military had insisted that the nation that struck first in a nuclear war would "win." Computer studies done later confirmed that. A well-conceived and executed first strike would knock out a substantial number of the other side's nuclear weapons, reducing its retaliatory capability. Time and again the computers came up with the same answer: the nation that struck first would sustain less damage and fewer casualties, and would wind up with more strategic weapons in reserve at the end of it all.

MIRV was extraordinarily attractive to the military for another reason as well. Military doctrine in the United States was at this time undergoing an enormously significant change. In the immediate postwar period, nuclear weapons were thought to be for deterrence only and unusable in any conventional sense. But gradually, over the decade of the 1970s, military doctrine shifted, postulating use of nuclear weapons to fulfill traditional military purposes such as the disruption of an enemy's communications network or his facilities for command and control of his forces. Simultaneously, "the services cooperated in emphasizing the importance of small-scale, theater-level, or even at-sea nuclear war."[45] So long as the armed services looked upon nuclear weapons as useful only for deterrence, they needed relatively few of them. But once they began developing strategies that involved using nuclear weapons in the ordinary course of war, MIRV became important because it provided the armed services with not hundreds, but thousands of deliverable warheads.

Caught between the demands of the defense establishment and an increasingly vocal anti-MIRV opposition, President Nixon vacillated briefly but then resolved the matter in favor of the military. He really had little choice. He needed the cooperation of the Joint Chiefs to complete a successful negotiation. Even more important, he would need their support in the event that a treaty actually went before the Senate for its approval.

But Nixon did not want to seem to be taking the military's side on this very controversial question. He therefore acted to lay responsibility for the failure to arrive at an agreement on Soviet shoulders by offering a plan for a mutual ban on MIRVs that he knew in advance would be rejected. During the preliminary talks between American and Soviet SALT delegations held in Helsinki at the end of 1969, the Soviets had made it abundantly clear that any agreements would have to be verified by national technical means only. On-site inspection was out of the question. "Methods of verification clearly had been a major concern of the Soviet delegation at Helsinki," Gerard Smith later explained. "U.S. non-insistence on on-site inspection may well have been a sine qua non for proceeding to Vienna" and the beginning of actual negotiations. Nixon's MIRV ban proposal, made long after he was aware of this, called for verification by an elaborate program of on-site inspection. Ironically, as the experts could and undoubtedly did tell the president, on-site inspection to verify that MIRVed missiles were not being deployed wouldn't work anyway. Missiles might be armed with a single warhead when inspectors came around. But, as one arms controller observed, after the inspection, "What's to prevent the Soviets from switching from a missile with one warhead . . . to a MIRV with ten warheads that's being stored in a shack nearby?" That of course was really beside the point. As one NSC staffer admitted, the on-site inspection provision was included in Nixon's MIRV proposal "to make it unacceptable. It was put in with no illusions that it would be accepted or" that it would be "much help with verification if it were."[46]

In private talks held between Smith and Vladimir Semenov early in the second round of SALT, the Russian diplomat charged "that the U.S. MIRV proposal had been designed to be rejected," and that it was "propagandistic." As a responsible diplomat, Smith had to defend the president's proposal. But in his recollections of SALT he has since admitted that "in fact, I felt Semenov's comment was not far from the mark." It was but the first of many disillusions Smith and the other SALT delegates would experience while working for Nixon and Kissinger. "Those of us who favored a ban had finally got the point," he wrote. "Our side did not want a MIRV ban."[47]

Once the Russians realized that President Nixon was not interested in pursuing a ban on MIRVs, they knew precisely how to respond to his proposal. The two powers had danced this particular minuet so often in the past that it was almost instinctive. The Kremlin proposed an unverified ban on the production and deployment of MIRVs but not on their testing. Such an agreement, which was of course totally unacceptable to Washington, would have allowed the Soviets to develop MIRV technology while prohibiting the United States from taking advantage of its lead in this area by deploying MIRVed missiles. After the United States rejected this proposal, the issue was laid to rest. The Soviets indicated that they remained interested in an arms control agreement—even one that did not include MIRV—and the negotiations got under way. The question that remained to be resolved was: What sort of an agreement could ignore the dangers posed by MIRV?

Henry Kissinger's role in the MIRV debate definitely will not go down in history as one of his finest hours. He of course understood the strategic significance of the new technology. But he was also very aware of the dangers inherent in not giving Richard Nixon exactly what he wanted. Very early in the debate, Kissinger told Gerard Smith that he might support a MIRV ban. But as the political implications of taking such a position became apparent, he went over to the other side. In his memoirs Kissinger attacks Smith and those others who stuck to their convictions. It was, he insisted, naïve to think that a unilateral moratorium on MIRV development could provide the basis for a negotiated ban on the technology. Kissinger was even more critical of those who argued that U.S. insistence on pursuing MIRV research and development damaged chances for a successful negotiation. He insisted in fact that the reverse was true. SALT I, he argued, stands as evidence that they were wrong.

The question, however, was not whether some agreement could be reached, but what sort of an agreement it would be. The SALT I treaty, which lacked a MIRV ban and therefore allowed for a massive expansion in the number of deliverable warheads on each side, was seriously flawed. Smith, always the gentleman, has written that administration leaders realized too late "that no stable agreement to limit offensive strategic arms could exist without stringent MIRV control."[48] But that was certainly not true of Kissinger, who understood from the outset that by exempting MIRV from the arms control talks, the government was in fact setting the stage for a major escalation of the arms race.

The debate over whether or not to continue the ABM program was even more intense than the one generated by MIRV. When Richard Nixon moved into the White House, the forces supporting ABM deployment had already won a major victory. Sentinel was a fact of life and the history of the arms race suggested that once the White House had decided to deploy a weapons system it became impossible to stop it. Moreover, Sentinel continued to have the unqualified support of the Department of Defense. Secretary Laird took the position that because the Soviet Union would soon be testing its own MIRVed missiles, an ABM system was essential to national security. This argument, which seemed convincing to many, in fact turned logic on its head. It was, after all, the American MIRV program and the Defense Department's opposition to a negotiated MIRV ban that forced the Soviets to MIRV their missiles in the first place.

President Nixon's decision to continue the ABM program was not simply a matter of rubber-stamping plans earlier laid by Johnson and McNamara. It was not until March 1969, after yet another Pentagon study, that he gave his assent. Renamed Safeguard, the ABM system would be deployed at twelve sites, including both offensive missile installations and major population centers. The president also announced that the program would be implemented in two phases, with the sparsely populated areas that were home to Minuteman missiles being the first to receive protection.

Nixon may have decided to proceed with this phased deployment in order to forestall the urban opposition that was certain to develop once ABM sites began cropping up in densely populated areas. If so, his strategy was almost immediately undermined by the Department of the Army, which went about acquiring land for all twelve installations at once. Citizens living in these areas, for whom the nuclear arms race had been merely an abstraction, suddenly realized that once the ABM installations were completed, they would become prime targets—lightning rods that would attract Soviet missiles.

The people of Seattle were among the earliest to raise an outcry when the army began acquiring land for an ABM site within a mile of the city's center. In November 1969, Chicago joined the protest. A group of local scientists organized the West Suburban Concerned Scientists Group and demanded that the army hold public hearings where interested citizens could air their views. The West Suburban group also publicized the dangers associated with placing an ABM site in a heavily populated area. A warhead might be detonated accidentally or go off over Chicago, thus destroying the city it was supposed to preserve. Boston was the best organized anti-ABM city. There, Professor Abram Chayes of the Harvard Law School, a former legal adviser to the state department, helped organize the New England Citizens Committee on ABM.

Inevitably, Congress began to feel the pressure. Even Mendel Rivers, chairman of the House Armed Services Committee and a friend to all things military, began to distance himself from ABM, expressing doubts about approving the projected sites for Washington and Chicago. In the Senate, the distinguished Republican senator from Kentucky, John Sherman Cooper, led a move to block ABM deployment. Edward Kennedy, one of the leaders of the anti-ABM campaign, not only endorsed but wrote the introduction to a new book that provided ammunition for those still attempting to head off deployment. *ABM: An Evaluation of the Decision to Deploy an Antiballistic Missile System,* edited by Abram Chayes and Jerome Wiesner, became an immensely useful source book for the enemies of ABM in the months that followed. In March 1969, six of this nation's leading weapons experts— Hans Bethe, Herbert York, George Kistiakowsky, James R. Killian, Wolfgang Panofsky, and George Rathjens—went before Congress to argue that Sentinel was not only unreliable but that the Soviets could easily overwhelm it by adding to their offensive strength. Other critics were less concerned with the system's technical weaknesses and more interested in how the Soviets would react to it. After all, they reasoned, the Soviets would have to assume (just as we had in the case of Galosh) that a system as costly and complex as Sentinel worked. Why would the United States spend so much time, money, and effort on it if it didn't? It was the destabilizing effect of an American ABM that troubled these opponents of Sentinel. In the logic of the nuclear arms race, stability is best guaranteed when each of the great nuclear powers believes that its deterrent remains credible. To the extent that the American ABM system raised questions about the effectiveness of the Soviet deterrent, it threatened stability.

While opposition kept the issue alive in the political arena, enthusiasm for Safeguard gradually waned inside the administration itself. There, technical considerations prevailed. In his earliest days at the Defense Department, Secretary Laird was a staunch defender of ABM. But within a year it became inescapably clear that McNamara, York, and the other critics of the technology were correct. No ABM system could defend against a sophisticated attack by MIRVed missiles. With the defense budget under unremitting attack, the administration could not afford to squander tens of billions on an expensive yet useless weapons system.

This might have marked the demise of Safeguard had it not been for the arguments of national security adviser Henry Kissinger, who in this case was strongly seconded by Gerard Smith of the Arms Control Agency. With an eye on the impending strategic arms limitation negotiations, Kissinger urged the importance of continuing the commitment to the ABM system. It wasn't until after the Johnson administration announced that it would proceed with Sentinel that the Soviets showed any interest in arms control talks. Moreover, in first raising the possibility of talks with the Nixon White House, the Soviets had indicated their particular interest in establishing some controls over defensive systems. Kissinger, believing that the threat posed by Sentinel had prompted the Soviets to agree to talks in the first place, hoped to use Safeguard both to strengthen the American negotiating position and as a bargaining counter—something to trade to the Soviets in return for a freeze on the deployment of new offensive weapons.

This "bargaining chip" philosophy—the idea that one builds weapons in order to improve one's bargaining position by trading them away at the negotiating table—was sharply criticized at the time by a number of arms control advocates including Paul Warnke (who subsequently became the head of President Carter's SALT II delegation) and the respected Soviet expert Marshall Shulman. In congressional testimony, Shulman argued that this policy forced the Soviets to match the U.S. program for program. The result could only intensify the arms race as each side committed itself to new weapons programs. The Soviets were no more willing than were we to negotiate from a position of weakness. Like us, they feared that if they agreed to talks while at a strategic disadvantage they might be "pressured into agreement." Therefore, they "felt obliged to match each step" taken by the United States "with comparable measures."[49] The bargaining-chip philosophy then, provided fuel for the arms race and not a basis for a sound arms control agreement. Unfortunately, administration leaders were completely out of sympathy with this point of view. Convinced that Safeguard provided an incentive for the Soviets to negotiate seriously, they clung to the program, fighting a two-year running battle with ABM opponents in the Senate who were determined to kill it.

Before April 1969, the Nixon administration had made a number of crucial decisions. It was prepared to negotiate an arms control treaty with the Soviets. In the negotiations, the United States would seek a comprehensive agreement limiting the number of offensive and defensive strategic weapons each side could deploy. It was prepared to use Safeguard as a bargaining counter to help achieve that end. But Washington was not interested in negotiating a ban on MIRV, the most dangerous threat of all to nuclear stability. It entered into strategic arms negotiations that winter with those assumptions providing the unshakable basis of the American bargaining position.

SALT opened in Helsinki on November 17, 1969. It was bleak and wintry in the Finnish capital, yet the city bustled in spite of the dreary conditions. Shops, hotels, and restaurants were crowded with the delegates, staff members, and over five hundred reporters who had come to cover the opening of what they billed as one of the most important international conferences since the end of World War II. It seemed as though after a generation of false starts, miscues, deception, and misunderstanding, the superpowers might at last be about to come to grips with at least some of the issues posed by the nuclear revolution.

President Nixon sent an experienced group of negotiators to Helsinki. Gerard Smith, onetime head of General Eisenhower's Policy Planning Council and director of the Arms Control and Disarmament Agency, led the delegation. Smith's involvement with the nuclear question began twenty years earlier when he signed on as an aide to AEC commissioner Thomas Murray, who was certainly no dove. Nor was Smith. But after witnessing nuclear tests in the Pacific in the early 1950s, he came to believe "that control of nuclear weapons was the most important business of the world," and devoted virtually all of his public life to that quest.[50] Philip Farley was the delegation's alternate chairman. Like Smith, Farley had extensive experience in nuclear affairs. His baptism came immediately after World War II when, as a member of the strategic bombing survey, he drafted that portion of the report dealing with the bombings of Hiroshima and Nagasaki. Later, during the Eisenhower administration, Farley served as special assistant to the president for atomic energy and disarmament. Still later he often filled in for Smith as acting head of the Arms Control and Disarmament Agency. Paul Nitze, another SALT delegate, had served with Farley on the strategic bombing survey. In 1949, he became the head of Dean Acheson's policy planning staff and was among the principal authors of

NSC-68. In 1957, Nitze was a member of the Gaither commission, which in the wake of Sputnik issued a report urging rapid preparations for nuclear war. Still later, he became President-elect Kennedy's national security adviser and then his assistant secretary of defense for international security affairs. He continued as a member of the national security bureaucracy under Lyndon Johnson, serving first as secretary of the navy and later as deputy secretary of defense.

Lieutenant General Royal Allison was the Joint Chiefs' delegate on the SALT team. Prior to taking on this diplomatic assignment, the ex–World War II fighter pilot had been assistant for strategic arms negotiations to the chairman of the Joint Chiefs. Smith, as well as others on the delegation more attuned to arms control than was Allison, often disagreed with him. That was to be expected. More important, they never lost their respect for him. Ambassador Llewellyn E. "Tommy" Thompson, the Soviet expert who conducted informal talks on arms limitation with Premier Kosygin in 1967, served as a member of the SALT delegation until poor health forced him to retire. He was replaced by Ambassador James Parsons, a career man in the State Department with considerable experience in northern and eastern European affairs. Harold Brown, the last of the SALT delegates, was at the time president of the California Institute of Technology. A physicist and nuclear weapons expert with outstanding credentials, Brown was later to become secretary of defense in the Carter administration.

The Helsinki meeting did not mark the beginning of detailed negotiations. After so many false starts, each side needed to feel the other out, to ascertain whether this was in fact to be the beginning of something important. The Americans quickly decided that the signs were promising. Ambassador Smith did note that the Soviet delegation was "loaded with intelligence people." But it also included a number of men who seemed "accustomed to lots of authority and who" were "seriously interested" in accomplishing something. Vladimir S. Semenov, a deputy foreign minister and expert in German affairs, headed the delegation. He was seconded by Colonel General Nikolai Ogarkov, who represented the Soviet general staff and Defense Minister Grechko.

Aleksandr Shchukin was an expert on defense research and a highly regarded Soviet academician. Others on the Soviet delegation included Petr Pleshakov, deputy minister of the radio industry of the Soviet Union; Colonel General of engineering-technical services Nikolai Alekseyev; Ambassador Georgi Korniyenko; and Oleg Grinevsky, a deputy chief of the international organizations division of the Ministry of Foreign Affairs. Ambassador Smith was particularly impressed with Semenov, who he thought was "a man bent on serious business and intent on getting through this preliminary phase without delay." The Soviet diplomat's opening remarks, which might have been written in the offices of the Arms Control and Disarmament Agency, reinforced this impression. "He spoke of nuclear war as a disaster for both sides—of the decrease of security as the number of weapons increases—of the costly results of rapid obsolescence of weapons—of the dangers of grave miscalculations—of unauthorized use of weapons—and of hostilities resulting from third power provocation."[43]

Though it soon became clear that the two sides were serious, it did not follow that agreement was going to come easily. Both delegations arrived in Helsinki seeking a comprehensive agreement that would limit offensive and defensive strategic weapons. Unfortunately, several weeks of fruitless discussions demonstrated that it was not going to be possible to define precisely what a strategic weapon was. Among its many objectives, the Nixon administration hoped to limit the number of medium and intermediate range missiles the Soviets had trained on western European targets. But because these weapons could not strike directly at the United States, the Soviets refused to consider them as strategic weapons to be limited under the agreement. On the other hand, the Soviets wanted to include American forward-based systems in the agreement. The United States had hundreds of nuclear armed aircraft stationed at bases throughout Europe or on-board aircraft carriers plying the Mediterranean and the Indian Ocean. These planes, if sent on one-way missions or refueled in midair, could strike at targets in the Soviet Union. As one Soviet delegate explained, it made little difference whether the bomb that killed him was delivered by a missile fired from a silo in the United States or a plane launched from an American air base in Europe. Dead was dead. These planes, which could deliver more megatonnage than the entire Soviet submarine fleet, certainly could not be left out of the agreement.

The American delegates were at first puzzled and suspicious about the Soviet insistence on including forward-based systems in the negotiations. Had they perhaps raised the issue in order to bargain it away later in return for some American concession? It was the construction of new missile launchers that was driving the arms race, not the medium range bombers stationed at forward bases. The number of operational warplanes so stationed had in fact declined in recent years. For weeks, the American delegates poked and prodded in an attempt to uncover the "real" reason the Soviets were so insistent on defining the forward-based systems as strategic. At length, the Americans concluded that they had no ulterior motive. The Soviets honestly viewed these weapons as an important element in the overall American strategic threat.

This proved to be a grave setback to Washington's hopes for a comprehensive arms control agreement. The overseas military bases of the United States had for years served several related functions. Their military purpose was obvious. But they were also important as political symbols, signals to the allies that the United States was serious about the defense of western Europe and Japan. Conventional wisdom held that if the Soviets succeeded in reducing the size of these forces as part of a general agreement limiting offensive weapons, America's allies would read this as a signal that the United States could no longer be relied upon. America's claim to leadership of NATO would be undermined.

Disagreement over the future of America's forward-based systems notwithstanding, the first two months of what became a three-year marathon negotiation proved productive. Each side came away convinced that the other was serious about limiting strategic weapons. It was also clear that the Soviets were particularly interested in blocking the deployment of Safeguard. Russian military leaders had evidently concluded that the American ABM might turn out to be the first installment of what could become a thick defensive system intended to blunt a Soviet missile attack. Such a system would raise questions about the credibility of Moscow's hard-won deterrent and force the Strategic Rocket Forces to increase the number of ICBMs it deployed. Finally, the principal trouble spot of future talks had been identified. A treaty limiting offensive weapons was going to be extremely difficult to achieve because of the American unwillingness to agree that the forward-based systems constituted a strategic threat to the Soviet Union.

On April 16, 1970, the second round of SALT began, this time in Vienna. The site of the negotiations was the Belvedere Palace, once the home of Prince Eugene of Savoy. The weather was fine and both delegations, whisked to their first meeting by smartly dressed motorcycle police, were in an optimistic frame of mind. Unhappily, as the talks proceeded it became obvious that the delegates' early optimism had more to do with the grandeur of the setting than possibilities for agreement. They found no way of reconciling differences over America's forward-based systems.

The failure of the delegates to resolve the problems of forward-based systems after hundreds of hours of talks frustrated both sides. At the same time, it illuminated a basic weakness in the American negotiating position. The Nixon administration was seeking an agreement that would limit the number of missile launchers in the Soviet arsenal and that would at the same time place a subceiling on the number of new "heavy" SS-9 missiles the Soviets could deploy. If the Russians deployed three hundred of these monsters as expected, when MIRVed they theoretically would pose a threat to the survivability of Minuteman and have a dangerously destabilizing effect on the nuclear balance. But what was Washington offering in return? The forward-based systems were not considered negotiable. Worse, the MIRV program was increasing the number of warheads in the American arsenal. The United States was then in the awkward position of seeking limits on the offensive capabilities of the Soviets while at the same time augmenting its own. For this reason, Gerard Smith had earlier urged the president to declare a moratorium on MIRV development, at least for the duration of the negotiations, and to allow him to use this technology as a bargaining counter. The

Soviets had not yet developed their own MIRVed missiles and were clearly concerned by the American lead in this area. Had the delegates been empowered to negotiate a MIRV ban, the world would have been better off and Smith would have had some leverage. As things stood, however, MIRV proved to be "the decisive asymmetry which ultimately prevented reaching meaningful controls over offensive forces in SALT I."[53]

Two months of exhausting negotiations did nothing to break the deadlock. At length, very reluctantly, the American delegation cabled Washington, proposing the so-called Vienna option —an attempt to bypass the forward-based systems issue by reducing the scope of the negotiations. Smith and his colleagues sought authorization to negotiate a partial agreement limiting ABMs as well as three strategic weapons systems: ICBMs, submarine-launched ballistic missiles (SLBM), and heavy bombers. Limits on medium and intermediate range missiles, cruise missiles, and the forward-based systems would be put off for the time being.

The American delegation had gone to Vienna hoping for a comprehensive agreement limiting offensive weaponry. They were now proposing a fundamental change in the nature of the negotiation under which the parties would seek a partial agreement while leaving more difficult questions for a later conference. They did so hoping that if the scope of SALT was thus reduced, chances for success would be improved. Simultaneously, however, they realized that certain technologies—especially MIRV—would be allowed to run dangerously free and that in the long run the less comprehensive approach they were recommending might end for all time the chance to limit these new dangers.

The Americans were not the only ones to recognize the need for a new approach. On the evening of July 4, 1969, Ambassador Smith was relaxing in his Vienna hotel room when he received a telephone call from the city's CIA section chief. An urgent message had been received from the White House that was just then being decoded. Smith jumped into some clothes while the CIA man drove over to pick him up. Together they drove through Vienna's empty streets to the SALT delegation's office. The cable was from Henry Kissinger. President Nixon had just received a proposal from Moscow suggesting the negotiation of a treaty limiting ABMs together with a broad agreement dealing with the problems of accidental attack or a provocative attack launched by some third power. The Soviets undoubtedly had China on their minds. If Washington was ready for such a partial approach to arms control, Moscow was prepared to guarantee a successful outcome to the Vienna talks. But the Kremlin made it clear that at least for the present it was prepared to go no further.

Sensing that the Nixon administration wanted an agreement for domestic political reasons, the Soviets were attempting to take advantage of an obvious weakness in the American negotiating position. The U.S. Senate was at that precise moment engaged in a furious debate over the future of America's ABM system. It seemed likely that the opposition would succeed in killing the entire program. But if that happened, the Soviets would have far less incentive to negotiate any sort of agreement limiting offensive or defensive weapons, and the president would lose the opportunity to get the arms control agreement he so obviously wanted. The Soviets seemed to be saying, "Take what you can get while you can get it."

President Nixon wanted to know what Smith thought of this new Soviet initiative. "Never before or after at SALT did I feel such a lonely responsibility," Smith later wrote. He sat for a long time alone in the office. Then he drafted a reply in longhand and gave it to the clerk for transmission. Smith did not believe that what the Soviets were offering, even in light of "the desirability of a positive Vienna outcome, should . . . lead us to premature commitment of our strongest bargaining counter, ABM." Once we had traded that away, the Soviets would have no reason for continuing the negotiations or agreeing to offensive limitations. Aware that the "future of SALT might be at stake," Smith returned to his hotel "hoping" that he "was right."[54] Right or wrong, Smith's views were seconded in Washington by Henry Kissinger, who thought the "Soviets wanted to stop the only strategic program we were actually building while they rejected all limitations on *offensive* missiles, which were our own principal concern."[55] President Nixon agreed and the Soviet proposal was rejected.

That could have spelled the end of SALT. The Senate came within an ace of killing Safeguard and probably would have done so had it not been for the last-second intervention of Gerard Smith. An avowed enemy of Safeguard, Smith nevertheless privately urged key senators, including Thomas McIntyre and James Pearson, to support continued funding for the program. Without the ABM as a bargaining counter, the head of the ACDA warned, his delegation would have no leverage at all. A few days later, on August 12, 1970, the Senate held its final debate on the issue. The program survived by the narrow margin of 52 to 47. In Vienna, Smith was still congratulating himself when *The New York Times* printed a story crediting him with influencing the vote. Smith was nearly beside himself. This leak jeopardized his position as head of the American SALT delegation as well as prospects for a successful outcome to the talks. It was only good fortune that the Soviets chose to overlook the incident.

Though elated by the president's victory over Senate foes of the ABM, Henry Kissinger nevertheless believed that the administration had won only a skirmish, not the war. The issue was certain to come up again during the 1971 debate on the defense budget. With the administration's Vietnam policy under attack and no end to the war in sight, it was reasonable to assume that the next time the Senate had the opportunity to kill Safeguard, it might well succeed. SALT would then surely collapse for, to quote Kissinger, "the Soviets would lose any incentive to halt their offensive buildup."[56] The United States, which was at least five years away from deploying any new offensive weapons of its own, had nothing else to trade. As far as Kissinger was concerned, then, a great deal was riding on the outcome of the third session of SALT, which opened in Helsinki in November 1970.

These talks proved hopelessly unproductive. Uninterested in the Vienna option, the Soviets insisted instead that because of Washington's unwillingness to include its forward-based systems in the negotiations, the two sides should take a two-track approach. Semenov suggested negotiating a treaty limiting the deployment of ABMs on both sides while carrying on parallel talks dealing with limits on offensive weapons. But it was clear that he now sought two separate treaties and that his priority was to achieve a limit on "defensive" systems first. The American delegates were disappointed but they could hardly have been surprised. They sought a freeze on Soviet offensive systems but offered only an ABM agreement in return. Nevertheless, the American delegation stuck to its instructions.

It was at this point, with the negotiations deadlocked and the ABM time bomb ticking away in the Senate, that Henry Kissinger became actively involved in the negotiations. It seemed clear to him that something would have to be done to move the negotiations off dead center. An agreement that limited offensive weapons, even one less restrictive than the Vienna option, might still be advantageous to the United States. Also, Kissinger viewed an arms limitation agreement as an important component of détente. Despite his many denials, Kissinger viewed the intense bargaining over numbers and definitions that had characterized SALT as largely pointless, since both powers had secure second strike capabilities. Moreover, the United States was in a weak bargaining position. Why not then accept an agreement that reflected the realities? This seemed reasonable, especially since the Soviets could continue to add to their strength while the Nixon administration, hamstrung by an obstreperous Congress, could not.

In a December 1970 memo to the president, Kissinger warned that if the SALT deadlock was not soon broken, Congress might well destroy the administration's bargaining position by abandoning Safeguard. He wanted authority to conduct a "back channel" negotiation with Anatoly Dobrynin that he hoped would get the negotiations moving again. Nixon was well aware of the threat posed by the Senate. And, like Kissinger, he realized that although at that time the two superpowers deployed about the same number of missile launchers, if something was not done to freeze Soviet deployment, the Kremlin would soon possess many more launchers than the United States and in time thousands more MIRVed warheads. Nixon once observed that he was not going to become the first president to lose a war. Neither was he willing to be the first president to allow the Soviets to gain the advantage in the nuclear arms competition. He therefore authorized Kissinger to go ahead and at the same time gave him far more flexibility than the official SALT delegation had been accorded. A few days later, Kissinger held the first of many secret meetings with the Soviet ambassador.

Kissinger's initial proposal to Dobrynin went a long way toward breaking the SALT impasse. He accomplished this by the simple expedient of modifying the American negotiating position so that it very nearly comported with Soviet proposals presented earlier to the SALT delegation in Helsinki. Whereas earlier the United States had sought one treaty of indefinite duration for the control of offensive as well as defensive strategic weapons, Kissinger now sharply curtailed what the administration hoped to gain from the talks. Implicitly accepting the Soviet claim that the American position regarding its forward-based systems made it impossible to negotiate a long-term agreement limiting offensive weapons, he sought instead only a temporary freeze on their deployment. He further agreed to conduct two parallel negotiations, one relating to limits on ABM deployments, the other focused on offensive weaponry. He did insist, however, that "the terms of an ABM agreement and the freeze . . . would have to be negotiated simultaneously and completed at the same time."[57] During the discussion of the proposed temporary freeze on offensive weapons, Paul Nitze recalls that "Dobrynin asked Henry whether the freeze would apply to ICBM and SLBM launchers." Though from the beginning of the negotiations the U.S. SALT delegation had insisted that SLBMs, like land-based missiles, would have to be limited, Kissinger told Dobrynin that he didn't know. He then checked with the president, came back and said, "I don't care." This was good news to the Soviets, who were at the time laying down eight modern missile-firing submarines yearly. Nitze later explained that although Kissinger understood the difference between land-based and submarine-launched missiles, "he didn't realize the significance of the difference and the problem that a large Soviet advantage in SLBMs was going to cause the Joint Chiefs of Staff."[58] If that was in fact the case, Kissinger was soon made to realize that he had gone too far. He was forced to take up the SLBM issue once again in a later back channel negotiation.

Kissinger had offered the Soviets a plan of negotiations that in some ways went even further than they dared hope. Nevertheless, the Soviet foreign ministry, now becoming downright greedy, refused to grasp the opportunity. Raising the ante, the Kremlin now insisted that the ABM agreement be signed *before* the beginning of negotiations on offensive weapons limitations. Still clinging to their one frail bargaining counter, however, Kissinger and Nixon refused to give any more ground. For the next four months, Dobrynin and Kissinger haggled until at length on May 15 they arrived at an agreement. Five days later, on May 20, 1971, it was solemnized by an exchange of letters between Nixon and Brezhnev.

Kissinger, who thought the May 20 accord had paved the way for the swift consummation of the first SALT agreement, was mistaken. He interpreted the accord to mean that negotiations for two agreements, one to limit ABMs and the other for offensive strategic weapons, would go forward in parallel and that the two treaties would be signed simultaneously. But the accord itself was imprecisely drafted. Even Kissinger seems somewhat apologetic about this, conceding in his memoirs that its "sparse (and somewhat convoluted) words scarcely did justice to the labors of the previous six months and to its intrinsic significance."[59]

A Tass news release issued just after President Nixon announced the agreement to the Washington press corps indicated that the ABM treaty would be negotiated first, with negotiations on offensive arms limitations to follow. Kissinger, who understood the agreement to mean something quite different, suspected that the Soviets were attempting to accomplish via a news release what they could not achieve at the bargaining table. He was right. It took four more months of negotiations at the delegation level to resolve the issue. At length, in September 1971, just ten days before the scheduled end of a long and arduous summer negotiation, the Soviet SALT delegation agreed to Kissinger's interpretation of the agreement.

The national media, where Kissinger's reputation as a miracle worker was already firmly established, viewed the back channel negotiations as a major accomplishment. But the members of the U.S. SALT delegation were less impressed. From March until May of 1971, they had conducted negotiations in Vienna unaware of the Kissinger–Dobrynin connection. Their instructions, which were narrowly conceived and far more unyielding on basic issues than the terms offered by Kissinger, made progress in the official channel impossible. Understandably, when they learned that the real negotiations had been taken out of their hands while they unwittingly conducted a hollow performance, they became bitter and disillusioned. "One can only conclude," Ambassador Smith later wrote, "that the SALT delegates were duped into believing that they were to be involved in a serious negotiation that winter in Vienna."[60] Nor did Smith view the May 20 agreement as the great achievement that some others did. After five months of talks, Kissinger and Dobrynin agreed on a plan nearly identical to one originally presented by the Russian SALT delegation the previous December. If this was what the president really wanted, Smith acidly remarked, the SALT delegation could have handed that to him months earlier and without the duplicity.

President Nixon would later argue that it was necessary to carry on these talks outside official channels because of the secretive way in which the Soviet government works. It is more likely, however, that Smith was correct in alleging that the president acted without the knowledge of anyone but Kissinger because of "his distrust of officials responsible for SALT—the Secretary of Defense, the Secretary of State, the Chairman of the Joint Chiefs of Staff, the Director of the Arms Control Agency, and our associates." Nixon's fear of leaks and the lengths to which he was prepared to go to stop them are a matter of record, as are his hostile feelings toward professional diplomats and, above all, arms controllers. "I thought the whole episode a sad reflection on the state of affairs in the administration," Smith wrote. "Kissinger and the President went the Soviets one better. At least in the Soviet Union the whole Politburo was consulted, on several occasions. The bulk of the American national security leadership was never consulted. It was informed after the fact."[61]

Someone might conclude, from what Kissinger has written of the back channel negotiations as well as from some of Smith's comments, that the SALT delegation was suffering primarily from a bad case of hurt feelings. To an extent, this was true. Having been ignored and upstaged at a key point in the talks, the delegation's morale was undermined. Its members, from Smith on down, assumed ever after "that other contacts with the Soviets were taking place which we could not be trusted to know about." This, Smith added ruefully, "proved to be the case."[62]

Yet Smith and the other delegates were responding to more than Kissinger's bad manners. They believed that he had made some serious errors in his negotiations with Dobrynin—especially regarding submarine-launched missiles. Kissinger's willingness to exclude SLBMs from the offensive freeze flew in the face of all previous American policy. There could be no doubt that these were strategic weapons. And all elements of the national security establishment, from the Arms Control and Disarmament Agency to the Joint Chiefs of Staff, insisted that they be limited. When it became clear that a treaty that did not include any reference to SLBMs would not be viewed enthusiastically by the Joint Chiefs and might not pass muster in the Senate, Kissinger reversed his field, instructing the SALT delegation to negotiate limits for SLBMs. But that was easier said than done. The Soviets, insisting upon "a strict interpretation of the May 20 accord," wouldn't budge. It was, as Gerard Smith observed, a "case of locking the stable door after the horse was gone."[63]

Largely because of this contradiction, the official SALT negotiations dragged on inconclusively for months. By early 1972, Kissinger and Nixon were growing edgy. A summit conference was planned for Moscow in May, just prior to the presidential campaigning season. It was important to have the negotiations wrapped up prior to the summit. The president wanted to sign a SALT agreement there as the capstone to his many foreign policy achievements. In spite of the fact that Kissinger had promised Ambassador Smith that he would keep him current and not engage in further secret negotiations on his own, he once again took to the back channel. In April 1972, he journeyed secretly to Moscow to conclude the negotiations. Two major issues remained. The first was the question of a limit on SLBMs. The second had to do with the number of ABM sites each side would be allowed to deploy under the terms of the treaty.

Kissinger and Brezhnev wasted little time resolving these problems. An agreement allowing each side to defend its national capital as well as one offensive missile site with ABMs was not considered objectionable in Washington. But the national security adviser's handling of the sensitive SLBM question was another matter entirely. Under terms of the agreement initialed in Moscow, the United States and its allies would be allowed as many as 50 modern submarines with a total of 800 launchers. (At the time, the United States had 41 boats with 656 launchers. The 9 British and French boats brought the total number of launchers to 800.) The Soviets, on the other hand, would be allowed some 62 modern submarines with 950 launchers.

Gerard Smith was unimpressed by the tentative SLBM accord. A recent intelligence estimate indicated that without any agreement the Soviets would probably have deployed 62 submarines and about 950 launchers over the five years of the freeze. If that was the case, then Kissinger had agreed to a limit that was no limit at all. Smith suspected that Kissinger had simply accepted a Soviet proposal that in fact allowed them to build missile-firing submarines without any restraints over the period of the freeze. He asked to see the interpreter's notes for the Kissinger–Brezhnev discussions in Moscow. To his amazement he learned that there were none. This astonishing breach of diplomatic practice led Smith to ask Kissinger for the memoranda he had kept on the Brezhnev talks. Kissinger promised but never produced them. Smith, of course, guessed that Kissinger had simply accepted a Soviet proposal on SLBM limits for the sake of having some agreement. The truth, however, may be even more bizarre. According to John Newhouse, Kissinger told him that it was he who supplied the proposed limits to Brezhnev and not the other way around.

Whoever initiated the proposal, Kissinger realized that it was going to be difficult to sell the package back home. On returning to Washington, he therefore ordered a revised national intelligence estimate that would indicate that if left to their own devices the Soviets would probably produce many more submarines and launchers than the tentative SLBM agreement allowed. "My clear task," one former NSC staffer has recalled, "was to make sure the Soviet proposals came up in the middle range." Another of Kissinger's aides admits to feeling "awkward as hell" while rigging the estimates. "What it was was Henry having struck a deal with the Soviets and then manipulating the bureaucracy to accept the deal." At length, after one false start, the CIA produced an estimate that indicated the Soviets might, if left unrestrained, produce between eighty and ninety submarines carrying some 1,150 launchers during the period of the freeze. "The numbers were not a complete sellout," one NSC aide is quoted as saying, "but they were close to a worst-case analysis of what the Soviets could do."[64]

Deliberately revising national intelligence estimates to serve political ends is an old game in Washington. It would be a mistake to make too much out of it. In any event, there were reasons for allowing the Soviets a larger number of SLBMs than the United States could have. As Kissinger pointed out, the Soviets suffered from geographic disadvantages that made it impossible for them to keep more than 10 percent of their submarines on station at any given time. America, on the other hand, with easy access to both the Atlantic and Pacific and in control of overseas submarine bases, was able to keep fully half of its boats at sea at all times. Kissinger also argued that the Soviets had nothing to match America's forward-based systems, which therefore served as a counterbalancing asymmetry.

Kissinger had no trouble winning the president's approval for the SLBM limits he had negotiated. Nixon was not only largely ignorant of the issues, he was anxious to sign a SALT agreement at the upcoming summit. The various national security bureaucracies were harder to convince. Admiral Elmo Zumwalt described the SLBM numbers Kissinger had agreed to as "appalling," adding that he thought it "necessary to watch with a very keen eye any agreement being negotiated by Henry Kissinger."[65] Secretary of State William Rogers and Gerard Smith were equally disappointed. Smith had no quarrel with Kissinger's agreement from the standpoint of national security. What concerned him was the danger that SALT's domestic enemies might use the numerically unequal SLBM agreement to defeat the whole SALT package, including the important ABM agreement, and that all future SALT negotiations might also be jeopardized.

Smith, who thought the United States would be better off without an agreement on SLBMs rather than the one Kissinger had produced, expressed his concerns at a meeting of the verification panel, an interagency group established at the insistence of the military to determine whether or not SALT agreements could be verified. Instead of holding to the course charted by Kissinger during his private negotiations in Moscow, Smith suggested renewing the talks for the purpose of establishing "an aggregate missile launcher freeze including both ICBM and SLBM launchers and specifying no numbers."[66] Kissinger, who chaired verification panel meetings, was furious. Reopening the talks at that point would make it impossible to sign a SALT treaty at the upcoming summit conference and might lead to a total breakdown in the negotiations. Other members of the verification panel, including Admiral Thomas Moorer, the chairman of the Joint Chiefs, and Secretary of Defense Laird, stood with Kissinger. They were not enthusiastic about the Kissinger–Brezhnev accord on SLBMs, but they did believe that having some outside limit on the number of submarine-launched missiles that the Soviets might deploy was better than nothing at all. Moreover, the freeze was to last just five years. The navy did not wish to deploy any more Polaris-type submarines and the first Trident submarine was at least six years from putting to sea. The agreement, then, had no effect on American planning.

A few days later, Smith and Secretary of State Rogers again aired their objections, this time at a meeting of the National Security Council. An irate president ended all talk of further negotiations on the SLBM issue when he responded to certain of Smith's objections with an emphatic "Bullshit!" As the participants left the cabinet room, Kissinger angrily told Smith that he found it "unbelievable" that after he had negotiated a SALT agreement Smith and Rogers should be attempting to block it.[67] Clearly both Kissinger and the president were extremely anxious for a successful summit meeting to include as its high point the signing of SALT I. In those last frenzied days before the president's party journeyed to Moscow, they were unwilling to allow anything to stand in the way.

With the date for the summit meeting already set, the two SALT delegations, meeting again in Helsinki, set frantically to work hoping to conclude the inevitable last-minute details of the long negotiation before the president's plane set down in Moscow. But a number of questions remained unresolved when President Nixon and his entourage arrived. From the beginning of his presidency, Richard Nixon had been obsessed with the importance of monopolizing the credit for the achievements of his administration. He was determined that this summit was to be his supreme triumph—his alone. He would share centerstage with no one—most especially the hard-working members of the SALT delegation. He therefore refused to bring the delegates to Moscow to finish their work, insisting instead on stumbling through the final highly technical details of the negotiations himself, aided only by Kissinger and others in his party who had some understanding of the issues. It was, an embittered Ambassador Smith thought, "a case of negotiations being too important to be left to the negotiators."[68]

Even after the last details of the treaty had been arranged, Nixon tried to limit the visibility of the SALT delegates at the signing ceremony. A cable from Moscow to Helsinki informed Smith that only he and one other delegate would be allowed to attend the formal signing. Infuriated, Smith telephoned Alexander Haig in Moscow and informed him in the clear, for the benefit of all Soviet eavesdroppers, that it would be up to the president to decide which of the agencies involved in the negotiations, state, defense, or the Joint Chiefs, he wanted to offend. Back came the reply. Ambassador Parsons, the State Department delegate, was to be left out. Smith thought it an act of "extreme heartlessness" on Nixon's part. Parsons had devoted two years of his life to the negotiations, only to be denied the privilege of being in at the conclusion. It was a lesson in how petty political leaders can sometimes be. Another lesson swiftly followed. Those delegates who were allowed to attend the Moscow summit were specifically instructed not to bring their wives.

The package of agreements known as SALT I was signed amidst great fanfare in Moscow on May 26, 1972. Later, President Nixon would claim that they prevented a major escalation in the arms race. Though Nixon overstated the case, it is nonetheless true that SALT I was a solid accomplishment. It included a number of important minor agreements including one to improve hot-line communications and another dealing with accident control. Both sides agreed to allow the use of national technical means (spy satellites and electronic eavesdropping devices) in gathering intelligence to verify treaty compliance, and a Soviet–American standing consultative commission was established "to clarify ambiguities and differences in treaty interpretation" as they developed.

The ABM treaty was the most important element in SALT I. The superpowers in effect agreed not to duplicate in the area of defensive weaponry the costly and futile competition that has characterized the arms race in offensive weapons. A total ban on ABM development would have been more significant. Nevertheless, the ABM treaty stands as a solid accomplishment. The five-year freeze on the deployment of new offensive weapons was useful but of far less significance. It was in effect a pause intended to provide the two sides with time for further negotiations that might produce truly substantive results. Since the United States had not intended to deploy any new weapons during the period of the freeze, it had everything to gain and nothing to lose.

These positive accomplishments of Salt I should not obscure the fact that the agreements left open some enormous loopholes that allowed the arms race to escalate sharply during the period of the five-year freeze. Most significantly, both sides agreed to allow qualitative improvements in their existing forces. As a result, the American missile force was so rapidly MIRVed that, whereas in 1967, 1,710 warheads were aimed at Soviet and Warsaw Pact targets, eight years later, with the same number of launchers the United States could fire upwards of 7,000 warheads. Similar developments were taking place in the Soviet Union. Additionally, as newer and more accurate guidance systems replaced older ones, each side developed what seemed to the other an increasing counterforce capability. Finally, SALT I was silent on the subject of cruise missiles. These small, extremely accurate weapons brought a frightening new dimension to the arms race. Once they were developed and deployed, there would be no way for either superpower to know exactly how many its adversary possessed because there was no method of accurately verifying the number or deployment of these easily concealed weapons. Obviously, much remained to be done if the arms race was actually to be brought under control.

12

"No Nukes"

RESISTANCE TO NUCLEAR POWER

THE PARTIAL TEST BAN TREATY and the limited success of SALT helped to allay public fears of military nuclear power somewhat. Just at the time those fears partially subsided, however, the American people began to voice concern over problems plaguing civilian nuclear power plants. Resistance to nuclear power grew out of the environmentalist movement of the late 1960s, pitting an ever more sophisticated antinuclear coalition against an increasingly embattled AEC and nuclear power industry. Antinuclear activists and the nuclear establishment fought to a stand-off on safety issues, but the hopeless economics of nuclear power brought the industry to its knees by 1980.

When environmentalists came to articulate their reasons for seeking to halt the growth of nuclear power, they found the safety issue ready-made and waiting to be exploited. From its very beginnings, the nuclear power industry suffered from mishaps that ranged from the minor but recurrent "incidents" of the sort detailed in the Union of Concerned Scientists' compilation, *The Nugget File,* to major accidents that killed people and threatened entire cities. By an irony, though, the world's first known reactor accident befell a nation that had renounced the military uses of nuclear energy for itself, and in a research reactor dedicated principally to nonmilitary programs. On December 12, 1952, at the Canadian Chalk River experimental reactor that was known as the NRX, a sequence of operator errors resulted in control rods being extracted from the reactor. This produced first a meltdown of some of the uranium fuel and then a hydrogen explosion that destroyed the core and dumped highly radioactive water into the reactor's substructure. The accident gave reactor operators their first experience with cleanup and decontamination procedures. The Canadians carried it off efficiently, restoring NRX to operation in fourteen months.

The first American meltdown followed not long after. On November 29, 1955, EBR-1, the little experimental reactor that had produced the nation's first electricity in a demonstration four years earlier, was being used to study the consequences of a rise in heat. At the end of the experiment, an operator dropped slow control rods, rather than the instantaneous "scram" rods, and the temperature in the core soared, melting fuel and cladding. Officials at the Idaho National Reactor Testing Station, the home of the EBR-1, failed to notify AEC chairman Lewis Strauss, and undertook cleanup on their own authority. The EBR-1 meltdown came at a most inconvenient time for the nascent nuclear power industry. As its initials indicate, EBR-1 was a breeder, which meant that it had a core of highly fissile material. Unlike conventional light water reactors, EBR-1 was therefore theoretically liable to explode in a serious accident. This unwelcome possibility haunted the consortium known as the Power Reactor Development Corporation.

PRDC included pillars of the American nuclear establishment: Westinghouse, Babcock & Wilcox, Combustion Engineering, Detroit Edison, and Philadelphia Electric. It was political force to be reckoned with, all the more so because it was headed by the dynamic Walker Cisler, chairman of Detroit Edison and the moving force behind the coalition. Cisler was excited about the prospects of a dual-purpose breeder reactor that would produce electricity for Detroit and plutonium for the AEC. He therefore proposed a 60 MWe fast breeder on the shores of Lake Erie south of Detroit. This project, America's first commercial breeder, Fermi-1, was in the planning stages at the time of the EBR-1 meltdown. Consequently, when a reporter asked Strauss about the EBR-1 meltdown and Strauss disclosed that he knew nothing about it, the AEC found itself with another public relations problem on its hands. This marked the beginning of Fermi-1's troubles.

PRDC filed an application with the AEC for a construction permit, the first step at that time in the process of licensing reactors, and the Commission referred it in due course to its Advisory Committee on Reactor Safeguards. On June 6, 1956, the ACRS gave the AEC a negative review of the request, stating that "there is insufficient information at this time to give assurance that the PRDC reactor can be operated at this site without public hazard."[1] It is not clear whether the ACRS had the EBR-1 meltdown in mind, but the committee up till then had insisted on remote siting for reactors, a policy originally adopted at the insistence of the ACRS's first chairman, Edward Teller. Despite this negative recommendation, on June 28 Strauss announced that he would attend groundbreaking ceremonies for Fermi-1 in August. The AEC issued a provisional construction permit for the Detroit breeder on August 3.

At this point, much to the discomfiture of the AEC, the issue suddenly became politicized, as well as entangled in the still-unresolved feud between the AEC and the JCAE. Michigan Governor G. Mennen Williams requested the AEC to assure the people of his state that Fermi-1 would be safe, and the AEC declined to do so, saying that it would be "inappropriate." Considering that a serious breeder accident at the Fermi-1 site could contaminate Detroit, Toledo, Cleveland, much of Lake Erie, and the Canadian cities of Windsor and Hamilton, the AEC's stonewalling was impolitic, to say the least. When JCAE chairman Clinton Anderson and JCAE member Chet Holifield learned of the AEC's posture, they reacted angrily, criticizing the AEC in public for its haste in granting the provisional permit. Anderson condemned the fact that AEC hearings at that time made no provision for public participation or even attendance. AEC regulatory and rule-making hearings were in effect secret sessions—"star chamber" proceedings, Anderson called them—with the first public notice of AEC actions coming when the AEC published its decision in the *Federal Register*. Anderson, wise in the ways of bureaucracy, warned that "from a practical standpoint, AEC might feel obligated to go through with a bad deal with respect to public safety because they will have permitted the expenditure of huge sums under the construction permit. It is my belief that decisions on safety should be made without any examination of dollars involved, but only from the standpoint of human lives."[2]

Anderson urged Walter Reuther, president of the United Auto Workers union, to begin legal proceedings to halt construction of Fermi-1, and Reuther delegated the assignment to his assistant in charge of energy matters, Leo Goodman, who was to play a prominent role in antinuclear activism throughout the next decade. These actions forced the AEC to designate a three-member Atomic Safety and Licensing Board to hold public hearings on the plant's safety. Goodman, the UAW, and two other unions participated in the hearings as "intervenors." This action set a precedent of the utmost importance: thenceforth, members of the public having neither scientific expertise nor any direct involvement with the proposed reactor had a right to intervene in licensing hearings, breaking through the closed circle of the nuclear establishment and upsetting the incestuous relationship between regulators and regulated.

The ASLB hearings dragged on for eleven months. During this period, at the request of the JCAE, a group of scientists, most of them associated with the Brookhaven National Lab, prepared an analysis of the consequences that might follow a major reactor accident. This report, published in March 1957 and commonly known as WASH-740, emphasized the supposedly remote possibility of a serious accident, but estimated that if one did occur, it would cause 3,400 deaths, 43,000 injures, and $7 billion in property damage. WASH-740 established the basic equation of reactor accidents—low probability: catastrophic consequences. The AEC published WASH-740, expecting that it would reassure the public on the low-probability point, but people in the Detroit area stressed the other side of the equation. They would have been even more appalled by a report commissioned by the PRDC that was prepared by the University of Michigan–Ann Arbor's Engineering Research Institute. The Michigan study posited an even worse worst-case scenario for a breeder accident, and projected that Detroit area residents would suffer 133,000 prompt fatalities, 181,000 likely or possible long-term fatalities, and 245,-000 massive somatic and genetic injuries, the last group being dosed with between 25 and 150 roentgens.[3]

It is instructive to contrast the uses made of worst-case scenarios by civilian and military nuclear planners. Pentagon officials have for twenty-five years justified the continued expansion of nuclear weaponry by envisioning a worst-case scenario in which the Soviets will outstrip the United States, developing a true nuclear superiority. The air force did this in 1956 during the flap over the bomber gap and again later during the long drawn out debate over the missile gap. A recent worst-case scenario involves the so-called "window of vulnerability." Because the Soviets may at some indeterminate date in the future be capable of launching a preemptive first strike against American land-based missiles, so the argument goes, we must develop new and more powerful nuclear forces ourselves. On the civilian side, worst-case scenarios are put to an entirely different use. Civilian scenarios warn of catastrophe from the dangers posed by nuclear development. Because of this they are ignored, as in the case of the PRDC-commissioned University of Michigan study. When worst-case studies encourage nuclear expansion they will be used; and when they do not, they will be dismissed.

Predictably, neither the ASLB nor its parent, the AEC, were deterred by WASH-740 or the Michigan study. In 1959, the AEC issued a construction permit for Fermi-1. The UAW appealed to the U. S. Court of Appeals for the District of Columbia circuit, and the court halted construction. PRDC appealed to the U.S. Supreme Court, which in 1961 reversed the court of appeals in a 7-to-2 decision upholding the validity of the licensing procedure then followed by the AEC, which in effect permitted issuance of a construction permit before safety questions were resolved. This case, *Power Reactor Development Corporation* v. *International Union of Electrical Workers,* marked the U.S. Supreme Court's first major involvement in nuclear power controversies. Its result, favoring nuclear development and upholding the pronuclear bias of federal procedures, set the tone for subsequent Supreme Court attitudes toward nuclear power. But this was not to be the last time that Fermi-1 was to make headlines.

As if to mock the AEC's easy assurances that reactor accidents were unlikely, one of Great Britain's plutonium production reactors at Windscale suffered a fuel fire on October 8, 1957, and spewed radioactive contaminants into its local environment. Again, operator error caused core temperatures to rise and ignite a fuel rod. Because the problem was not discovered for forty-two hours, eventually a total of eleven tons of uranium fuel were set ablaze. Firemen squelched the blaze twenty-four hours later, but not before radioactive materials belched out the plant's stack. Iodine-131, already implicated as a sinister component of fallout from weapons testing, had fallen on grass near the plant and passed into local milk supplies via grazing dairy herds. British authorities dumped half a million gallons of the hot milk into local rivers, producing a sour-milk stench that lingered for weeks. The total radioactive inventory going through the stacks was estimated at approximately a tenth of that released by the Hiroshima bomb. It drifted in a cloud that deposited fallout in Denmark, Belgium, the Netherlands, France, and Germany.[4] Windscale was an unusual reactor design—uranium fuel elements encased in graphite, and cooled by air—and more advanced designs obviated the type of accident that occurred in 1957. The British government later shut down the damaged reactor as well as its twin and then entombed them.

Apart from the Chelyabinsk disaster in the Soviet Union, the first reactor accident resulting in immediate fatalities occurred at the National Reactor Testing Station in Idaho. A small (3 MWe) prototype military reactor was down, and on January 3, 1961, three young navy men, Richard Legg, Richard McKinley, and John Byrnes, were reassembling it by manually lifting and reengaging control rods. AEC investigators could only speculate as to what happened. Perhaps a rod became jammed; perhaps the sailors were just horsing around; some AEC investigators have even speculated that the accident was a deliberate suicide-murder, committed by one of the men who was distraught because he thought his wife was having an affair with another operator.[5] Whatever the cause, someone jerked a rod up too far—eighteen inches rather than four. The little reactor instantly went supercritical and caused a steam explosion. All three men were killed immediately. A control rod speared McKinley through his groin to the roof of the containment structure. The aftermath was more gruesome: only the parts of the men's bodies that had been covered by clothing could be handled, and then only after twenty days had elapsed. The corpses were buried in lead-lined coffins sealed in lead-lined burial vaults, but their exposed heads and hands had to be severed before burial and disposed of with high-level radioactive waste.[6] No other reactor accident in the United States has produced immediate fatalities, but the April 1963 sinking of the U.S.S. *Thresher,* a nuclear submarine, off Cape Cod killed all 129 men aboard. The cause of the disaster remains unknown; it may have been an accident in the vessel's propulsion reactor.

These accidents and the beginnings of public controversy disturbed AEC officials. Consequently in 1964, the Commission ordered a review and update of WASH-740, the 1957 accident study that attempted to quantify the consequences of a serious reactor mishap, in hopes of coming up with more reassuring projections. To its dismay, the AEC found that the 1964 conclusions turned out to be far more pessimistic. Where the 1957 study estimated 3,400 deaths, the 1964 update predicted 45,000. Clifford Beck, the AEC's assistant director of regulation, summed up the 1964 conclusions for the commission: "Damages would result possibly 10 times as large as those calculated in the previous study." The affected area "would be the size of the state of Pennsylvania." Coming as it did after several accidents, this report was, to say the least, disheartening to the AEC and its clients. The AEC staffers preparing the report met twice with a group from the Atomic Industrial Forum, the nuclear industry's chief lobbying and propaganda arm. The AIF recommended that the AEC not publish the revisions, but rather extend the study for "another year or two" and in the meantime report cursorily to the JCAE "that if major accidents are assumed to occur without regard to the improbability of such events, very large damages, of course, would be calculated to happen." The AEC squelched the 1964 revision for seven years. In the meantime, AEC chairman Glenn Seaborg was free to state, as he did in a 1971 speech, that reactor "problems will only cause a temporary shutdown of the plant for the necessary repairs and corrective action and will not harm the public."[7]

In 1973, David D. Comey, a nuclear critic, forced the AEC to disgorge its 1964 revisions by threatening to sue under the Freedom of Information Act. Even then, the Commission denied that a final study had been completed in 1964 and released only selected portions of what it called a "draft." It simultaneously issued a press release deriding the "grossly unrealistic assumptions" of the original 1957 study. Through the seven years of the cover-up, AEC officials repeatedly stressed that the discouraging impact of the 1964 report was not the magnitude of the catastrophe, the lives lost, the people coming down with cancer, but instead the public relations consequences. Howard Hembree, an AEC official, stated that the estimated "consequences could be projected downward to planned reactors, such as Nine-Mile Point and Oyster Creek, and that such projections could affect their building and site locations." Another AEC staffer worried about the link between the Siamese twins of military and civilian nuclear power. The results of an accident conjured up in the 1964 study "are more severe than those equivalent to a good-sized weapon and the correlation can readily be made by experts."

AEC officials were especially touchy about public relations problems at this time because the nuclear power industry was poised to take a great quantitative leap. Early reactors had all been small by today's standards, in the 100 to 500 MWe range. But in the mid-1960s, orders were pouring in for mammoth stations that trebled previous sizes to come in at 1,000 MWe range, such as Browns Ferry I and II, ordered by TVA for northern Alabama, or Zion I and II north of Chicago. The industry was growing, as the AEC later admitted, "from Kittyhawk to the Boeing 747 in two decades."[8] Such scaling-up posed uncertainties, and the AEC did not want the industry subjected to public skepticism at this vulnerable moment. Even before the 1964 study was begun, Allan Lough, a member of the study's steering committee, warned Clifford Beck that

> Great care should be exercised in any revision to avoid establishing and/or reinforcing the popular notion that reactors are unsafe.

Though this is a public-information or promotional problem that the A.E.C. now faces with less than desirable success, I feel that by calculating the consequences of hypothetical accidents the A.E.C. should not place itself in the position of making the location of reactors near urban areas nearly indefensible.[9]

Lough's viewpoint prevailed, obliterating the caution that had hitherto led the AEC to require that even tiny experimental or research reactors be sited remotely in the Idaho desert. Today, seven large reactors ring New York City, Philadelphia is surrounded by five, and five sit in the environs of Chicago.

The passage of time did not make the estimates of nuclear catastrophe any more palatable to the nuclear establishment. A 1975 Nuclear Regulatory Commission update assumed 3,300 prompt fatalities and $14 billion in property damage, but a study only recently completed by Sandia National Labs concluded that a worst-case accident at Salem I or II in New Jersey might kill more than 100,000 people, and a worst-case accident at one of the Indian Point plants on the Hudson River above New York City could cause $300 billion in property damage.[10] In the face of these projections, Stalin's aphorism comes to mind: A single death is a tragedy, a million deaths is a statistic.

The AEC had good reason to fear public reaction, for in 1966 an accident occurred that vindicated the pessimistic views of nuclear critics. Having at last overcome all political and legal hurdles, the Fermi-1 fast breeder was built on the shores of Lake Erie at Lagoona Beach, a town midway between Detroit and Toledo (twenty-five miles from each). It went critical in August 1963, but a series of problems prevented it from being raised to full power output until 1966. On October 5, Fermi-1's operators cautiously raised it toward full power. But at low power levels (20 and 34 MWt), controls indicated incomprehensible abnormalities occurring in the core. Radiation alarms went off, and the bewildered operators scrammed the reactor. This shut down the reaction, but it left the operators in an extremely delicate situation. They had no idea what was going on in the core, a small cylinder about thirty inches high by thirty inches in diameter. They could not peer in, even by remote means, because the coolant was sodium, an opaque molten metal. Walter Patterson dramatically describes the technical dimensions of the problem they faced in those nerve-wracking hours: the reactor's slender fuel pins,

14,700 of them, made of 28 per cent enriched uranium clad in stainless steel, had to be aligned to meticulous tolerances, no more than a millimetre or so apart. Furthermore this configuration had to be maintained at a temperature of over 400°C, while submerged in an upflowing torrent of liquid sodium passing through the minuscule channels between the pins. Any disturbance of the Fermi core geometry could impede the flow of coolant, leading to unbalanced thermal expansions and more distortion.

The core geometry had another crucial characteristic, common to fast breeders. Unlike a thermal reactor, whose fuel is usually arranged in an optimum geometry to maximize reactivity, a fast reactor has its fuel in a configuration which may be considerably short of the maximum theoretical reactivity it can exhibit. If the Fermi core had been distorted and melted, it might thereafter be susceptible to local surges of reactivity, intense hot spots, which could lead in turn to chemical reactions between fuel, cladding and coolant, and even to violent chemical explosions. Such chemical explosions, rebounding in a collapsing mass of highly enriched fissile fuel, might even cause a full-fledged nuclear explosion.

No one at the Fermi plant had any very persuasive idea of what to do. Any attempt to enter the reactor with the usual remote handling gear might disturb the precarious equilibrium in the ruptured core.[11]

As might be expected, the nuclear industry and its critics sharply disagree on what ensued. John G. Fuller, a prize-winning science writer who covered the Fermi "meltdown"—the term preferred by nuclear critics—in his detailed narrative *We Almost Lost Detroit* states that an evacuation alert went out to the local sheriff's office and that preliminary steps were under way to attempt an evacuation of Detroit. But no record of such orders exists, fueling the suspicion that evidence of the accident's seriousness was destroyed in the aftermath. Quoting an unnamed area nuclear engineer, Fuller evaluates the consequences succinctly in the title of his book.

The American Nuclear Society, by contrast, takes a much more benign view. It scoffs at what it considers rumors of evacuation orders, and dismisses the "incident"—its preferred term—on October 5 as demonstrating "that thoughtful preparation for reasonable malfunctions coupled with a design philosophy that incorporates redundancy and defense-in-depth provides a safeguards envelope that will adequately respond to the real accident and provide ample margin between actual consequences and public harm even though reactor accidents seldom occur."[12] The occurrence was simply a troublesome malfunction that posed no danger to anyone in the plant, much less to Detroit area residents off-site, though it did have serious financial and political repercussions.

Fermi-1 was down four years for repairs. Its restart produced only an anemic performance, and in 1972, the PRDC, Fermi-1's parent organization, decided to dismantle the core and decommission the reactor. This decision was made principally because the AEC, under its then chairman James Schlesinger, declined to provide direct cash subsidies to the crippled reactor of the magnitude that Chairman Cisler of Detroit Edison was demanding. The dead reactor still stands today on the shores of Lake Erie, under perpetual guard, empty and foreboding. America's first effort at running a full-scale breeder had failed.

The next near miss came at a military plant: the Rocky Flats, Colorado, factory that fabricated plutonium triggers for nuclear warheads and, as an adjunct to this manufacturing operation, recycled plutonium. Plutonium, fiendishly dangerous in so many other ways, has yet another sinister physical characteristic: it is pyrophoric, that is, it can spontaneously ignite. Hence industrial fires pose extraordinary dangers in plutonium facilities. Dow Chemical ran Rocky Flats as a contractor to the AEC from 1953 to 1975. During that period, Dow monitored for radiation, but paid no particular attention to the escape of plutonium particles as such, except as they might show up in radiation checks at the plant site. Numerous small fires occurred in the plant, and plutonium-bearing industrial oil leaked off-site, but the plant's most dangerous eruption occurred in the fire of May 11, 1969. This became one of the costliest industrial fires in American history, with a total cost possibly approaching $70 million—$50 million for damage to the plant and $20 million for plutonium damaged by the fire. The fire did not breach the roof of the plant; if it had, the residents of Denver and its environs would have received lethal doses of airborne plutonium particles. As it was, the AEC claimed that 99.97 percent of the plutonium particles had been contained. However, a group of scientists in the area organized themselves as the Colorado Committee for Environmental Information and set about learning more about the fire. While they did not reject the AEC's general contention that the plutonium had been contained, the group stressed the warning given by Air Force General Edward B. Giller, head of the AEC's Division of Military Applications, in Senate hearings in 1970, who said that if the fire had burned through the roof—it almost had —"then hundreds of square miles could be involved in radiation exposure and involve cleanup at an astronomical cost as well as creating a very intense reaction by the general public."[13] But like the plutonium, public reaction was contained.

As if these troublesome accidents did not give it enough cause for concern, the AEC also had to fend off challenges from citizens' groups objecting to the siting of particular reactors. After the licensing controversy at Fermi-1, the next major siting confrontation between nuclear activists and a utility occurred at the proposed Bodega Head reactor fifty miles north of San Francisco. In 1958, Pacific Gas & Electric, the nation's largest privately owned utility, began buying up land around Bodega Bay, but it remained secretive about its plans for the site until 1961, when it announced that it intended to locate a reactor there.[14] Opposition immediately crystallized on the aesthetics issue: Bodega Bay is a spot of great natural coastal beauty, too rare to be sacrificed as an industrial site. Then a second issue arose: the proposed site was only 1,000 feet from the San Andreas fault, the world's most active earthquake fault zone. This in itself was a violation of AEC siting regulations. While PG&E was excavating, two members of a U.S. Geological Survey team discovered that an auxiliary fault ran directly through the site itself. Finally in 1964, PG&E threw in the towel, canceling the Bodega reactor.

The controversy was replicated at another site near the San

Andreas fault, Diablo Canyon, near San Luis Obispo, two hundred miles north of Los Angeles. Thanks to clever tactics, PG&E won a short term victory, at least. It proposed reactors at both Nipomo Dunes and Diablo Canyon, and met with the Sierra Club board of directors and other conservation organizations. After some bargaining, PG&E agreed to drop the Nipomo site and a majority of the Sierra Club directors acquiesced in the Diablo Canyon project, which PG&E eventually built. But protests continued to bedevil the choice, and in 1981, massive peaceful resistance at the Diablo Canyon site brought national attention to PG&E and its controversial reactors. Shortly afterward, the Nuclear Regulatory Commission discovered serious construction defects in the reactor itself and denied an operating permit. At the time of this writing, it is uncertain whether Diablo Canyon will ever go on stream.

The Bodega–Diablo controversy had another far-reaching effect. A minority of the Sierra Club directors refused to go along with the original compromise and broke away from the organization. Led by David Brower, they formed Friends of the Earth, an influential organizational sibling that adopted a stance of resistance to all forms of commercial nuclear power. Hard feelings between the breakaway FOE group and the parent Sierra Club were overcome by the late 1970s, and both organizations provided weighty opposition to nuclear projects throughout the country. FOE's national publication, *Not Man Apart,* became one of the nation's most influential environmentalist publications, and its section "The Nuclear Blowdown" provides a monthly survey of the on-going struggle against nuclear power that began on the granite spit at Bodega Head.

On the other side of the continent, another siting controversy erupted in 1962 when New York City's principal utility, Consolidated Edison, announced plans for a 700 MWe reactor in the borough of Queens, on the East River just across from 72nd Street in Manhattan. Fierce opposition from the city council and from former AEC chairman David Lilienthal aborted the project in its earliest stage.

As the 1960s wore on, public challenges to nuclear power gravitated toward administrative hearings and then to courts. In

1836, Alexis de Tocqueville wrote that "scarcely any question arises in the United States which does not become, sooner or later, a subject of judicial debate."[15] Americans are a legalistic and litigious people, accustomed to carrying on their policy debates around criteria of legality, constitutionality, and legitimacy. Nuclear power was no exception to this national trait. The administrative and judicial struggles over nuclear power began with a state's-rights controversy involving the Northern States Power Company's Monticello reactor in Minnesota. Monticello is a medium-sized (545 MWe) reactor located on the Mississippi River approximately forty miles northwest of the Twin Cities. The Minnesota Pollution Control Agency attempted to set standards for its discharge of radioactive waters into the Mississippi. The state sought to impose the ceiling on discharges recommended by the reactor's vendor, General Electric, which were fifty times more stringent than AEC national standards. The utility resisted, insisting that such discharge standards were the exclusive responsibility of the federal government—which meant the AEC.

This controversy was resolved by the Eighth Circuit Court of Appeals in an important precedent, *Northern States Power Co.* v. *Minnesota* (1971).[16] The court sided with the utility, holding that on the question of radioactive waste discharges, federal authority had preempted the states. "Preemption" is a well-established constitutional doctrine, providing one of several means of adjusting the balance of national and state powers within the American system. It is grounded on the need for national supremacy and uniformity in the regulation of interstate commerce. *Northern States* extended this familiar concept to the problems of regulating nuclear power. Nuclear advocates, especially those in the legal community, hopefully concluded that the *Northern States Power* case had extended the preemption doctrine to cover all aspects of nuclear power, thus voiding all state efforts to control reactors and the nuclear fuel cycle. To this extent, *Northern States Power* provided legal succor to utilities and others in the nuclear establishment who resist citizen initiatives.

But industry hopes that *Northern States* presaged blanket preemption were dashed by an April 1983 decision of the U.S.

Supreme Court, which upheld the constitutionality of a California statute that conditioned construction of nuclear reactors on a certification by a state commission that adequate means exist for the "permanent and terminal disposal" of high-level radioactive waste. The majority upheld the statute because of the economic motivation for the requirement, though in dictum it stated that preemption covered all safety issues.[17]

Other federal courts did not treat the AEC kindly. In the famous *Calvert Cliffs* litigation, Judge J. Skelly Wright of the U.S. Court of Appeals, District of Columbia Circuit, chastised the AEC for its arrogant disregard of the recently enacted National Environmental Policy Act (NEPA). When Congress passed NEPA in 1969, it required that federal agencies prepare an environmental impact statement for actions that will have an adverse impact on the environment. Baltimore Gas & Electric proposed to build two 850 MWe reactors on Chesapeake Bay. Intervenors, the Calvert Cliffs Committee, demanded the AEC consider problems of nonradioactive thermal pollution of the waters of the bay. The AEC refused, on the altogether arbitrary grounds that it had authority to exclude consideration of nonradioactive problems for plants that applied for construction licenses before March 4, 1971. Throughout, the AEC adopted a reluctant, grudging, and hostile posture toward NEPA, issuing rules that required as narrow a compliance as possible with its provisions.

Skelly Wright was no stranger to controversy. After the 1954 *Brown* v. *Board of Education* decision outlawing legally mandated racial segregation in public schools, Wright, as a judge of the U.S. District Court for the eastern district of Louisiana, enforced racial integration and made a national reputation for himself as a fearless activist judge. These personal qualities shone through his *Calvert Cliffs* opinion. Rarely has a federal judge so harshly criticized a federal agency. Declaring that the AEC rules would "subvert" NEPA, Wright stated that "the Commission's crabbed interpretation of NEPA makes a mockery of the Act." In the introductory section of his opinion, Wright broadly construed the environmental protection emphases of NEPA to force federal agencies to comply to the letter with its provisions mandating environmental protection.[18] Lawyers and laypeople interpreted

Calvert Cliffs as a sharp rebuke to the agency. Observers believed that AEC chairman Seaborg intended to have the decision appealed to the U.S. Supreme Court if it was adverse to the agency, but he resigned just before Wright handed down his opinion and was replaced by James Schlesinger, a man of more compliant temperament, who ordered the Commission to revise its rules to embody the full compliance with NEPA that Wright had ordered.

In the late sixties and early seventies, the AEC was stymied by criticism. Scientists inside the agency and out exposed its policies as unfounded. Lay critics began to scrutinize its record of errors and lies. Activists thwarted some of its projects. The AEC itself was abolished in 1974, but nuclear critics only grew more vociferous in their opposition to what they were coming to call the "plutonium economy."

The AEC throughout the 1960s was accustomed to dismissing its few critics as uninformed cranks. It came as a shock, then, when physicists, nuclear chemists, and eventually even nuclear engineers offered a scientific critique of AEC actions. Caught unprepared and in a political climate inhospitable to red-baiting, AEC supporters could only fume impotently. The earliest public scientific criticisms of agency policy came from a physicist at the University of Pittsburgh, Ernest Sternglass, who by 1969 reached a shocking conclusion: probably 400,000 infants had died up to that time because of medical problems caused by fallout—chiefly lowered resistance to disease and reductions in birth weight. Sternglass bearded the nuclear lion in its den, announcing these findings at an AEC symposium held at the production reactor site in Hanford, Washington, one of the shrines of nuclear power in America. Worse yet, Sternglass carried these findings to the general public in two articles published in the *Bulletin of Atomic Scientists* that year, and another reaching a broader public in *Esquire*, titled "The Death of All Children."[19] Even in an era conditioned to megadeaths, the thought of hundreds of thousands of babies dying could not go unchallenged, and the AEC assigned one of its staffers, the biologist Arthur Tamplin, to refute Sternglass.

Tamplin did so in October 1969, arguing that Sternglass's estimate was at least 100 times too high. From an AEC point of view, though, that was little comfort, for it meant that by Tamplin's estimates, 4,000 infants had died from fallout. AEC dogma of the era proclaimed that no one died from fallout, so the Commission pressured Tamplin to recant. He refused, and in his refusal he was backed by John Gofman, the physician and nuclear chemist who was associate director of the AEC's Lawrence Livermore lab where Tamplin worked. The AEC now found itself facing a fearsome pair of opponents. For six years, Gofman had been working on health problems of nonmilitary nuclear applications at the behest of AEC chairman James Schlesinger. His earlier experience in 1963 with the committee reviewing the Knapp iodine-131 findings might have left him skeptical of the AEC's good faith in handling studies critical of its policies. But he labored on until 1969–70, when he joined Tamplin, Sternglass, and others in criticizing the supposedly safe levels of exposure to radiation, and promptly found himself an outcast of the nuclear community.

More criticism from within the nuclear community stopped the AEC in its tracks in a controversy involving nuclear waste. Because of their extremely high toxicity and their permanence, high-level radioactive wastes must be secured, effectively forever, from both human meddling and escape into the biosphere. The AEC at first, however, declined to regard the wastes problem this way. Instead, it viewed radioactive wastes as a valuable commodity, bearing recoverable amounts of uranium and plutonium. As for the irreducible residue left after these had been extracted in some recycling process, the AEC shrugged:

> A point is finally reached at which a decision must be made between the economics of further decontamination and the realities as to public health risks involved in release of these wastes to nature.

The AEC cautioned, though, that it would be prudent to follow "a conservative course of action in favor of protection of public health."[20]

Conservatism in practice meant virtually ignoring the problem until the number of civilian reactors coming on stream in the 1960s made some sort of solution to the waste problem urgent. Gone was the attitude that equated waste with valuable commodities, not to be resurrected until AEC chairman Dixie Lee Ray hawked the notion in the 1970s that Americans ought to view wastes as a "resource." Until then, the AEC tried to rid itself of them. In the late 1960s, the solution favored by the AEC was to reduce wastes to liquid form, pour the hot slop into canisters that would not disintegrate for a few years, and then dump them somewhere, out of sight, out of mind. Among the various options for long-term waste disposal, salt formations scored high. Nuclear spokesmen claim that they are permanent, inexpensive, and, best of all, isolated from the biosphere. Abandoned mines are often scouted as desirable candidate sites, and the German Federal Republic has actually begun to use one for this purpose at Asse. Proponents of salt formations claim that their very existence testifies to their immunity from water leaching, which is the most likely route by which radioactive wastes would find their way back into the environment. In putting forth its salt proposals, the AEC and its successors have always relied on a piece of simplistic reasoning: the very fact that the salt formation is there is proof that it is dry and stable for eons. If it were not, so the logic goes, water would have leached it away already. This ignores the fact that the salt may have already been penetrated by drilling, and that the ferocious heat given off by the waste might cause water already present in the salt to migrate to the waste containers, helping to corrode them. But the salt disposal method is relatively cheap, sites are plentiful, and the technology of drilling into salt is comparatively well along.

Consequently, the AEC enthusiastically pursued the hope of finding a salt repository through the sixties, and by the end of the decade concluded it had found one in a salt formation at Lyons, a town of some 5,000 souls near the geographic center of Kansas. The AEC apparently never remembered that the area around Lyons is the semi-fabulous Quivira, sought by the conquistador Coronado in the deluded belief that it was the land where gold, silver, and jewels were as plentiful as pebbles. Lyons turned out to be a Quivira for the AEC, though the modern conquistadores were after something a good deal more mundane: dry, remote salt.

The AEC was at this time under intense pressure to find a

permanent solution for the problems of high-level radioactive waste, and to do so quickly. The National Academy of Sciences condemned its plans to dispose of high-level wastes from Rocky Flats at the National Reactor Testing Station site near Idaho Falls, Idaho, and it had been embarrassed over revelations of leaking radioactivity in its Hanford, Washington, disposal trenches. Hence the AEC moved with unique speed to get the Lyons, Kansas, site in operation. Milton Shaw, head of the AEC's Division of Reactor Development and Technology, informed the JCAE that further research on the suitability of the Lyons site "will not be particularly productive. We need the project and are ready to proceed with it."[21] The residents of the area seemed quite happy to have the AEC locate its radioactive dump in their backyards, but the area's congressman, Joe Skubitz, Kansas governor Robert Docking, and the Kansas Geological Survey were dubious and worried. Geologists and nuclear engineers from Kansas and Missouri condemned the choice. The American Salt Company, proprietor of an abandoned mine in the salt formation, warned that it had injected water into the bores. The Kansas Geological Survey discovered oil and gas bore holes throughout the area as well, making the formation what they called a "leaky sieve." By fall of 1971, the AEC was ready to throw in the towel. It claimed that new information ("discovery" of the bore holes) made it necessary to consider alternatives to Lyons, and the whole problem was back to square one, where it remains today.

The Lyons fiasco demonstrated a pattern that has repeated itself subsequently. Nuclear proponents declare that a solution to the problem of wastes is either certain or imminent. Then in a flurry of enthusiasm, the AEC or the Department of Energy announces that it has discovered a site or a technique, or both, to implement the solution, and it rushes ahead with plans to make its solution a reality. Then scientist critics, some of them inside the nuclear establishment, point out fatal technical flaws in the scheme. Congress or the president recommends that the project be dropped, and nuclear proponents return to the beginning of the cycle, promising an imminent solution and declaring that the problems are only political, not technical. The search begins once again for a technical fix and/or a politically feasible site.

The assault from within the scientific community was paralleled by a sudden deluge of popular criticism in books and the periodical press. The AEC's public relations counterassault proved wholly inadequate to this new challenge. First came Sheldon Novick's *The Careless Atom* (1969), which, compared with what succeeded it, was a moderate, reasoned, even gentle critique. In the same year, Nuel Pharr Davis, a professor of English at the University of Illinois–Champaign, published *Lawrence and Oppenheimer*, a subtle, allusive, beautifully written quasi-biography that was merciless to Oppenheimer's tormenters, many of them pillars of the nuclear establishment. In the same vein was the Austrian Robert Jungk's *Brighter Than a Thousand Suns: A Personal History of the Atomic Scientists* (1970), a book precisely summed up in its subtitle. Norman Moss's *Men Who Play God: The Story of the H Bomb & How the World Came to Live With It* (1969) injected a strong but largely implicit moral critique, as well as an international perspective, of the military side of nuclear power.

Overtly polemical books followed. In 1970, Richard Curtis and Elizabeth Hogan published *Perils of the Peaceful Atom: The Myth of Safe Nuclear Power Plants.* John Gofman and Arthur Tamplin made their debut as nuclear critics with their mordantly titled *Population Control Through Nuclear Pollution* (1970), a gloves-off condemnation of nonmilitary nuclear power. They emphasized the effects of routine radioactive emissions, and condemned the hubris of a scientific community that substituted wishful thinking for an honest appraisal of evidence. Another scientist, Barry Commoner, like Sheldon Novick a member of the St. Louis group that created the Scientists' Institute for Public Information, brought out *The Closing Circle: Nature, Man, and Technology* (1971), a comprehensive and enduring survey of our environmental muddling that was especially hard on nuclear power. Roger Rapoport criticized the AEC's military activities in *The Great American Bomb Machine* (1971). Peter Metzger condemned the AEC in toto in *The Atomic Establishment* (1973). John Gofman and Arthur Tamplin reentered the antinuclear fray with *Poisoned Power: The Case Against Nuclear Power Plants* (1971), a devastating critique from nuclear insiders. Another scientist's attack, embodying his research of the previous decade, was Ernest Sternglass's *Secret Fallout* (originally published as *Low-level Radiation*) (1972), a popular rather than technical survey. Sternglass warned of the dangers posed by routine emissions from nuclear plants, including fetal deaths, congenital abnormalities, increased infant mortality, childhood leukemia, and later-appearing disorders, among them heart disease and cancer. He brought out a second edition of this book in 1981 to include a survey of the effects of the Three Mile Island accident and a retrospective on his decade's experiences as a nuclear critic. Richard Lewis cheered on intervenors and other activists in *The Nuclear-Power Rebellion: Citizens vs. the Atomic Industrial Establishment* (1972).

In the next few years, the issues broadened. In an influential short collection of essays, the British economist E. F. Schumacher introduced the idea of "appropriate technology" in *Small Is Beautiful: Economics as if People Mattered* (1973), one of the earliest approaches that went beyond antinuclear negativism to offer a persuasive positive alternative. Then in 1974, Ted Taylor devastatingly introduced the sinister question of nuclear terrorism in Mason Willrich and Theodore Taylor, *Nuclear Theft: Risks and Safeguards* (1974). Though this was a technical book read only by a limited audience, the topic reached a wider readership through John McPhee's quasi-biography of Taylor, *The Curve of Binding Energy* (1974), originally published as articles in *The New Yorker*.

Then, at a most inopportune time from the AEC's perspective, the issue of nuclear weapons tests came back into the headlines. The Partial Test Ban Treaty had not entirely stifled critics of the AEC's testing policy, and the continuation of testing underground even created new ones, including some extremely unlikely individuals such as reclusive millionaire Howard Hughes, who feared earthquake damage near his Nevada residence set off by underground shots.[22] A 1970 test, "Baneberry," resulted in a venting accident, producing an atmospheric release of radioactivity. Nevadans were scarcely more hospitable to underground testing than to atmospheric shots. The AEC was under pressure to find another test site, and since the late 1960s, it had been investigating Amchitka Island, one of the most remote members of Alaska's Aleutian chain. An in-house evaluation recommended against the site because the island sits above one of the most active earthquake fault zones on earth and is therefore an un-dependable long-term repository for the remains of an under-ground shot. The AEC went ahead with this shot anyway, code-named Cannikin, in November 1971. Most Pacific nations protested vigorously, none more so than Canada. A third of the U.S. Senate objected. U.S. editorial cartoonists began depicting AEC personnel as mad-scientist stereotypes, wearing lab coats and lunatic expressions on their faces. A group of Canadian and U.S. activists, concerned primarily about the fate of the oceans, sailed a small vessel, the *Greenpeace,* into the test zone in a futile effort to halt the shot. Out of this experience the movement known as Greenpeace emerged, to enjoy spectacular success two years later. The AEC won a short-term victory, but the damage to its reputation proved lasting.

The French joined the nuclear club in 1966 and had been carrying out atmospheric tests on Mururoa, a French protector-ate in the South Pacific. Greenpeace repeatedly sailed into the off-limits zone in an effort to stop the tests. In 1972, a French war vessel, *La Paimpolaise,* harassed and rammed the *Greenpeace III,* and the next year, a boarding party of goons from the French navy intercepted the vessel and beat the two male members of the party with truncheons, nearly putting out the eye of one of them, while one of the female members surreptitiously filmed the pro-ceedings. Greenpeace members managed to hide the film from French naval and police officials and to publish shots of the boarding and beating, a public embarrassment to the French government that, together with vociferous protests from the Pa-cific-rim nations, halted the French tests.[23] Greenpeace, the "Rainbow Warriors," as they style themselves, remain a potent force in the international antinuclear movement working for the Comprehensive Test Ban Treaty.

The AEC found its hands full combating antinuclear activists closer to home. One principal focus of resistance was the string of ill-conceived ideas known as "Project Plowshare." In 1957, AEC technicians proposed that nuclear explosives be used for "peaceful" civil engineering projects, such as digging a new isth-mian canal or creating artificial harbors. The problem of radioac-tive contamination of the site did not worry them, though none of their aboveground projects ever became a reality. Underground civil-engineering schemes looked more feasible. The AEC touted proposals for "stimulating" natural gas to the surface by nuclear detonations that shattered rock formations in which the gas is trapped. Two demonstration shots, Gasbuggy in New Mexico (1967) and Rulison in Colorado (1969), produced only indifferent results. All the Gasbuggy gas had to be flared off (burned) at the wellhead because it was too radioactive for industrial or domestic use; this flaring, of course, just released this radioactivity into the air. The Rulison gas supposedly would lose its radioactivity in eight years, but the city councils of Glenwood Springs and Aspen, Colorado, declined to permit its use without a referendum. As usual, the AEC was not deterred, and announced another Colorado shot, Rio Blanco, for 1973. This galvanized public protest, centered around the university community of Boulder. Encouraged by the 1972 initiative campaign that rejected the Winter Olympics for Colorado, the activists organized an initiative that would prohibit gas-stimulation shots in Colorado. They were helped significantly by the AEC's own estimate that some shots would trigger earthquakes, and by Edward Teller's vehement opposition to the initiative. Coloradoans enacted the initiative measure by a 60 to 40 margin. It was the most significant setback to Plowshare to date, and its success stimulated the later antinuclear initiatives.[24]

Fears of nuclear power in all its forms were well advanced throughout Colorado by the time of the Rio Blanco initiative. Denver residents looked uneasily over their shoulders at Rocky Flats, remembering the 1969 fire there. As if that were not enough, the Grand Junction tailings pile fiasco stirred the state through the late 1960s. During the glory days of wildcat uranium prospecting along the Colorado Plateau in the 1950s, Amax Uranium Corporation, the nuclear arm of the giant hard-rock mining company, Amax, operated a uranium mill near Grand Junction in western Colorado and simply dumped the tailings nearby as an ordinary by-product. The AEC ignored the radioactive tailings piles, insisting it had no jurisdictional responsibility for them. Grand Junction building contractors saw the piles as a free and accessible source of sand to be used in batching concrete and hauled off some 300,000 tons of it. Then, in 1966, state and federal public health service officials discovered that Grand Junction buildings were "hot," and traced the source of radioactivity in their foundations to the uranium decay cycle.

Through a series of alpha- and beta-particle emissions, uranium-238 decays to radium-226, which decays to radon-222, which in turn disintegrates into what are called the "daughters of radon": polonium-218, lead-214, bismuth-214, polonium-214, lead-210, bismuth-210, polonium-210, and lead-206. All but lead-206 are radioactive. Though radon is a gas, its daughters are tiny solid particles that become attached to dust, which, in turn, people inhale. Since the daughters are alpha- and beta-emitters, they are most dangerous to internal organs, particularly the lungs. The state promptly prohibited further use of the tailings and in the 1970s, the federal government began a program of destroying, removing, and replacing the hot foundations of houses and schools. The people of Grand Junction remain of two minds about this expensive and inconvenient operation. Most are determined that schools should be decontaminated, but others think that worries over the low levels of radioactivity caused by leaking radon are misplaced. Jim Temple, a general manager for the Public Service Company, a telephone utility, expressed the views of the latter group to an interviewer: "The human body is a pretty marvelous thing. It has a potential of building up a tolerance to almost anything. Perhaps the body can absorb the little bit of radiation that's around here, build up a tolerance to it. Besides, I'm a fatalist. We've all got to go someday; we're all going to die of something."[25]

The uranium decay cycle posed a far more lethal problem for others in the Colorado Plateau: uranium miners. As with the tailings piles, the AEC considered uranium mines outside the boundary of its regulatory responsibility because the 1946 Atomic Energy Act limited its licensing authority over "source materials," that is ores, "after removal from its place of deposit in nature." Responding predictably to this regulation-free environment, the uranium mining corporations—Kerr-McGee, Conoco, United Nuclear, Mobil, Utah International, Anaconda—hired cheap nonunion laborers, many of them unemployed

Navajo Indians in the Four Corners area, and sent them down to unventilated mines. There the decay cycle did its deadly work. Tony Mazzocchi, director of health and safety for the Oil, Chemical, and Atomic Workers Union, summed it up: "Those mines are nothing but cancer factories."[26]

The AEC did not adopt standards for radiation levels in the mines until 1972. It took no action to require that the mine shafts be ventilated, insuring that the daughters of radon would be contained and concentrated in the miners' work environment. AEC officials understood what they were doing; they did not act in ignorance. Medical researchers had traced the etiology of lung cancer in the Joachimsthal miners since the 1930s. The U.S. Public Health Service began sampling the air in uranium mines in the early 1950s and reported in 1955 that radioactivity exceeded international standards. In 1956, it reported that 65 percent of the miners in the shafts it surveyed were exposed to concentrations of radon's daughters comparable to the Joachimsthal mines. But nothing happened until 1967, when Leo Goodman, the AFL-CIO union officer having primary responsibility for occupational safety and health matters, identified the risks in a speech to the American Public Health Association. Just at this time, abnormal rates of lung cancer began showing up among the miners, especially the relatively cancer-free Navajos. Victor Archer, a physician with the National Institute of Occupational Safety and Health, has estimated that one out of every six uranium miners, a thousand men in all, will succumb to lung cancer.[27] The AEC finally began moving, reluctantly, to impose radiation standards on the mines, adopting exposure ceilings in 1972 and requiring that underground mines be ventilated.

By the late 1960s, an organized antinuclear movement appeared, providing informed scientific criticism of AEC policies at public hearings. Sometimes they confronted AEC nonscientist officials with challenges beyond their depth. A sense of the AEC's frustration, and its responsive tactics, is contained in a bit of dialogue between JCAE chairman Holifield and AEC commissioner James Ramey, a former executive director of the JCAE whom the Committee forced President Kennedy to nominate to the AEC. At JCAE hearings on reactor safety issues in

1969, Ramey described his experiences at public hearings on the Monticello reactor in Minnesota and Vermont Yankee in Vermont:

> *Chairman Holifield:* Will you give us a little bit of a report? I know you have participated in a number of public hearings in Vermont, New Hampshire and Minnesota. Would you give us an analysis of what these meetings have been like?
>
> I know some of them have been kind of rough and maybe some of them not quite so rough.
>
> *Mr. Ramey:* I could give you a few, shall we say, impressions. . . . At each of these meetings that I have gone through—the Vermont and Minnesota ones—there has been a convergence of certain factors. I will be fairly candid, if I may, on this. One of these factors is that there are some professional "stirrer-uppers" involved in each one of the meetings.
>
> *Chairman Holifield:* That is a good name, "stirrer-uppers."
>
> *Mr. Ramey:* Gentlemen from some "paper" conservation organizations that you can hardly find an address for to persons associated with the coal industry who always seem to be around these days.
>
> Second, there is a group of younger scientists, some of whom might be a little bit on the extremist side who seem to always be talking on matters beyond their own professional competence. They discuss and comment on areas in which they have not performed their scientific work.
>
> *Chairman Holifield:* Well, we have a certain number of book writers, too, of sensational books.
>
> *Mr. Ramey:* They are usually journalists and public relations men.
>
> *Chairman Holifield:* That is right; with no scientific background or competence.
>
> *Mr. Ramey:* None whatsoever; that is right.
>
> *Chairman Holifield:* But we must not forget that there are some competent people from some of the universities and these people, I think, we mustn't brush this off, we are going to have people before this committee that do have responsible concerns. . . .

Mr. Ramey: We usually start out the other way and end up on the irresponsible fellows. I thought I would just start out on the other side first.

One of the things that has struck me, though, on these is the number of really phony arguments that have been submitted in these meetings.

As you know, Mr. Chairman, I am not a scientist but I have been in this game for a long time. I went through the whole fallout controversy and other controversies when I was Staff Director of the Joint Committee. I may have gotten a pretty good ear for detecting phonies and phony arguments.[28]

Ramey's dismissal of AEC scientific critics as unqualified extremists represented wishful thinking on his part, for the AEC could now expect to find itself confronting articulate, informed technical experts at every licensing hearing it conducted. Scientific opposition crystallized around the Union of Concerned Scientists, an organization centered in the Harvard–MIT nexus in Cambridge, Massachusetts. Led by Henry W. Kendall, an MIT physicist, UCS raised the particularly troublesome issue of emergency core-cooling systems, usually referred to in the press as ECCS.

The controversy over ECCS had been heating up throughout the 1960s because the "maximum credible accident" against which engineers design reactors includes a meltdown of the reactor core following a loss-of-coolant accident (LOCA). The meltdown scenario, applicable to both types of light water reactors, begins with a rupture of the principal pipe or pipes carrying cooling water to the reactor core. Without coolant, the uranium fuel pellets and the zircaloy cladding that keeps them in the long, narrow fuel pins would both melt. The fuel pins would deform and bunch together in spots, preventing circulation of coolant. Core melting would begin about sixty seconds after the original loss of coolant. The entire core would melt in about fifteen minutes, forming a hideous blob weighing some hundreds of tons. Heat from its uncontrolled reaction would melt everything it came in contact with, and the blob would burn its way through the reactor vessel and housing, and down into the substrate rock for some unknown distance, possibly hundreds of feet, or, in the popular image, all the way to China: the China Syndrome.

Even this is not the worst imaginable possibility. Nuclear proponents insist that a reactor cannot explode like a bomb. True—its fissile fuel is not sufficiently enriched. But a reactor may be subject to a steam explosion that would be almost as lethal. In this scenario, water, possibly the leaked coolant, would collect in a pool below the reactor vessel. The meltdown core would reach it on its journey to China, possibly creating a chemical reaction that would have the effect of an explosion. If this occurred, the core's path would be reversed and it would be blasted upward like a molten artillery shell, through the top of the reactor vessel and the containment structure itself, into the environment where it would contaminate air, land, and water in unimaginable ways.

All that stands between humanity and this ghastly possibility is the emergency core-cooling system, an auxiliary and deliberately redundant network of pumps, waterlines, and valves designed to force cooling water into the core in case of a rupture in the primary coolant loop. But the ECCS must do its job reliably and quickly—within a matter of seconds. For if the core gets hot enough, it will vaporize any incoming cooling water, and this steam, under pressure, would block the entry of more coolant. Even if the water was injected in time, it might cause a thermal shock reaction similar to that which causes a hot glass to break when plunged into cool water, except that the rupture in a LOCA would be in the containment vessel.

Because the ECCS is so absolutely critical, the AEC had made some token beginnings at trying to find out what happens in a LOCA by constructing the loss-of-fluid-test (LOFT) reactor in Idaho. But construction delays, cost overruns, and shifts in AEC policy, especially after the advent of Milton Shaw to the Reactor Development and Technology division of the AEC, all contributed to postpone the LOFT experiment. By an absurd irony, when the LOFT reactor was finally completed in 1978, the investment in it had become so great that DOE decided it was too costly to be destroyed in a sacrificial experiment. So in 1970, the AEC commissioned Aerojet Nuclear, contractor at the Idaho Falls facility, to run a series of simulated ECCS tests. All failed, and

372 · NUCLEAR AMERICA

Aerojet Nuclear concluded that it was beyond current capability to predict the course of a LOCA.

The AEC at this time was pushed and pulled in inconsistent directions on the ECCS problem. On the one hand, it was subject to intense pressures from the nuclear industry and its political abettors to minimize costs to suppliers and utilities that would be associated with stringent safety requirements. AEC chairman Glenn Seaborg warned against "going to extremes [in safety regulation] without consideration of costs." Ramey warned the Advisory Committee on Reactor Safeguards that "utilities and equipment manufacturers have held discussions with the Commission and have expressed their concern over snowballing safeguards requirements leading to increased costs." California congressman Craig Hosmer, a fervent nuclear supporter in the House of Representatives, in a speech to a joint meeting of the Atomic Industrial Forum and the American Nuclear Society, called for "burning the Advisory Committee on Reactor Safeguards at the stake." Even ACRS consultants conceded that "there are limits on how far one can go in this direction [safety] in a price-competitive industry." Milton Shaw of the AEC's Reactor Development and Technology division complained that ORNL safety researchers were "causing more problems than they were solving" and accordingly stinted on funding safety research.[29]

But on the other hand, the Union of Concerned Scientists and other intervenors were bringing pressure to bear on the AEC for a thorough and honest review of safety problems, principally those associated with the ECCS. The UCS, under Kendall and Daniel Ford, an economist, had begun to prepare its own evaluation of the consequences of a meltdown, essentially an update of the old WASH-740 figures. They labored in ignorance of the fact that the AEC had already done this in 1964 and then suppressed the results. The AEC knew it could expect more unpleasant surprises at licensing hearings of the sort Ramey complained about in the Monticello and Vermont Yankee hearings. Some of its own staff were growing restless at the ostrich attitude that the Commission was taking toward safety problems. Intervenors in licensing hearings for Pilgrim (Massachusetts), Indian Point II (New

York), and Midland (Michigan) reactors were about to raise the entire ECCS issue.

The AEC responded by scheduling generic rulemaking hearings on the ECCS to begin in January 1972. (A generic hearing deals with a problem common to all reactors, in contrast with the more usual hearing that is concerned only with a particular reactor and its specific problems. A rulemaking hearing is one whose function is to produce rules applicable to all reactors, rather than "orders" specific to a particular reactor.) But as Daniel Ford, a member of the UCS team at the hearings, has observed, the generic hearings "were an administrative maneuver aimed at limiting public questioning of E.C.C.S. adequacy."[30] The AEC painstakingly circumscribed the scope of testimony and questioning permitted, inhibited its own staff from speaking with unfriendly participants, removed AEC staffers it considered unreliable, suppressed critical in-house reports, and formally instructed all its witnesses at the hearings in a written memorandum: "Never disagree with established policy."[31] The president of Aerojet Nuclear, one of the AEC's captive contractors that ran the Idaho NRTS facility, warned his employees that they might be fired or demoted for embarrassing testimony.

Despite these pressures, the 1972 generic hearings became an acute embarrassment for the AEC, as its own staffers and documents provided ample testimony about the inadequacy of safety assurances for the ECCS. As might have been predicted, the AEC remained unmoved by these disclosures, and made no significant changes in its safety regulations. But ventilating the existence of the problem in itself was a major setback to AEC promotional activities. By this time, public confidence in nuclear power had begun to corrode into skepticism, which in turn decayed into suspicion, which degenerated into hostility. No amount of AEC cheerleading could overcome the airing of doubt and criticism. The generic hearings were a perfect megaphone for these criticisms. Sixty groups of intervenors testified, led by the prestigious critics of the UCS. No longer could the AEC deride skeptics as uninformed, emotional layfolk: they now found themselves confronted by physicists, chemists, mathematicians, geologists, and others from the nation's most prestigious research institutions who combatted AEC propaganda with computer printouts.

Recognizing that the generic hearings convinced no one who was not already a believer, the AEC then decided to prepare an update of its 1957 WASH-740 risk assessment and the still-secret 1964 update. It determined to keep the study in-house so as to control its conclusions, and it retained a veto over the final report, but it also recognized that this would impair the credibility of the study. It therefore persuaded a member of the nuclear engineering faculty at MIT, Norman Rasmussen, to chair the committee that was to oversee the new assessment, and it opportunistically encouraged use of the phrase "MIT study" to describe it, though Rasmussen actually had little to do with its substance and his institution played no role at all. Rasmussen was a physicist, not a statistician or mathematician, and had done no work on problems of reactor safety. But he was a member of the nuclear complex, having served as a board member of Americans for Energy Independence, a pronuclear pressure group funded by Westinghouse, manufacturer of pressurized water reactors.

The product of this tightly controlled effort was a document completed in August 1974 that was known as the *Reactor Safety Study* or the Rasmussen report or WASH-1400. The Rasmussen report heartened the AEC and the nuclear community because it made the chances of a serious accident seem infinitesimally remote. It compared the chance of being killed or injured in a reactor accident to various commonplace accidents such as household fires and automobile collisions, as well as to exotic ones. It was the latter that journalists pounced on: the report concluded that an individual's chance of being killed in a reactor accident was equivalent to his chance of being hit by a meteorite. In numbers, an individual's chance of being killed was estimated at one in 300,000,000 and injured, one in 150,000,000. The report also scaled down the scope of damage caused by a meltdown: 3,300 prompt fatalities, 1,500 latent ones, 45,000 injuries, 290 square miles of contamination serious enough to require evacuation.

But the Rasmussen report did not stand up well to criticism. Its fundamental statistical technique was fault-tree analysis, a method derived from NASA's needs for comparison of differing space systems. Fault-tree analysis is comparable to constructing a genealogical chart: beginning with the accident, the analyst lists in a second tier all of the major causes (faults) of that accident, then in the next tier all of the causes of each of those faults, and so on down the tiers of causality until the most elementary failings (such as a bolt shearing) are reached. Each fault is assigned a probability, and by computer manipulation, these probabilities are evaluated together to predict the likelihood of an accident. But fault-tree analysis is useful for comparative purposes only. In the words of William Bryan, a mechanical engineer at the National Institute for Applied Research:

> If you're consistent in the use of these numbers in the fault tree, when you get done you can certainly compare one design against another and say this design is better than the other, if you used a common data base. But only for comparison. The absolute value of the number is totally meaningless. There is just no way that the number can mean anything in terms of the real-world probability of failure.[32]

The Rasmussen report also limited itself exclusively to mechanical and systems failures, excluding human error; to meltdowns and not other kinds of reactor accidents; to reactor accidents and not to other steps in the fuel cycle; to land-based light water reactors and not other kinds, such as the breeder. Finally and most devastatingly, the report either missed entirely certain kinds of accidents, such as the one that occurred at Three Mile Island, or grossly underestimated the possibility of accidents that had already occurred. *The Bulletin of the Atomic Scientists,* the Union of Concerned Scientists, and the American Physical Society all commented critically on the report or the way in which it was produced. WASH-1400 served the AEC well in the short term as fodder for propaganda, but so obviously flawed an analysis could not long survive serious scrutiny. In 1979, the Nuclear Regulatory Commission tried to bury the study, repudiating its conclusions with as little publicity as possible: "The Commission does not regard as reliable the Reactor Safety Study's numerical estimate of overall risk of reactor accident" and "withdraws any explicit or implicit past endorsement of the Executive Summary,"[33] a sanitized condensation of the report that omitted all potentially adverse data.

Meanwhile, the AEC's problems continued to mount. Adopting a suggestion made more than a decade before, Congress in 1973 divided the AEC's regulatory and promotional functions, and in the next year abolished the agency itself, assigning its regulatory functions to the Nuclear Regulatory Commission and its promotional activities to the Energy Research and Development Administration (ERDA), a short-lived body whose functions in turn were absorbed by the Department of Energy. In 1976, Congress abolished the JCAE. With the retirement, death, or defeat of prominent nuclear spokesmen in Congress like Chet Holifield, Craig Hosmer, Clinton Anderson, John Pastore, and Mike McCormack, the nuclear industry lost invaluable legislative support. By the time of the Carter administration, the NRC had begun to take its regulatory responsibilities far more seriously than its predecessor. Two of Carter's appointees to the NRC were publicly critical of the industry, leading nuclear spokesmen to make the unfounded complaint that the NRC was hostile to the expansion of nuclear power. The regulatory climate of the late 1970s was cooler from the industry's viewpoint, and the warm incestuous relationships of the atomic-industrial complex that characterized the 1950s and 1960s were gone.

The year 1974 was a dismal one for the nuclear power industry. The maiden voyage of the Japanese nuclear powered merchant ship N.S. *Mutsu* turned into a public relations nightmare. Intense local hostility among the fishermen of Mutsu Bay prevented the vessel from sailing out of its port; they feared radioactive contamination of their scallops. The ship, under auxiliary nonnuclear power, had to sneak out of the bay at night after a typhoon scattered the civilian blockade. As soon as the propulsion reactor was raised toward full power, a radiation leak developed. The ship's engineers first tried to plug the leak with boiled rice. When this did not work, they turned to even more desperate expedients, including dirty socks. But more sophisticated measures were needed, and the vessel tried to return to its home port. The fishermen refused to let it do so, and the *Mutsu* wallowed at sea for forty-five days until negotiations permitted its reentry, but only on conditions that it be permanently excluded from the bay within half a year. So little did the fishermen trust the nuclear vessel and Japanese authorities that the agreement specified that the town's mayor had to have exclusive possession of the keys to the fuel-loading crane.[34]

Marx Brothers nuclear technology is not a monopoly of the Japanese. Dale Bridenbaugh, a GE nuclear engineer, related an incident where he had to construct a container to ship radioactive pipe insulation that was leaking. He ordered a technician to line the container with sanitary napkins. He explained that they are "one of the most expendable materials used in a nuclear power plant. We used it for things you wouldn't believe. We bought it by the truckload, almost by the railroad-car full. What keeps a nuclear plant running is lots of Kotex, lots of masking tape, and lots of plastic bags."[35]

The *Mutsu* incident may have been slapstick farce, but there was nothing funny about the 1975 Browns Ferry fire. TVA, which had become the world's foremost nuclear utility, operated twin 1,100 MWe reactors at Browns Ferry in northern Alabama. An electrician was checking for drafts by holding a candle near suspect sites, when a draft caught the flame and ignited some flammable insulation. The fire spread rapidly through the cable systems, requiring that both reactors be scrammed. It destroyed all five ECCS of one of the units, knocked out 15 percent of capacity on the TVA grid, and raised the electricity bills of TVA's customers for the cost of replacement electricity, which must often be bought off the national grid at premium prices.[36] Browns Ferry was a multiple disaster for the nuclear-industrial complex. It showed up the inadequacies of the AEC's defense-in-depth/redundancy approach to safety design. It conclusively proved that common-fault accidents could happen, even if they were officially classified as improbable. It brought an abrupt end to the public relations honeymoon that the new Nuclear Regulatory Commission enjoyed for a few months after taking over from the old AEC. Finally, it pricked the conscience of many in industry and government about the lighthearted, indifferent attitudes toward safety that characterized the AEC's regulatory approach.

In 1976, three nuclear engineers employed by General Electric, Dale Bridenbaugh, Gregory Minor, and Richard Hubbard, quit their well-paying managerial jobs in protest against their company's complacent approach to nuclear problems. Browns Ferry did it for Minor, who had worked on the TVA reactor. When GE declared it to be a "non-accident" because no one was killed and no radiation leaked off-site, Minor responded: "But to me it was a disaster. All the safety systems were gone! All of our backup systems gone! I felt we were very, very lucky that we hadn't had a major catastrophe." Among the many things bothering Bridenbaugh was the obvious use to which the government of India was putting its Tarapur reactor, the first "peaceful" application of nuclear power in the Third World. The Indian government was reprocessing plutonium out of the spent fuel to build a bomb, while the official stance of the U.S. government was a string of grotesque contortions denying this unlawful but obvious diversion.[37] At the same time, Robert Pollard, another nuclear engineer who had worked for the AEC/NRC six years, also resigned, explaining in a formal statement to the JCAE that NRC officials knew of safety problems in plants but tried to hurry along the licensing process anyway. "Historically," he said, "the regulatory policy has been to avoid major problems that are expensive to solve or would delay" the plants coming on line.[38] Industry, the JCAE, and the NRC could only try to contain the damage these resignations did to their credibility.

The presidential election year, 1976, also saw a proliferation of citizen initiatives on nuclear policy questions. In California, Ohio, Montana, Washington State, Oregon, Colorado, and Arizona, complex initiative proposals restricted or prohibited the operation of nuclear power plants unless specific safety conditions were met, particularly with respect to waste. Each of these initiatives was soundly defeated, some by landslide margins. Dispirited nuclear opponents attributed their defeat to the costly "no" campaigns waged by the nuclear industry, which outspent their pathetically underfunded opponents by margins of as much as a hundred to one. The measures were all complex, and the nuclear power industry was far more persuasive than their opponents on all economic aspects of the initiatives, including jobs, projected demand for electricity, impact on standard of living, and utility bills.

The antinuclear movement did have one bright spot in the disappointing 1976 elections, though it was overlooked nationally. Missouri voters enacted an initiative measure that prohibited something known as CWIP (pronounced "kwip"): Construction Work In Progress. Utilities building plants demand authority to charge their ratepayers costs for construction in progress; that is, to pass through immediately to the ratepayers a capital cost, rather than waiting till the plant goes on line to recoup it through the rate base. Union Electric, the St. Louis–based utility building the Callaway nuclear plant in central Missouri, warned that if the initiative defeated CWIP, ratepayers would pay more in the long run. But the Missouri voters, caught up in a ratepayers' rebellion, enacted the initiative anyhow. When Union Electric canceled the Callaway II plant in 1981, they blamed their decision in part on the CWIP initiative. The CWIP issue has surfaced elsewhere, most notably as part of the controversy surrounding the Seabrook, New Hampshire, nuclear plant, and promises to persist until resolved at the national level.

The disappointments of 1976 did not slow the antinuclear movement for long. Jimmy Carter ran that year on a platform that demoted nuclear power to an option "of last resort"—an odd position for a man who began his adult life as a navy nuclear engineer under Hyman Rickover. His victory heartened antinuclear activists and environmentalists, who enjoyed a four-year thaw in the Washington climate of hostility that characterized the Republican administrations that preceded and succeeded Carter. Nuclear opponents applauded Carter's efforts to deal with the related problems of nuclear proliferation and terrorism, resulting in withdrawal of support for plutonium recycling and in the administration's outright opposition to the Clinch River breeder reactor.

An unexpected issue surfaced in the mid-1970s: civil liberties problems stemming from nuclear power. European activists, more sensitive than their American brethren to this issue, had been warning for some time that, in the slogan of German nuclear opponents, "The nuclear state is a police state." As if to corroborate the European warning, civil liberties questions popped up as offshoots of the problem of terrorism. To cope with persons who might try to divert fissile bomb material, nuclear utilities began tightening their security measures by screening nonemployees who visited plants. Employees at nuclear installations found themselves subjected to background investigations, which included inquiries about their sexual orientation, drinking habits, credit ratings, friendships, associations, and political opinions. Some utilities experimented with psychological profiling, compiled personnel dossiers, and imposed lie detector tests. They conducted personal searches, detention, and interrogation.

So much for "friendlies." To cope with "hostiles," that is, terrorists or lunatics, private corporations and public law enforcement agencies made plans to conduct routine information gathering, to infiltrate suspect groups, to conduct covert surveillance, and to wiretap—something expressly authorized under the federal 1968 Omnibus Crime Control Act, if done with a warrant, for all offenses under the Atomic Energy acts.

Such intelligence gathering was a serious enough threat to First Amendment liberties even when conducted in scrupulous compliance with the law. But such activities have a way of getting out of hand, pushing against the boundaries of legality. In California alone, public and private intelligence agencies have mounted an extensive campaign against antinuclear activists. Former state attorney-general George Deukmejian, who has since been elected governor, used twenty agents from the state bureau of investigation to spy on demonstrators at the Diablo Canyon protests. Local sheriffs' and police agents have infiltrated legitimate groups and acted as spies and agents provocateurs, organizing rallies, demonstrations, and exhorting individuals to commit illegal acts. Agents from the Los Angeles Police Department secretly attempted to videotape a meeting of the city council to gather intelligence about persons testifying against licensing of the Sun Desert reactor; they were discovered and thrown out of the meeting.

Private intelligence corporations, who are doing a booming business in matters of corporate espionage, as well as the nuclear utilities themselves, are conducting their own surveillance operations, outside the control of law. In 1975, the Virginia legislature debated, but did not pass, a bill that would permit the state's largest utility, Virginia Electric Power Company, to establish its own private police force having arrest powers and access to all public law enforcement records. In the same year, the Atomic Industrial Forum, the industry's trade association, combined forces with the New York firm of Charles Yulish Associates to collect intelligence on persons and groups opposing nuclear power. The Georgia Power Company, another nuclear utility, set up its "risk management" section in 1973, with a $750,000 budget spent on wiretapping gear and James Bond–type surveillance equipment, such as cars that can change their headlight configuration to confuse the driver they are tailing. PG&E used a company called Research West to investigate its numerous opponents in California, while on the other side of the country, an organization called Information Digest infiltrated the antinuclear Clamshell Alliance in New Hampshire.

The FBI has authority, under the 1946 and 1954 Atomic Energy acts, for law enforcement involving nuclear facilities and materials. The CIA's authority extends to foreign operations. State police, particularly those of Texas, California, Oklahoma, and New Hampshire, have conducted nuclear surveillance. The Law Enforcement Intelligence Unit, a computerized pool of intelligence, is shared by 225 local police agencies and includes data on nuclear activists.

The principal danger that all this monitoring capability poses to American liberty is the inevitable confusion of actual terrorists with legitimate opponents of nuclear power. As one example of such confusion, in 1976 congressional hearings, James Adams, a deputy assistant director of the FBI, asserted that the "Communist Party of the United States, which is dominated and controlled by the Soviet Union . . . has a program to try to discourage the use of nuclear energy in the United States."[39]

The real extent and danger of nuclear-industrial covert operations was revealed in connection with the death of Karen Silkwood, a lab worker at the Kerr-McGee plutonium processing plant in Crescent, Oklahoma. For several months, Silkwood, who was a representative of the Oil, Chemical and Atomic Workers Union, had been compiling information on health and safety violations at the Crescent plant. She may also have inadvertently come across information on diversion of plutonium from the plant. At one point, supposedly forty-four pounds of plutonium was MUF: materials unaccounted for. The Silkwood investigators suspected it had found its way to the international black market. On November 13, 1974, she was driving from Crescent to Oklahoma City with a file folder of evidence on the health and safety problems, mostly relating to defective equipment like leaking gloveboxes, careless practices like horseplay with uranium, and faulty ventilation systems. En route, her car smashed into a culvert wing, and she was killed. The incriminating file was never found.

Silkwood's death and its fascinating, frightening aftermath have been extensively investigated and reported.[40] The cause of her death is still disputed; the band of feminists and antinuclear activists, lawyers, union officers, priests, and investigative reporters who have pursued the details of her life and death are convinced that Kerr-McGee officials or police deliberately contaminated her with plutonium, and then caused her death, intentionally or not, by running her little Honda off the road. The first issue, her contamination, was resolved in her favor by a 1979 jury verdict in an Oklahoma federal district court against the Kerr-McGee Corporation that awarded her heirs an extraordinary $10 million in punitive damages. Just as frightening is the strange and extensive network of surveillance abuses that haunted Silkwood during her lifetime and her champions later.

Kerr-McGee security officials, the Oklahoma City Police Department, which supplied many of its alumni to the Kerr-McGee security operation, the Oklahoma State Police, and the FBI were all involved in the investigations of her death. Eventually hints cropped up that the CIA or its front operations might have had their hand in, plus Savak, the secret police of the Iranian Shah, and possibly even Israel's foreign intelligence agency, Mossad. A Silkwood investigator traced Oklahoma City Police Department connections to two secretive private intelligence operations in Fort Lauderdale, Florida, the Audio Intelligence Devices Corporation, a supplier of high-tech snooping equipment, and the National Intelligence Academy, a training center for foreign intelligence operatives. Silkwood's life and death were crossed by break-ins, black-bag operations including the one that contaminated her refrigerator with plutonium, cover-ups, employee harassment, theft and destruction of evidence, intimidations, threats, false rumors, FBI undercover agents, and agents provocateurs. The Silkwood case threw a spotlight on the nuclear police state in a comparatively early phase of its existence. In the long run, such freewheeling tactics backfire. Robert Luke, the manager of corporate planning for Kerr-McGee, observed that "Karen Silkwood is to the nuclear industry what the movie 'Jaws' had been to the beaches."[41]

The Silkwood abuses were not a fluke, as the experience of Rosalie Bertell demonstrates. Bertell, a Roman Catholic nun and mathematician, is an associate of Irwin Bross at the Roswell Park Memorial Institute in Buffalo, New York, and a leading epidemiological investigator of the links between nuclear power and cancer. On October 4, 1979, as she was returning from a debate at the Ginna reactor site near Rochester, New York, a car tailing her pulled ahead and dropped a gascan-sized object in her path, causing one of her tires to blow. She managed to pull off the road. A mysterious vehicle followed her; its occupants questioned her, and drove off. The Rochester police refused to investigate. Bertell is convinced that her harassment was committed by security forces trying to stop her confrontation with nuclear power.[42]

Matters continued to go downhill for the nuclear industry in 1979. Besides the $10 million Kerr-McGee verdict, the industry had to absorb Three Mile Island and the film *The China Syndrome,* which by an extraordinary coincidence came to public attention simultaneously. At four in the morning on March 28, 1979, a minor problem in the second unit of Metropolitan Edison's Three Mile Island nuclear plant near Harrisburg, Pennsylvania, set off a sequence of mechanical and human errors that produced the worst reactor accident outside the Soviet Union in the history of nuclear power, caused the gravest release of radiation in a nonmilitary setting, and staggered the nuclear industry. The American public got a grim and expensive lesson in the problems of nuclear power with Three Mile Island. Daniel Ford, formerly executive director of the Union of Concerned Scientists, who wrote the best popular account of the accident, has observed that "the long-lived radioactive material in a modern commercial reactor would approximate the long-lived radioactive fallout produced by the detonation of more than a thousand nuclear weapons equivalent in size to the bomb dropped on Hiroshima."[43] If reactors cannot explode like a nuclear weapon, they can do other unpleasant things that dump this horrifying inventory into the biosphere that sustains life on earth.

The problems at TMI began when pumps forcing coolant water through the primary loop tripped—that is, shut down—thus stopping the course of coolant from the reactor core to a heat exchanger. Such a pump trip is a common and expectable transient in the ordinary routine of a reactor, and emergency systems are designed to cope with it in course. When the flow stopped, temperatures began to rise in the core because the coolant was no longer flowing and therefore not able to carry off the heat. This in turn caused pressure to rise in the core, and that pressure opened a relief valve at the top of the containment structure. At the same time, the reactor automatically scrammed, shutting off the fission reaction but not the decay heat.

So far, so good. But now the malfunctions and operator errors began in earnest. The pressure valve failed to close when it should have, causing a continuous loss of coolant for almost two and a half hours into the accident. Worse, the control panel light indicating that the valve was open blinked off, leading the operators to assume erroneously that the valve had closed. They were not at fault for this mechanical failure, but they compounded it with a human error of their own. Another indicator revealed abnormally high pipe temperatures near the relief valve. The operators shrugged off this sign of trouble, later explaining that the temperatures regularly registered high because of a leak in the system. While all this was going on, a preaccident human error intervened to complicate matters. Two valves in emergency pumps designed to force water into the heat exchanger, which were to be left open at all times in normal operating procedures, had been closed several days before the accident, and stayed closed, causing feedwater in the secondary loop to boil dry.

The operators on duty then made several more serious errors. They shut down the emergency core-cooling system, in the mistaken belief that there was too much coolant in the core rather than too little. Then they shut down circulation pumps that moved the coolant through the core. This caused the upper part of the core to be uncovered, leading to a partial meltdown. That was bad enough, but steam in the core reacted with the zircaloy cladding of the fuel rods to produce hydrogen, which first erupted in a small chemical explosion and then later formed a large bubble at the top of the containment building. The NRC at first treated this as a potentially explosive situation. That response, eventually proven unnecessary, dragged the emergency out several days and provided the dramatic element that was easiest for the American public to follow in the media's reporting. Much of the coolant spilled down into the sump of the containment building, whence it was pumped into an adjacent auxiliary building. From there, some of it escaped into the environment.

Three days into the accident, monitoring helicopters discovered that an airborne plume of radioactivity from the plant was drifting over nearby Middletown. At this point, Governor Richard Thornburgh of Pennsylvania, the NRC commissioners, and the NRC's director of nuclear reactor regulation, Harold Denton, gave serious thought to evacuation and to lesser population control measures, such as warning people to stay indoors. Thornburgh urged pregnant women and preschoolers to evacuate the area within a five-mile radius of the down reactor. An estimated 140,000 people fled the TMI area that weekend in response to this evacuation advisory. Other signs of panic appeared. The Federal Reserve Bank of Philadelphia had to pump $7 million into the area to cover panic withdrawals from local banks. A teacher at a Harrisburg school found that while she stepped out of her fourth grade classroom briefly, her children started to write their own wills. One little girl wrote: "My bed go to my sister Susie and my soul go to heaven." A used-car dealer sold twenty-one vehicles in one day alone, with some of his buyers paying cash, in tens and twenties. The dealer noted that most of his purchasers were physicians.[44]

Investigators were not able to form reliable estimates of the extent and nature of the damage to the reactor until they were able to manipulate remote-control television cameras into the core during the summer of 1982. Then they were appalled to discover that an almost complete core melt had taken place, with 90 percent of the fuel rods damaged, with a large lump of uranium fuel and zircaloy cladding melted, slumped, and fused at the bottom of the core.[45]

Governments, industry, and people learned several long-term lessons from TMI, none of them encouraging. The first was partially revealed in the day by day news coverage of the accident, and fully disclosed when verbatim transcripts of NRC deliberations during the crisis were published several months later. No government or its agencies—not the state of Pennsylvania, the Carter White House, the Nuclear Regulatory Commission, the Pennsylvania Emergency Management Agency, to say nothing of the reactor's owner, Metropolitan Edison—displayed any ability to cope with the crisis effectively. On the contrary: handicapped by a lack of information and by industry's confident assumption that a serious core meltdown was a remote and unlikely eventuality, government officials found themselves impotent and foundering in the crisis. In such a situation, communications problems loomed large, and the press, not hostile at first, came to treat government spokesmen with a skepticism that bordered on contempt.

Many of the principal actors in the TMI drama have testified to the enervating blend of ignorance, willful self-deception, and misplaced wishful thinking that permeated official response to the accident. Roy Yeager, a TMI instrument technician and therefore near the bottom of the decisionmaking hierarchy, shrewdly guessed what was going on in the echelons above him: "The general consensus throughout the whole first day was, number one, nobody really knew what was actually happening; number two, some that had an inkling of what was happening didn't really want to believe what was going on." Unfounded optimism or skepticism displaced straightforward observation. Presented with evidence of radiation levels in the containment dome of 20,000 rads (450 rads is a lethal dose), Lee Gossick, head of the NRC's Incident Response Center in a Washington suburb, nevertheless recommended to his superiors downtown that the reading was an abnormality and should be disregarded. Later that day, Victor Gilinsky, an NRC commissioner, and Victor Stello, a high-ranking staffer, suspected a partial core melt from data on superheated steam in the containment structure, but Harold Denton pooh-poohed their concerns, attributing the data to relatively minor technical malfunctions. Commenting on such responses, Roger Mattson, NRC director of systems safety, observed that "people still wanted to believe the best. The NRC, for the first couple of days, wanted to believe something better was going on. The 'want-to-believe' mind-set evolved. Nobody would believe that what was actually happening could happen."[46]

By the second day of the accident, NRC officials were beginning to despair about their lack of information and control. Mattson lamented, "It is the same way every partial core meltdown has gone. People haven't believed the instrumentation as they went along. It took us until midnight last night to convince anybody that those goddamn temperature measurements meant something. By four o'clock this morning B and W [Babcock & Wilcox, the engineering firm that built the reactor] agreed." That same day, NRC commissioner Joseph Hendrie bewailed his position:

> We are operating almost totally in the blind, his [Pennsylvania governor Richard Thornburgh] information is ambiguous, mine is nonexistent, and—I don't know, it's like a couple of blind men staggering around making decisions.[47]

The ignorance and lack of information that handicapped the NRC throughout the crisis derived in large measure from an attitude that the Commission inherited from the AEC, and that had characterized federal nuclear regulatory policy since the 1950s, namely, reliance on industry to regulate itself. The consequence, as Commissioner Peter Bradford noted acidulously, was that the AEC/NRC ignored evidence of flaws in reactor safety systems "because its long-standing rationalization has been that 'no chain is weaker than its strongest link.' "[48]

Intense local hostility to nuclear power was another long-term consequence of the accident. Reaction flared immediately, on the second day of the crisis, when Middletown residents learned that the utility faced a potential core meltdown and did not notify area residents of the potential dangers. An area resident, Jessie Sanders, said, "When they built it here, I was ignorant about the dangers. We never realized how dangerous it was. Person after person now says to me, 'If there's an antinuclear club, I'm a member.' We're volunteering for an organization we don't even know the name of."[49] Area farmers insisted their livestock and even orchards were damaged by TMI off-site radiation. Ernest Sternglass appeared at a news conference in Harrisburg to warn of the consequences of low-level radiation and inadvertently set off a panicky reaction, especially among pregnant women and the parents of small children.[50] Local opposition persisted: on May 18, 1982, voters in the three counties surrounding TMI voted in a nonbinding referendum by a 2 to 1 margin to reject the restart of TMI Unit 1, which was undamaged by the accident at its twin and had been shut down earlier for routine maintenance.

Reaction by leaders of the nuclear establishment, like Edward Teller and Congressman Mike McCormack, also increased public skepticism. Lewis Perelman of Cal Tech's Jet Propulsion Lab summed up this official response: nothing happened, the incident proves that nuclear reactors are safe, and in any event we cannot abandon nuclear power. These are, Perelman notes, "the psychological processes of denial, rationalization, and fatalism, a pattern characteristic of the pathology of addiction." Perelman pointed out that when airline hijackers release their hostages, no one "proclaimed that 'nothing happened' simply because none of the passengers had been killed, or that the incident proved that airline security measures were effective" because the hostages finally emerged physically unharmed.[51]

From industry's point of view, it was an appalling coincidence that the popular and overtly antinuclear film, *The China Syndrome,* was released just at the time of the TMI accident. Jack Lemmon and Jane Fonda, its stars, had been involved in the antinuclear movement for some time, but their acting did far more for the cause than their activism. The movie educated countless Americans in the jargon of high technology. The phenomenon of the film's title, core melts, the notorious phrase "an area the size of Pennsylvania," weld inspections, and other technical concepts that had previously been the domain of engineers and dedicated activists now became familiar to people who had no opinions on nuclear power but who enjoyed a good story.

The 1970s were a decade of troubles for the nuclear industry. Orders for new reactors declined to zero, and utilities canceled previously ordered reactors. American consumption of energy not only failed to grow to meet 1960s predictions; it actually declined. Soaring interest rates combined with increasing construction lead times to make reactor capital cost overruns of 300 percent and more commonplace. Nuclear waste remained an unsolvable but unavoidable problem. Antinuclear political movements grew in strength and sophistication, forcing cancellation of most of the projected Washington State Public Power System and thrusting many communities and small utilities close to bankruptcy. Public confidence in the industry slid into a steady and seemingly irreversible decline. Even the Reagan administration, unquestioningly committed to the cause of nuclear power, could offer no effective, tangible assistance to the moribund industry.

13

"A Wolf Playing a Cello"

THE ARMS RACE AND THE DEMISE OF SALT II

WHILE PUBLIC OPPOSITION AND economic stagnation during the 1970s combined to bring development of civilian nuclear power to a near standstill, the arms race sped along. Henry Kissinger had originally hoped that the SALT I agreement to freeze offensive weapons for five years would provide a breathing space during which the two nuclear giants might be able to arrive at a more effective program. But it did not work out that way. SALT I left a gaping loophole that both superpowers used to modernize and augment existing strategic nuclear forces. Confronted by Soviet suspicions, potent opposition from the military-industrial complex, and technological developments that threatened the nuclear balance, first Kissinger and then Jimmy Carter tried and failed in separate attempts to find some method of checking the arms race. Salt II, which was at best only a modest step in the right direction, was never ratified. While both the Soviet Union and the United States have so far found it convenient to continue observing its terms, nothing binds them. The nuclear arms race continues to be a major feature of life in the second half of the twentieth century. Meanwhile, policymakers on both sides remain trapped in their nuclear dilemma, unwilling to divest themselves of these weapons of genocide.

SALT I demonstrated that it was possible for the superpowers to agree on arms control measures. The treaty banning full-scale deployment of ABM systems was a significant accomplishment.

But the interim freeze on offensive weaponry left the door open for major additions to each side's nuclear arsenal. During the Nixon, Ford, and Carter presidencies, the United States added an enormous number of warheads to its strategic forces. In 1970, when serious SALT negotiations first began at Vienna, the United States deployed 1,710 warheads on strategic missiles. By the end of the decade, that number had increased to over seven thousand. Similar developments were taking place inside the Soviet Union.

The loophole in the interim freeze agreement through which both sides so deftly squeezed was the stipulation that existing strategic forces could be modernized. The Soviets interpreted this to mean that so long as they did not exceed agreed-upon quantitative ceilings, they could replace obsolescent missiles with more reliable and accurate ones then being tested. In the months following the signing of the agreement, the American intelligence community began gathering data on these new Soviet systems. Washington took no comfort from what it learned. The SS-17 could be MIRVed three or perhaps four times. The SS-18, a behemoth capable of carrying a twenty-five megaton payload, was MIRVed from eight to ten times. The SS-19, somewhat smaller but more technically advanced than the SS-18, carried six MIRVed warheads. Just as significantly, intelligence gathered by satellites and via listening posts positioned near the Soviet border revealed that the new Soviet missiles were considerably more accurate than those they were to replace, having a CEP of somewhere between 0.23 and 0.30 nautical miles.*

Defense planners, who inveterately think in terms of "worst case" possibilities, concluded that once these new missiles were deployed, the Soviets would have a strategic force that might be capable of attacking and destroying a large percentage of Amer-

*Missile accuracy is measured in terms of what weapons experts call CEP—circular error probable. This describes the radius of a circle in which half of the warheads aimed at a specific point and fired from the same place will fall. Conversely, it also means that it is probable that half of the warheads aimed at the same spot will fall outside that circle. To say then that a type of missile has a CEP of 0.25 nautical miles is to say that half of the warheads carried by that missile will land within a circle the diameter of which is one-half nautical mile and that half of them will not. A nautical mile is 6,076 feet, 796 feet more than the statutory land mile.

ica's Minuteman missiles in a preemptive strike. Though these fixed land-based missiles accounted for only 25 percent of the strategic nuclear forces at Washington's disposal, cautious planners nevertheless considered the potential threat to Minuteman to be strategically dangerous.

Henry Kissinger believed that the Soviets were stretching the modernization clause of the interim freeze agreement beyond reasonable limits by replacing older, single-warhead weapons with these newer and more accurate MIRVed versions. But Washington was in no position to object, because modernization programs that also threatened the nuclear balance were moving steadily ahead on this side of the Atlantic as well. Five hundred fifty Minuteman missiles were even then being MIRVed. In addition, the Pentagon planned to replace existing Minuteman warheads with the new, more powerful model MK 12A. Fitted with this new warhead, the Minuteman III would have a CEP of 0.12 nautical miles and might itself be considered a counterforce weapon, capable of successfully attacking Soviet missile silos. Polaris submarines, moreover, were soon to be replaced by the more powerful Trident. When fitted with the Trident II missile, then in the planning stage, the Trident sub would also have a counterforce capability. The air force planned to replace the B-52 fleet with the newer B-1 and hoped to add the MX missile to its arsenal. With a throw weight* of over 8,000 pounds, the MX was four times as powerful as the Minuteman and considerably more accurate. Its estimated CEP was from three hundred to five hundred feet.

The fact that both sides were taking advantage of the loophole in the interim freeze to improve their strategic forces demonstrated how difficult it would be to replace that flawed agreement with something better. Kissinger hoped for a treaty that would extend the credibility of Minuteman as a deterrent by banning or at least limiting the number of heavy SS-18 missiles that the Soviets could MIRV. The outline for such an agreement was

*The throw weight of a missile is the total weight of its reentry vehicles and determines the number and power of MIRVed warheads that a single missile can carry. The MX as of this writing is expected to carry ten 335-kiloton warheads. Because of its extraordinary accuracy, it must be viewed as a counterforce weapon.

reasonably clear in his mind. Because of the advanced state of its MIRV program, the United States would seek an advantage over the Soviets in the number of deliverable warheads it could possess. The MIRVing of Soviet missiles would be restricted. To compensate for this, the Soviets would be allowed a larger number of missile launchers than the United States. Their overall force, however, would be kept at a level insufficient to threaten the credibility of Minuteman.

Before he could hope to convince the Soviets to enter into such an agreement, however, Kissinger believed that Congress would have to make it clear to the Kremlin that unless an agreement could be reached, the United States was prepared to proceed with the development of an entire new generation of weapons systems. Congress had already approved the Trident submarine program, but Kissinger wanted funding for two other programs, the B-1 bomber and the cruise missile. An updated version of the German buzz bomb of World War II, the cruise was a subsonic, air-breathing, nuclear-capable pilotless aircraft. After being released from a mother plane a thousand or fifteen hundred miles from its intended target, the cruise was programmed to fly at low levels to avoid enemy radar. Its guidance system was so well designed that its builders expected the missile to land within yards of its target. If the Russians became convinced that the United States had the will to stay ahead in the arms race, Kissinger reasoned, they would be more willing to call the race off. To further improve his bargaining position, Kissinger hoped to use the cruise, a weapon the Soviets were much concerned about but one that the air force seemed willing to sacrifice, as a bargaining counter to be traded away in return for Soviet concessions.

It has become a commonplace to observe that Henry Kissinger patterned himself after the great nineteenth-century European diplomatists who restructured Europe's political order following the wars of Napoleon. Had Kissinger operated in a nineteenth-century political context, his plan might have succeeded. But his problem was more complex. The Vietnam war had created a strong antimilitary bias in Congress. Aside from the Trident submarine, congressional support for other military programs was at best problematic.

While congressional opponents of the defense establishment threatened Kissinger's plans, critics on the right made life equally difficult for him. Senator Henry Jackson, whose views on national security matters were extremely influential, was strongly opposed to Kissinger's policy of détente, which may be described as an effort at reducing tensions with the Kremlin while simultaneously structuring a global political order that Moscow and Washington would both want to defend. Jackson had also fought against SALT I, and for the same reason. A dedicated cold warrior, the senator from Washington State viewed these policies as threats to American national security because, to the extent that they tended to convince Congress and the public that peace was possible, they sapped support for Defense Department programs. Jackson was convinced that signs of weakening resolve in the United States would encourage Soviet aggressiveness. Jackson had not been influential enough to kill the SALT I treaty. But he was able to attach an amendment to the Senate's statement of approval requiring that, in future arms control agreements the United States not accept "levels of intercontinental strategic forces inferior" to those held by the Soviets.[1] Jackson, who had been quite skeptical of the SLBM agreement in SALT I, was sending a loud, clear message to the White House. Kissinger would not be allowed the privilege of playing with the numbers or, as he preferred to view it, "balancing asymmetries" again.

Early in 1973 American and Soviet delegations met in Geneva for the beginning of SALT II. Though this earliest session was purely preliminary in nature, it was nevertheless premature because Washington's various national security bureaucracies had not as yet agreed upon a mutually acceptable negotiating position. While the delegations killed time dealing with matters of little consequence, Henry Kissinger found himself in the midst of an intra-administration struggle and unable to pull the strands of policy together into a coherent plan of action. The State Department and the Arms Control and Disarmament Agency were strongly opposed to Kissinger's view that new weapons programs would provide the leverage and bargaining power essential to a successful negotiation. The prevailing view at Foggy Bottom was that the threat of new weapons would only escalate the arms race while making negotiations with the Soviets more difficult. Arms controllers continued to urge, as they had during the SALT I talks, that the United States immediately stop all further MIRV testing and deployment and seek a negotiated MIRV ban with the Soviets. Only in this way, they insisted, could the United States hope to head off the MIRVing of Soviet missiles that would make Minuteman vulnerable to a counterforce blow.

The Defense Department and the Joint Chiefs took the opposite position first because of their continued commitment to the MIRVing of Minuteman. In addition, as Admiral Thomas Moorer candidly pointed out, if MIRVs were banned, Congress would certainly kill the Trident submarine, which would have no real reason for existing without multiple-warhead missiles. Even more significantly, the chiefs, who stood firmly behind the Jackson amendment, made it clear that they would oppose any treaty that did not guarantee the United States as many launch vehicles as the Soviets.

Kissinger was hopelessly isolated. The military was sticking by the principle of equal aggregates, Congress would not approve the weapons programs he believed necessary for a successful negotiation, and the diplomats were attacking his bargaining-counter philosophy while calling for an end to all MIRV testing. "Our dilemma," Kissinger has since explained, "was that we were constrained by domestic pressures from choosing either of two options that made strategic sense: building up massively to bring about Soviet restraint through the threat of a counter-force capability, or freezing the status quo while we still had an edge in warheads."[2]

In his memoirs, Kissinger blames both the advocates of arms control and the defense establishment for refusing to agree upon a realistic negotiating position. Yet while it may be true that the arms controllers disagreed with his approach, it is clear that they had no influence in deciding which bargaining position was finally adopted. The defense establishment was calling the shots. Under the terms of the American proposal put on the table at Geneva, each party would be allowed a total of 2,350 delivery vehicles. The only other significant aspect of the American plan was a recommended freeze as well as a ban on the further testing of land-based MIRVs.

Kissinger was not surprised when the Soviets showed no interest in the American proposal. To reach the figure of 2,350 total launch vehicles, the Russians would be required to dismantle 250 existing weapons. The United States, on the other hand, would be able to add to its forces. The United States had already MIRVed 60 percent of its land-based missile force and had no plans to proceed any further. But the Soviets had as yet MIRVed none of theirs. Thus the American proposal would have barred the Soviets from MIRVing their land-based missiles (at the time 85 percent of their total force) while allowing the United States to retain its already MIRVed land-based force and MIRV the Trident I, a submarine-launched missile. Kissinger thought the Russians would be better off without an arms control agreement than the one dreamed up by the defense establishment. Obviously, so did the Russians.

The whole situation was by turns frustrating and ludicrous. "No agency was willing to face the root fact that in the absence of an agreement the Soviets would exceed us in the number of MIRVed missiles in the early part of the eighties and would have many more warheads than we."[3] It was a "strategic absurdity" but there was nothing the embattled national security adviser could do about it. A bitter Kissinger subsequently wrote:

> The proposal was put forward despite its implausibility because it was a good way to stifle our domestic debate. No one could be accused of softness if we asked for a number of delivery vehicles beyond our intention to build while restricting the Soviets to levels of MIRVs far below their capacity. It was fairy-tale diplomacy. If one wished hard enough, one could achieve all one's aims without having to pay any price.[4]

With the negotiations going nowhere, Kissinger did a curious thing. In May 1973, while at Zavidovo, the Politburo's hunting preserve near Moscow, he proposed that the United States and the Soviet Union set the end of 1974 as a deadline for signing the next SALT agreement. He believed that such a deadline was the only way to "stop endless procrastination within our government and at Geneva." A skeptical Andrei Gromyko, who evidently feared that failure to meet the deadline might sour Soviet–American relations, nevertheless reluctantly agreed. Kissinger hoped that by establishing a time limit he would strengthen his own hand at home, forcing the State and Defense Department bureaucracies to be reasonable about establishing what he viewed as a legitimate bargaining position. He was sadly mistaken, however. During the remainder of 1973 and most of 1974 the SALT negotiations remained stalemated, primarily because the various agencies involved could not agree on a realistic bargaining position and the president, increasingly preoccupied with the Watergate affair, was either unwilling or unable to discipline his administration.

On August 8, 1974, fifteen months after he had been reelected by an overwhelming popular majority, Richard M. Nixon resigned in disgrace and was replaced by Vice-President Gerald R. Ford. Nixon's resignation and his subsequent pardon in effect ended the national fixation on Watergate and gave Kissinger an opportunity to meet the SALT deadline established over a year before. But the November 1974 Vladivostok communiqué, which was intended to establish the framework for a second SALT treaty, was no triumph for Henry Kissinger. On the contrary, the key feature of this latest accord was an agreement to set a ceiling of 2,400 missile launchers for each side with a subceiling of 1,320 launchers that could be MIRVed. The Soviets thus agreed to dismantle some two hundred older strategic missiles, and conceded the principle of equal aggregates demanded by Senator Jackson, the Defense Department, and the Joint Chiefs. The Soviets also agreed to drop their long-standing demand that America's forward-based systems be included under these limitations. But Kissinger was forced to make major concessions in return. First, he agreed to give up further attempts to limit the number of heavy ICBMs the Soviets could deploy. This issue, central to American concerns about Minuteman vulnerability, was a truly major change in administration policy. Second, and of lesser significance, Kissinger agreed to count heavy bombers as strategic weapons to be limited under an accord.

Even if Vladivostok had become the basis for SALT II, it would have meant little in terms of true arms control. The ceilings it established were high enough to accommodate all of the ambitions of both Soviet and American defense establishments. The United States would be able to MIRV as many land-based missiles as it desired while continuing with the Trident MIRV program. On their part, the Soviets would have been able to MIRV as many heavy missiles as they wished. Kissinger, who believed that he could have negotiated lower overall levels had he been granted some flexibility, was discouraged. He thought that as new Soviet missiles became operational during the 1980s, the Minuteman force would become increasingly vulnerable.

The Vladivostok accords, he wrote, "enshrined the principle of equal aggregates" and did so "just when multiple warheads made the number of delivery vehicles a less and less reliable criterion of strategic equivalence." To "achieve a paper equality in overall totals we let the Soviets have an additional 2,400 or more warheads they would not otherwise have had. It was a triumph of theology over analysis."[5]

To make matters worse, the Vladivostok communiqué sidestepped certain slippery questions raised by two new weapons systems that had come to prominence during the early 1970s. One was the Backfire bomber of the Soviet Air Force. This plane, a nuclear-capable medium range jet bomber, which the U.S. Air Force claimed was more advanced than its own FB-111, was intended for use in the European theater and for antisubmarine warfare. In spite of its design, which suggested clearly that it was not to be used against the continental United States, the Joint Chiefs believed that the Backfire should be counted as a strategic weapons system and included under the limits tentatively established at Vladivostok. Their reasoning was that Backfires could be stationed in western Siberia and, if flown on one-way missions or refueled in midair, could attack American targets. In a perfect example of worst-case planning, the chiefs insisted that the Backfire should be judged not on the basis of what it was designed to do but of what it was capable of doing under the most extreme circumstances.

The long-range cruise missile was another matter entirely. In the early 1970s, the air force considered abandoning work on the cruise because opponents of the B-1 bomber were promoting the little drone as a cost-effective alternative. The air force was convinced not to do this, however, by Henry Kissinger, among others, who saw the cruise as a valuable bargaining counter in future negotiations with the Soviets. Kissinger erred in not considering the possibility that air force leaders might change their minds about the cruise. That is precisely what happened. Not only did the air force insist on keeping the weapon; the Joint Chiefs were strongly opposed to limiting the number of cruise missiles to be deployed under an arms limitation agreement. "Those geniuses," Kissinger acidly remarked while commenting on the intellectual capabilities of air force planners, "think the goddamn thing is a cure for cancer and the common cold."[6]

At the height of his fame following the American withdrawal from Vietnam in 1973, a Gallup poll found that Henry Kissinger was the most popular man in the United States. Another poll conducted by a British firm proclaimed him the most popular man in the world. He shared the Nobel peace prize, and one *Newsweek* magazine cover even portrayed him, cartoon-style, costumed as Superman. But as Kissinger himself clearly understood, political power that is based on celebrity status doesn't last. By the end of 1975, his ability to get things done had been significantly reduced. Things had not gone well in the intervening two years. Watergate had thrown a shadow over everyone associated with Richard Nixon, South Vietnam had collapsed, and perhaps most significantly, numerous Americans had come to question the value of détente because of increasing Soviet aggressiveness around the world.

During the 1973 Arab–Israeli War, Moscow provided military advisers and massive aid for Egypt and Syria. Some Americans even thought that the Soviets helped plan the war. When the surprised Israeli forces counterattacked, surrounded, and then seemed about to destroy an entire Egyptian army in the desert, the Russians threatened direct military intervention. Only a worldwide American military alert, along with considerable White House pressure on the Israelis to keep them from going too far, deterred the Kremlin. In 1975, the Soviets again revealed their expansionist inclinations, this time in Africa. After the Portuguese pulled out of Angola, the country was thrown into chaos as three competing factions struggled for power. The Soviets provided military aid for the Marxist Augostino Neto and his Popular Movement for the Liberation of Angola (MPLA). The United States funneled aid to the other two groups, the National Front for the Liberation of Angola (FNLA) headed by Holden Roberto, and Jonas Savimbi's National Union for the Total Independence of Angola (UNITA). Another "secret war" seemed to be shaping up until in December 1975, Congress learned of the CIA involvement in Angola and promptly cut off funding, leaving the field to the Soviets. The war in Angola continued and the MPLA's victory was not assured until after the Soviets had ferried in somewhere between 20,000 and 25,000 Cuban combat troops. At the same time that the Russians and their Cuban surrogates were becoming heavily involved in Angola, they established a close relationship with the government of Somalia and showed considerable interest in establishing a naval presence in the Indian Ocean. Then, after a coup overthrew Ethiopia's aged emperor, Haile Selassie, Moscow established an even stronger connection with Ethiopia's new Marxist ruler, Mengistu Haile-Mariam.

The Kremlin's expanding role in Africa, especially its willingness to use Cuban troops to accomplish its aims, substantially strengthened Kissinger's critics on the right, who claimed that détente was "a one-way street" and that the Soviets were using it to create a false sense of security in the West so that they could expand more easily. Détente, once a popular idea, became a dirty word, so loaded politically that President Ford actually abandoned it.

It was against this background that Kissinger, now secretary of state, made one final attempt to resolve the Backfire–cruise problem. In January 1976, he journeyed to Moscow where he negotiated a tentative compromise on these two troublesome issues. The Soviets agreed to accept constraints on the Backfire bomber. In return, the secretary of state agreed to count B-52s that were equipped to carry cruise missiles against the subceiling of 1,320 MIRVed missiles agreed upon at Vladivostok. In Washington, however, Kissinger's plan ran afoul of Secretary of Defense Donald Rumsfeld and Fred Iklé, the director of the Arms Control and Disarmament Agency, who managed to kill it. The defense establishment made a counteroffer to the Soviets—ratification of the Vladivostok accords along with a temporary three-year agreement limiting Backfire and cruise. But the Soviets, who had already deployed Backfire and who undoubtedly realized that it would take at least three years for the United States to begin producing cruise missiles for deployment, angrily rejected the proposal. It was the end for SALT as far as the Ford administration was concerned. The next phase in the on-going negotiations would be undertaken by the new Democratic administration.

Jimmy Carter's narrow victory in the 1976 presidential election once again threw the SALT process into turmoil. The Soviets, for all their revolutionary rhetoric, do not like change. They had grown comfortable with Henry Kissinger over the preceding eight years. He was a practical man who understood that relationships are built incrementally. He seldom asked too much and understood that success in negotiation depended upon patience, flexibility, and an appreciation of what was possible. Carter, however, appeared to operate on an entirely different set of premises, so different in fact that Soviet leaders wondered if his election did not signal a return to the tensions of the Cold War era.

Carter hoped to pursue détente. But as a result of Soviet adventurism in Africa and a growing popular belief in this country that Kissinger's celebrated policy was not paying off, during the campaign Carter felt compelled to take some relatively strong anti-Soviet positions. Moreover, he was quite earnest about the question of human rights, which was central to his entire approach to foreign policy. And that, of course, did not go over particularly well in Moscow, where candidate Carter was viewed as meddling in the internal affairs of the Soviet state. Carter's choice of Zbigniew Brzezinski to be his national security adviser was another bad omen to the men in the Kremlin. A Polish expatriate who grew up in Canada before emigrating to the United States, Brzezinski, a professor of political science at Columbia University, was a hard-line cold warrior, who urged a revitalization of the alliances that bound the United States to western Europe and Japan. Brzezinski called his policy "trilateralism," but the Soviets had another name for it; they called it capitalist encirclement.

Even before Jimmy Carter moved into the Oval Office then, the men in the Kremlin were prepared for the worst. They seem to have taken him for a traditional cold warrior who disguised his hard-line attitudes with a rhetoric that smacked to them of pious hypocrisy. They became so suspicious that even harmless platitudes, when they fell from Carter's lips, took on sinister meaning. Thus, when in his inaugural address the new president expressed the hope that his administration would be able to end the arms race and purge the earth of nuclear weapons, Moscow read these remarks as pure propaganda. "Already we felt Carter was maneuvering for publicity," wrote a Soviet diplomat. "We felt he was weaseling out of the Vladivostok promises. We felt that he was insincere."[7] Nor did it help when, in the early weeks of his administration, Carter sent an encouraging letter to the leading Soviet dissident, Andrei Sakharov, and received Vladimir Bukovsky, a prominent exiled dissident, in the Oval Office.

Despite Soviet suspicions, though, Carter was seriously interested in ending the arms race. Even before his inauguration he stunned the members of the Joint Chiefs of Staff, asking whether they believed national security and the nuclear balance could be maintained if both the Soviet Union and the United States reduced their nuclear arsenals to two hundred ICBMs each. Zbigniew Brzezinski, who happened to be present when this amazing exchange took place, later wryly observed, "It was unclear to me at the time whether the JCS were more astonished by this notion or more tempted to exploit it to avoid any progress on arms control altogether."[8]

Nor was there any difference of opinion inside the administration with regard to the fundamental objective. The United States would pursue an aggressive arms control policy aimed at achieving deep cuts in the nuclear arsenals of both superpowers. The really divisive question was how to go about this. Should the administration press forward, negotiate a treaty based on the Vladivostok accords, and then in a new negotiation seek reductions in existing nuclear arsenals? Or should Vladivostok be scrapped and a new negotiation be undertaken to achieve significant reductions sooner?

Cyrus Vance, the new secretary of state, who had been a McNamara deputy during SALT's birth pangs, favored a two-stage approach in which Vladivostok would be ratified first. The secretary warned that Brezhnev believed binding commitments had been made at Vladivostok. If Carter now backed away, Soviet leaders might interpret this as some sort of trap. Vance thus considered it wiser to move cautiously by stages rather than to seek a major breakthrough. "My preference," Vance later wrote, "was to take advantage of the political strength and momentum of a new administration, and the traditional honeymoon with Congress, to attempt to conclude an agreement based essentially on Vladivostok." Vance wanted to put the potentially troublesome issues of the cruise missile and the Backfire bomber on the back burner for the moment and deal with them in SALT III. "In my view, the modest alternative—accepting the Vladivostok framework—offered the best prospect for a rapid conclusion of a SALT II Treaty that would limit Soviet strategic forces and provide a more stable foundation for US–Soviet relations in what could well be a rough period ahead."[9]

Brzezinski disagreed. He was justifiably impatient with the tedious pace of the SALT negotiations and loath to begin his career as national security adviser by ratifying an agreement negotiated by Kissinger. "Why should Zbig just accept Henry Kissinger's straitjacket?"[10] asked one Brzezinski loyalist. Brzezinski and Kissinger had been rivals for years, first as academics and later as foreign policy advisers to important political figures. The former Columbia University political scientist wanted to demonstrate that Henry Kissinger wasn't the only one capable of doing some creative work in the area of foreign policy. What better way to do that than by negotiating a better SALT treaty than Kissinger had managed?

Like Brzezinski, Secretary of Defense Harold Brown also wanted to bypass Vladivostok. Brown's primary concern was the possible vulnerability of Minuteman. He realized that the president, who was committed to restraining Pentagon spending, was unlikely to support the mobile MX missile system, which was intended to guarantee the invulnerability of America's land-based missile force. This meant that Minuteman's credibility as a viable element in the so-called strategic triad would have to be assured, and the best method of accomplishing that was to limit the number of warheads the Soviets could deploy on their latest generation of missiles. Brown feared that a two-stage negotiation would move too slowly for that. A former member of the SALT I delegation, he realized that when negotiating with the Russians it can sometimes take months or years to reach agreement on even the most cut-and-dried matters. Assuming the Senate approved a treaty based on the Vladivostok formula, the administration might then attempt to negotiate deep cuts in the strategic arsenals of both sides. But long before the second stage could begin, the Soviets would have deployed their latest generation of MIRVed ICBMs, Minuteman would be at least theoretically vulnerable, and it would probably be impossible to convince the Russians to dismantle missiles only recently deployed.

Every administration ought to have a gadfly, someone willing to challenge established dogma. In the Carter administration, that place was filled by Paul Warnke, the head of the Arms Control and Disarmament Agency. Warnke, a dedicated arms controller, played the part with a joie de vivre not often found in Washington's inner circle, which may explain why he survived for only twenty months. Warnke was ungracious enough to point out that when Moses descended from Sinai, nowhere on those stone tablets he brought with him was there engraved anything about the triad. Yet somehow, since the 1960s, it had become an unquestioned assumption that America would depend upon three separate deterrent forces: land-based missiles, strategic bombers, and missile-firing submarines. Minuteman constituted about 25 percent of the American deterrent. But submarines alone could devastate the Soviet Union. Even if Minuteman was becoming vulnerable, as long as the United States could rely on the invulnerability of its submarines as well as a portion of the strategic bomber fleet, its security was assured.

Warnke thought the "theologians" who spent their time constructing worst-case scenarios in the cloistered chambers of the Pentagon had lost touch with the real world and the real dangers.

While they concerned themselves with hypothetical threats to Minuteman, a new threat had emerged, and as usual it was the result of advancing American technology. The long-range cruise missile was small (only 21 feet long), inexpensive to manufacture, easily hidden from the prying eyes of spy satellites, and deadly. At that moment, this technology was still in the developmental stage in the United States. The Russians, as usual trailing in the arms race, were far behind. Warnke wanted the cruise banned before any further developments could take place. He recalled that only a few years before, a similar situation had existed with regard to MIRV technology. Rather than negotiate a MIRV ban, the Nixon administration had insisted on pursuing its advantage. And the result? The Soviets MIRVed their missiles, the number of deployed warheads on both sides escalated sharply, and the Defense Department found itself warning of Minuteman vulnerability. The long-range cruise missile, Warnke insisted, posed a similar danger. Once the Soviets developed their own version, an uncontrollable race would begin. Thousands would be produced and deployed on each side and arms control would be a dead issue; because these weapons were so easily hidden, there would be no method of verifying any agreement for their limitation.

Vance agreed. Brown and others in the defense establishment, he believed, were making far too much of the supposed impending threat to Minuteman. While it was true that the Soviets might develop the theoretical capability to launch a preemptive attack against America's land-based missiles, it would be virtually impossible for them to "coordinate the simultaneous arrival on widely dispersed targets of hundreds of missiles and thousands of warheads." They would have no opportunity to test their plans beforehand "to be sure that an attack of such magnitude and complexity could actually be carried out." The reliability of their missiles could not be guaranteed. Moreover, in a real attack "the flight paths of attacking missiles would be along axes that were subject to geophysical forces whose influence on statistically derived accuracy estimates was highly uncertain." These imponderables, Vance believed, made it most unlikely that the Soviets would ever be tempted to take such a cosmic risk.[11]

Together Vance and Warnke made a convincing case. But they

had argued the strategic realities of the situation. And political considerations would determine how the administration reacted. In the first place, President Carter himself, as yet unaware of how difficult negotiations with the Kremlin could sometimes be, was attracted by the prospect of achieving a foreign policy coup early in his administration. In a diary entry dated February 1, 1977, he expressed enormous enthusiasm for a variety of diplomatic initiatives including "deep cuts in total nuclear weapons."[12] But aside from the president's personal political ambitions, it was obvious that if reductions in the size of the Soviet missile force were not soon forthcoming, those who advocated the deployment of a new generation of weapons systems would be able to use the strategically questionable but politically potent issue of Minuteman vulnerability to bludgeon the administration into concessions. Not long after President Carter took office, Washington State's Senator Henry Jackson made the alternatives clear. In a memo to the President, Jackson urged the importance of achieving major reductions in the size of the Soviet Union's strategic forces as the only method of avoiding Minuteman vulnerability and the further escalation of the arms race. Carter and his staff realized that Jackson could be a valuable ally or a dangerous foe in a treaty fight. It seemed essential to keep him in the fold. But a SALT treaty based on the Vladivostok accords would not meet Jackson's minimums. He and a number of other like-minded senators would oppose such a treaty. Failing a negotiation in which major reductions were made in the size of the Soviet force, it was certain that Jackson would use his considerable influence to support further increases in America's strategic capabilities.

In mid-February President Carter wrote directly to President Brezhnev hoping to find out how the Kremlin would respond to an American proposal to abandon the Vladivostok formula and open a new negotiation aimed at achieving major reductions in strategic forces. According to Carter, Brezhnev's reply "was very negative concerning our ideas about nuclear arms control." Brzezinski described it as "brutal, cynical, sneering, and even patronizing . . . a very sharp rebuff."[13] Obviously the Soviets thought they had an agreement and were sticking grimly to the Vladivostok formula.

But not even Brezhnev's point-blank rejection of new talks resolved issues inside the administration. On the contrary, policymakers continued to debate the issues almost as though the Soviet leader had said nothing. On March 12, at a secret high-level meeting held in the White House cabinet room, the president finally came down on the side of those who wanted to try for a new agreement. Secretary of State Vance, who opposed the decision, was not optimistic. "I knew that the president's attempt to 'jump over SALT II' was a long shot," he later explained. Then again, he had to admit that there was an outside chance that "the Soviets, confronting a new president and the prospect of having to deal with him for at least four and perhaps eight years, would be willing to take a bold step. And success would mean a dramatic breakthrough in turning around the arms race." As Vance prepared for his mission to Moscow, he tried to look on the positive side. He would do his best.[14]

Though perhaps ill-advised, the decision to scrap Vladivostok is at least understandable. The president could not ignore what he viewed as the political realities. America's land-based missiles might not be vulnerable to a Soviet attack; but the fear of missile vulnerability was an argument that could only be met by achieving significant reductions in the size of the Russian forces or by augmenting our own. Then too, at the beginning of his administration, Carter wanted desperately to establish himself as an effective leader. He could hardly hope to accomplish that by simply ratifying a foreign policy initiative authored by his predecessor. Finally, Carter, a Christian moralist, seems to have had difficulty believing that the Russians could really distrust him or doubt his motives. In 1982, a sadder but wiser Jimmy Carter wrote that "in light of what I now know about the Soviet leaders it is easier for me to understand why the boldness of these first proposals would cause them concern." They "seemed to have doubted my motives, believing that I wanted to abandon the Vladivostok agreement and merely achieve some advantages over them in future negotiations."[15]

Carter turned responsibility for drafting the new American plan for arms control over to Brzezinski's Special Coordinating Committee of the National Security Council. William Hyland, a

holdover from Henry Kissinger's days as national security adviser, was assigned the task of actually drafting the proposal. The
Hyland draft called for reductions in both the overall ceiling and
subceilings proposed for MIRVed missiles outlined earlier in the
Vladivostok accord. Whereas Kissinger had agreed to a limit of
2,400 missile launchers for each side, Carter hoped to reduce
that figure to somewhere between 1,800 and 2,000. In like fashion, he wanted to reduce the number of MIRVed missiles in each
arsenal to 1,200 at most. Vladivostok stipulated a maximum of
1,320 MIRVed missiles.

The Carter plan added a new wrinkle with regard to MIRVs.
Each side would be restricted to 550 land-based MIRVed ICBMs.
Of these, the Soviets would be required to limit the number of
heavy SS-18s they deployed to 150. (The SS-18, which could be
MIRVed thirty times, was the largest of the modern missiles that
the Soviets deployed and the one of greatest concern to Senator
Jackson and others who believed that the Minuteman force was
becoming vulnerable to attack.) In order to slow development of
new missiles, the plan also called for restrictions on flight tests
and a ban on the testing of mobile ICBMs as well as any new
ICBMs. The last major aspect of the plan was a 2,500-kilometer
limit on the range of cruise missiles. As a concession to the
Soviets, the Backfire bomber would not be considered a strategic
weapons system for the purpose of the negotiation.

The Carter initiative struck at the very basis of the Vladivostok
accords. In 1974, the Soviets had made two major concessions.
First, they had agreed to drop their insistence that America's
forward-based systems be considered strategic weapons. Second,
they had conceded the principle of equal aggregates and in so
doing had agreed to dismantle upwards of 200 launch vehicles.
Since the United States did not have 2,400 strategic missiles
deployed, the agreement would not have required a similar sacrifice on its part. In return, Kissinger and Ford had abandoned
their insistence that the Soviets reduce the number of heavy
missiles they were planning to deploy. Conveniently ignoring
commitments made earlier by Kissinger and Ford, the Carter
administration was now proposing that the Soviets reduce the
number of MIRVed "heavies" in their inventories from 300 to

150 while dismantling another 150 modern operational missiles to meet the lower ceiling being proposed. For its part, the United States would agree to abandon plans to develop the MX missile while accepting limits in certain other areas of research and development. The inequity of the proposal was obvious. The Soviets would abandon costly forces in being. The United States would abandon plans. As one American arms controller put it, "We would be giving up future draft choices in exchange for cuts in their starting lineup."[16]

Whatever doubts Jimmy Carter had about this new approach to arms control were considerably eased by, of all people, Henry Kissinger. On the evening of March 18, the Carters, Brzezinski, and Henry and Nancy Kissinger dined together at the White House. Perhaps inevitably, the conversation turned to arms control and the president outlined the proposal he was about to make to the Soviets. He then asked Kissinger whether he thought the Kremlin would go for the idea. Kissinger raised his eyes toward the ceiling, seemed to think for a moment or two, and then, according to the president, said that he thought the plan "had a good chance to be accepted by the Soviets if they are sincere and want to make progress on disarmament."[17] No one can recall whether the former secretary of state had his tongue planted in his cheek as he spoke.

Practically no one in the administration, with the possible exception of the president himself, held out much hope that the Soviets would budge. Neither Brzezinski, nor Vance, nor even William Hyland, who drafted the American proposal, thought there was any but the most remote possibility of success. Because of this, Vance urged the president to establish a fall-back position for the purpose of keeping the negotiations alive. If the Soviets proved willing to go no further, the secretary was empowered to negotiate a second SALT treaty establishing the ceilings agreed upon at Vladivostok but deferring the cruise and Backfire issues for SALT III. Vance seems to have envisioned a scenario in which he would place the Carter plan on the table at the opening of the impending Moscow negotiations largely for purposes of establishing a bargaining position. He assumed that the Soviets would make a counterproposal and that the real negotiations could then begin in earnest with the bottom line approximating the original Vladivostok accord. The secretary of state was in for a rude awakening.

President Jimmy Carter took great pride in the openness of his administration. Perhaps that was good domestic politics after the revelations of the Vietnam era and Watergate. But it was not a sensible approach to the conduct of Soviet–American relations. The men in the Kremlin are by nature suspicious; they do not like surprises, and they do not approve of conducting serious negotiations in public. Yet this is precisely what Carter attempted to do. In a speech given before the United Nations General Assembly in mid-March 1977, he announced that in upcoming negotiations with the Soviets, the United States would seek strict controls or even a freeze on new types and new generations of weaponry, as well as "a deep reduction in the strategic arms of both sides." At the same time, he made it clear that he did not consider the Vladivostok accords as binding when he remarked that if a comprehensive arms reduction plan could not be arranged he would agree to "a limited agreement based on those elements of the Vladivostok accord on which we can find a complete consensus."[18]

These and other public statements by administration leaders struck the Soviets as not only inappropriate, but threatening. Brezhnev viewed the Vladivostok accords as binding. Now Carter seemed to be squirming free not only of Kissinger's commitments but of promises the president himself had earlier conveyed through Averell Harriman, who visited Moscow during the election campaign. Moreover, by publicizing his plan for major cuts in delivery systems, Carter seemed to be attempting to put the Soviets on the defensive in exactly the same way that he had over human rights. It would be difficult to reject the Carter plan without running the risk of being branded as uninterested obstructionists by a significant element of world public opinion. The United States had played this game before. The Baruch plan and more recently Nixon's fraudulent proposal for a MIRV ban were but two of a number of schemes that the Soviets believed had been designed to be rejected. The Kremlin knew the rules of the game. When Secretary of State Vance arrived in Moscow to open negotiations, they would be ready. Again Carter's Christian naïveté cost him dearly. It evidently never occurred to him that the Kremlin might view his public posturing as an indication that he was not serious. He still seems almost surprised as he tells us in his memoirs that the "Soviet leaders seemed to suspect that by making our positions known, we were waging a propaganda battle instead of negotiating in good faith."[19]

Although they did not receive the same VIP treatment earlier accorded Kissinger and Nixon, Cyrus Vance and his party were given a warm and friendly reception on arriving in Moscow. At the opening of this latest round of high-level SALT negotiations, however, it quickly became evident that the Soviet leadership was definitely not in a cordial mood. Brezhnev opened the festivities by making it clear that linkages existed between the various aspects of the Soviet–American relationship and that the United States could not expect progress in certain areas while attacking the Soviet Union elsewhere. He denounced President Carter's human rights campaign, especially his active encouragement of Soviet dissidents, as an unjustifiable interference in the internal affairs of the Soviet Union. If the SALT process was currently moribund, and it was, Brezhnev explained that this was the result of the rapid deterioration of the Soviet–American relationship that had set in since the new American administration came to power. Brezhnev then took pains to laud the Vladivostok accords as a triumph of statesmanship while stating categorically that future progress in the area of arms control would depend upon sticking to the 1974 agreement.

At the first working session of the Moscow conference, Andrei Gromyko echoed the Communist party chief's strong endorsement of Vladivostok and sternly warned that any attempt by the Carter administration to go further before formally ratifying earlier accords would place the entire SALT process in jeopardy. Having rejected the Carter plan for arms reduction before it was even placed on the table, the Soviet foreign minister then called a recess to give the stunned Americans time to consider their next move. Leslie Gelb, director of the State Department's Bureau of Political-Military Affairs, turned to Vance and said, "I think you just heard their answer." "You mean they're not going

to come back with a counterproposal?" Vance asked, disbeliev-
ing. "That's right," said Gelb, who bet a dollar on it.[20] Three
days of unproductive talks proved that Gelb was right. The Soviets would not consider a new negotiation. Nor were they attracted to the administration's fall-back position, which called for
the ceilings established at Vladivostok but without reference to
cruise missile deployments.

Why were the Soviets so adamant on the subject of new
negotiations? They had no interest in scoring some sort of propaganda coup by blaming the Carter administration for repudiating
Vladivostok. On the contrary, the Tass communiqué issued at the
end of the conference was a model of diplomatic propriety. Tass
played down the fact that the meeting had been a failure and
made no mention whatsoever of Vladivostok. The communiqué
said only that "the two sides agreed to continue their exchange
of views on SALT and other subjects." Moreover, when it became
clear that the negotiations were stalled, Gromyko and Vance
cooperated to create at least the appearance of progress. They
established eight joint working groups to investigate a whole
range of issues from the negotiation of the long-deferred comprehensive test ban treaty to the possibility of demilitarizing the
Indian Ocean. Clearly Brezhnev and Gromyko did not want
SALT to collapse.

Why then did they show so little flexibility? The answer that in
retrospect seems most credible is that they had very little room
for maneuver. As Nikita Khrushchev pointed out to Norman
Cousins during the period prior to the negotiation of the Partial
Test Ban Treaty, Russian leaders have political limits too. Henry
Kissinger believed that prior to signing the Vladivostok accords,
Brezhnev had been required to "knock heads" within his own
government, especially among the military, to get a consensus in
favor of "equal aggregates" at a time when the Soviets enjoyed
a significant advantage in the number of launch vehicles they
deployed. The Carter administration, ignoring this, was seeking
increased cuts and a strict limit on the deployment of SS-18s
while offering nothing in return. Even if Brezhnev had wanted to
go along with Carter's plan for deeper cuts, he probably did not
have sufficient political capital left to persuade the Politburo and

the military. As Gromyko's deputy, Georgi Kornienko, told Paul Warnke near the end of the conference: "You shouldn't have disregarded the fact that Brezhnev had to spill political blood to get the Vladivostok accords."[21] The United States was going to have to offer concessions in return.

But wasn't Secretary Vance prepared to negotiate a treaty based on what had been agreed to at Vladivostok? Why did Foreign Minister Gromyko pass up that opportunity? The answer seems to be that Washington and Moscow disagreed on the real meaning of Vladivostok. The Soviets insisted that Henry Kissinger's abortive 1976 agreement to count long-range bombers equipped with cruise missiles against the approved subceiling of 1,320 MIRVed missiles was integral to the entire package. They were unwilling to accept the overall ceilings agreed upon at Vladivostok without some limits on the number of air-launched cruise missiles the United States could deploy. The evidence clearly suggests that had Vance been empowered to offer concessions regarding the cruise, something might have come of the Moscow talks. Gromyko hinted during the negotiations that he might even be willing to reduce the overall ceiling on launchers established at Vladivostok by another two hundred missiles, but insisted on discussing this within the overall context of the abortive agreement he had worked out with Henry Kissinger in 1976. But Vance hadn't the authority. After the fact, sadder but wiser, Vance observed that "a prolonged negotiation was inevitable" for "the Soviets considered stringent cruise missile limits integral to the Vladivostok framework while we did not."[22]

The Moscow talks ended on a sour note. In the final meeting before the American delegation returned to Washington, Brezhnev blustered while the secretary of state grew angry "at the vehemence and finality with which [he] rejected our SALT proposals. There was not even a hint of a counter-proposal. He called our position 'unconstructive and one-sided' and 'harmful to Soviet Security.' . . . It was evident," Vance continued, that "there was no point in attempting to pursue serious negotiations on this trip." Later that evening, Vance let his anger get the better of him—a luxury good attornies don't often allow themselves. At a press conference held at Spasso House, the residence of Malcolm Toon, the American ambassador, he explained to the assembled reporters that the negotiations had collapsed. "They told us they had examined our proposals and did not find either acceptable. They proposed nothing new on their side."[23] After having laid total responsibility for the failure of the talks on the Soviet Union, Vance then described in broad outline the plan advanced by the administration. He did not speak in complete candor, however, for he neglected to include in his remarks those details that might have made the inequities in the Carter plan clear. Nor did he explain that the Soviets viewed limits on the cruise missile as an important component of the Vladivostok agreement.

The Russian leaders were furious. Carter and Vance may have seen themselves as neo-Wilsonians, practicing democratic diplomacy, but Brezhnev and the Politburo saw them as political tricksters attempting to lay the responsibility for the collapse of SALT on their doorstep. This was how the game had been played ever since the United States went public with the Baruch plan in 1946. Andrei Gromyko, who had been the Soviet UN representative when the United States made its first hopelessly unacceptable proposal for nuclear disarmament, knew exactly how to respond. He called a press conference of his own where he denounced the Carter plan as a "cheap and shady maneuver," and to prove his point he noted that while insisting on sharp reductions in the number of heavy missiles in the Soviet arsenal, the Carter administration would not consider limits on its own forward-based systems, nor would it agree to include in the limits established the nuclear arsenals of its allies Britain and France. If the United States continued to insist on reductions in the Soviet heavy missile force, he warned, the Soviets would certainly have the right to insist upon commensurate reductions in these areas. Gromyko then informed the press that while under the Carter plan the Soviet Union would be required to dismantle over three hundred weapons systems, the United States could actually add to its arsenal. Although the angry foreign minister indicated that the Soviet Union remained willing to negotiate, it was clear that SALT was in desperate trouble.

The final word on the outcome of the Moscow conference was James Earl Carter's, and it was not reassuring. He explained that he was pleased to learn that the Soviet government was willing to continue to discuss SALT, but warned that if he should conclude that the Soviets were not sincere, he would "be forced to consider a much more deep commitment to the development and deployment of additional weapons." To Anatoly Dobrynin, watching transfixed as the whole fragile structure of SALT seemed to come tumbling down about him, "President Carter seemed to be saying, 'Either you accept our position or we start the arms race and the cold war again.' His statement was taken as a *diktat* or ultimatum."[24]

It was a grim and dispirited group of arms controllers who returned to the United States from this foray to Moscow. Secretary Vance had made some serious mistakes. But now it was he who gently took the reins. Neo-Wilsonianism would have to go. Open covenants could only be openly arrived at if all sides agreed to play by the same rules. Otherwise, it was good rhetoric but bad diplomacy. Since the Soviets were not going to negotiate in front of the footlights, Henry Kissinger's back channel would have to be reopened. The American ambassador in Moscow, Malcolm Toon, did not have ready access to the Kremlin hierarchy, so Anatoly Dobrynin would again have to serve as the conduit. Neither Carter nor Brzezinski liked the idea, but in the end they acquiesced.

Working quietly through Dobrynin, Vance sought to convince the Soviets that the Carter administration was genuinely interested in pursuing arms control negotiations. Meanwhile, William Hyland, Leslie Gelb, and others at the State Department tried to work out a new bargaining formula that would include the fundamental objectives of the Carter administration as well as obvious Soviet concerns, particularly the cruise missile. Once it became clear that the administration was prepared to include the cruise in its new approach, the door was swiftly opened for an entirely new negotiation. Two years of complex, often frustrating discussions followed. At length, in the spring of 1979 the SALT II agreement finally came together. Like all such agreements it was a bundle of compromises, first among the competing bureaucracies that constituted each government, and then between the governments themselves.

The agreement scarcely resembled the first Carter plan, but it did represent a marginally useful step in the right direction. The agreed-upon total of strategic weapons that each side could possess was lower than had been agreed upon at Vladivostok. There were subceilings for MIRVed missiles and a lower subceiling for MIRVed ICBMs. Heavy bombers equipped with long range cruise missiles were to be counted under the MIRV subceiling. Because MIRV technology made the actual number of missile launchers on each side less significant, it would be a mistake to overemphasize the importance of these numerical limits. Nevertheless, under the terms of SALT II the Soviets would have been required to dismantle 270 strategic delivery vehicles while the United States, which was under the overall ceilings, could still augment its forces.

More important than these quantitative limits were restrictions on the right of each side to modernize strategic nuclear forces then in being. The two sides agreed to a fractionization freeze under which neither side could MIRV its missiles to a greater extent than had already been established through testing. This was important to Harold Brown and the Joint Chiefs, for it meant that the Soviet SS-18, which was theoretically capable of carrying anywhere from twenty to as many as forty warheads, would be limited to ten. The Trident SLBM would similarly be limited to fourteen separate warheads. Limits were also established for the future increase in size and payload capacity of existing missiles. Finally, each side would be permitted to test and deploy one new type of ICBM—a stipulation that would allow the United States to develop the MX missile.

A more limited part of the overall agreement, designated the Protocol, which was scheduled to expire at the end of 1981, banned the deployment of mobile ICBMs as well as the flight testing of ICBMs from mobile launchers. Flight testing and deployment of air-to-surface ballistic missiles with ranges greater than 600 kilometers were banned, and the ground-launched cruise missiles were limited to a range of 600 kilometers.

SALT II, like its predecessor, established no restraints on the technical and scientific developments that have so consistently fueled the arms race. Nor did the treaty limit the number of heavy ICBMs the Soviets could deploy. This is not to say, however, that the treaty lacked merit. The quantitative limits combined with the freeze on fractionization placed a definable maximum on the actual number of MIRVed warheads each side could deploy. Had the treaty been ratified, it would have been a simple matter for each side to accurately estimate the number of warheads in the other's arsenal and plan its own needs accordingly. When one considers how often in the past the arms race has been escalated because one side or the other overestimated its adversary's capabilities, it is clear that this was significant. Still, SALT II was no cause for rejoicing. No one, not even its friends, described the treaty as a major achievement.

President Carter and Leonid Brezhnev signed the SALT II treaty in Vienna on June 18, 1979. The Soviet leader could then relax; his battles were behind him. Carter, on the other hand, had yet another hurdle to face: he had to convince two thirds of the U.S. Senate to approve the agreement. As soon as it became clear that a treaty was going to be signed, the administration swung into action, unleashing a major lobbying campaign. According to President Carter:

> Thousands of speeches, news interviews, and private briefings were held. The personal and political interests of each senator were analyzed as we assessed the prospects of the ultimate vote for SALT II. It was obvious that we faced formidable opposition, but we had a good chance of success if we and the Soviets could demonstrate good faith, and if there were no obstacles to Senate confidence in the Soviet leaders.[25]

A well-organized opposition moved into high gear as well. One of the most active groups opposing the treaty was the American Security Council, which at the time had a national membership of some 230,000 persons including a great many retired military officers. The political action arm of the ASC, the Coalition for Peace Through Strength, included on its rolls some 232 congressmen and senators and was committed to a "national strategy based on over-all military and technological superiority over the Soviet Union." The Coalition was extremely well funded. It lobbied actively in Congress and ran a public information program that produced and distributed propaganda films in which the Soviet Union was depicted as streaking ahead in the arms race while the United States went about naïvely disarming itself unilaterally. One such film, *The Price of Peace and Freedom*, was broadcast by about 200 local television stations around the country and may have been seen by as many as 50 million Americans.

Another influential group, the Committee on the Present Danger, was founded in late 1976 by Paul Nitze (as of this writing, President Reagan's head negotiator at the Geneva talks in the reduction of medium and intermediate range missiles), Eugene Rostow (until recently the head of President Reagan's Arms Control and Disarmament Agency), and former Secretary of Defense James Schlesinger. The committee was not a large organization: membership was by invitation only. But those inside the charmed circle were influential people. These included among others Richard Perle, Senator Henry Jackson's aide and an assistant secretary of defense for President Reagan; former Deputy Secretary of Defense David Packard; Lane Kirkland, the head of the AFL-CIO; Professor Richard Pipes of Harvard University; and Richard Allen, Ronald Reagan's first national security adviser.

Like the American Security Council, the Committee on the Present Danger placed heavy emphasis on the importance of maintaining American military superiority over the Soviet Union. The committee claimed that

> our country is in a period of danger, and the danger is increasing. Unless decisive steps are taken to alert the nation, and to change the course of its policy, our economic and military capacity will become inadequate to assure peace and security.... The principal threat to our nation, to world peace, and to the cause of human freedom is the Soviet drive for dominance based upon an unparalleled military build-up.... If we continue to drift, we shall become second-best to the Soviet Union in overall military strength, our alliances will weaken, our promising rapprochement with China will be reversed. Then we could find ourselves isolated in a hostile world, facing the unremitting pressures of Soviet policy backed by

an overwhelming preponderance of power. Our national survival itself would be in peril, and we should face, one after another, bitter choices between war and acquiescence under pressure.[26]

If this statement sounds familiar, it should. Save for the Chinese reference, it might almost have been lifted from NSC-68 or the Gaither report. Scare tactics had worked repeatedly in the past. There was no reason to believe they would not work again.

In anticipation of a major national debate on arms control, some congressmen and senators began to stake out their territory early. Representative Charles H. Wilson, a member of the House Armed Services Committee, a full year and a half before the treaty was signed, was already parroting the views of the American Security Council. The treaty would, Wilson charged, "guarantee Soviet strategic superiority" over the United States for the remainder of the century. Wilson claimed to be deeply troubled by the fact that the terms of the agreement were to be policed by each side using national technical means of verification only. This meant that each side would have to rely on data collected by spy satellites, electronic eavesdropping equipment, and the like to assure itself that the other side was living up to its agreements. There would be no on-site inspections. Numerous representatives of the American intelligence community were satisfied that with the overlapping technical means of verification at their disposal, they could assess whether or not the Soviets were abiding by the agreement. Indeed, for years it had been an unspoken rule at arms control negotiations that nothing of significance would be seriously considered for inclusion in a treaty that could not be checked by national technical means. The history of SALT I had already demonstrated that a system of verification without on-site inspections could work, indeed was working. In 1972, the superpowers established the Standing Consultative Commission to enforce SALT I. Between then and 1980, both sides brought complaints to the SCC for adjudication. Yet despite meticulous investigation, no evidence was ever uncovered "of deliberate cheating by either party." Both sides had "engaged in inadvertant or minor transgressions" but in every instance these had "been corrected after referral to the commission."[27]

But neither Wilson nor the many others who used the old

on-site inspection argument were stayed from attacking SALT II
either by the record of the SCC or the sworn testimony of Defense Secretary Harold Brown and Admiral Stansfield Turner,
the head of the CIA. They were looking for a politically potent
argument with which to defeat the treaty. What might be described as the "You can't trust the Russians" approach to foreign
policy had been consistently effective for many years. And it was
about to work its magic again, even though SALT II had nothing
to do with trust.

With the treaty at last before the Senate Foreign Relations
Committee, the nation's newspapers ran numberless articles
debating the pros and cons of SALT II and arms control. One
news release issued by the Coalition for Peace Through Strength
claimed that, if ratified, SALT II would give the Soviets a two to
one advantage in strategic offensive weapons, a forty-seven to
one advantage in strategic defensive weapons, a six to one advantage in total megatonnage, and vast superiority over the United
States with regard to the accuracy of its missiles. To accept such
a claim one would also have to believe that the entire national
security establishment from the president and the Joint Chiefs on
down was filled with either traitors or fools. In part, that was
exactly what David Sullivan, a former CIA analyst, did argue. He
insisted that those two babes in the woods, Richard Nixon and
Henry Kissinger, had been consistently outmaneuvered and
outsmarted by the wily Soviets during the SALT I negotiations.
As a result, by taking advantage of loopholes in the agreement
and concealing their activities, the Russians had been able to
outstrip the United States in developing new weaponry. Warning
of Soviet guile and "deceit," Sullivan cautioned against making
the same mistake again. Other extreme critics claimed that the
Soviets had violated the SALT I accords by constructing new
missile silos, attempting to conceal the testing and deployment
of new missiles, and failing to dismantle older weapons as required under terms of the agreement. None of these charges was
corroborated, however, and all were categorically denied by the
Carter administration.

At a somewhat more rarified level, Professor Richard Pipes,
house intellectual for the Committee on the Present Danger,

published a number of pieces on the Op Ed page of *The New York Times* urging the defeat of the treaty. The Harvard political scientist insisted that the Soviets were preparing to fight and win a nuclear war, that the new heavy missiles gave them the capability they needed, and that unless the United States moved quickly to strengthen its civil defense and build an entire new generation of strategic delivery systems, all would be lost. Pipes constructed a terrifying scenario in which the Soviets would strike first at the United States and in the process destroy a major portion of our retaliatory forces. The American response, therefore, would be substantially reduced and its effectiveness would be further curtailed by Soviet civil defense preparations. A mere thirty million Russians, Pipes calculated, would be killed. According to Professor Pipes,

> the USSR could absorb the loss of 30 million of its people and be no worse off, in terms of human casualties, than it had been at the conclusion of World War II. In other words all of the USSR's multimillion cities could be destroyed without trace or survivors, and provided that its essential cadres have been saved it would emerge less hurt in terms of casualties than it was in 1945.[28]

The defenders of SALT quickly rebutted Pipes and other critics. Arthur Macy Cox, a staunch defender of arms control, insisted that the Soviets have no intention of deliberately initiating a nuclear war. Their strategic buildup, he argued, was an attempt to keep up with the United States. He quoted Marshal Victor Kulikov, one time Soviet chief of staff, who wrote that "the Soviet state effectively looking after its defense, is not seeking to achieve military superiority over the other side, but at the same time it cannot permit the approximate balance which has taken shape between the USSR and the US to be upset, to the disadvantage of our security."[29] Cox's view was seconded by Raymond L. Garthoff, a member of the SALT I delegation and an expert on Soviet military affairs, who wrote:

> The record indicates that the Soviet political and military leadership accepts a strategic nuclear balance between the Soviet Union and the United States as a fact, and as the probable and desirable

prospect for the foreseeable future. They are pursuing extensive military programs to ensure that they do not fail to maintain their side of the balance, which they see as in some jeopardy, given planned American programs. They seek to stabilize and to maintain mutual deterrence. In Marxist–Leninist eyes, military power is not and should not be the driving element in world politics. With "imperialist" military power held in check, the decisive social-economic forces of history would determine the future of the world.[30]

The defenders of SALT II and arms control received help from an unexpected source as two well-known Soviet dissidents spoke out against the hard-line view. Aleksandr Solzhenitsyn, who obviously has no love for the Soviet regime, nevertheless did not believe that the men who ruled the Soviet state had taken leave of their senses. Consequently, when he read Professor Pipes's version of reality behind the Kremlin's walls he explained that it affected him "in much the same way as I imagine Rostropovich would feel if he had to listen to a wolf playing a cello."[31] And in a 1980 "Letter from Exile" published in *The New York Times*, Andrei Sakharov, the leading Soviet dissident and the father of the Soviet hydrogen bomb, wrote:

> Despite all that has happened, I feel that the questions of war and peace and disarmament are so crucial that they must be given absolute priority even in the most difficult circumstances. It is imperative that all possible means be used to solve these questions and to lay the groundwork for further progress. Most urgent of all are steps to avert a nuclear war, which is the greatest peril confronting the modern world.[32]

Sakharov would never have offered such advice had he the slightest suspicion that the Soviet regime, which he more than most men had reason to despise, was planning to fight and win a nuclear war.

Other critics of the hard-line view disputed the claim that the Soviets were about to achieve the capability of launching a successful surprise attack against American missile installations. While serving as professor of strategy at the Naval War College, Thomas Etzold noted that the Soviets did not possess, nor were they ever likely to possess, a missile force reliable enough to accomplish this aim. Missile systems are too complex, the possibility that something might go wrong is too distinct for any sane Soviet (or American) strategist to ever willingly take the gamble of launching a first strike. Etzold explained:

> Simply put, for a nuclear weapon really to do what it theoretically is capable of doing, its delivery system must be "on line" rather than down for maintenance; it must work when activated; and all the electronics of the weapon itself must function in sequence and as programmed to bring about specific weapons effects necessary. In addition, the bomb must arrive in the proper sequence and timing in relation to other weapons in use in the area if it is not to be blown off course or otherwise prevented from operating properly. Finally, the weapon must detonate at the proper altitude, to obtain the desired overpressure at the exact target area.[33]

Etzold also explained that even though Soviet and American missiles have become increasingly accurate, they will never be accurate enough to guarantee a successful attack against hardened missile installations:

> Bias is the term for the distance, or difference, between the intended target and the center of the circle within which half the reentry vehicles fall. Course deviations result from variations in the electromagnetic spectrum and gravity fields around the earth. They may be caused as well by variations in atmospheric density, temperature, wind, and, in large-scale nuclear war, perhaps also by the heat, dust, concussion, debris, and radiation caused by other nuclear devices.[34]

Because there is no scientific method of correcting for bias, Secretary of Defense Harold Brown insisted that "a number of our ICBMs could be expected to survive even a well-executed Soviet surprise attack."[35] And the then secretary of defense, James Schlesinger, one of the founders of the Committee on the Present Danger, told Congress in secret testimony in 1974 that

> I believe there is some misunderstanding about the degree of reliability and accuracy of missiles. . . . It is impossible for either side to acquire the degree of accuracy that would give them a high confidence first strike, because we will not know what the actual

accuracy would be like in a real world context. As you know, we have acquired from the Western Test Range a fairly precise accuracy, but in the real world we would have to fly from operational bases to targets in the Soviet Union. The parameters of the flight from the Western Test Range are not really very helpful in determining those accuracies to the Soviet Union. We can never know what degrees of accuracy would be achieved in the real world. . . .

The point I would like to make is that if you have any degradation in operational accuracy, American counter-force capability goes to the dogs very quickly. We know that, and the Soviets should know it, and that is one of the reasons that I can publicly state that neither side can acquire a high confidence first strike capability. I want the President of the United States to know that for all the future years, and I want the Soviet leadership to know that for all future years.[36]

The best efforts of friends and enemies of SALT II notwithstanding, the treaty's fate was not decided as a result of public pressure. Despite the fear-mongering and propaganda, the general public remained uninterested in SALT. The issues involved seemed so complex, the mysteries of nuclear strategy so utterly esoteric, that the public gave what amounted to a collective yawn and refused to become involved. By the time the treaty reached the Senate in the summer of 1979, public attention was fixed on the Iranian revolution and the seeming collapse of American influence in the Middle East. This left the Senate with wide latitude to debate the treaty. That should have provided the administration with an advantage, since the Democrats held a majority in the upper House. A fractious group under the best of circumstances, however, Senate Democrats fully lived up to their reputation, splitting badly over SALT. Indeed, the treaty debate produced some surprising bedfellows as extremes of left and right joined together to oppose the president's handiwork.

Two conservative Democratic opponents of SALT II whose views deserve close analysis are Senator Henry Jackson of Washington and Paul Nitze. Long before the treaty had been signed it was clear that Nitze would oppose it. The Committee on the Present Danger, an organization he helped found, had been urging the administration to abandon SALT for months. Despite his "superhawk" reputation, Nitze neither was nor is opposed to all arms control agreements. He did insist, however, that such agreements provide what in his estimation were real advantages for the United States. And on balance he gave SALT II low marks in this regard. Nitze was particularly concerned about the danger of Minuteman vulnerability, which he saw as an inevitable outgrowth of the deployment of the Soviet Union's newer heavy missiles. Because the treaty left the Soviets free to deploy these weapons in sufficient numbers to launch a disarming first strike, he opposed it. Nitze seems to have believed that the administration had settled for too little, that the Kremlin's leaders needed an arms control agreement as much or more than the United States did, and that they could be made to pay for it. He realized that some proponents of the treaty viewed it as a means of checking further Soviet military expansion and feared that without the treaty the Soviets would streak ahead of the United States militarily. But he dismissed that possibility, arguing that the Soviet economy, which was already showing signs of stress, could not stand the added pressure. Holding to views developed almost thirty years before when he headed the State–Defense Department study group that produced NSC-68, Nitze argued that the United States should abandon SALT II and instead devote its energies to increasing its military capabilities. Such pressure, he seems to have believed, would bring the Kremlin to the point where it would be willing to make significant concessions.

Nitze's opposition to the treaty, though not unexpected, was nonetheless a blow to the Carter administration. He was a prestigious Democrat who had been a key policymaker in the Truman administration, a member of the SALT I negotiating team, and an adviser on international security affairs to Presidents Kennedy and Johnson. His views carried considerable weight with conservatives as well as some moderates in the party. Even so, Henry Jackson's persistent attacks on the treaty were far more disturbing. Jackson was a powerful senator, the second-ranking member of the Armed Services Committee and a man who exerted considerable influence over the Joint Chiefs of Staff. Moreover, he was widely reputed to be among the most knowledgeable in the upper House on the subjects of nuclear weaponry.

Even before the negotiations had begun, the Carter people, aware that Jackson had strongly opposed SALT I, consulted the senator on the terms he thought ought to be included in the agreement. But the treaty bore little resemblance to Jackson's views. He came out in opposition three months before the agreement had been signed. Later, just before the president's scheduled flight to Vienna for the summit conference where he was to sign SALT II, Jackson unleashed a scathing attack.

> To enter a treaty which favors the Soviets as this one does on the ground that we will be in a worse position without it, is appeasement in its purest form. . . . Against overwhelming evidence of a continuing Soviet strategic and conventional military buildup, there has been a flow of official administration explanations, extenuations, excuses. It is all ominously reminiscent of Great Britain in the 1930's when one government pronouncement after another was issued to assure the British public that Hitler's Germany would never achieve military equality—let alone superiority. The failure to face reality today, like the failure to do so then—that is the mark of appeasement.[37]

It was absurd to compare the United States in 1979, a nation that wielded military power unparalleled in human history, with the Great Britain of 1938. Yet Jackson's speech by turns worried and infuriated the president. Appeasement was such a loaded word, and so effective. It was raining in Vienna when the official entourage boarded *Air Force One* for the flight to the summit. But Carter, who recalled that British Prime Minister Neville Chamberlain had returned from the Munich Conference carrying an umbrella to protect himself against London's wet weather, forbade any umbrellas on the flight. "I'd rather drown than carry an umbrella," he said.[38]

Senator Jackson was a man of the World War II generation whose adult recollections spanned the period from the 1930s to the present. He viewed the Soviet Union as America's inveterate enemy and saw the two superpowers as being in a continuing struggle for global supremacy. He also remembered a time when isolationism was predominant in the United States and the

American military establishment was of no consequence. The SALT process, he feared, might lead to a reemergence of traditional American attitudes toward international affairs and defense policy. If the American people were to become convinced as a result of SALT that peace with the Soviets was likely, Jackson feared that they would abandon the assertive foreign and military policies of the postwar era. He was equally convinced that if American military power withered in relation to that of the Soviet Union, the ability of the United States to influence the course of political and economic events beyond its shores would be seriously circumscribed and the Soviets would gain the upper hand in the global struggle for political influence and power that had been the central fact of international life since 1945. There was really little President Carter could have done short of abandoning SALT that would have satisfied Jackson.

Treaties do not ordinarily pass the U.S. Senate, where a two-thirds majority is required, unless presidents do their homework. Even then, Senate approval of an important agreement is by no means assured. John Hay, secretary of state during the McKinley and Theodore Roosevelt administrations, remarked in 1903 that "there will always be 34% of the Senate on the blackguard side of every question." "A treaty entering the Senate," he said, "is like a bull going into the arena: no one can say just how or when the final blow will fall—but one thing is certain—it will never leave the arena alive."[39]

Not much had changed in the intervening seventy-six years. The Carter administration was of course doing an intensive job of lobbying on behalf of the treaty. But that was not nearly enough. The president realized even before he set pen to treaty in Vienna that he was going to have to make major concessions to a number of interested parties in order to win Senate approval. Waiting first in line were the Joint Chiefs of Staff, who were none too enthusiastic about the new agreement. If they testified against the treaty before the Senate Foreign Relations Committee, the full Senate would never approve it. Just prior to his departure for the Vienna summit, Carter made a bid for the military's support by approving the development of the MX missile. Two days after signing SALT II he announced that the new system would be deployed in a controversial mode that would cover thousands of square miles of the desert Southwest. The estimated cost of this gargantuan project was $40 billion. The history of military procurement in the postwar period suggested that actual costs would probably come to at least twice that.

Carter's decision to build the MX missile points up one of the persistent ironies in the history of arms control. In order to win support for an agreement that is theoretically supposed to limit the arms race somehow, presidents have repeatedly found themselves compelled to support escalation. President Nixon could not have sold SALT I to the Senate without excluding a MIRV ban from the negotiations. SALT I produced an ABM treaty, to be sure. But it also paved the way for the massive augmentation of deployed warheads on both sides that subsequently took place. Seven years later, President Carter was forced to pay an equally high price, one that had enormous implications for the future of the arms race.

Although the United States had officially adopted an assured destruction strategy in 1964 and never publicly strayed from that position, in fact targeting policies had undergone significant changes over the years. When he first announced the new strategy, Secretary of Defense McNamara explained that America's retaliatory capability would be assured if, in the event of an attack by the Soviet Union, the United States could strike back destroying 50 percent of the Soviet Union's industrial capacity (he later increased the figure to 70 percent) and 25 percent of her population. To accomplish this, Defense Department experts calculated that the United States would need to deliver four hundred warheads on target. Because assured destruction included as a secondary consideration a minimal offensive damage-limiting capability, the Johnson administration actually deployed more weapons than this. The extra warheads were targeted on certain Soviet military installations. Nevertheless, during the Johnson administration, when strategic planners discussed assured destruction they spoke in terms of hundreds, not thousands of warheads.

Ten years later, during the Ford administration, Secretary of Defense James Schlesinger engineered a significant change in nuclear strategy that at the time went largely unchallenged. Schlesinger insisted that assured destruction placed too much emphasis on deterrence and not enough on national survival in the event of a nuclear war. Like McNamara during the early months of the Kennedy administration, he believed policymakers ought to be armed with nuclear options, and that they ought to have the capability of fighting limited nuclear wars. MIRV as well as the increasing accuracy of ballistic missiles, moreover, made this seem possible. Schlesinger never publicly abandoned assured destruction, which remained the official policy of the United States. But he did modify it in a most significant way. Not only would Washington seek to deter the Soviets from attacking, but if a nuclear war should break out, the United States needed to be certain that the Soviets would not recover at a faster rate than the United States. This, Defense Department analysts explained, would require an immense expansion of America's nuclear arsenal. Where once policymakers had agreed that a successful retaliatory attack by four hundred warheads would do, the Schlesinger Defense Department supported the deployment of some 8,500 warheads.

Though Schlesinger described this change as a mere modification of the assured destruction strategy, it represented a good deal more than that. The increased number and accuracy of American weapons deployed in the mid-1970s demonstrated that while giving lip service to deterrence, the defense establishment was developing a nuclear-war fighting and perhaps even a first strike capability.

That was the situation when President Carter decided to build and deploy two hundred new MX missiles, each armed with ten 330-kiloton warheads. Because these were to be additional forces, the president had to explain why they were needed. This he did in August 1980, with Presidential Directive Number 59, which announced still another modification in nuclear strategy. This new directive moved the United States further in the direction set earlier by Secretary Schlesinger. It called for more Soviet military bases to be targeted (especially missile silos) and a heavy emphasis on developing the capability to destroy Soviet command and control facilities as well as the shelters that would be used by Soviet leaders in the event of a nuclear attack. By degrees over a period of a decade, the United States has moved from a commitment to deterrence to the development of a limited nuclear-war fighting capability. It is a change of monumental consequence, one that may result in catastrophe. In his memoirs, President Carter portrays himself as a man absolutely dedicated to ending the nuclear arms race. And perhaps intellectually and emotionally he is. But as Thomas Etzold has pointed out, PD-59, which remains to this day the strategy of the United States, is *"a recipe for fighting, not avoiding nuclear war."*[40]

President Carter's change of heart with regard to the MX was not the only concession he felt called upon to make in pursuit of the ratification of SALT II. Senator Sam Nunn, from the president's home state of Georgia, warned that he would not support the treaty unless there was a more substantial increase in overall defense expenditures than the president had planned. When Henry Kissinger, the father of SALT I, told the Senate Foreign Relations Committee that like Nunn he could not support the agreement unless it was tied to increased defense spending, Carter again bent to the pressure, promising that he would approve a 5 percent annual real increase in defense spending over the next five years. By the time he had finished making the compromises he deemed essential to win Senate approval of SALT II, President Carter had done as much as any president before him to escalate the arms race.

The irony and the danger that resulted from Carter's single-minded pursuit of the treaty's ratification was not lost on a number of senators who soon concluded that, far from helping to check the arms race, SALT II was likely to fuel it. In a letter to the president published in *The New York Times,* two Democrats, George McGovern of North Dakota and William Proxmire of Wisconsin, joined Republican Mark Hatfield of Oregon in announcing that they would vote against the treaty because it left the door open for the development of a new generation of weapons systems. Cruise missile technology alone might have produced this reaction. But it was the president's MX decision that evoked the loudest outcry, for the senators believed that this weapon, when added to the American arsenal, would have a sharply destabilizing effect on the nuclear balance. With three times the throw weight of the Minuteman and a CEP of about four hundred feet, the MX would have been the deadliest missile deployed by either side and would have given the United States something very close to true counterforce capability. Critics of the MX even envisioned a scenario that began with a Soviet–American crisis and ended in all-out nuclear war merely because of the existence of the new missile. Arms controller Earl Ravenal, writing in *The New York Times,* explained that MIRVed ten times, the MX posed a direct threat to the survivability of Soviet land-based missiles. The difference was that while the United States had 50 percent of its warheads at sea and another 25 percent on manned bombers, the Soviets had placed most of their nuclear eggs in the land-based basket. In 1979, fully 85 percent of their warheads were deployed aboard fixed, land-based missiles. Because of this, Ravenal believed the Soviets would be almost compelled to launch their ICBMS early in a crisis, fearing that if they did not, their weapons would be destroyed in an American first strike.

Not only would the people of the United States be less secure with SALT II and MX than without it, William Proxmire pointed out, there was another irony—they would have to pay through the nose for the privilege. The senator from Wisconsin, whose Golden Fleece Award regularly annoys members of the academic community while winning him invaluable publicity, pointed out that SALT II would be accompanied by huge and needless increases in defense spending. Proxmire's guess was that before the bargaining was over, the treaty might end up costing the public as much as $100 billion. He might have inquired, though he refrained from doing so, how much the administration would have been required to spend on new weapons had it not just entered into a major arms control agreement.

Many Republicans were quick to join in criticism of the treaty. According to Carter, both former President Ford and Howard Baker, minority leader in the Senate, informed him almost two years before the treaty was ready for consideration that they would oppose it. It was not that they disapproved of the contents of the treaty—in fact they had no precise idea what it might contain. As Baker explained, he had supported the president on the controversial Panama Canal Treaty and simply could not afford to back him up again. Carter takes a jaundiced view of such Republican opposition in his memoirs, commenting that to "support a Democratic President on two such difficult issues would have been almost suicidal for those whose political future depended on rich extremists who finance a lot of Republican campaigns."[41]

Carter may have been wrong about who finances Republican party politics. But he was certainly accurate in suggesting that a great many of those Republicans who opposed SALT II did so for political reasons. The Democrats took advantage of the missile gap during the Eisenhower administration, proving that national security questions, if they are important enough, almost inevitably become partisan issues. The Republicans would have been saints had they ignored this opportunity. Carter was already in political difficulties when the treaty debate began in earnest. His inability to deal effectively with a variety of problems including inflation, unemployment, a rising federal deficit, and the energy crisis, had raised serious questions about his leadership abilities. His vacillation when dealing with the revolution in Iran, and his decision not to attempt to save the Shah from the forces of Islamic fundamentalism, had further eroded public confidence in him. For the Republicans, SALT II was an irresistible target of opportunity.

The Republican opposition enjoyed one great advantage provided gratis by the Soviet government. SALT II was supposed to reflect the continuing spirit of détente between Moscow and Washington. But what did détente actually mean? Since 1977, the Kremlin had intervened in the war between Ethiopia and Somalia, vastly increased its aid program to the Marxist government of South Yemen, and given aid and encouragement to the Vietnamese who were then fighting a war against the Khmer Rouge in Cambodia. Could this be the record of a nation truly interested in reducing global tensions? Henry Kissinger had popularized the idea of linkage and practiced it where possible. In 1977, the Kremlin demonstrated that it too believed in linkage when it insisted that President Carter could not take a strong position on human rights, encouraging Russian dissidents such as Andrei Sakharov, and still expect arms control negotiations to go smoothly. Now it was the turn of the Republicans in the Senate. Howard Baker and his colleague Robert Dole of Kansas, both presidential aspirants, urged other senators to vote for or against the treaty on the basis of an overall judgment of Soviet behavior around the world. Emulating Henry Cabot Lodge, Sr., another Republican Senate leader of an earlier age who had fought the Treaty of Versailles by indirection, Baker also threatened to play the amendment game. Even before the treaty had been reported out of committee, he proposed a number of sweeping changes in the agreement. One, which would have required the Soviets to reduce by one half the number of heavy missiles they could deploy, would certainly have killed the treaty instantaneously.

Cyrus Vance was frustrated and annoyed by all the partisan maneuvering. SALT had been the work of three administrations representing both major political parties. Democrats and Republicans alike sought arms control agreements "out of a cold assessment of American security interests." To argue then that SALT could be used as "a reward for good behavior on the part of Moscow" made no sense. Both nations would benefit by ratifying the agreement or, contrariwise, suffer for refusing to do so.[42]

Still, all the sound and fury of the opposition notwithstanding, Vance, like other administration leaders including the president himself, believed the treaty would be ratified. It had widespread public support as well as the endorsement of the Joint Chiefs and America's allies abroad. Besides, the administration had orchestrated its part of the ratification debate expertly. Lloyd Cutler, a close friend of Vance and a well-known Washington attorney, was doing a superb job of lobbying in the Senate, while "Zbig" Brzezinski provided valuable backup from the White House. Moreover, a "ratification bargain" had all but come together in the weeks after the Vienna summit. "Politically," Secretary Vance later wrote, "I believed the MX production decision, to be followed shortly by a basing decision, would relieve the Joint Chiefs' concern about the long-term trends in the strategic balance and strengthen their endorsement of SALT. The MX decision, when added to our planned growth in defense spending," he continued, "would also reassure those senators concerned about trends in the military balance."[43]

But Vance's optimism gave way to serious concern in mid-July when events took a nasty turn. That perennial political hot potato, the Soviet presence in Cuba, suddenly became a factor in the treaty debate. On July 17, during a public hearing on the SALT treaty, Senator Richard Stone of Florida pointedly remarked that the presence of Russian combat forces on the island would pose a serious threat to America's security. Shortly thereafter he called upon the administration to reveal what it knew about the possibility that Fidel Castro was playing host to Soviet combat units. Stone was obviously getting classified information from someone inside the American intelligence community. For several months, American operatives had been gathering information on this very subject. While the data was still fragmentary, it did appear that some Russian combat troops were stationed in Cuba.

By the end of July, the rumor that the Soviets had actual combat forces in Cuba had gained wide currency. The State Department and the intelligence people were working overtime to come up with something concrete, and Secretary Vance thought the situation serious enough to warn the Soviets "that the presence of a combat unit in Cuba would inflame U.S.–Soviet relations at a critical moment in the Senate debate on the SALT II treaty."[44]

Before the end of August, the stepped-up efforts of the intelligence services had produced results. On August 25, the secretary of state was informed that a Soviet motorized combat brigade of some two to three thousand men was stationed in Cuba and had been there at least since 1975 or 1976. It seemed certain to Vance that when this information reached the public, treaty opponents would use it for their own purposes since, as he later explained, "in the political climate of 1979, a rational separation of the brigade issue and SALT was not possible."[45]

With the treaty now clearly in trouble, the secretary took the unusual step of summoning Anatoly Dobrynin, who was then in the Soviet Union, back to Washington. He next lodged a formal protest with the Soviet embassy and instructed Under Secretary of State David Newsom to call the leaders of both houses of

Congress to catch them up on these fast-moving developments. Senator Frank Church, the chairman of the Committee on Foreign Relations, received Newsom's call at home in Idaho where he was combining a short vacation with some political campaigning. Church believed that when the Cuban news broke in the press it would "sink SALT." He feared it might sink him too since he was in serious political trouble at the time. In a panic, he telephoned Vance, urging him to go public before the story leaked. When Vance demurred, Church, whose record on defense spending and SALT was under unremitting attack by his conservative opponents, broke the story himself. In a transparent attempt to preempt his political opponents, Church called a press conference and told the assembled reporters that the Senate would refuse to ratify SALT II until the Soviets removed their troops from Cuba. He also warned that the members of the upper House would probably demand proof of a Soviet evacuation before even considering the agreement.

Of course the Russian brigade, which had actually been in Cuba since 1962, was no threat to the United States. In addition, its presence in no way violated earlier agreements between Washington and Moscow relative to the Soviet presence in Cuba. Nevertheless, opponents of the treaty were quick to take advantage of the situation, echoing Church's demands.

Initially, President Carter hoped to play down the significance of the Soviet contingent in Cuba, hoping that the furor would die away. But the Cuban story, which remained in the headlines for days, could not be dismissed so easily. Something had to be done. But what? Obviously, the Soviets would not withdraw the brigade; under the circumstances, that would have been humiliating. Secretary Vance had in mind a compromise involving the removal of the brigade's command structure and its heavy weapons so that it could no longer be considered as having any offensive capabilities. But Vance, struggling to find some way out of this utterly ludicrous yet politically difficult situation, turned out to be his own worst enemy. At his regularly scheduled press conference, held on September 5, he was asked what the administration was going to do about those Soviet forces in Cuba. His reply, which was intended to "preserve negotiating flexibility while conveying seriousness," was that he would "not be satisfied with the maintenance of the status quo."[46] To the secretary's everlasting chagrin, that statement was instantaneously interpreted to mean that the United States would demand the removal of the troops from Cuba. Of course that was not what Vance had in mind. But the administration, already under attack for its vacillating foreign policy, could not explain its true intentions without appearing to vacillate once again, this time over a highly charged emotional issue.

During the remainder of the month of September, Vance met several times with Ambassador Dobrynin and Foreign Minister Gromyko, hoping that the Russians would help him find some way out of this embarrassing imbroglio. But the Soviets were in no mood to remove a unit that had been in Cuba for nearly twenty years simply because the U.S. Senate insisted upon it. Nor would they withdraw the brigade's heavy weapons or dismantle its command structure. Brezhnev did write President Carter assuring him that the brigade was a training unit and that Moscow had "no intention of changing its status as such in the future." But that was as far as he would go. President Carter had suffered another humiliating blow to his prestige, for to most observers it appeared that the administration had issued an ultimatum to the Soviets, been rebuffed, and then simply backed away. An already unpopular president thus lost even more standing with the public and the SALT II treaty had suffered what to many seemed a mortal wound.

Frank Church (who was defeated in his bid for reelection) kept the treaty in committee until November, by which time the storm over Soviet troops in Cuba had more or less blown itself out. Then, by a vote of nine to six the Foreign Relations Committee recommended that the full Senate approve the agreement. But that was the end of the road for SALT II. After testing Senate waters, Robert Byrd of West Virginia, the majority leader, announced that the treaty would not be debated immediately. Byrd was indefinite about when the debate might begin except to say it would take place sometime in 1980. When queried by reporters, he denied that the president did not have the votes. What else could he say?

It will always remain a moot question whether the administration would have brought the treaty to a vote in 1980. On December 20, 1979, Soviet forces invaded Afghanistan and two weeks later the president asked Senator Byrd to defer consideration of the treaty. If the Cuban episode did not kill the chances for ratification of SALT II, the invasion of Afghanistan certainly did. As Secretary Vance would later sorrowfully admit: "Ratification was blocked because the opponents were successful in creating political linkage between the treaty and the problem of restraining Moscow's attempts to expand its influence." Vance was depressed not only at his own failure but because the enemies of the treaty had "legitimized the fallacy that the United States could use the treaty to punish the Soviet Union for actions in areas that were unrelated to the strategic balance." That certainly did not bode well for the future of arms control.[43]

Historian Thomas A. Bailey has described Woodrow Wilson's decision to kill the Treaty of Versailles rather than see it enacted with Republican reservations as the "supreme infanticide." SALT II died a squalid death in comparison, the victim of an intensive lobbying campaign by such groups as the American Security Council, partisan opposition, administration bungling, and a desperate political ploy by a single Democratic senator. There is an ironic epilogue to the story, however. Even though SALT II was not approved by the Senate, as of this writing it remains unofficially in effect. After the debacle, President Carter announced that he would abide by its terms so long as the Soviets agreed to do the same. They did. President Reagan, who during the election campaign proclaimed the treaty "fatally flawed," has nevertheless followed suit.

A decade of efforts to achieve significant arms control has produced little substantive result, and greater insecurity for both superpowers. More nuclear weapons are deployed now than ever before and each side continues to add to its arsenal. Assuming that the leaders of both the Soviet Union and the United States were honestly concerned about reducing the danger posed by nuclear weapons, how may we account for their meager accomplishments? The radical critic Dwight MacDonald offered what is the best answer to these questions more than thirty years ago in the immediate aftermath of the attacks on Hiroshima and Nagasaki. MacDonald was angered by the naïveté of some like Robert Oppenheimer, who argued that nuclear weapons were nothing to worry about because they were too terrifying to be used in warfare. Rational leaders would recognize this, Oppenheimer believed, and would therefore use nuclear energy for peaceful purposes only. MacDonald insisted that, on the contrary, nuclear weapons would change nothing. National leaders would use them just as they had used conventional armaments to attain their ends. Presidents, prime ministers, even dictators, functioned within an institutional structure that governed their behavior. It was the nation-state that had to be changed, Mac-Donald insisted. "We must get the modern national state before it gets us."[48]

Epilogue: The Chariot of the Sun

Leo Szilard, Niels Bohr, Robert Oppenheimer, and Albert Einstein all realized that the nuclear power they had helped release wrought a revolution in human affairs. In its military applications, it inverted the logic of warfare. Its civilian uses held out a Faustian promise of limitless energy, but at the cost of eternal caretaking. Men groped for images to explain this revolution, and ransacked the attics of mythology to find a figure awesome enough to personify the change in the human condition. The figure most frequently chosen was the Titan Prometheus, who stole fire from the forge of the god Hephaestus and gave it to humanity, only to be punished for his presumption by being chained to a mountaintop in the Caucasus. There each day an eagle alit on the rebellious Titan and devoured his liver, which regenerated each night. (When the artificial element with atomic number 61 was definitively synthesized and identified at the Oak Ridge laboratories in 1945 as part of experiments with uranium, it was named promethium.) Among many others, *The New York Times* science reporter William Laurence used the image of humanity's benefactor to describe uranium as the "new substance, a veritable Prometheus bringing to man a new form of Olympic fire."[1]

But another image drawn from Greek mythology may have been more appropriate: the fate of Phaëthon, child of the sun god Helios. When the boy asked that his father prove his paternity, Helios rashly agreed, swearing an unbreakable oath. Phaëthon then demanded to be allowed to drive his father's chariot for one day. The appalled Helios, bound by his oath, had to let the boy have his way. The exhilarating ride up the vault of the sky quickly turned to terror as the horses of the sun went out of control. The boy had seized more power than he was capable of handling. The steeds leaped up, then plunged down to earth, scorching all living things and drying up rivers, creating the Libyan desert in once-fertile Africa. Zeus himself had to put an end to the mad ride by killing Phaëthon with a thunderbolt. Our military, political, and scientific leaders seem to be latter-day Phaëthons, holding reins of power that they are too immature to control.

A middle-level official in the Reagan administration, T. K. Jones, blithely assures us that we can survive a nuclear war by digging holes in our backyards and driving our automobiles over them. Somehow, by cowering under our cars, we will emerge to resume life after what Nukespeak blandly labels a "nuclear exchange." But a scientist who has studied the effects of nuclear war somberly warns: "If the civil defense budget were in my hands, I would spend all $120 billion on morphine."[2]

American and Soviet policymakers alike have failed to develop constructive approaches to the nuclear revolution. They behave like sleepwalkers unable to rouse themselves to the realization that the very existence of nuclear weapons has fundamentally changed international political affairs. Their instinct, from Roosevelt to Reagan, from Stalin to Chernenko has been to integrate nuclear weapons into national military arsenals as though these instruments of mass destruction were nothing more than conventional weapons of war writ large. President Truman explained this view simplemindedly when he remarked that the atomic bomb was "just another artillery weapon." This "bigger bullet" rationalization is the refuge of small minds dwarfed even more by the immensity of the power they control.

No president save Ronald Reagan has ever admitted that he was uninterested in arms control or disarmament. Even Reagan quickly learned that was bad politics. So every administration beginning with Truman's and now including Reagan's has spent a certain amount of time posturing, pretending to be genuinely interested in arms reduction. But they have pursued arms control within the confines of a narrow, conventional definition of the national interest. Neither the United States nor the Soviet Union has accepted the premise that they have a shared interest in eliminating nuclear weapons from the world. Each side has pursued arms control negotiations for traditional political reasons— because each hopes to gain some narrowly defined advantage, which in reality means either gaining superiority or staying close in the arms race. Why, after all, did the Soviets consent to negotiate an arms control agreement in 1968? They feared that the United States was about to deploy a new technology, ABM, that would threaten the credibility of their deterrent. Why did President Nixon agree to negotiate a SALT agreement? The Soviet buildup in offensive weaponry threatened to outstrip American forces unless checked through diplomacy. The negotiations we know as SALT came about because both sides felt that an agreement would be to their advantage.

Advantage, however, is always defined within the context of the ongoing arms race. It is the arms race itself that is the problem. It must be attacked directly. That can only take place as part of a more broadly based effort to reduce tensions and create a general community of interest between the Soviet Union and the United States. Of all the leaders of the postwar era, only a few —Dwight Eisenhower and Henry Kissinger come immediately to mind—have understood this. But not even these leaders were able to stand up to the political and institutional forces arrayed against them and mount a successful assault against the dynamic of the arms race.

Where policymakers have failed to comprehend the new world created by nuclear weaponry, military leaders have complicated the problem by their tireless pursuit of armaments that are useless in war, but that threaten to eliminate life on the planet. Britain's Prime Minister Lord Salisbury remarked in 1892, "If you believe the soldiers, nothing is safe. . . . If they were allowed full scope they would insist on the garrisoning of the moon to protect us from Mars." Salisbury undoubtedly thought at the time that this was a bit of ironic humor, a Jules Verne fantasy. Yet less than a century later, the American military is actually demanding the militarization of outer space. For the past thirty years, Pentagon planners have used the concept of national security to justify the development of a bewildering array of high-technology weapons systems—many of them useless. America's military leaders have developed a thirst for state-of-the-art weaponry that seemingly knows no limits. As a result, strategic weapons and delivery systems have proliferated out of all proportion to need.

But in spite of all its expensive hardware, the American defense establishment has not understood the significance of the nuclear revolution. As early as 1946, the strategist Bernard Brodie realized that nuclear weapons, when combined with modern delivery systems, would revolutionize warfare. They could serve only as a deterrent. The military side of the nuclear paradox stated that we had to develop weapons *not* to use them. Difficult to grasp at best, this idea seems to have altogether eluded current military strategists in the United States. Early strategic thinkers like Brodie also emphasized the importance of preserving a firebreak between conventional and nuclear weapons because the use of nuclear weapons, even at the tactical level, would quickly escalate to all-out war. Even in the early years of the arms race, the military establishment never entirely accepted these views. As the quest for improved weapons and delivery systems succeeded and the instruments of mass destruction proliferated, the military's original wavering acceptance of deterrence and the firebreak dissolved. MIRV, which the defense establishment demanded, produced thousands of new warheads. As their numbers increased, military leaders naturally had to find some justifiable use for these new weapons. So strategic doctrine shifted from deterrence to the development of a nuclear-war fighting capability. Nuclear weapons have been integrated into strategic planning and will be used for conventional military purposes in the event of war. Deterrence has been undermined and the firebreak has disappeared as current American planners, insisting on more, as well as more accurate, nuclear weapons, reject the understanding of an earlier generation. Never has the American military establishment labored with so much determination to deploy weapons that are so useless in warfare.

Even when not actually used in warfare, nuclear fire has been lethal. We realize now that the decisions made by the military services, the Department of Defense, and the AEC between 1945 and 1963 were, at best, extremely risky for thousands, perhaps millions, of persons exposed to fallout from nuclear weapons testing. Abnormally high rates of cancer, birth defects in their children, and other disorders have plagued the military person-nel and civilians most directly exposed to test fallout. The haunt-ing question remains: What did those men really know when they made the decisions that exposed their fellow humans to such horrific risks? Robert Minogue, the research director of the Nu-clear Regulatory Commission, declared in a 1981 interview that "high AEC officials knew very well the biological effects of low-level radiation in the 1950s. They can't use ignorance as an excuse."[3] But this judgment is not precise enough. What exactly did they know in fact, and what should they have known in 1950 when they made their first explicit attempts to play nuclear rou-lette with American soldiers and civilians?

At the very least, these were risky exposures—so much so that none of the persons making the decisions ever permitted them-selves to be exposed in the same way. American officials consis-tently adopted the most optimistic view of risks possible; they denied reality and common sense; they placed an impossible burden of proof on their critics; they shut their eyes to scientific evidence that they should have considered; they manipulated data to produce results they wanted; they tried to suppress inves-tigations that they feared would produce unwelcome news. The most charitable view would say that they acted in optimistic igno-rance of what they were doing. A more critical person would conclude that they were criminally negligent. Perhaps all these things will lead some in the future to condemn them for crimes against humanity. But the most that we can say now, as historians working exclusively from printed records, is that they acted with extreme and willful carelessness, with a monstrous disregard for the possible sufferings of innocent people.

The development of nonmilitary applications of nuclear power poses related questions to the historian. Why did government bureaucracies and legislative committees—the AEC and the JCAE—persist in policies that they ought to have known would pose grave risks to the American people? A partial answer is that the AEC was a bureaucracy that simply behaved like any other bureaucracy. It existed to carry out its statutory mandate, and it could not be expected to do anything inconsistent with that mandate. Like all bureaucracies, it could respond only to clientele interests, not to some abstraction like "the public safety and health." The Atomic Energy acts directed the AEC to develop and promote nuclear power. American defense policies concurrently developed in the executive branch gave military nuclear applications a decisive priority over civilian. Assuming (probably contrary to fact) that the AEC could even have imagined that the goals of nuclear development, the primacy of military applications, the growth of private sector enterprise, and public health could come into conflict with each other, the Commission's overriding mandate, repeatedly reaffirmed by both the Joint Committee on Atomic Energy and the executive branch, was military nuclear development. Rather than admitting that this conflicted with public health and safety, the AEC simply declared that public safety was compatible with nuclear development because the latter was the unquestionable priority. The AEC's lies, its deliberate exposure of the American people to the risks of cancer and nuclear catastrophe, all follow from that fundamental commitment.

The substantive goals of the AEC were predetermined, and, given the nature of bureaucracies as systems, were unchallengeable. But if the goals were preordained, the means were not. Why did the AEC opt for a regime of industry self-regulation? In the 1950s, the AEC might have chosen to regulate the emergence of the nuclear power industry with a firm hand, much as Hyman Rickover insisted on strict quality control for the nuclear navy. Some recognized the need for strict regulation from the earliest days of nuclear power. Vannevar Bush, testifying to Congress in October 1945, put it in vividly homey terms: "I certainly do not wish to think that some group of experimenters might set up a laboratory half a mile from my house and family and experiment on atomic energy carelessly, poison the neighborhood, or possibly blow it up."[4] Yet only a decade later, the AEC was enthusiastically promoting the siting of reactors in and near major cities. Despite its statutory mandate, the AEC was reluctant to regulate industry, because its commissioners assumed that would impede military and industrial nuclear development. Commissioner Willard Libby set the AEC's basic course when he declared in 1955 that "our great hazard is that this great benefit to mankind [nuclear power] will be killed aborning by unnecessary regulation."[5]

The AEC waived its regulatory responsibilities because its commissioners were dedicated to some vague ideology of unregulated private enterprise. For some like Lewis Strauss, this belief was almost mystical; for others, like his successors James Schlesinger and Dixie Lee Ray, it was merely an axiom. They believed that the nuclear industry was sincerely concerned about public safety, and therefore dismissed those who did not share their beliefs as cranks or mischievous malcontents.

Ideology alone might not have driven the AEC to the extremes it reached in pursuing policies that harmed the American people. Its clients also played a decisive role in shoving it in that direction. Commissioners and bureaucrats are human; they respond to the most immediate pressures around them. They are particularly susceptible to being led when they lack expertise in the highly technological aspects of nuclear power. Ignorant and uninformed as most of them were, they took their direction from the only available source of knowledge: the nuclear industry and its scientific abettors. Such clients would have had a decisive influence in any event, but their monopoly of scientific and technological understanding made them irresistible. Alvin Weinberg, who has pondered these matters more deeply than anyone else inside the nuclear community, has provided us with an unforgettable image to explain this power: scientists and engineers constitute the "nuclear priesthood," a caste of men who can call upon superhuman forces by means of hidden mysteries known and comprehensible only to themselves.

We have committed our fate to this priesthood because of our faith in our technology. We were already a technological people before World War II. Along with optimism, faith in progress, and individualism, technological faith is one of our most conspicuous traits as a people. It is as impossible for us to call that faith into question as it is for the devotee of any other religion to doubt his own beliefs.

Thus deprived of an ability to question technical systems that we imagine to be vital, we must live with delusions. One of the most enduring, dating from the scientists' reaction to Hiroshima and Nagasaki, has been the idea that military and civilian applications of nuclear power are separable. We have forgotten the 1940 prediction of the unnamed Imperial Chemical Industries executive that "there must always be a very close relation between the exploitation of nuclear energy for military explosive purposes and for power production." In its place, we have substituted that fond hope formalized in Eisenhower's Atoms for Peace program, the will-o'-the-wisp of the "peaceful atom." In reality, the linkages between military and civilian nuclear power are so intimate that the developments of one are interdependent with the other. When we tried to implement the 1950s idea of exporting nuclear reactors to underdeveloped nations, we only succeeded in giving unstable nations like South Africa, Pakistan, Argentina, India, and now even Brazil the capability of producing plutonium for weapons. Driven by the Cold War and NSC-68 to embrace the idea of the "national security state," we have reinforced the bonds between the Siamese twins of military and civilian nuclear power. The interests supporting nuclear power—banks, manufacturers, international conglomerates, academics, scientists, engineers, the armed services, congressmen, and bureaucrats— have formed an establishment of irresistible power, making it impossible to pull the plug of the taxpayer- and ratepayer-funded economic life-support machine that is essential to keep nuclear power alive.

Alvin Weinberg warns us that we have struck a Faustian bargain with nuclear power.[6] In return for the limitless benefits that fission power seemed to promise, we have committed ourselves to superhuman and perpetual responsibilities. In our collective hubris, we have taunted the gods by boasting that we can do what humanity has never done before and what all human experience counsels us we probably cannot do. We confidently proclaim that we can safeguard nuclear wastes forever; we pretend that we have an accurate understanding of what happens in the core of a nuclear reactor; we experiment with megadeath weapons that approach doomsday machines; we computer-generate "sce-

THE CHARIOT OF THE SUN · 447

narios" of universal nuclear catastrophe and proclaim that somehow we, godlike and immortal, will survive the holocaust. Meanwhile, our children dream nightmares of nuclear war—and President Reagan blames that on the nuclear freeze movement.
Veterans and downwind people suffer insidious cancers and mu-
tations caused by fallout from weapons testing. Reactors threaten
us with accidents unlike any ever seen on earth. We are tor-
mented by visions of the end of human life, a universal dance of
death that will make the epidemiological catastrophes of the Middle Ages seem like the sniffles by comparison. This is the price
we pay for demanding to ride the chariot of the sun.

Appendix

1. POWER REACTOR TYPES

We refer in text to a variety of nuclear reactors. To clarify our terms, we offer this elementary description of the differing types of reactors that concern historians. These are all commercial power reactors, designed to produce electricity. Other sorts of reactors include: weapons or production reactors, designed to produce plutonium; research reactors, designed principally to produce neutrons, which are used in various kinds of physical, chemical, agricultural, industrial, and even criminal and archaeological research; and propulsion reactors, whose purpose is providing the motive source for naval surface and submarine vessels.

American power reactors are predominantly of two kinds: boiling water reactors (BWR) and pressurized water reactors (PWR). Because both use ordinary water as the coolant and transfer medium, water just like that coming out of a household tap, they are generically called light water reactors (LWRs), to distinguish them from reactors that use deuterium, so-called heavy water.

The PWR is the more common type of light water reactor. It is manufactured by Westinghouse. As its name indicates, the water that serves as a neutron moderator, coolant, and transfer medium circulates through the core around the fuel rods under high pressure—approximately 150 atmospheres. Being under pressure, this water does not boil, a design feature that avoids the problems of having the coolant boiling around the core. It circulates through a route called the primary loop, into a steam generator (which is a heat exchanger), where it gives off the heat that it has transported out of the core to other water contained in the secondary loop. The water in the secondary loop is not pressurized, and so it boils and turns into steam. Meanwhile, the cooled water in the primary loop is routed back to the core to repeat the cooling cycle. The steam in the secondary loop goes from the exchanger to a turbine, which it spins to power a generator that produces electricity. The water in the two loops do not intermingle. The primary loop must therefore be leak-proof.

The boiling water reactor, manufactured by General Electric, is simpler in design. The water again serves as moderator, coolant, and transfer vehicle, but it is allowed to vaporize into steam, which goes directly to the turbine. Thence it is condensed back to water, which reenters the core. This makes the two-loop system and the steam generator unnecessary, saving some capital costs.

The British and French reactor types that were displaced by the American LWRs are gas graphite reactors, so-called because their coolant is a gas (carbon dioxide), and the fuel rods are encased in a graphite core that serves as a moderator. The British design is usually called a "Magnox," from the name of the magnesium alloy that serves as cladding for the fuel rods. Because gas has a low density, it is not as effective a coolant as water, and the early Magnox designs had to operate at a low heat level. British engineers worked on a more sophisticated design, the advanced gas reactor, using stainless steel as a cladding and uranium dioxide as a fuel. The United States built two variations on gas cooled reactors, called high temperature gas reactors. The first, Peach Bottom near Philadelphia, went critical in 1965; the second and last, Fort St. Vrain in Colorado, went critical in 1974.

The Canadians have designed a reactor using heavy water as a coolant-moderator, calling it CANDU (for Canadian Deuterium Uranium, after its coolant and fuel). The CANDU reactors resemble PWRs in that their heavy water coolant circulates through a closed primary loop into a steam generator; but unlike the PWR, the faggots of its fuel rods lie horizontally in a stainless steel tank called a calandria.

One other type of reactor design is assuming ever-increasing importance: the liquid metal fast breeder reactor (LMFBR). Nuclear industry sources sometimes claim that production of uranium fuel from currently identified sources will be inadequate to meet the needs of light water reactors by 2025. Consequently, nuclear proponents look hopefully to a new generation of reactors that "breed": they produce more fissionable plutonium than they consume. The breeder reactor holds promise of a virtually limitless fuel supply, if its technological problems can be overcome. In a breeder, a compact core containing as much fuel as possible relative to other components is cooled by a metal in molten state, usually sodium, which dissipates heat more effectively than gases or liquids. The problem with this design, however, as most persons remember from their high school chemistry, is that sodium reacts violently with water and other materials. To cope with this problem, engineers surround it with a cloud of an inert material, such as argon. But this argon can mix with sodium in the form of bubbles. Moreover, sodium is opaque, and hence prohibits remote visual inspection of reactor cores. These and other technical problems of LMFBRs are daunting. But the British, French, and Soviets have constructed operating breeders. The United States has had less luck with the breeder. Both the first breeder, EBR-1 at the National Reactor Test Station in Idaho, and the first commercial breeder, Fermi-1 near Detroit, suffered disastrous accidents. Despite these discouraging experiences, the nuclear industry continues to promote the breeder, generally with support from Republicans (e.g., the Reagan administration) and over the opposition of most Democrats (e.g., the Carter administration). Because of the uncertainty of political support, America's only projected breeder, the Clinch River Breeder Reactor near Oak Ridge, faces a dubious future, due in large measure to inflation and anticipated cost overruns. In late 1983, Congress mandated its termination.

Appendix

2. THE NUCLEAR FUEL CYCLE

The history of nuclear power is closely bound to the nuclear fuel cycle, and a picture of the "life cycle" of uranium will help clarify problems and controversies that have arisen since commercialization. The following diagram gives an overview of the steps in the nuclear fuel cycle, and we will follow them in sequence.

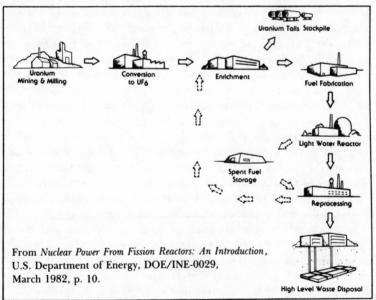

Uranium Tails Stockpile

Uranium Mining & Milling

Conversion to UF₆

Enrichment

Fuel Fabrication

Light Water Reactor

Spent Fuel Storage

Reprocessing

High Level Waste Disposal

From *Nuclear Power From Fission Reactors: An Introduction*, U.S. Department of Energy, DOE/INE-0029, March 1982, p. 10.

Mining and Milling. Uranium is found in ores scattered throughout the earth, but with important concentrations in the Colorado Plateau of the United States, a vast stretch of land in Arizona, New Mexico, Colorado, and Utah, and in adjacent regions such as Wyoming. Elsewhere, significant uranium deposits are found in Canada, South Africa, Australia, France, and the Soviet Union. Uranium-bearing ores are mined either in surface or underground mines, and the ore is crushed to the consistency of sand. Chemical solvents then extract the uranium, in the form of a mix of uranium oxides with a formula of U_3O_8. These oxides, yellowish and in a wet consistency resembling concrete, are called "yellowcake." Yellowcake is trucked on to the next step in the process, but back at the mining/milling site, two waste products remain: liquid waste left over from the process, which is both radioactive and chemically toxic; and the leftover "sand" from the ores, which is also radioactive. This latter product, called "tailings," was at first simply left unattended in great heaps near the mouths of uranium mine shafts. These radioactive tailings piles, which even today retain about 85 percent of their original radioactivity, pose two problems. First, being dry sand, they are blown about by the winds that prevail on the southwestern plains, or sift down into rivers, producing serious radioactive contamination of drinking water in the Colorado River basin. Not until 1972 did the AEC even acknowledge that these were problems and begin to provide funds to attempt to deal with them. So far, efforts to prevent airborne circulation of radioactive tailings have resulted in little success. The other problem of the tailings piles at first presented itself in the guise of an opportunity: building contractors, particularly around Grand Junction, a city of 20,000 people in western Colorado, unaware of or indifferent to the radioactivity of the piles, used the sandlike material in the concrete of foundations for houses, schools, and commercial buildings. These "hot" foundations emitted a steady discharge of radioactivity to the occupants above them. In the mid-1970s, the federal government bore the expense of destroying these foundations and replacing them with nonradioactive substitutes. The residents of Grand Junction greeted this program with mixed feelings, some glad to be rid of the radiation-emitters beneath them, others annoyed at the inconvenience of having their homes literally dug up from beneath them and skeptical about the insistence of health physicists that the foundations did pose a real problem.

Uranium mining underground poses yet another problem, this one assuredly lethal. Early in the nineteenth century, miners from the Joachimsthal mines in Bohemia spoke in bewildered horror of the *Bergkrankheit:* the "mountain sickness," diagnosed back in 1879 as lung cancer, that struck the miners. Medical investigation disclosed before World War II that the disease originated when, in the poorly vented shaft mines, uranium-238 was constantly emitting alpha particles and decaying down into a succession of "daughters": elements below it in the decay chain, including radium-226 (a solid), radon-222 (a gas), and polonium-218 (a solid). The gas radon mixes with air. When it decays, its polonium daughter is electrically charged and adheres to air-borne dust. In this form, it is inhaled into the lungs of miners, where it undergoes further alpha-particle decay, causing cancer. Though this etiology was well documented by 1950, the great uranium boom of the period led the AEC to ignore the problem, with the result that thousands of hard-rock miners in the Colorado Plateau, many of them American Indians, have contracted lung cancer.

Conversion and enrichment. The yellowcake must be transported to the next step in the reactor cycle, enrichment. Transportation here, as between every other step of the cycle, is by commercial truck transport over ordinary roads. This in itself poses a problem for the last transport leg, when highly radioactive materials must be hauled on roads amidst ordinary private traffic, with the hazards of accidents and spills. Some cities, notably New York, have attempted to ban transport of these materials through their jurisdictions, but this action has been challenged by the industry as an interference with federal supremacy in the area. In any event, yellowcake is trucked to a conversion plant where it is converted to the gas uranium hexafluoride, UF_6, familiarly called "hex." This gas is then shipped to massive gaseous diffusion plants at Oak Ridge, Tennessee; Paducah, Kentucky; or Portsmouth, Ohio. Here the hex is passed through metal membranes with tiny pores; an ever larger proportion of U-235 passes through the membranes, going repeatedly through successive "cascades" until it is enriched from its natural level of 7 parts per 1,000 to 30 parts per 1,000. (For weapons applications, the enrichment must be carried to 900 parts per 1,000.) Gaseous diffusion consumes prodigious quantities of electricity: the Oak Ridge

Plant requires its own 2,000 MWe coal-fired power plant, the rough equivalent of two modern nuclear plants. This immense consumption of electricity should be, but seldom is, debited against the amount of electricity finally produced from nuclear power, in net energy accounting. Several technological challengers to gaseous diffusion exist on the horizon. One, a centrifugation process in which the heavier U-238 tends to get spun outward in a centrifuge, may soon be economically competitive. The other, a laser technology, will probably never be, because it can deal with only minute quantities of hex at a time. Enrichment by whatever process is heavily shrouded in secrecy because it is so intimately linked to the Siamese twin of nuclear weapons power.

Fuel fabrication. The enriched uranium is next transported to industrial plants that convert the enriched hex to yet another form of uranium, uranium dioxide, UO_2, in powder form, which is baked into small pellets the size of a cigarette filter that are then stacked in rods made of a zirconium alloy called zircaloy. These fuel rods are then assembled into a configuration called fuel assemblies, which are carefully and firmly stacked in their next transport phase to prevent them from coming anywhere near enough to each other to reach criticality, and are hauled on to the reactors where they will be consumed.

Fuel consumption: the reactors. Lowered into the core of light water reactors, the fuel assemblies are exposed to the fissioning process. There they have a useful life of about three years. At the end of this time, the fission reactions that have taken place in them leave them not only practically depleted of fissile uranium, but also swollen, caked with highly radioactive residues that nuclear engineers with disarming simplicity call "crud," and engorged with fission products and actinides. In this condition, they are ferociously radioactive, but many of the fission products responsible for this radioactivity have relatively short half-lives. The spent fuel assemblies are pulled out of the core and transferred with extreme care to temporary cooling ponds of water, called "swimming pools" because of their close resemblance to their more mundane cousins, where circulating water cools them while the shorter-lived decay products run through their half-lives and decay to harmless levels. But the longer-lived actinides and fission products still leave the fuel assemblies quite hot.

Reprocessing. At present, irradiated fuel assemblies are being held at the reactor sites, pending decisions on what to do with them in the mid- and long terms. But they contain significant amounts of U-235 and plutonium, which can be recycled back into the streams of fuel and weapons use. Some high-level radioisotopes are transported for burial or processing off-site. This transport stage, unlike all those preceding it, is tricky and expensive. Yellowcake and fresh fuel rods are only mildly radioactive, but the decay products in spent rods are fiercely hot, and hence must be transported in massive fifty-ton casks containing lead shielding. The consequences of a transportation accident involving these casks is terrifying, but the Nuclear Regulatory Commission has confidence that the casks it has developed can withstand the impact of a locomotive engine crashing into them.

When commercial fuel reprocessing took place, the spent rods were hauled to a reprocessing facility, chopped up, and bathed in a solvent such as nitric acid. This acid stream passed through various other solvent stages, the U-235 parted company with the plutonium, and both were eventually separated out from the remaining wastes. The valuable remains thence went by different routes, the U-235 back to the conversion stage, the plutonium either to fuel fabrication or to weapons use. The remaining high-level wastes are commercially useless at present: no way has been found to convert their intense thermal heat to beneficial forms, so they must be trucked off for interim "management" pending the development of technologies that will make the last stage of the fuel cycle a reality.

Long-term waste storage. Nuclear engineers have admitted to us in private conversations that this stage is what one of them called the Achilles' heel of the nuclear power industry. Opponents of nuclear power insist that we do not know what to do about long-term storage of high-level radioactive wastes, and point to some of the nuttier possibilities that have been favored with serious consideration by the AEC, such as shooting them into the sun by rocket, or placing them atop Arctic icecaps, where their thermal heat will melt them down to some permanent stratum, somewhere this side of Antarctica, it was hoped. They contend that these bizarre schemes suggest a desperation that marks the death throes of the industry. Nuclear engineers and their allies in government, for their part, have expressed confidence for thirty years that waste technologies do exist, or, alternatively, are just around the corner. At present, no long-term waste dumps exist in the United States. The West Germans are experimenting with a worked-out salt mine at Asse, while their American colleagues contemplate various granite and salt formations. In December 1982, the lame-duck Congress then sitting authorized the president to designate a permanent waste dump, but this long-delayed legislative decision does not assure engineering feasibility. About all the statute guarantees are further procrastination, political wrangling, and litigation.

Glossary

Nuclear power is a highly technical subject, and like all such subjects, it is replete with acronyms, jargon, and other sorts of unintelligible terminology. We have written this book for a general reading audience, and so have avoided obscure terms as much as possible. But there is an irreducible minimum of esoteric terminology that is inevitable in writing about nuclear power. We have usually defined these at their first appearance in the text unless the context has made their meaning obvious or unless they are so commonly used that we may presume that the general reader is familiar with them. Below we have culled out all acronyms, etc., that are not household words and identified or defined them here.

ABM antiballistic missile

ACRS Advisory Committee on Reactor Safeguards. A nominally autonomous advisory body appointed by the AEC that rendered nonbinding technical opinions. It was charged with advising the AEC/NRC on all safety-related aspects of the civilian nuclear program.

ADA Atomic Development Authority. Proposed as part of the 1946 Acheson–Lilienthal plan.

AEC Atomic Energy Commission (1946–1974)

AIF Atomic Industrial Forum. The nuclear industry's trade association and an organization designed to promote civilian nuclear power. Its membership roster is a Who's Who of the nuclear-industrial complex.

459

ANL   Argonne National Laboratories

ANS   American Nuclear Society. A professional association of scientists, engineers, health physicists, and industry executives who promote the expansion of nuclear power through publications, awards, and other forms of support. Unlike the AIF, ANS is not a trade association or a lobbying group, though some of its members are politically active.

ASLB   Atomic Safety and Licensing Board. A review committee that is part of the licensing process for reactors.

Atlas   America's first liquid fueled intercontinental ballistic missile.

breeder reactor   A nuclear reactor designed to produce more plutonium (through the transmutation of elements) than it consumes. None currently exist in the United States, Fermi-1 having been a gigantic failure and the proposed Clinch River breeder facing an uncertain future. Breeders are operational in France and the Soviet Union, nations that display less official concern about terrorism and proliferation than the U.S.A.

CANDU   A unique Canadian design for reactors. The letters stand for Canadian-Deuterium-Uranium.

CIA   Central Intelligence Agency

cladding   The metal sheath enclosing uranium fuel pellets in the core of a nuclear reactor. See also, *zircaloy*.

CND   Campaign for Nuclear Disarmament

CNI   Committee on Nuclear Information

CP-1   Chicago Pile Number One, the world's first nuclear reactor, which went critical in 1942.

criticality   The point at which a nuclear reaction becomes self-sustaining.

CWIP   Construction Work In Progress, the designation of an effort by utilities to force their ratepayers to pay current interest charges while a nuclear or fossil plant is under construction, rather than waiting to pay the interest only after the plant goes on line.

DOE   Department of Energy

EBR-1   Experimental Breeder Reactor Number One

ECCS Emergency Core-Cooling Systems

FCDA Federal Civil Defense Administration

FRC Federal Radiation Council

GAC General Advisory Committee (to the AEC)

Galosh An ineffective antiballistic missile system deployed by the Soviets around Moscow.

GE General Electric

HUAC House Un-American Activities Committee

IAEA International Atomic Energy Agency

ICBM intercontinental ballistic missile

IRBM intermediate range ballistic missile

isotope Forms of elements can have the same atomic number (established by the number of protons in the nucleus of their atom), which determines their place in the atomic table, but differing atomic weights due to differing numbers of neutrons. For example, carbon-12 has six protons and six neutrons; its radioactive sibling, carbon-14, has six protons but eight neutrons. Each is an isotope of the element carbon. Because they occupy the same place in the atomic table, they have identical chemical properties, but display different physical behavior. The word *isotope* was coined by the discoverer of isotopes, Frederick Soddy, from Greek roots meaning "same place" (in the atomic table). For his work with isotopes, Soddy received the Nobel in chemistry in 1921.

JCAE Joint Committee on Atomic Energy

JCS Joint Chiefs of Staff

kiloton 1,000 tons

LMFBR Liquid Metal Fast Breeder Reactor. See also, *breeder reactor.*

LOCA Loss of Coolant Accident

LOFT Loss of Fluid Test. A proposed experiment in which a reactor would be deliberately destroyed by a LOCA to provide data on performance of reactors in accidents.

LWR light water reactor

MAUD See ch. 1, n. 14.

MED Manhattan Engineering District, the official code name for the World War II effort to build an atomic bomb; also called the Manhattan Project.

megawatt A measure of electrical power equal to one million watts, abbrev. MW. There are two principal measures of the power output of a nuclear reactor: megawatts electric (MWe) and megawatts thermal (MWt).

Met Lab Metallurgical Laboratory. The code name for the branch of the Manhattan Project located at the University of Chicago.

Minuteman A solid-fueled ICBM deployed in reinforced concrete silos.

MIRV Multiple Independently Targeted Reentry Vehicle; nuclear warheads.

MIT Massachusetts Institute of Technology

MWe See *megawatt*

NATO North Atlantic Treaty Organization

NCRP National Council on Radiation Protection

NDRC National Defense Research Committee

NEPA Nuclear Energy for the Propulsion of Aircraft *or* National Environmental Protection Act

Nike Zeus The army's first-generation ballistic missile defense system

NRC Nuclear Regulatory Commission

NRTS National Reactor Testing Station, Idaho Falls, Idaho

NSC National Security Council

NSC-68 A 1950 National Security Council policy paper calling for massive and costly U.S. rearmament

O&M Operating and maintenance; a category of costs.

OPEC Organization of Petroleum Exporting Countries

ORNL Oak Ridge National Laboratory

OSD Office of the Secretary of Defense

OSRD Office of Scientific Research and Development

OSS   Office of Strategic Services, a World War II forerunner of the CIA.

PG&E   Pacific Gas & Electric Co., a California utility

Polaris   A submarine-launched ballistic missile.

Poseidon   A MIRVed submarine-launched ballistic missile.

PRDC   Power Reactor Development Corporation

rad   A physical measure of radiation. It is an acronym for radiation absorbed dose or an abbreviation for radiation.

R&D   research and development

Rad-Safe   Off-Site Radiological Safety Organization, an AEC cover-up at the Nevada test site

RAF   Royal Air Force

RDT   Division of Reactor Development and Technology, AEC

rem   A biological measure of radiation. It is an acronym for roentgen equivalent man.

roentgen   (*R*) a measure of radiation. See p. 202.

SAC   Strategic Air Command, U.S. Air Force

Safeguard   The ABM system that President Nixon first planned to deploy.

SALT   Strategic Arms Limitation Talks

SAM   Substitute Alloy Materials, World War II code name for Columbia University laboratories that were a part of the Manhattan Project.

SANE   Committee for a Sane Nuclear Policy

SCAP   Supreme Commander, Allied Powers. This was General MacArthur's official title during the Japanese occupation.

scram   Emergency shutdown of a nuclear reaction. Daniel Ford, in *Cult of the Atom,* p. 28, states that the word is an acronym for Safety Control Rod Ax Man. For the meaning of this odd phrase, see Prologue, description of CP-1.

Sentinel   The ABM system President Johnson planned to deploy.

SIPI   Scientists' Institute for Public Information

SLBM   Submarine-Launched Ballistic Missile

Sr-90   strontium-90, a radioactive isotope

tailings   Sand-like dross or other residue left over from mining and milling operations.

Tallinn   An air defense system deployed around Leningrad.

Titan   A large silo-based liquid-fueled ICBM.

TMI   Three Mile Island

TVA   Tennessee Valley Authority

U-235, U-238   isotopes of uranium

UCS   Union of Concerned Scientists

VA   Veterans Administration

wing   A division of the United States Air Force, which in the 1950s contained a total of 54 to 72 planes, the exact number depending on the mission of the particular wing (fighter, bomber, reconnaissance, etc.).

yellowcake   A mixture of uranium oxides having the equivalent chemical formula U_3O_8, resembling wet yellow concrete. This is the form uranium takes between the milling and conversion processes discussed in appendix 2, "The Nuclear Fuel Cycle."

zircaloy   A zirconium alloy used for fuel-rod cladding.

Suggestions for Further Reading

Dean G. Acheson, *Present at the Creation: My Years in the State Department* (New York: Norton, 1969). Like all memoirs, Acheson's must be used with care. It nevertheless remains one of the most useful autobiographies for Cold War subjects. It is particularly important with regard to early disarmament efforts, as well as the 1950 decision to rearm.

Gar Alperovitz, *Atomic Diplomacy: Hiroshima and Potsdam* (New York: Simon & Schuster, 1965). In this revisionist analysis of Truman's decision to use the atomic bomb against Japan, Alperovitz argues that Cold War considerations predominated. The bomb was used not to force the Japanese to surrender, the author argues, but to impress the Russians and make them more willing to accept a European peace settlement in the American mode.

Stephen E. Ambrose, *Rise to Globalism: American Foreign Policy, 1938–1980*, 2nd rev. ed. (New York: Penguin, 1980). This excellent survey of American foreign policy covers the nuclear years, relating national security questions to foreign policy. *Rise to Globalism* emphasizes American responsibility for the Cold War.

Isaac Asimov, *Asimov's Guide to Science* (New York: Basic Books, 1972). An excellent, readily accessible layperson's introduction to most of the scientific concepts mentioned in this book. Asimov writes intelligibly for the nonscientist reader, and develops all his themes historically, a refreshing and unusual approach in scientific writing.

Desmond Ball, *Politics and Force Levels: The Strategic Missile Program of the Kennedy Administration* (Berkeley, Calif.: University of California

Press, 1980). This is the most complete account available of the Kennedy administration's decision to expand its strategic nuclear forces and escalate the arms race.

Barton J. Bernstein, ed., *The Atomic Bomb* (Boston: Houghton Mifflin, 1976). Bernstein has collected a number of important essays and selections from longer studies dealing with the major questions surrounding the decision to use the atomic bomb against Japan.

Bernard Brodie, *The Absolute Weapon* (New York: Harcourt, Brace, 1946). This is one of the first major works dealing with strategy in the nuclear age. Brodie, who became one of this country's foremost early nuclear strategists, was also one of the first to perceive that nuclear weapons could only be used for deterrence. He argued that nuclear weapons had changed the nature of warfare and that in the future the principal purpose of the military would be to deter rather than fight wars.

Irvin C. Bupp and Jean-Claude Derian, *Light Water: How the Nuclear Dream Dissolved* (New York: Basic Books, 1978). The authors, both economists, take a critical view of the economics of nuclear power in its early commercialization phase. Bupp, currently associated with the Harvard Business School, was a member of the secretariat of the AEC from 1963 to 1966, and after that a consultant to the Commission. His co-author served as an adviser to the CEA (Commissariat à l'Energie Atomique), the French equivalent of the AEC. The blending of American and continental perspectives heightens the interest of this book. *Light Water* is the only book-length study of the economics of nuclear power that manages to be both relatively detached, and written in language accessible to laypeople. The authors support the development of commercial nuclear power but regret the abnormal promotion that attended its debut.

Robert J. C. Butow, *Japan's Decision to Surrender* (Palo Alto, Calif.: Stanford University Press, 1954). Still the best study of the weeks preceding Japan's surrender, Butow's book suggests strongly that the atomic bombs were not decisive in forcing the Japanese to surrender; that at most they only speeded by a few days or weeks a process that was already under way.

Jimmy Carter, *Keeping Faith: Memoirs of a President* (New York: Bantam, 1982). While not as enlightening as it might have been, Carter's memoirs are especially revealing with regard to the way his own naïveté influenced the conduct of the SALT II negotiations in a negative way. On balance, however, this is one of the more disappointing of the several memoirs produced by leading statesmen in recent years.

Ronald W. Clark, *The Greatest Power on Earth: The International Race for Nuclear Supremacy* (New York: Harper & Row, 1980). A history of the early years of nuclear power, from the 1930s through Super. Because of the period it covers, the book necessarily emphasizes military aspects. The author writes from a British perspective, but he includes much material on American matters and treats the topic as international in scope. This is an extremely well-written book, novelistic in its pace and detail.

The Committee for the Compilation of Materials on Damage Caused by the Atomic Bombs in Hiroshima and Nagasaki, *Hiroshima and Nagasaki: The Physical, Medical, and Social Effects of the Atomic Bombings,* Eisei Ishikawa and David L. Swain, trans. (New York: Basic Books, 1981). Probably the definitive assessment of the subject of its subtitle, this study, by a Japanese group, refutes the deliberately benign official American view by demonstrating painstakingly that the destruction of people, society, and life in the world's only nuclear attacks to date were far more profound and horrifying than the United States has cared to admit. This book is must reading for any who think that nuclear war in any form is "acceptable." The study is extensively illustrated, and is not for the squeamish. Statistics are converted into suffering, dying human beings, without sentimentality or moralizing. This book combines scientific, social-scientific, and historical analysis, expressed in a flat and understated prose that is ably translated from the original Japanese.

Nuel Pharr Davis, *Lawrence and Oppenheimer* (New York: Simon & Schuster, 1968). Less a dual biography than a history of an era, this sensitive, exquisite study recreates a dualism in the approach of scientists to public policy that was personified in these two men. The author, a professor of English at the University of Illinois, writes with subtlety and grace. Lawrence evolves into a monster of ambition, while Oppenheimer becomes more and more a figure out of Greek tragedy, seeing his relentless doom approaching and unable to avert it. This brief book has no competitor in its ability to evoke the mood of the era, and to suggest allusively the possibilities thrown away in the tragedies surrounding Oppenheimer.

Frank G. Dawson, *Nuclear Power: Control and Management of a Technology* (Seattle: University of Washington Press, 1976). One of the earliest histories of commercial nuclear power, this study originated as a doctoral dissertation by a nuclear engineer and was published under the auspices of the Battelle Institute. The author's engineering background gives him a more assured grasp of the technical aspects of nuclear power but renders him uncritical of nuclear policymaking. This study was path-breaking at the time it was prepared, there being then no adequate histories of nonmilitary nuclear power. But it is aging rapidly, suffering the fate of contemporary histories, which tend to become a part of the events they chronicle. It nonetheless remains valuable as an early attempt to make sense out of an obscure topic.

Robert A. Divine, *Blowing on the Wind: The Nuclear Test Ban Debate, 1954–1960* (New York: Oxford University Press, 1978). An historian's survey of the debates attending the fallout controversy. It is especially valuable for demonstrating patterns of rhetorical escalation by nuclear proponents. Predictions of irreversible Soviet advantage if the United States discontinues this or that item in the nuclear armamentarium were to be repeated often in later years. The reader gets a dismaying sense of *déjà vu* comparing incidents in this book with current headlines.

Dwight D. Eisenhower, *Waging Peace, 1956–1961: The White House Years* (Garden City, N.Y.: Doubleday, 1965). This volume of Eisenhower's memoirs, which covers the period from 1956 to 1961, is particularly useful for the president's reaction to the missile gap and the Gaither Commission report.

Alain C. Enthoven and K. Wayne Smith, *How Much Is Enough?: Shaping the Defense Program, 1961–1969* (New York: Harper & Row, 1971). Enthoven and Smith were members of the McNamara defense department. Their book explains what they found wanting in the strategy of massive retaliation and what they tried to do about it. It is also useful for understanding the conflict between the Office of the Secretary of Defense and the military during this period.

Thomas H. Etzold, *Defense or Delusion?: America's Military in the 1980s* (New York: Harper & Row, 1982). This is a superlative analysis of the many current weaknesses of America's military establishment, with excellent chapters on weaponry and the nuclear issue. Etzold, professor of strategy at the Naval War College, is an extraordinarily effective critic of current military and strategic policy.

Daniel Ford, *The Cult of the Atom: The Secret Papers of the Atomic Energy Commission* (New York: Simon & Schuster, 1982). This book lives up to the promise of its somewhat lurid subtitle. The author, an economist who was formerly director of the Union of Concerned Scientists, used the Freedom of Information Act to pry thousands of documents loose from the AEC's successor, the NRC, and discovered thick veins of gold in the bureaucratic ores. The documents confirm the worst suspicions of the AEC's critics, revealing an agency that long before Watergate resorted to coverup, the Big Lie, harassment of critics, and suppression of evidence. Ford's account, as a participant, of the 1972 generic ECCS hearings makes especially gripping reading.

Daniel Ford, *Three Mile Island: Thirty Minutes to Meltdown* (New York: Viking, 1982). This is the best of the numerous books that recounted the events at Three Mile Island for the American public, and pointed out lessons we ought to have learned from the event. Enjoying the double advantage of being a skilled writer but not an engineer, Ford was able to translate arcane data into images comprehensible to people who are not technically trained. His reprise and judgments are thoughtful, critical, but fair. Ford identifies regulatory failure and industry cost-cutting as the principal villains.

John G. Fuller, *We Almost Lost Detroit* (New York: Reader's Digest Press, 1975). The author, a prize-winning veteran science writer, has here compiled a history of Fermi-1, America's first commercial breeder reactor, with emphasis on the 1966 near blowdown. He writes in a novelistic style, supported by the persistence of an investigative reporter in gathering evidence. His conclusion, summed up in the evaluation of an unnamed nuclear engineer who provides the book's title, is sharply challenged by industry spokesmen, who claim that there was never any serious danger to the Detroit-Windsor-Toledo-Cleveland area, and that the safety mechanisms of Fermi-1 worked admirably.

Bertrand Goldschmidt, *The Atomic Complex: A Worldwide Political History of Nuclear Energy* (La Grange, Ill.: American Nuclear Society, 1982). A relatively brief survey of the history of nuclear power, Goldschmidt's volume is something between a memoir (he was a nuclear chemist and French CEA official who participated in the story he relates) and an official history, its American publication being under the aegis of the American Nuclear Society. Because of its brevity, it tells little of the factual story found in more comprehensive studies, and it carries no scholarly apparatus. It is nonetheless interesting for its author's opinions (many of them purely speculative) and for its distinctively French point of view.

Margaret Gowing, *Britain and Atomic Energy, 1939–1945* (London, England: 1964); and *Independence and Deterrence: Britain and Atomic Energy, 1945–1952* (London, England: MacMillan, 1974). These two volumes constitute the official history of the British nuclear program. Although detailed, they are highly readable and provide a vivid review of Great Britain's debut as a nuclear power. The author retains balance, together with a critical distance from her subject and its actors, thus greatly enhancing the value of her effort. Regrettably, nothing comparable exists for France or, for obvious reasons, the Soviet Union. The author's emotional and intellectual detachment from her topic stands in marked contrast with that of her American counterparts.

Gregg Herken, *The Winning Weapon* (New York: Knopf, 1980). This is by far the best study of the relationship between the development of nuclear weaponry and foreign policy in the Truman administration. It focuses on the nuclear question from the end of World War II through 1950. The most useful material deals with the first reaction of the administration to its newfound power and how it came to propose the Baruch plan for nuclear disarmament.

Richard G. Hewlett, *A History of the United States Atomic Energy Commission*, vol. I, with Oscar E. Anderson, Jr., *The New World, 1939/1946;* and vol. II, with Francis Duncan, *Atomic Shield, 1947/1952* (University Park, Penn.: Pennsylvania State University Press, 1962 and 1969, respectively). The official history of the AEC, these two volumes are exhaustive, thoroughly researched, and meticulously detailed, probably too much so for the casual reader. But unlike their British counterpart, they are weakened by a lack of critical distance from their subject. They are useful in presenting the canonical views of the nuclear establishment, but the reader will look in vain for even the suggestion of an attitude that nuclear power, in either its military or civilian manifestations, might threaten the survival of millions, or that the nuclear Fathers might have erred. The tone throughout verges on the apologetic, and the authors waspishly dismiss the work of those who are more critical than they, like Robert Jungk and Nuell Pharr Davis.

Richard G. Hewlett and Francis Duncan, *Nuclear Navy, 1946–1962* (Chicago: University of Chicago Press, 1974). Like the authors' *Atomic Shield,* this is a masterly technical study. Its subject, the nuclear navy, is narrower, but crucial, and the authors enjoyed the same access and research assistance that made the official history of the AEC such a comprehensive effort. *Nuclear Navy,* like the official AEC history, suffers from the same defects of its virtues: the authors' emotional proximity to their subject renders them uncritical of the larger problems of nuclear power.

Stephen Hilgartner et al., *Nukespeak: Nuclear Language, Visions, and Mindset* (San Francisco: Sierra Club Books, 1982). A fascinating application of George Orwell's perceptions about the political misuse of language in the development of nuclear power. At once an analysis of ideology and official dogma, a history of nuclear power, and a book-length piece of investigative journalism, *Nukespeak* demonstrates how closely technological development is tied to the manipulation of thought. As far as nuclear power is concerned, *1984* arrived long ago. Regrettably, this provocative book came into our hands too late to influence the writing of our study.

Robert Jungk, *Brighter Than a Thousand Suns: A Personal History of the Atomic Scientists,* James Cleugh, trans. (New York: Harcourt, Brace, 1956, 1958). One of the earliest histories of the development of nuclear power, this book delivers exactly what its subtitle promises, tracing the topic through the personal interactions of the men who developed the bomb. In this respect, it is similar to Davis's *Lawrence and Oppenheimer,* and like that study it is implicitly critical of the decisions unthinkingly made to build bigger bombs and light water reactors. Unlike Davis's book, this study, originally written in German, tells its story from a central European cultural perspective, which adds to its interest. Nuclear spokesmen have unsparingly criticized it for relatively minor technical errors.

Jerome H. Kahan, *Security in the Nuclear Age: Developing U.S. Strategic Arms Policy* (Washington, D.C.: Brookings Institution, 1975). This work, one of the many fine studies produced by the Brookings Institution, provides an excellent introduction to the problem of national security and nuclear weapons. It is especially useful for the period of the Eisenhower and Kennedy administrations.

William W. Kaufmann, *The McNamara Strategy* (New York: Harper & Row, 1964). Kaufmann, the principal architect of the No Cities doctrine, reviews the problems of nuclear strategy in the Eisenhower and Kennedy years.

Daniel J. Kevles, *The Physicists: The History of a Scientific Community in Modern America* (New York: Knopf, 1978). One of the best-written contributions in the new field of the sociology of science. Less a history of twentieth-century physics than a study of the interaction between a scientific community and the larger political world outside the laboratory, *The Physicists* is an absorbing survey of the political and intellectual maturation of American scientists.

Henry Kissinger, *The White House Years* (Boston: Little, Brown, 1979). This, the first volume of Kissinger's memoirs, is extremely useful for the history of SALT I. Kissinger writes with style and grace and here defends himself against critics on the left and right who disagreed with his approach to arms control.

Howard Kohn, *Who Killed Karen Silkwood?* (New York: Summit Books, 1981). A fascinating reconstruction of Silkwood's life, and death, plus an account of the efforts of the investigating and litigating team that tried to discover exactly what happened to her in the last weeks of her life, and to identify those responsible for her plutonium poisoning and death. The author, a reporter for *Rolling Stone,* was a member of this team, but manages to keep himself out of the narrative while at the same time enriching it with vivid personal vignettes and a readable journalistic style. An equally good book, concentrating on Silkwood rather than the investigations after her death, is by

Richard Rashke, *The Killing of Karen Silkwood: The Story Behind the Kerr-McGee Plutonium Case* (Boston: Houghton Mifflin, 1981).

Joseph I. Lieberman, *The Scorpion and the Tarantula: The Struggle to Control Atomic Weapons, 1945–1949* (Boston: Houghton Mifflin, 1970). This is a readable account of the early efforts of the Truman administration to find some method of controlling nuclear weapons.

David E. Lilienthal, *Atomic Energy: A New Start* (New York: Harper & Row, 1980). A jaded retrospective by the first chairman of the AEC. Lilienthal supports continued development of nuclear power, but is concerned that the hothouse promotional atmosphere surrounding the debut of light water reactors led to too hasty development, with the result that safety problems were swept under the rug. He favors intensive investigation of alternative reactor types.

David E. Lilienthal, *The Atomic Energy Years, 1945–1950* (New York: Harper & Row, 1964). This is the second volume of Lilienthal's memoirs, covering the period when he served as chairman of the AEC. His daily diary entries provide a fascinating, candid inside view of the earliest years of the nuclear establishment. For his more chastened views of nuclear power, see the previous entry.

Amory B. Lovins, *Soft Energy Paths: Toward a Durable Peace* (San Francisco: Friends of the Earth, 1977). This book unnerved the nuclear-industrial complex when it first appeared in condensed form in *Foreign Affairs*. Lovins, a young physicist of astonishing energy, demonstrates that the world must choose between "hard," high-tech sources of energy and the soft paths that rely on renewable energy sources. He is no soft-headed idealist: his technical data appalled nuclear spokesmen, and they have mounted an unending effort to refute his contention that the nuclear power industry is like a brontosaur with its head lopped off—it is dead, but is not yet aware of the fact. Lovins is the foremost exponent of a principal theme of the present study, the vital linkages between civilian and military nuclear power.

Michael Mandelbaum, *The Nuclear Question: The United States and Nuclear Weapons, 1946–1976* (New York: Cambridge University Press, 1979). This is the most complete analysis we have found of the

Kennedy administration's attempts to deal with the problems of military strategy in the nuclear age.

H. Peter Metzger, *The Atomic Establishment* (New York: Simon & Schuster, 1972). One of the earliest attacks on the AEC and both military and civilian nuclear power. Written in a journalist's exposé style, the book is nonetheless solidly researched and documented. It was instrumental in the disbanding of the AEC, which it discredited by demonstrating the carelessness and duplicity of the commissioners and staff.

Alva Myrdal, *The Game of Disarmament: How the United States and Russia Run the Arms Race* (New York: Pantheon, 1976). Myrdal, who has won the Nobel peace prize for her continuing efforts for nuclear disarmament, has produced a scathing denunciation of the United States and the Soviet Union for their joint failure to seriously address the problem of nuclear disarmament.

John Newhouse, *Cold Dawn: The Story of SALT* (New York: Holt, Rinehart and Winston, 1973). This is an excellent analysis of the origins of the Strategic Arms Limitation Talks. It begins with the McNamara defense department and progresses from there through the negotiations themselves. The book is most valuable as a view of how institutional pressures and bureaucratic politics work to make arms control almost impossible to achieve.

Walter Patterson, *Nuclear Power* (New York: Penguin, 1976). This remains, for the layperson, the best brief one-volume introduction to both the science and the policy questions concerning nuclear power. The author, a Canadian physicist associated with Friends of the Earth, writes from a British perspective. The first half of the book is a technical survey of reactor types and the fuel cycle, explaining clearly how reactors work and what challenges they pose. The second half is an historically organized survey of the development of nuclear power, with an emphasis on accidents and other problems. The author is skeptical about the nuclear promise, and even more so about those who make the promises. Yet the book is scrupulously accurate and fair. A bonus for the reader is the muscular yet sparkling prose, presented in a British idiom.

Samuel B. Payne, Jr., *The Soviet Union and SALT* (Cambridge: MIT Press, 1980). One of the few good studies of Soviet policy with regard to arms control, Payne's book quotes numerous important statements by Soviet military and political leaders.

Peter Pringle and James Spigelman, *The Nuclear Barons* (New York: Holt, Rinehart and Winston, 1981). The authors, a journalist and a lawyer, perform the extraordinary and daunting feat of writing a worldwide overview of military and civilian nuclear policy from the 1930s to the present, with particular attention to the linkages between military and civilian nuclear power. Written in a journalistic style, the book is heavily researched, including personal interviews with figures like Soviet emigré scientists. The authors' central thesis is that an international technological elite composed of scientists, engineers, politicians, academics, and military men emerged to promote military/civilian nuclear power, creating a nuclear establishment that suppressed all normal political checks on its operations, especially those related to budget and information.

George H. Quester, *Nuclear Diplomacy: The First Twenty-Five Years* (New York: Dunellen, 1970). This is a brief survey of the relationship between nuclear weaponry and diplomacy from 1945 to 1970. While not as thorough as other studies, it is nevertheless a sound introduction to the problem and contains much useful information.

Howard L. Rosenberg, *Atomic Soldiers: American Victims of Nuclear Experiments* (Boston: Beacon, 1980). The most thorough investigation to date of the fates of American military personnel exposed to radiation from the atomic bombing of Hiroshima and Nagasaki and from subsequent weapons tests. Explicitly partisan, the book demonstrates the criminally careless use of soldiers and seamen for military and scientific experimentation by the Department of Defense, its constituent services, and the AEC. It also explores the indifferent or willfully blind attitudes of the Veterans Administration in withholding treatment and compensation from these victims of the American weapons testing program.

Jonathan Schell, *The Fate of the Earth* (New York: Knopf, 1982). This widely-noted description of the consequences of nuclear war is written in a spare, relentless prose that forces even the most reluctant person to confront the unthinkable: the destruction of humanity, possibly even most life on earth. It had a profound impact on the nuclear freeze movement.

Glenn Seaborg, *Kennedy, Khrushchev, and the Test Ban* (Berkeley, Calif.: University of California Press, 1981). An insider's account of the origins of the movement for a test ban agreement. It is most useful for the diary entries that appear throughout the text.

Martin Sherwin, *A World Destroyed: The Atomic Bomb and the Grand Alliance* (New York: Knopf, 1977). This book tells the arresting story of the development of the atomic bomb and the ways in which Roosevelt and Churchill formed an early nuclear alliance against the Soviet Union. It also analyzes why President Truman used the bomb against Japan and the ways in which the existence of nuclear weapons affected Soviet–American relations at the end of the war.

Alice K. Smith, *A Peril and a Hope: The Scientists' Movement in America, 1945–1947* (Chicago: University of Chicago Press, 1965). This is a well-researched narrative of the effort of nuclear scientists after World War II to achieve civilian control over the development of nuclear power. The author, a professional historian, is married to one of the participants of the movement she writes about, so she writes with the authority and the access of a quasi-insider.

Gerard C. Smith, *Doubletalk: The Story of the First Strategic Arms Limitation Talks* (Garden City, N.Y.: Doubleday, 1980). Smith, who headed President Nixon's Arms Control and Disarmament Agency and led the SALT delegation, provides a vivid memoir of the negotiations. He takes an extremely critical look at Kissinger and Nixon and their roles in the SALT negotiations.

Strobe Talbott, *Endgame: The Inside Story of SALT II* (New York: Harper & Row, 1979, 1980). Over the past several years, policymakers have proven increasingly willing to discuss major policy developments in off-the-record or sometimes on-the-record interviews. Talbott has taken advantage of this to produce what is the best history we have yet of the SALT II negotiations.

Henry L. Trewhitt, *McNamara* (New York: Harper & Row, 1971). This admiring biography is useful for understanding McNamara's thinking with regard to the developing arms race. It is also important for the origins of SALT.

Harvey Wasserman and Norman Solomon, *Killing Our Own: The Disaster of America's Experience with Atomic Radiation* (New York: Delacorte, 1982). A journalistic account, relying almost entirely on published sources, of the damage done by radiation in warfare, nuclear testing, medical X rays, workplace exposure, waste disposal, routine reactor releases, and nuclear accidents. The study is thorough, and presents its story as much as possible through the experiences of radiation's victims.

Daniel Yergin, *The Shattered Peace: The Origins of the Cold War and the National Security State* (Boston: Houghton Mifflin, 1977). An extraordinarily readable account of the early years of the Cold War that includes an enlightening analysis of the origins of the national security state.

Herbert York, *Race to Oblivion: A Participant's View of the Arms Race* (New York: Simon & Schuster, 1970). Once a protegé of Edward Teller, York served as director of the Livermore Weapons Laboratory and later as director of defense research and engineering in the Eisenhower administration. This little book is an extremely critical look at how technology and the military-industrial complex drive the arms race. It is filled with useful insights, especially with regard to the period of the missile gap.

In addition to the foregoing books, the files of four serial publications contain a wealth of material on the historical development of nuclear power:

The Bulletin of the Atomic Scientists, a publication that was the child of postwar scientists' movement, provides penetrating analyses of problems of military and civilian nuclear power, chiefly the former. It is opposed to the arms race and is generally supportive of civilian nuclear power, but critical of the errors that have marked its development.

Environment, a publication born of the St. Louis–based Committee on Nuclear Information. Of all the publications that deal with environmental matters, this is one of the best, and one that devotes an extensive amount of coverage to nuclear matters.

Not Man Apart, a publication of Friends of the Earth, contains a section in every issue called "Nuclear Blowdown" that provides a detailed and highly critical review of problems in the nuclear power industry, culled from other publications, newspapers, and leaked documents.

Nucleonics Week is the organ of the nuclear power industry. Like other industry publications, it has much valuable and interesting material —favorable to the industry, of course—buried in masses of highly technical and/or ephemeral bits of industry news.

Notes

Prologue: The Italian Navigator

1. Arthur H. Compton, *Atomic Quest: A Personal Narrative* (New York: Oxford University Press, 1956), p. 144.

2. A 1933 speech to the British Association for the Advancement of Science, quoted in Ronald W. Clark, *The Greatest Power on Earth: The International Race for Nuclear Supremacy* (New York: Harper & Row, 1980), p. 33. It is unclear whether the word "moonshine" appeared in the speech Rutherford actually gave or whether it was an interpolation by the London *Times*. In any event, the word caught the popular imagination so forcefully that the speech is still known as the "moonshine speech."

3. Compton, *Atomic Quest*, p. 138.

4. Richard G. Hewlett and Oscar E. Anderson, Jr., *The New World, 1939/1946*, vol. I of *A History of the United States Atomic Energy Commission* (University Park, Pa.: Pennsylvania State University Press, 1962), p. 109.

5. A good journalistic account of December 2, 1942, is Stephane Groueff, *Manhattan Project: The Untold Story of the Making of the Atomic Bomb* (Boston: Little, Brown, 1967), pp. 82–89.

1 $E = mc^2$

1. H. G. Wells, *The World Set Free And Other War Papers*, vol. XXI of *The Works of H. G. Wells* (New York: Scribner's, 1926), pp. 23–25.

2. Quoted in Clark, *The Greatest Power on Earth*, pp. 6–7.

3. *Ibid.*, p. 24.

4. Aston quoted in *ibid.*, p. 24; A. S. Eve, *Rutherford: Being the Life and Letters of the Rt. Hon. Lord Rutherford* (New York: Cambridge University Press, 1939), p. 102.

5. Churchill and Lodge quoted in Clark, *Greatest Power on Earth*, pp. 24 and 18 respectively.

6. Quoted in James Stokely, *The New World of the Atom*, rev. ed. (New York: Washburn, 1970), pp. 53–54.

7. Lise Meitner and O. R. Frisch, letter to editor, *Nature* (11 February 1939) p. 239.

8. Quoted from an interview with Fermi's officemate by Daniel J. Kevles, *The Physicists: The History of a Scientific Community in Modern America* (New York: Knopf, 1978), p. 324.

9. Spencer R. Weart and Gertrud W. Szilard, eds., *Leo Szilard: His Version of the Facts* (Cambridge, Mass.: MIT Press, 1978), p. xvii.

10. The Szilard–Einstein letter is reproduced in Morton Grodzins and Eugene Rabinowitch, *The Atomic Age: Scientists in National and World Affairs* (New York: Basic Books, 1963), pp. 11–12.

11. Richard G. Hewlett and Oscar E. Anderson, Jr., *The New World* (vol. I of *A History of the United States Atomic Energy Commission* (University Park, Pa.: Pennsylvania State University Press, 1962), p. 17.

12. From Szilard's account of the meeting contained in his "Reminiscences," in *The Intellectual Migration: Europe and America, 1930–1960*, vol. II of *Perspectives in American History* (Cambridge, Mass.: Harvard University Press, 1968), p. 115.

13. The memorandum consisted of two parts. The first part, dealing with technical questions, is reprinted as appendix 1 in Margaret Gowing, *Britain and Atomic Energy, 1939–1945* (London: MacMillan 1965). The second part, from which the quotation in text is taken, is quoted in Clark, *Greatest Power on Earth*, p. 90.

14. The meaning of the acronym and accounts of its origins vary. It has variously been translated as Military Application of Uranium Detonator or Ministry of Aircraft Uranium Development. The British government later did little to rebut the charming story that the name was adopted as an in joke among British scientists, who had earlier misunderstood a telegram from Niels Bohr inquiring about a former family nurse named Maud as an obscure effort to transmit secret scientific data.

15. The MAUD report is reproduced in Gowing, *Britain and Atomic Energy*, pp. 396–436; quotation at p. 429.

16. Quoted from a note by Imperial Chemical Industries printed as appendix VII to the MAUD report, reprinted in Gowing, *Britain and Atomic Energy*, at p. 435.

17. *Ibid.*, p. 86.

18. Kevles, *The Physicists*, p. 324.

19. Quoted in Ralph E. Lapp, *Atoms and People* (New York: Harper, 1956), p. 25.

20. Hewlett & Anderson, *New World*, p. 109.

2 The Radiance of a Thousand Suns

1. Leslie R. Groves, *Now It Can Be Told: The Story of the Manhattan Project* (New York: Harper, 1962), pp. 3–4.

2. Quoted in John Purcell, *The Best-Kept Secret: The Story of the Atomic Bomb* (New York: Vanguard, 1963), p. 15.

3. Hewlett & Anderson, *New World*, p. 142.

4. Kevles, *The Physicists*, p. 342.

5. Hewlett & Anderson, *New World*, p. 187. It should be pointed out, however, that DuPont insisted that its fixed fee for involvement with the Manhattan Project be limited to one dollar. The chemical giant was anxious to avoid implications of war-profiteering.

6. Harold Orlans, *Contracting for Atoms* (Washington, D.C.: Brookings Institution, 1967), p. 13. The Sandia consortium, which operated the Sandia Laboratories near Albuquerque, New Mexico, was a subsidiary of Western Electric, Bell Telephone Labs, and AT&T.

7. *Ibid.*, pp. 19–20.

8. Charles W. Johnson and Charles O. Jackson, *City Behind a Fence: Oak Ridge, Tennessee, 1942–1946* (Knoxville: University of Tennessee Press, 1981) is a detailed narrative, copiously illustrated, of the conditions of life at wartime Oak Ridge.

9. Carmine A. Prioli, "The Fu-Go Project," *American Heritage*, 33 (1982), pp. 89–92.

10. Groves, *Now it Can Be Told*, p. 64.

11. James W. Kunetka, *City of Fire: Los Alamos and the Birth of the Atomic Age, 1943–1945* (Englewood Cliffs, N.J.: Prentice-Hall, 1978), p. 96.

12. Rabi and Tuck quoted in Nuel Pharr Davis, *Lawrence and Oppenheimer* (New York: Simon & Schuster, 1968), pp. 183, 185.

13. Alice K. Smith, "Los Alamos: Focus of an Age," in Richard S. Lewis and Jane Wilson, eds., *Alamogordo Plus Twenty-Five Years* (New York: Viking, 1970), pp. 45, 34.

14. Pash and DeSilva are quoted in Davis, *Lawrence and Oppenheimer*, pp. 148–149, 187, respectively.

15. Sherwin, *A World Destroyed*, pp. 62–63.

16. David Irving, *The German Atomic Bomb: The History of Nuclear Research in Nazi Germany* (New York: Simon & Schuster, 1967), p. 120.

17. On *Alsos*, see Groves, *Now it Can Be Told*, chapters 13, 15, 17, and the chatty, anecdotal reminiscences of Samuel Goudsmit, *Alsos* (New York: H. Schuman, 1947).

18. Groves, *Now It Can Be Told,* p. 242.

19. Sherwin, *A World Destroyed,* p. 62.

20. Daniel Yergin, *Shattered Peace: The Origins of the Cold War and the National Security State* (Boston: Houghton Mifflin, 1977), pp. 18–41, 50–51, 52, 74–76.

21. James McGregor Burns, *Roosevelt: The Soldier of Freedom* (New York: Harcourt, Brace, Jovanovich, 1970), pp. 406–414; Herbert Feis, *Churchill, Roosevelt, Stalin: The War They Waged and the Peace They Sought* (Princeton: Princeton University Press, 1957), pp. 269–279.

22. Yergin, *Shattered Peace,* pp. 42–68.

23. Gowing, *Britain and Atomic Energy,* p. 95.

24. Sherwin, *A World Destroyed,* pp. 71, 80–81.

25. The Quebec Agreement is reproduced in Gowing, *Britain and Atomic Energy,* pp. 439–440.

26. Quoted in Sherwin, *A World Destroyed,* p. 93.

27. *Ibid.,* pp. 98–103; Joseph I. Lieberman, *The Scorpion and the Tarantula: The Struggle to Control Atomic Weapons, 1945–1949* (Boston: Houghton Mifflin, 1970), pp. 14–43.

28. Quoted in Sherwin, *A World Destroyed,* p. 100.

29. *Ibid.,* pp. 105–108; Lieberman, *The Scorpion and the Tarantula,* pp. 34–35.

30. Quoted in Sherwin, *A World Destroyed,* p. 110.

31. *Ibid.,* pp. 109–111; Lieberman, *The Scorpion and the Tarantula,* pp. 42–43.

32. Sherwin, *A World Destroyed,* p. 7.

33. Quoted in Lansing Lamont, *Day of Trinity* (New York: Atheneum, 1965), p. 192.

34. Davis, *Lawrence and Oppenheimer,* pp. 128–130.

35. Lamont, *Day of Trinity,* p. 194.

36. *Ibid.,* pp. 236, 246.

37. *Ibid.,* pp. 235, 237, 242, 244.

3 A Destroyer of Worlds

1. Quoted in Gordon Thomas and Max Morgan Witts, *Enola Gay* (New York: Stein and Day, 1977), p. 239.

2. *Ibid.,* p. 264.

3. These figures are from the Committee for the Compilation of Materials on Damage Caused by the Atomic Bombs in Hiroshima and Nagasaki, *Hiroshima and Nagasaki: The Physical, Medical, and Social Effects of the Atomic Bombings,* Eisei Ishikawa and David L. Swain, trans. (New York: Basic Books, 1981), pp. 364–369. These latest definitive figures, compiled by a Japanese commission, double

the official American estimates, which were the numbers hitherto conventionally cited.

4. Walter Gerlach diary entry, 7 August 1945, quoted in Robert Jungk, *Brighter Than a Thousand Suns: A Personal History of the Atomic Scientists* (New York: Harcourt, Brace, 1971), p. 220.

5. "America's Atomic Atrocity," *Christian Century* (29 August 1945), pp. 974–76; "Honor and Shame," *Commonweal,* (24 August 1945), p. 443–44.

6. "Godless Götterdämmerung," *Time* (15 October 1945), pp. 62–63.

7. Editorial, *Politics* (August 1945); and "The Bomb," *Politics,* (September 1945). Both reprinted in Barton J. Bernstein, ed., *The Atomic Bomb: The Critical Issues* (Boston: Little, Brown, 1976), pp. 144–150.

8. "A Beginning for Sanity," *Saturday Review of Literature* (15 June 1946), pp. 5–9, 38–40.

9. P. M. S. Blackett, *Fear, War, and the Bomb* (New York: McGraw-Hill, 1949), pp. 130–143.

10. Sherwin, *A World Destroyed,* p. 203.

11. Kenneth M. Glazier, Jr., "The Decision to Use Atomic Weapons Against Hiroshima and Nagasaki," *Public Policy* (Summer 1970), p. 472.

12. *Ibid.;* Robert J. C. Butow, *Japan's Decision to Surrender* (Palo Alto, Calif.: Stanford University Press, 1954), pp. 115–118.

13. Sherwin, *A World Destroyed,* p. 208.

14. Butow, *Japan's Decision to Surrender,* p. 111.

15. Labour's victory in Britain's July 5, 1945, national elections retired Winston Churchill. Attlee replaced him as prime minister.

16. Stimson & Bundy, *On Active Service* (New York: Harper & Brothers, 1947), pp. 631–32.

17. Edwin A. Locke, Jr., to Truman, Oct. 19, 1945, Papers of Harry S Truman, The President's Secretary's Files, Truman Library, Independence, Mo.

18. Dwight D. Eisenhower, *The White House Years: Mandate for Change, 1953–56* (New York: Doubleday 1963), p. 313.

19. Quoted in Glazier, "Decision to Use Atomic Weapons," p. 474.

20. William D. Leahy, *I Was There* (New York: Whittlesey House, 1950), p. 441.

21. Quoted in Jungk, *Brighter Than a Thousand Suns,* p. 171.

22. *Ibid.,* p. 178.

23. Reprinted in Grodzins & Rabinowitch, *Atomic Age,* pp. 13–18.

24. "A Petition to the President of the United States," dated July 17, 1945, reprinted in Grodzins & Rabinowitch, *Atomic Age,* pp. 28–29.

484 · NOTES

25. These quotations from the Franck report are taken from the version published as appendix B in Smith, *A Peril and a Hope,* pp. 560–572.

26. Quoted in Jungk, *Brighter Than a Thousand Suns,* p. 186.

27. Leo Szilard, "Reminiscences," in *Intellectual Migration: Europe and America, 1930–1960* (Cambridge, Mass.: Harvard University Press, 1968), pp. 128–129.

28. Bernstein, *The Atomic Bomb,* p. 113.

29. Richard B. Russell to Harry S Truman, August 8, 1945, Papers of Harry S Truman, Truman Library, Independence, Mo.

30. Bernstein, *The Atomic Bomb,* p. 112.

31. Glazier, "Decision to Use Atomic Weapons," p. 480.

32. Joseph C. Grew, *Turbulent Era* (Boston: Houghton-Mifflin, 1952), pp. 1421–26.

33. Henry H. Arnold, *Global Mission* (New York: Harper & Row, 1949), p. 589.

34. Butow, *Japan's Decision to Surrender,* pp. 244–245.

35. *Ibid.,* pp. 243–244.

36. *Ibid.,* p. 245.

4   Just Another Piece of Artillery

1. Quoted in Stephen E. Ambrose, *Rise to Globalism: American Foreign Policy, 1938–1980* (Baltimore: Penguin, 1980), p. 100.

2. Quoted in Colin Gray, *Strategic Studies and Public Policy* (Lexington, Ky.: University Press of Kentucky, 1982), pp. 31–32.

3. Quoted in Yergin, *The Shattered Peace,* p. 169.

4. Quoted in Warren R. Shilling, Paul Y. Hammond, and Glenn H. Snyder, *Strategy, Politics, and Defense Budgets* (New York: Columbia University Press, 1962), p. 201.

5. Quoted in George H. Quester, *Nuclear Diplomacy: The First Twenty-Five Years* (New York: Dunellen, 1970), p. 56.

6. Quoted in Davis, *Lawrence and Oppenheimer,* p. 260.

7. Walter Millis, ed., *The Forrestal Diaries* (New York: Viking, 1951), pp. 93–96.

8. Acheson to Truman, Sept. 25, 1945, *Foreign Relations of the U.S. (FRUS),* 1945, II (Washington, D.C.: GPO, 1947), p. 48.

9. Minutes of a Discussion, 10 October 1945, *ibid.,* p. 56.

10. Dean Acheson, *Present at the Creation: My Years in the State Department* (New York: Norton, 1969), p. 155.

11. *Ibid.,* p. 155.

12. Quoted in Lawrence Freedman, *The Evolution of Nuclear Strategy* (New York: St. Martins Press, 1981), pp. 39–40.

13. Alice K. Smith, *A Peril and a Hope: The Scientists' Movement in America, 1945–1947* (Chicago: University of Chicago Press, 1965), p. 16.

14. Four sections of the "Prospectus on Nucleonics" are reprinted as an appendix in *ibid.*, quotations from pp. 553, 554.

15. Aaron Novick, "A Plea for Atomic Freedom," *New Republic*, 114 (25 March 1946), pp. 399–400.

16. Quoted in Victor D. McElheny, "Kapitsa's Visit to England," *Science* 153 (12 August 1966), pp. 725–727.

17. Fermi quoted in Hewlett & Anderson, *New World*, p. 422.

18. For a fictionalized account of Slotin's death, see Dexter Masters, *The Accident* (New York: Knopf, 1955).

19. Quoted in Jungk, *Brighter Than a Thousand Suns*, p. 228.

20. Quoted in Hewlett & Anderson, *New World*, p. 421.

21. Reprinted as appendix C in Smith, *A Peril and a Hope*, pp. 573–575.

22. *Ibid.*, pp. 77–78.

23. Edward Teller and Allen Brown, *The Legacy of Hiroshima* (Garden City, N.Y.: Doubleday, 1962), pp. 13–14.

24. Smith, *A Peril and a Hope*, p. 90.

25. *The New York Times*, 22 September 1945, p. 5. Groves later claimed that the press had misquoted him.

26. As a government publication, the Smyth report was titled *General Account of the Development of Methods of Using Atomic Energy for Military Purposes* (1945). It was subsequently published as *Atomic Energy for Military Purposes* (Princeton: Princeton University Press, 1945).

27. David Lilienthal, *The Atomic Energy Years, 1945–1950* (New York: Harper, 1964), p. 134.

28. For a concise organizational history of the scientists' movement, see Donald A. Strickland, *Scientists in Politics: The Atomic Scientists Movement, 1945–46* (West Lafayette, Ind.: Purdue University Press, 1968). But Smith, *A Peril and a Hope*, is not likely to be superceded as the definitive study of the movement.

29. The text of Truman's 3 October 1945 message is in Harry S Truman, *Year of Decision* (Garden City, N.Y.: Doubleday, 1955), pp. 530–533.

30. Quoted in Hewlett & Anderson, *New World*, p. 430.

31. Quoted in Smith, *A Peril and a Hope*, p. 135.

32. House Committee on Military Affairs, *Atomic Energy*, Hearings on H.R. 4280, Oct. 9, 18, 1945 (Washington, D.C.: GPO, 1945), p. 129.

33. Herbert Anderson to Willie Higginbotham, 11 October 1945, quoted in Hewlett & Anderson, *New World*, p. 432.

34. "Scientists' Revolt Reported," *The New York Times*, 12 October 1945, p. 5.

35. Quoted in Smith, *A Peril and a Hope*, p. 157.

36. Quoted in Davis, *Lawrence and Oppenheimer*, p. 227.

37. Wallace to Truman, 9 November 1945, quoted in Hewlett & Anderson, *New World*, p. 444.

38. Wallace quoted in Hewlett & Anderson, *New World*, p. 490; Herblock in Washington *Post*, 14 March 1946.

39. Groves, Luce, Thomas, and Adamson quoted in Hewlett & Anderson, *New World*, pp. 502, 519, 524, 422 respectively.

40. Act of 1 August 1946, ch. 724, 60 Stat. 755.

41. Quoted in Sidney Lens, *The Day Before Doomsday: An Anatomy of the Nuclear Arms Race* (Garden City, N.Y.: Doubleday, 1977), p. 177.

5 Super

1. Richard G. Hewlett and Francis Duncan, *Atomic Shield, 1947/1952*, vol. II of the official *History of the United States Atomic Energy Commission* (University Park, Pa.: Pennsylvania State University Press, 1969), p. xiii.

2. The adjectives are John M. Blum's: *V Was for Victory: Politics and American Culture During World War II* (New York: Harcourt, Brace, Jovanovich, 1976), p. 240.

3. All quotations from Hewlett & Duncan, *Atomic Shield*, pp. 8–11.

4. Lilienthal reprinted this little speech with pride in the second volume of his journals, *The Atomic Energy Years*, pp. 647–648.

5. Hewlett & Duncan, *Atomic Shield*, p. xiv.

6. Quoted in Stephen E. Ambrose, *Rise to Globalism: American Foreign Policy, 1938–1980*, 2nd rev. ed. (New York: Penguin, 1980), p. 122.

7. Quoted in Corbin Allardice and Edward R. Trapnell, *The Atomic Energy Commission* (New York: Praeger, 1974), p. 80.

8. Quoted in Hewlett & Duncan, *Atomic Shield*, pp. 116–117.

9. *Ibid.*, pp. 186–187, 202–203.

10. Herbert F. York, *The Advisors: Oppenheimer, Teller, and the Superbomb* (San Francisco: W. H. Freeman, 1976), pp. 34, 162. Truman's 1952 statement is quoted in Lewis Strauss, *Men and Decisions* (New York: Popular Library, 1962), p. 331. (Strauss, however, chose to believe that Truman was misquoted.)

11. Lilienthal, *Atomic Energy Years*, p. 577 (diary entry of 10 October 1949).

12. This account of the Super debates is derived from Hewlett & Duncan, *Atomic Shield*, pp. 373–409 and York, *Advisors*, pp. 46–74. Norman Moss recounts the debates from the perspective of a British journalist in *Men Who Play God: The Story*

of the Hydrogen Bomb & How the World Came to Live with It (New York: Harper & Row, 1969), chs. 1–3.

13. The GAC opinion and its addenda are reproduced in York, *Advisors*, pp. 152–159, with the deletion of nonrelevant classified information.

14. The absent Seaborg was the exception. By letter, he informed Lilienthal that he would have to know more before he would oppose going ahead with Super.

15. Quoted in York, *Advisors*, p. 60.

16. Lilienthal, *Atomic Energy Years*, p. 585 (diary entry of 1 November 1949).

17. Quoted in Kenneth W. Condit, *The History of the Joint Chiefs of Staff: The Joint Chiefs of Staff and National Policy: Volume II, 1947–1949* (Wilmington, Del.: M. Glazier, n.d.), p. 556.

18. Acheson, *Present at the Creation*, p. 346.

19. Quoted in Michael Mandelbaum, *The Nuclear Question: The United States and Nuclear Weapons, 1946–1976* (New York: Cambridge University Press, 1979), p. 49.

20. *The New York Times*, 1 February 1950, p. 3.

21. Truman to Acheson, Jan. 31, 1950, *Foreign Relations of the United States*, 1950, I, pp. 141–142.

22. NSC-68, April 14, 1950, *Foreign Relations of the United States*, I, p. 237.

23. Nathan F. Twining, *Neither Liberty Nor Safety* (New York: Holt, Rinehart, Winston, 1966), pp. 48–49.

24. *Ibid.*, pp. 49–50.

25. Paul Y. Hammond, *Cold War and Détente* (New York: Harcourt, Brace, Jovanovich, 1975), p. 62.

26. Quoted in Yergin, *The Shattered Peace*, p. 403.

27. Princeton Seminars, 10 October 1954, Harry S Truman Library.

28. Acheson, *Present at the Creation*, p. 374; Princeton Seminars, statement by Edward Barrett, 10 October 1954, Truman Library.

29. The phrase is from David Caute, *The Great Fear: The Anti-communist Purge under Truman and Eisenhower* (New York: Simon & Schuster, 1978), p. 466.

30. Quoted in Philip M. Stern, *The Oppenheimer Case: Security on Trial* (New York: Harper & Row, 1969), p. 15.

31. York, *Advisors*, p. 60.

32. Quotation is from Hewlett & Duncan, *Atomic Shield*, p. 372.

33. Borden's letter is substantially excerpted in Stern, *Oppenheimer Case*, pp. 214–219.

6 Massive Retaliation

1. Quoted in Richard A. Aliano, *American Defense Policy from Eisenhower to Kennedy* (Athens, Ohio: Ohio University Press, 1975), pp. 30–31.

2. *Ibid.*, p. 32.

3. *Ibid.*, p. 27.

4. Quoted in Douglas Kinnard, *President Eisenhower and Strategy Management* (Lexington, Ky.: University of Kentucky Press, 1977), p. 8.

5. Sherman Adams, *First-Hand Report* (New York: Harper & Row, 1961), p. 398.

6. Quoted in Desmond Ball, *Politics and Force Levels: The Strategic Missile Program of the Kennedy Administration* (Berkeley, Calif.: University of California Press, 1980), p. 190.

7. Quoted in E. Bruce Geelhoed, *Charles E. Wilson and the Controversy at the Pentagon* (Detroit, Mich.: Wayne State University Press, 1979), p. 73.

8. *Ibid.*, pp. 108–109.

9. *U.S. Department of State Bulletin,* XXX, No. 761 (June 25, 1954), p. 108.

10. Quoted in Kinnard, *Eisenhower and Strategy Management,* p. 27.

11. Quoted in Mandelbaum, *The Nuclear Question,* p. 57.

12. Gerard C. Smith, *Doubletalk: The Story of the First Strategic Arms Limitation Talks* (Garden City, N.Y.: Doubleday 1980), pp. 10–11.

13. Dwight D. Eisenhower, *Mandate for Change* (Garden City, N.Y.: Doubleday 1963), p. 454.

14. Twining, *Neither Liberty Nor Safety,* p. 148.

15. *Ibid.*, p. 148.

16. Aliano, *American Defense Policy,* p. 46.

17. Quoted in Jerome H. Kahan, *Security in the Nuclear Age: Developing U.S. Strategic Arms Policy* (Washington, D.C.: The Brookings Institution, 1975), p. 33.

18. Harland B. Moulton, *From Superiority to Parity: The United States and the Strategic Arms Race 1961–1971* (Westport, Conn.: Greenwood Press, 1973), p. 19.

19. Eisenhower, *Mandate for Change,* p. 455.

20. Quoted in Aliano, *American Defense Policy,* p. 50.

21. *Ibid.*, pp. 49–50.

22. Quoted in Edgar M. Bottome, *The Missile Gap* (Rutherford, N.J.: Fairleigh Dickinson University Press, 1971), pp. 56–59.

23. Quoted in Kahan, *Security in the Nuclear Age,* p. 42.

24. Quoted in Aliano, *American Defense Policy,* pp. 133–134.

25. The Redstone Arsenal, a 38,000-acre military preserve near Huntsville, Alabama, is the home of the Army Missile Command, which is responsible for the rocket and guided missile program, as well as the Army Missile and Munitions Center and School, and NASA's Marshall Space Flight Center.

26. Quoted in Aliano, *American Defense Policy,* pp. 50–53.

27. Dwight D. Eisenhower, *Waging Peace, 1956–1961: The White House Years* (Garden City, N.Y.: Doubleday, 1965), pp. 221–222.

28. *Ibid.,* p. 222.

29. Ball, *Politics and Force Levels,* pp. 53–55.

30. *Ibid.,* p. 44.

31. Herbert York, *Race to Oblivion: A Participant's View of the Arms Race* (New York: Simon & Schuster, 1971), pp. 62–64.

32. *Ibid.,* p. 30.

33. *Ibid.,* pp. 71–72.

34. *Ibid.,* p. 146.

35. *Ibid.,* p. 70.

36. *Ibid.* pp. 73, 68.

37. *Ibid.* p. 146.

38. *Ibid.*

7 Atoms for Peace

1. Daniel Ford, *The Cult of the Atom: The Secret Papers of the Atomic Energy Commission* (New York: Simon & Schuster, 1982), p. 29.

2. Quoted in *ibid.,* p. 30.

3. Quoted in Hewlett & Duncan, *Atomic Shield,* p. 498.

4. This account of the navy's role in the origins of nonmilitary power reactors follows Richard G. Hewlett and Francis Duncan, *Nuclear Navy, 1946–1962* (Chicago: University of Chicago Press, 1974), ch. 8, "Nuclear Power Beyond the Navy."

5. The British reaction and response is told in fascinating detail by Margaret Gowing in her *Independence and Deterrence: Britain and Atomic Energy, 1945–1952* (London: MacMillan, 1974), the second segment of her official history of the British nuclear program.

6. The bases of dissatisfaction with the 1946 act are reviewed in John Gorham Palfrey, "Atomic Energy: A New Experiment in Government-Industry Relations," *Columbia Law Review,* 56 (1956), pp. 367–392.

7. The Atoms for Peace address is excerpted in Henry S. Commager, comp., *Documents of American History*, 9th ed. (Englewood Cliffs, N.J.: Prentice-Hall, 1973), II, pp. 586–589.

8. David Lilienthal, "We Must Grasp the Facts About the Atom," *The New York Times Magazine*, 4 May 1947, p. 7.

9. Harold P. Green, "The Strange Case of Nuclear Power," *Federal Bar Journal*, 17 (1957), pp. 100–128, at p. 102.

10. Jack M. Holl, "Eisenhower's Peaceful Atomic Diplomacy: Atoms for Peace in the Public Interest," unpublished paper delivered at the Conference on Energy in American History, Blacksburg, Virginia, October 1982, p. 3.

11. Philip Mullenbach, *Civilian Nuclear Power: Economic Issues and Policy Formation* (New York: Twentieth Century Fund, 1963), p. 147.

12. Atomic Energy Act of 1954, ch. 1073, 68 Stat. 919.

13. Herbert Marks and George F. Trowbridge, *Framework for Atomic Industry: A Commentary on the Atomic Energy Act of 1954* (Washington, D.C.: BNA, 1955), pp. 17–25.

14. Quoted in Allardice & Trapnell, *Atomic Energy Commission*, p. 43.

15. Lewis Strauss, "My Faith in the Atomic Future," *Reader's Digest* (August 1955), pp. 17–21, at p. 21.

16. See Strauss's views expressed in the semi-autobiographical *Men and Decisions*, chs. 14 and 15.

17. This account of the EBR-1 meltdown follows Walter Patterson, *Nuclear Power* (New York: Penguin, 1976), pp. 167–169.

18. Clinton P. Anderson, "Atoms for Peace: The Dream, the Reality," *The New York Times Magazine*, 1 August 1965, pp. 10–14, at p. 13.

19. For Fermi-1's early troubles, see John G. Fuller, *We Almost Lost Detroit* (New York: Reader's Digest Press, 1975), chs. 2–4.

20. Anderson and Holifield quoted in McKinley C. Olson, *Unacceptable Risk: The Nuclear Power Controversy* (New York: Bantam, 1976), pp. 59–60; see pp. 57–62 on the first phase of the Fermi struggle.

21. *Power Reactor Development Co.* v. *International Union of Electrical, Radio and Machine Workers*, 367 U.S. 396 (1961); quotation at p. 419.

22. Government technical publications are often known by unlikely shorthand designations derived from cataloguers' terms. So with WASH-740, which simply stands for Washington, report number 740.

23. Patterson, *Nuclear Power*, p. 171.

24. Quoted in Olson, *Unacceptable Risk*, p. 56.

25. Quoted in Peter Faulkner, ed., *The Silent Bomb: A Guide to the Nuclear Controversy* (New York: Random House, 1977), p. 223.

26. Harold P. Green, "The Strange Case of Nuclear Power," *Federal Bar Journal,* 17 (1957), pp. 100–128, at p. 103.

27. U.S. Congress, Joint Committee on Atomic Energy, "Selected Materials on Atomic Energy Indemnity Legislation," 89 Cong. 1 sess., June 1965, p. 104.

28. *Ibid.,* p. 180, at p. 181.

29. Quoted in Harold P. Green, "Nuclear Power: Risk, Liability, and Indemnity," *Michigan Law Review,* 71 (1973), pp. 479–510, at p. 485.

30. Act of 2 Sept. 1957, P.L. 85–256, 71 Stat. 576.

31. *Duke Power Co.* v. *Carolina Environmental Study Group, Inc.,* 438 U.S. 59 (1978). The quotation is from the 1966 revision of Price–Anderson, at 42 U.S.C. §2210(e).

8 Sunshine Units

1. AP news story, run as "Protection Called Lax in Atomic Test," Columbia, Missouri *Daily Tribune,* 24 May 1983.

2. Quoted in Patrick Huyghe and David Konigsberg, "Grim Legacy of Nuclear Testing," *The New York Times Magazine,* 22 April 1979.

3. From a 1953 AEC pamphlet, *Assuring Public Safety in Continental Weapons Tests,* quoted in H. Peter Metzger, *The Atomic Establishment* (New York: Simon and Schuster, 1972), pp. 84–85.

4. Ralph Lapp, "Sunshine and Darkness," *Bulletin of the Atomic Scientists,* 15 (1959), pp. 27–29, especially fn. 9.

5. Quoted in Howard L. Rosenberg, *Atomic Soldiers: American Victims of Nuclear Experiments* (Boston: Beacon, 1980), p. 30.

6. Huyghe & Konigsberg, "Grim Legacy."

7. Quoted in Rosenberg, *Atomic Soldiers,* p. 61.

8. *Ibid.,* p. 54.

9. A. O. Sulzberger, Jr., "Early Radiation Safety Problems Laid to A-Bomb Program's Pace," *The New York Times,* 20 June 1979.

10. Rosenberg, *Atomic Soldiers,* pp. 58–59.

11. Quoted in *ibid.,* p. 64.

12. Diary of Gordon Dean, quoted in *ibid.,* p. 65.

13. Quoted in Metzger, *Atomic Establishment,* p. 97.

14. As recorded in the diary of Eisenhower's press secretary, James Hagerty, quoted in Robert A. Divine, *Blowing on the Wind: The Nuclear Test Ban Debate, 1954–1960* (New York: Oxford University Press, 1978), p. 11.

15. *Sixteenth Semiannual Report of the Atomic Energy Commission* (Washington, D.C.: GPO, 1954), p. 52.

16. Giff Johnson, "Paradise Lost," *Bulletin of the Atomic Scientists,* 36 (December 1980), pp. 24–29, at p. 28.

17. Ralph Lapp, *The Voyage of the Lucky Dragon* (New York: Harper, 1957).

18. "The Children of John Wayne, Susan Hayward, and Dick Powell Fear That Fallout Killed Their Parents," *People* (10 November 1982), pp. 42–46.

19. *Thirteenth Semiannual Report of the Atomic Energy Commission* (Washington, D.C.: GPO 1953), p. 125.

20. Speech of 23 September 1954, quoted in Metzger, *Atomic Establishment,* p. 92.

21. Stakman to acting AEC chairman Thomas Murray, 25 March 1954, quoted in Harvey Wasserman and Norman Solomon, *Killing Our Own: The Disaster of America's Experience with Atomic Radiation* (New York: Delacorte, 1982), p. 80.

22. *Ibid.,* p. 80.

23. W. F. Libby, "Radioactive Fallout and Radioactive Strontium," *Science,* 123 (20 April 1956), pp. 657–660, at p. 660.

24. The Russell-Einstein Manifesto is reprinted in Grodzins and Rabinowitch, *Atomic Age,* pp. 539–541.

25. Quoted in Rosenberg, *Atomic Soldiers,* p. 72.

26. All quoted in *ibid.,* pp. 66, 70, 72.

27. *Ibid.,* pp. 72–73.

28. Quoted in Wasserman & Solomon, *Killing Our Own,* p. 95.

29. Patterson, *Nuclear Power,* p. 142.

30. Quoted in Rosenberg, *Atomic Soldiers,* pp. 77–78.

31. Joseph L. Lyon et al., "Childhood Leukemias Associated with Fallout from Nuclear Testing," *New England Journal of Medicine,* 300 (1979), pp. 397–402; quotation at p. 399.

32. Quoted in Michael Uhl and Tod Ensign, *GI Guinea Pigs: How the Pentagon Exposed Our Troops to Dangers More Deadly Than War: Agent Orange and Atomic Radiation* (n.p.: Playboy Press, 1980), pp. 3–4. A film released in 1982, *The Atomic Café,* ran this footage and similar propaganda material. Stills from the film were published in *The Atomic Café: The Book of the Film* (New York: Bantam, 1982).

33. All quotes from Wasserman & Solomon, *Killing Our Own,* pp. 92–98, 105.

34. This phrase is quoted in Metzger, *Atomic Establishment,* p. 83.

35. Chet Holifield, "Who Should Judge the Atom?," *Saturday Review* (3 August 1957), pp. 34–37, at p. 36.

36. Quoted in Metzger, *Atomic Establishment,* p. 98.

37. Kelly tells his story and that of other atomic soldiers in Thomas H. Saffer and Orville E. Kelly, *Countdown Zero* (New York: Putnam, 1982).

38. All quotations from Rosenberg, *Atomic Soldiers*, pp. 99, 105.

39. Quoted from interviews with Dann in *ibid.*, pp. 119–120.

40. Quoted in Metzger, *Atomic Establishment*, p. 229.

41. Edward Teller, "The Compelling Need for Nuclear Tests," *Life* (13 February 1958), pp. 64–68, at p. 66.

42. Quoted in Wasserman & Solomon, *Killing Our Own*, p. 105.

43. Quoted in Rosenberg, *Atomic Soldiers*, pp. 86–87.

44. Quoted in *ibid.*, p. 135.

45. John Gofman, *An Irreverent, Illustrated View of Nuclear Power* (San Francisco: Committee for Nuclear Responsibility, 1979), pp. 227–228.

46. Zhores A. Medvedev, *Nuclear Disaster in the Urals* (New York: Norton, 1979), p. 7.

47. *Ibid.*, p. 16.

48. Quoted in Divine, *Blowing on the Wind*, pp. 204–205.

49. Quoted in Wasserman & Solomon, *Killing Our Own*, p. 107.

50. Quoted in Divine, *Blowing on the Wind*, p. 271.

51. *Ibid.*, p. 272.

52. "Radiation Protection Guidance for Federal Agencies," *Federal Register* (18 May 1960), p. 4402.

53. Gofman interview in Leslie J. Freeman, *Nuclear Witnesses: Insiders Speak Out* (New York: Norton, 1981), pp. 90–91.

54. "U.S. Doubts Peril in A-Test Fallout," *The New York Times*, 18 September 1962.

55. Quoted in Metzger, *Atomic Establishment*, p. 106.

56. E. J. Sternglass, "Cancer: Relation of Pre-Natal Radiation to Development of the Disease in Childhood," *Science*, 140 (7 June 1963), pp. 1102–1104.

9 Mutually Assured Destruction

1. Quoted in Moulton, *From Superiority to Parity*, p. 37.

2. Quoted in George C. Herring, *America's Longest War* (New York: John Wiley, 1979), p. 73.

3. Quoted in Moulton, *From Superiority to Parity*, p. 38.

4. Theodore Sorensen, *Kennedy* (New York: Harper & Row, 1965), p. 524.

5. Quoted in William W. Kaufmann, *The McNamara Strategy* (New York: Harper & Row, 1964), p. 40.

6. Quoted in Sorensen, *Kennedy*, p. 512.

7. *Ibid.*, p. 513.

8. Quoted in Kaufmann, *The McNamara Strategy*, p. 24.

9. Quoted in Moulton, *From Superiority to Parity*, p. 38.

10. Quoted in Henry L. Trewhitt, *McNamara* (New York: Harper & Row, 1971), p. 18.

11. Kaufmann, *The McNamara Strategy*, p. 171.

12. Quoted in Thomas G. Paterson et. al., *American Foreign Policy, A History* (Lexington, Mass.: D. C. Heath, 1977), p. 532.

13. Arthur M. Schlesinger, Jr., *A Thousand Days* (Boston: Houghton Mifflin, 1965), p. 217.

14. Quoted in Trewhitt, *McNamara*, p. 13.

15. Quoted in Kaufmann, *The McNamara Strategy*, p. 2.

16. Trewhitt, *McNamara*, p. 18.

17. Quoted in Alain C. Enthoven and K. Wayne Smith, *How Much Is Enough?: Shaping the Defense Program, 1961–1969* (New York: Harper & Row, 1971), p. 78.

18. Quoted in Kaufmann, *The McNamara Strategy*, pp. 170–171.

19. York, *Race to Oblivion*, pp. 129–130.

20. *Ibid.*, p. 130.

21. Roger Hilsman, *To Move a Nation: The Politics of Foreign Policy in the Administration of John F. Kennedy* (Garden City, N.Y.: Doubleday, 1964), p. 44.

22. Kaufmann, *The McNamara Strategy*, p. 104.

23. Sorensen, *Kennedy*, p. 626.

24. Quoted in Enthoven & Smith, *How Much Is Enough?*, p. 124.

25. Schlesinger, *A Thousand Days*, p. 835.

26. *Ibid.*, p. 353.

27. *Ibid.*, p. 354.

28. Quoted in Alva Myrdal, *The Game of Disarmament: How the United States and Russia Run the Arms Race* (New York: Pantheon, 1976), p. 39.

29. Quoted in Schlesinger, *A Thousand Days*, p. 853.

30. Quoted in Ball, *Politics and Force Levels*, p. 237.

31. Seymour Melman, *Pentagon Capitalism: The Political Economy of War* (New York: McGraw-Hill, 1970), p. 108.

32. Quoted in Ball, *Politics and Force Levels*, p. 34.

33. Quoted in Lens, *The Day Before Doomsday*, pp. 130–131.

34. Herman Kahn, *On Thermonuclear War* (Princeton, N.J.: Princeton University Press, 1960), p. 213.

35. Quoted in Ball, *Politics and Force Levels*, p. 192.

36. Quoted in Moulton, *From Superiority to Parity*, p. 72.

37. Quoted in *ibid.*, p. 78.

38. Quoted in *ibid.*, p. 86.

39. Quoted in Lawrence Freedman, *The Evolution of Nuclear Strategy* (New York: St. Martins Press, 1981), p. 239.

40. Quoted in *ibid.*, p. 240.

41. Quoted in Trewhitt, *McNamara*, p. 115.

42. Quoted in Moulton, *From Superiority to Parity*, p. 64.

43. Quoted in Robert F. Kennedy, *Thirteen Days: A Memoir of the Cuban Missile Crisis* (New York: Norton, 1968), p. 156.

44. Quoted in Kaufmann, *The McNamara Strategy*, p. 148.

45. Quoted in Trewhitt, *McNamara*, p. 115.

46. Quoted in Kahan, *Security in the Nuclear Age*, p. 93; Moulton, *From Superiority to Parity*, p. 234.

47. Quoted in Schlesinger, *A Thousand Days*, p. 315.

48. Quoted in Kahan, *Security in the Nuclear Age*, p. 94.

49. Quoted in Moulton, *From Superiority to Parity*, p. 197.

50. Quoted in Ball, *Politics and Force Levels*, p. 245.

51. Schlesinger, *A Thousand Days*, p. 438.

52. Quoted in Ball, *Politics and Force Levels*, p. 247.

53. Quoted in Solly Zuckerman, *Nuclear Illusion and Reality*, (New York: Vintage Books, 1983) p. 46–47.

54. *Ibid.*, p. 251.

55. Glenn Seaborg, *Kennedy, Khrushchev, and the Test Ban* (Berkeley, Calif.: University of California Press, 1981), p. 166.

56. Quoted in *ibid.*, p. 179.

57. Quoted in *ibid.*, p. 180.

58. Quoted in *ibid.*, p. 208.

59. Quoted in *ibid.*, p. 209.

60. Quoted in *ibid.*, p. 209.

61. Quoted in Schlesinger, *A Thousand Days*, pp. 900–902.

62. Quoted in *ibid.*, p. 904.

63. Quoted in Seaborg, *Kennedy, Khrushchev, and the Test Ban*, p. 195.

64. Quoted in *ibid.*, p. 227.

65. *The New York Times*, 27 July 1963.

66. Myrdal, *The Game of Disarmament*, p. 96.

10 Too Cheap to Meter

1. Hewlett & Duncan, *Nuclear Navy*, p. 255.

2. U.S. Congress, Joint Committee on Atomic Energy, *Comments of Reactor Designers and Industrial Representatives on the Proposed Expanded Civilian Nuclear Power Program*, 85 Cong. 2 sess. December 1958, p. 60.

3. Quoted in Irvin C. Bupp and Jean-Claude Derian, *Light Water: How the Nuclear Dream Dissolved* (New York: Basic Books, 1978), p. 35.

4. Henry Nau, *National Politics and International Technology: Nuclear Reactor Development in Western Europe* (Baltimore: The John Hopkins University Press, 1974), pp. 132–133.

5. Bupp & Derian, *Light Water*, p. 29.

6. *Ibid.*, ch. 1.

7. The phrase "Great Bandwagon Market" was coined by Philip Sporn, president of American Electric Power Co., a giant utility. Sporn was one of the few experts in the early 1960s who displayed any degree of skepticism about the projected economics of nuclear power. The phrase appears in U.S. Congress, Joint Committee on Atomic Energy, *Nuclear Power Economics—1962 through 1967*, 90 Cong. 2 sess., February 1968, p. 15.

8. Reprinted in *ibid.*, pp. 95–253. The figures are at p. 226 (pagination is of the JCAE report, not the AEC document it reprinted).

9. Bupp & Derian, *Light Water*, p. 47.

10. Strauss speech of 16 September 1954, quoted in Ford, *Cult of the Atom*, p. 50.

11. Bupp & Derian, *Light Water*, p. 49.

12. Quoted by Philip Sporn in JCAE, *Nuclear Power Economics—1962 through 1967*, p. 5.

13. Bupp & Derian, *Light Water*, p. 74.

14. *Ibid.*, p. 76.

15. Quoted in table 5-10 of John M. Fowler, *Energy-Environment Source Book* (Washington, D.C.: National Science Teachers Association, 1975). The fixed charges include depreciation, interest, return on equity, and taxes. The assumption of a 70 percent capacity factor for nuclear plants is optimistic. The capacity factor is the rate at which the plant might be run if it were never shut down for maintenance, refueling, and operating problems. For comparison purposes, a 235 MWe coal-fired plant in Missouri coming on line in 1982 cost $781 per kw of installed capacity.

16. From a table in Frank G. Dawson, *Nuclear Power: Control and Management of a Technology* (Seattle: University of Washington Press, 1976), p. 141.

17. Paul L. Joskow, "Commercial Impossibility, the Uranium Market and the Westinghouse Case," *Journal of Legal Studies*, 6 (1977), pp. 119–176.

18. William H. Berman and Lee M. Hydeman, *The Atomic Energy Commission and Regulating Nuclear Facilities* (Ann Arbor: University of Michigan Law School, 1961), pp. 300–336.

19. David E. Lilienthal, *Atomic Energy: A New Start* (New York: Harper & Row, 1980), p. 30.

20. Richard S. Olney to Charles Perkins, 28 Dec. 1892, excerpted in James M. Smith and Paul L. Murphy, *Liberty and Justice: The Modern Constitution: American Constitutional Development Since 1865* (New York: Knopf 1968), pp. 292–293.

21. Bupp & Derian, *Light Water*, p. 180.

22. Dawson, *Nuclear Power*, p. 205.

23. JCAE, *Nuclear Power Economics—1962 through 1967*, pp. 86, 90.

24. Robert Gillette, "Nuclear Safety (II): The Years of Delay," *Science,* 177 (1972), pp. 867–871, at p. 870.

25. Robert Gillette, "Nuclear Safety (I): The Roots of Dissent," *Science,* 177 (1972), pp. 771–776, at p. 776.

26. Robert Gillette, "Nuclear Safety (III): Critics Charge Conflict of Interest," *Science* 177 (1972), pp. 972–975, at p. 972.

27. Both quoted in Gillette, "Nuclear Safety (III)," p. 974.

28. Robert Gillette, "Nuclear Safety (IV): Barriers to Communication," *Science* 177 (1972), pp. 1080–1082.

11 Strategic Sufficiency

1. Quoted in Ernest Yanarella, *The Missile Defense Controversy: Strategy, Technology, and Politics, 1955–1972* (Lexington, Ky.: University of Kentucky Press, 1977), p. 62.

2. *Ibid.* p. 70.

3. Quoted in Smith, *Doubletalk*, p. 35.

4. Quoted in Trewhitt, *McNamara*, p. 127.

5. *Ibid.*

6. York, *Race to Oblivion*, p. 178.

7. Quoted in John Newhouse, *Cold Dawn: The Story of SALT* (New York: Holt, Rinehart & Winston, 1973), p. 84.

8. Quoted in *ibid.*, p. 84.

9. York, *Race to Oblivion*, pp. 194–195.

10. *The New York Times*, 27 July 1967.

11. Quoted in Henry Kissinger, *The White House Years* (Boston: Little, Brown, 1979), p. 208.

12. Quoted in Newhouse, *Cold Dawn*, pp. 92–93.

13. Quoted in *ibid.*, p. 96.

14. Quoted in Trewhitt, *McNamara*, p. 131.

15. Newhouse, *Cold Dawn*, p. 101.

16. *Ibid.*, p. 98.

17. *Ibid.*, p. 101.

18. *Ibid.*, p. 102.

19. Quoted in Samuel B. Payne, Jr., *The Soviet Union and SALT* (Cambridge, Mass.: M.I.T. Press, 1980), p. 35.

20. Quoted in *ibid.*, p. 32.

21. Quoted in Newhouse, *Cold Dawn*, p. 104.

22. Quoted in Smith, *Doubletalk*, p. 34.

23. Kissinger, *The White House Years*, p. 199.

24. Quoted in Myrdal, *The Game of Disarmament*, p. 29.

25. Quoted in Freedman, *The Evolution of Nuclear Strategy*, p. 350.

26. Quoted in *ibid.*, pp. 349–350.

27. Quoted in *ibid.*, p. 376.

28. Quoted in *ibid.*, p. 348.

29. Quoted in *ibid.*

30. Kissinger, *The White House Years*, p. 218.

31. Quoted in Zuckerman, *Nuclear Illusion and Reality*, p. 70.

32. Quoted in *ibid.*, p. 71.

33. Quoted in *ibid.*, p. 73.

34. Quoted in *ibid.*, p. 74–75.

35. Freedman, *The Evolution of Nuclear Strategy*, p. 381.

36. Kissinger, *The White House Years*, pp. 217–218.

37. *Ibid.*

38. *Ibid.*, p. 399.

39. Quoted in Newhouse, *Cold Dawn*, p. 140.

40. Smith, *Doubletalk*, p. 22.

41. Quoted in Kissinger, *The White House Years,* p. 546.

42. Smith, *Doubletalk,* p. 23.

43. Quoted in Kissinger, *The White House Years,* p. 211.

44. Quoted in Smith, *Doubletalk,* p. 160.

45. Etzold, *Defense or Delusion,* p. 139.

46. Quoted in Seymour M. Hersh, *The Price of Power: Kissinger in the Nixon White House* (New York: Summit Books, 1983), p. 165.

47. Quoted in Smith, *Doubletalk,* p. 176.

48. *Ibid.,* p. 177.

49. Quoted in Kahan, *Security in the Nuclear Age,* p. 175.

50. *Ibid.* p. 7.

51. *Ibid.* p. 84.

52. *Ibid.*

53. Quoted in *ibid.,* p. 156.

54. *Ibid.,* p. 147.

55. Kissinger, *The White House Years,* p. 547.

56. *Ibid.*

57. *Ibid.,* p. 819.

58. Quoted in Hersh, *The Price of Power,* p. 347.

59. *Ibid.,* p. 815.

60. Smith, *Doubletalk,* p. 233.

61. *Ibid.,* p. 234.

62. *Ibid.,* p. 235.

63. Quoted in Hersh, *The Price of Power,* p. 532.

64. Quoted in *ibid.,* p. 540.

65. Quoted in *ibid.,* p. 537.

66. Smith, *Doubletalk,* p. 373.

67. *Ibid.,* p. 376.

68. *Ibid.* p. 408.

12 No Nukes

1. "Safety Questions Will Delay Detroit Reactor Plant, AEC Member Says," *Wall Street Journal,* 22 July 1956, p. 22.

2. Quoted in Richard Curtis and Elizabeth Hogan, *Perils of the Peaceful Atom: The Myth of Safe Nuclear Power* (Garden City, N.Y.: Doubleday, 1969), p. 10.

3. The PRDC-commissioned study is discussed in Patterson, *Nuclear Power*, p. 171.

4. For an account of the Windscale fire, see Sheldon Novick, *The Careless Atom* (Boston: Houghton Mifflin, 1968), pp. 5–10.

5. Ford, *Cult of the Atom*, p. 204.

6. AEC, "Operational Accidents and Radiation Exposure Experience" (1965), reproduced in Karl Grossman, *Cover Up: What You Are Not Supposed to Know About Nuclear Power* (Sagaponack, N.Y.: Permanent Press, 1980), p. 35.

7. All quotations concerning the 1964 revisions and its cover-up are from David Burnham, "A.E.C. Files Show Effort to Conceal Safety Perils," *The New York Times*, 10 November 1974.

8. Quoted in Ford, *Cult of the Atom*, p. 66.

9. Quoted in *ibid.*, pp. 68–69.

10. "Nuclear Study Raises Estimates of Accident Tolls," Washington *Post*, 1 November 1982, p. 1.

11. Patterson, *Nuclear Power*, p. 181.

12. E. Pauline Alexanderson, ed., *Fermi-1: New Age for Nuclear Power* (La Grange Park, Ill.: American Nuclear Society, 1979), p. 250.

13. Quoted in Metzger, *Atomic Establishment*, pp. 149–150; on the fire, see Olson, *Unacceptable Risk*, pp. 109–113.

14. This account of the Bodega Head controversy is based on Novick, *Careless Atom*, pp. 35–58.

15. Alexis de Tocqueville, *Democracy in America*, Henry Reeve, trans. (1836; rpt. New York: Knopf, 1945), I, 284.

16. *Northern States Power Co.* v. *Minnesota*, 447, F.2d 1143 (8 Cir., 1971), aff'd. without opinion, 405 U.S. 1035 (1972).

17. *Pacific Gas & Electric Co.* v. *State Energy Resources Conservation and Development Commission*, 103 S.Ct. 1713 (1983), Blackmun and Stevens, JJ. dissenting on the point raised in dictum.

18. *Calvert Cliffs Coordinating Committee* v. *AEC*, 449 F.2d 1109 (1971).

19. Ernest J. Sternglass, *Secret Fallout: Low-Level Radiation from Hiroshima to Three-Mile Island* (New York: McGraw-Hill, 1981). This is a revised edition of the book that originally appeared in 1972.

20. Quoted in Robert O. Pohl, "Waste Disposal: Will It Stay Put?," *Physics Today* (December 1982), pp. 37–45, at p. 37.

21. Quoted in Metzger, *Atomic Establishment*, p. 156.

22. "Howard Hughes Raises New Question About Atomic Test Blasts in Nevada," *The New York Times*, 18 April 1969, p. 21.

23. David McTaggart, *Greenpeace III: Journey into the Bomb* (New York: Morrow, 1979), is a gripping account, complete with photographs of the incidents, by the Canadian who nearly lost his eye in the beating.

24. James Robertson and John Lewallen, *The Grassroots Primer* (San Francisco: Sierra Club Books, 1975), pp. 125–135.

25. Quoted in Olson, *Unacceptable Risk*, p. 47.

26. Quoted in Leslie J. Freeman, *Nuclear Witnesses: Insiders Speak Out* (New York: Norton, 1981), p. 168.

27. Freeman, *Nuclear Witnesses*, p. 144.

28. JCAE, *Environmental Effects of Producing Electric Power: Hearings* . . . 91 Cong., 1 sess., October–November 1969, part 1, p. 129.

29. All quotes in Ford, *Cult of the Atom*, pp. 94, 98.

30. *Ibid.*, p. 115.

31. Quoted in *ibid.*, p. 119.

32. Quoted in Anna Gyorgy, *No Nukes: Everyone's Guide to Nuclear Power* (Boston: South End Press, 1979), p. 116.

33. Daniel Ford, *The Cult of the Atom: The Secret Papers of the Atomic Energy Commission* (New York: Simon & Schuster, 1982), p. 172.

34. Patterson, *Nuclear Power*, pp. 210–212.

35. Quoted in Freeman, *Nuclear Witnesses*, p. 261.

36. David D. Comey, "The Incident at Brown's Ferry," in Faulkner, *Silent Bomb*, pp. 3–18.

37. On these men, see Freeman, *Nuclear Witnesses*, pp. 258–292; Minor quoted at p. 277.

38. Pollard's statement is printed in Faulkner, *Silent Bomb*, pp. 315–319.

39. Quoted in Donna Warnock, "Waving Goodbye to the Bill of Rights," in Environmental Action Foundation, *Accidents Will Happen: The Case Against Nuclear Power* (New York: Harper & Row, 1979), p. 169.

40. Richard Rashke, *The Killing of Karen Silkwood: The Story Behind the Kerr-McGee Plutonium Case* (Boston: Houghton Mifflin, 1981); Howard Kohn, *Who Killed Karen Silkwood?* (New York: Summit Books, 1981)

41. Quoted in John S. Ezell, *Innovations in Energy: The Story of Kerr-McGee* (Norman, Okla. University of Oklahoma Press, 1979), p. 448.

42. Peter B. Chowka, "A Tale of Nuclear Tyranny," *New Age* (August 1980), pp. 26 ff.

43. Daniel Ford, *Three Mile Island: Thirty Minutes to Meltdown* (New York: Viking, 1982), p. 32.

44. Mark Stephens, *Three Mile Island*, pp. 162–163.

45. "Core Melted, 3 Mile Island TV Reveals," Washington *Post*, 22 July 1982.

46. Yeager, Gossick, Denton, Mattson quoted in Ford, *Three Mile Island*, pp. 191, 170–171.

47. Mattson and Hendrie quoted in Sternglass, *Secret Fallout* (1981), pp. 226, 221.

48. Quoted in Ford, *Three Mile Island*, p. 178.

49. Quoted in Stephens, *Three Mile Island*, p. 174.

50. Sternglass, *Secret Fallout* (1981), ch. 17, "Incident at Three Mile Island."

51. Quoted in Amory B. Lovins and L. Hunter Lovins, *Energy/War: Breaking the Nuclear Link* (San Francisco: Friends of the Earth, 1980), p. 58.

13 A Wolf Playing a Cello

1. Hersh, *The Price of Power*, p. 558.

2. Henry Kissinger, *Years of Upheaval* (Boston: Little, Brown, 1982), p. 264.

3. *Ibid.* p. 1015.

4. *Ibid.*, p. 1012.

5. *Ibid.*, p. 1173.

6. Strobe Talbot, *Endgame: The Inside Story of SALT II* (New York: Harper & Row, 1979). p. 35.

7. Quoted in Talbot, *Endgame*, p. 39.

8. Zbigniew Brzezinski, *Power and Principle* (New York: Farrar, Straus, Giroux, 1983), p. 157.

9. Cyrus Vance, *Hard Choices* (New York: Simon & Schuster, 1983), p. 49.

10. Quoted in Talbot, *Endgame*, p. 49.

11. Vance, *Hard Choices*, p. 49–50.

12. James Earl Carter, *Keeping Faith: Memoirs of a President* (New York: Bantam Books, 1982), p. 217.

13. Quoted in *ibid.*, p. 218; Brzezinski, *Power and Principle*, p. 155.

14. Vance, *Hard Choices*, p. 49.

15. Carter, *Keeping Faith*, p. 218.

16. Quoted in Talbot, *Endgame*, p. 61.

17. Carter, *Keeping Faith*, p. 219.

18. Quoted in Talbot, *Endgame*, p. 66.

19. Carter, *Keeping Faith*, p. 218.

20. Quoted in Talbot, *Endgame*, p. 70.

21. Quoted in *ibid.*, p. 73.

22. Vance, *Hard Choices*, p. 55.

23. Quoted in Talbot, *Endgame*, p. 74.

24. Quoted in *ibid.*, p. 74.

25. Carter, *Keeping Faith*, p. 262.

26. Quoted in Arthur Macy Cox, *Russian Roulette: The Superpower Game* (New York, Times Books, 1982), p. 77.

27. Wolfgang Panofsky, *Arms Control and SALT II* (Seattle: University of Washington Press, 1979), pp. 48–49.

28. Quoted in Cox, *Russian Roulette*, p. 114.

29. Quoted in *ibid.*, p. 117.

30. Quoted in *ibid.*, p. 118.

31. Quoted in *ibid.*, p. 114.

32. Quoted in *ibid.*, p. 172.

33. Thomas H. Etzold, *Defense or Delusion?: America's Military in the 1980s* (New York: Harper & Row, 1982), pp. 159–160.

34. *Ibid.*, pp. 161–162.

35. Quoted in *ibid.*, p. 162.

36. Quoted in James Fallows, *National Defense* (New York: Vintage Books, 1982), pp. 155–156.

37. Quoted in Talbot, *Endgame*, p. 5.

38. Quoted in *ibid.*, p. 7.

39. Quoted in Thomas A. Bailey, *Diplomatic History of the American People*, 10th ed. (Englewood Cliffs, N.J.: Prentice-Hall, 1980), p. 488.

40. Etzold, *Defense or Delusion*, p. 140.

41. Carter, *Keeping Faith*, p. 224.

42. Vance, *Hard Choices*, p. 350.

43. *Ibid.*, p. 138.

44. *Ibid.*, p. 360.

45. *Ibid.*, p. 361.

46. *Ibid.*, p. 362.

47. *Ibid.*, p. 350.

48. Dwight MacDonald, editorial in *Politics* (August 1945), quoted in Bernstein, ed., *The Atomic Bomb*, p. 145.

Epilogue: The Chariot of the Sun

1. William L. Laurence, "The Atom Gives Up," *Saturday Evening Post* (7 September 1940), pp. 12–13, at p. 12.

2. Quoted in Philip J. Hilts, "In Event of Nuclear War, Health Prognosis Is Hopeless, Doctors Say," Washington *Post*, 21 November 1980.

3. Quoted in Wasserman & Solomon, *Killing Our Own*, p. 101.

4. Quoted in Hewlett & Anderson, *New World*, pp. 430–431.

5. Quoted in George T. Mazuzan and J. Samuel Walker, "Developing Nuclear Power in an Age of Energy Abundance, 1946–1952," p. 9, in *Papers Presented at the Conference on Energy in American History, 30 September–3 October 1982*, at the Virginia Polytechnic Institute Center for the Study of Science in Society.

6. Alvin Weinberg, "Social Institutions and Nuclear Energy," *Science*, 177 (7 July 1972), pp. 27–34, at p. 34.

Index

505

Wilson, Charles H., 419–420
Wilson, Harold, 270
"window of vulnerability," 348
Windscale reactor, 183, 224, 349
Winne, Harry A., 92
Wohlstetter, Albert, 168–169,
    300–301, 307–308
World Set Free, The, 5
worst-case scenarios, 348
Wright, J. Skelly, 358–359

xenophobia, 34
X rays, 8, 213

Yeager, Roy, 386
Yalta Conference, 42
York, Herbert, 147, 172–175,
    237–238, 292–296, 298–299, 323
Yount, Herbert W., 198
Yucca Flats, 202

Zavidovo, 396–397
Zinn, Walter H., 119–120, 121, 126,
    180, 194
Zion reactors, 351
Zuckerman, Solly, 262
Zuckert, Eugene, 189, 205, 206